BEAST COMPLEX
Volume I

Story & Art by
Paru Itagaki

BEAST
COMPLEX
Volume I
CONTENTS

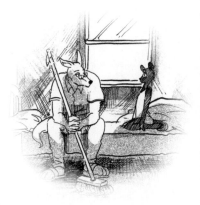

Story 1
The Lion and the Bat

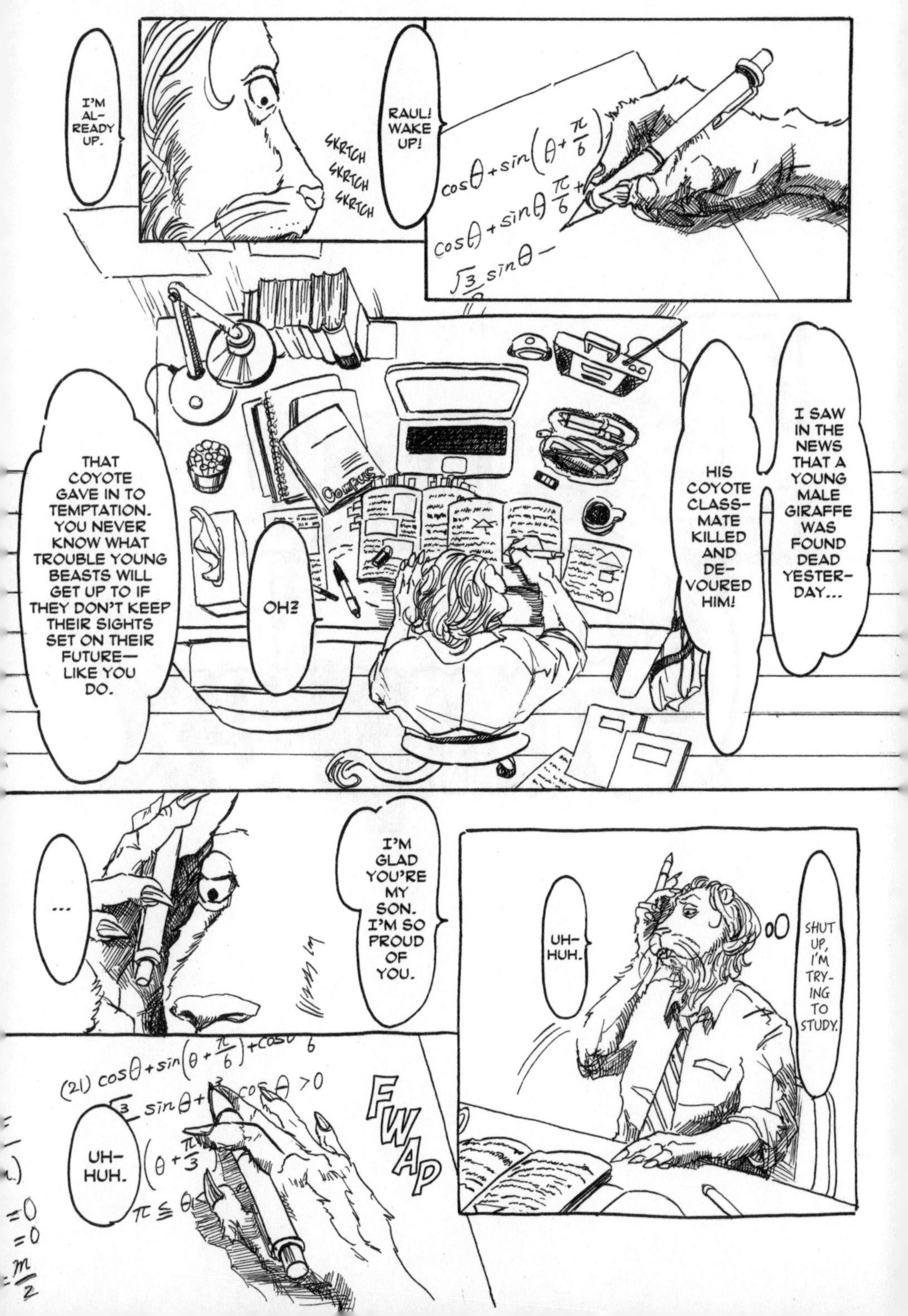
RAUL! WAKE UP!
SKRTCH SKRTCH SKRTCH
I'M ALREADY UP.
I SAW IN THE NEWS THAT A YOUNG MALE GIRAFFE WAS FOUND DEAD YESTERDAY...
HIS COYOTE CLASSMATE KILLED AND DEVOURED HIM!
OH?
THAT COYOTE GAVE IN TO TEMPTATION. YOU NEVER KNOW WHAT TROUBLE YOUNG BEASTS WILL GET UP TO IF THEY DON'T KEEP THEIR SIGHTS SET ON THEIR FUTURE—LIKE YOU DO.
SHUT UP, I'M TRYING TO STUDY.
UH-HUH.
I'M GLAD YOU'RE MY SON. I'M SO PROUD OF YOU.
...
FWAP
UH-HUH.

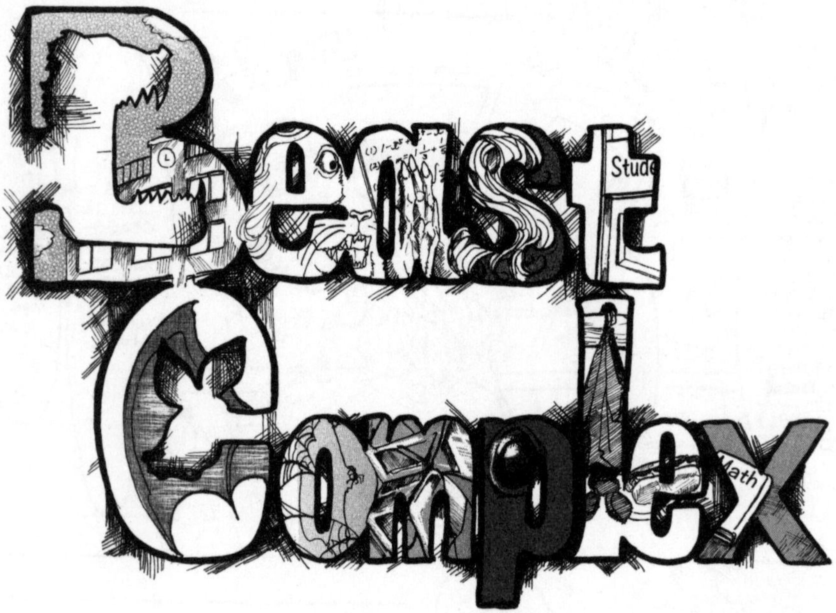
Beast
Complex
Stude
Math

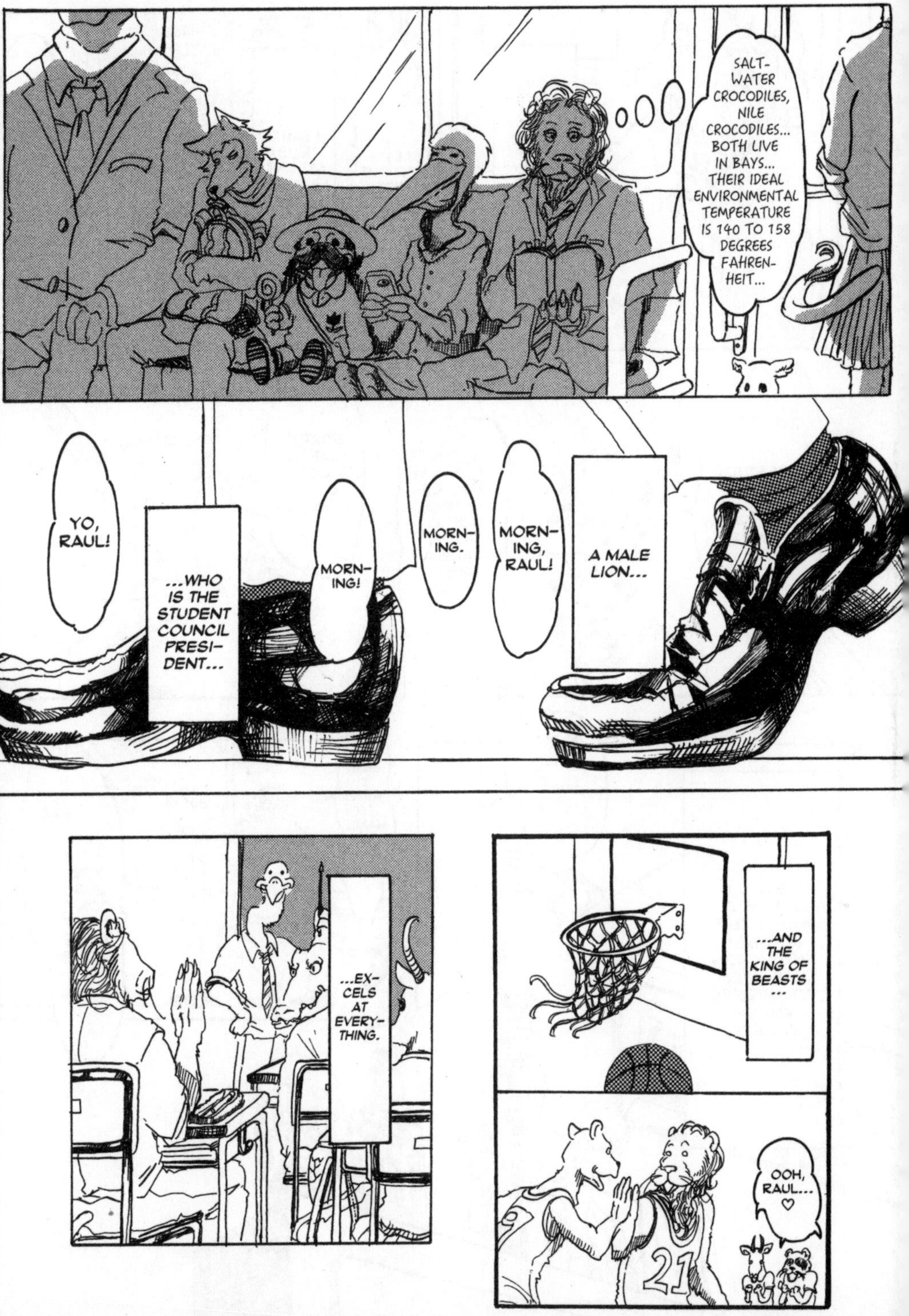
SALT-WATER CROCODILES, NILE CROCODILES... BOTH LIVE IN BAYS... THEIR IDEAL ENVIRONMENTAL TEMPERATURE IS 140 TO 158 DEGREES FAHRENHEIT...
A MALE LION...
MORNING, RAUL!
MORNING.
MORNING!
...WHO IS THE STUDENT COUNCIL PRESIDENT...
YO, RAUL!
...AND THE KING OF BEASTS...
OOH, RAUL... ♡
...EXCELS AT EVERYTHING.

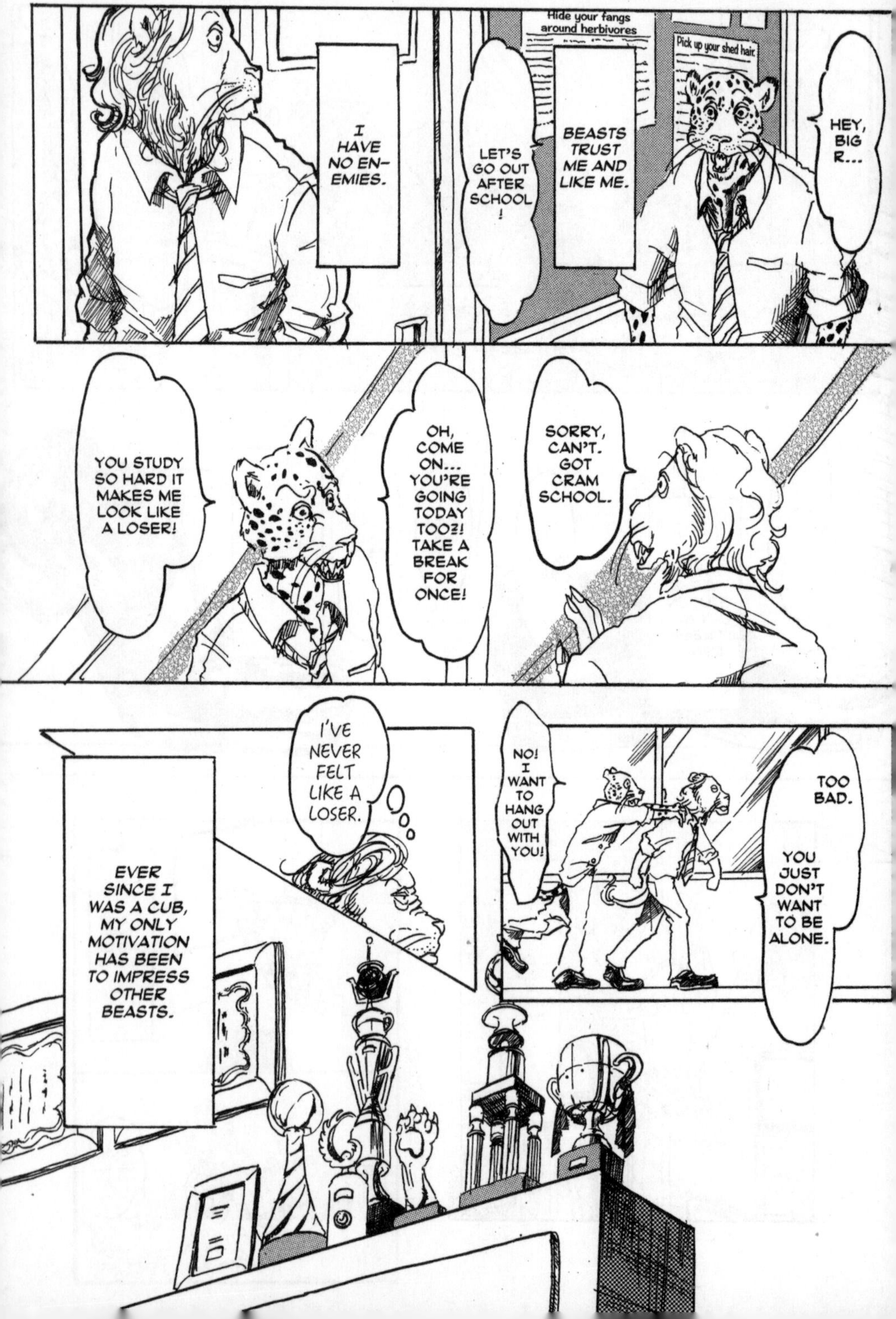
Pick up your shed hair.
Hide your fangs around herbivores
HEY, BIG R...
BEASTS TRUST ME AND LIKE ME.
LET'S GO OUT AFTER SCHOOL!
I HAVE NO ENEMIES.
SORRY, CAN'T. GOT CRAM SCHOOL.
OH, COME ON... YOU'RE GOING TODAY TOO?! TAKE A BREAK FOR ONCE!
YOU STUDY SO HARD IT MAKES ME LOOK LIKE A LOSER!
TOO BAD.
YOU JUST DON'T WANT TO BE ALONE.
NO! I WANT TO HANG OUT WITH YOU!
I'VE NEVER FELT LIKE A LOSER.
EVER SINCE I WAS A CUB, MY ONLY MOTIVATION HAS BEEN TO IMPRESS OTHER BEASTS.

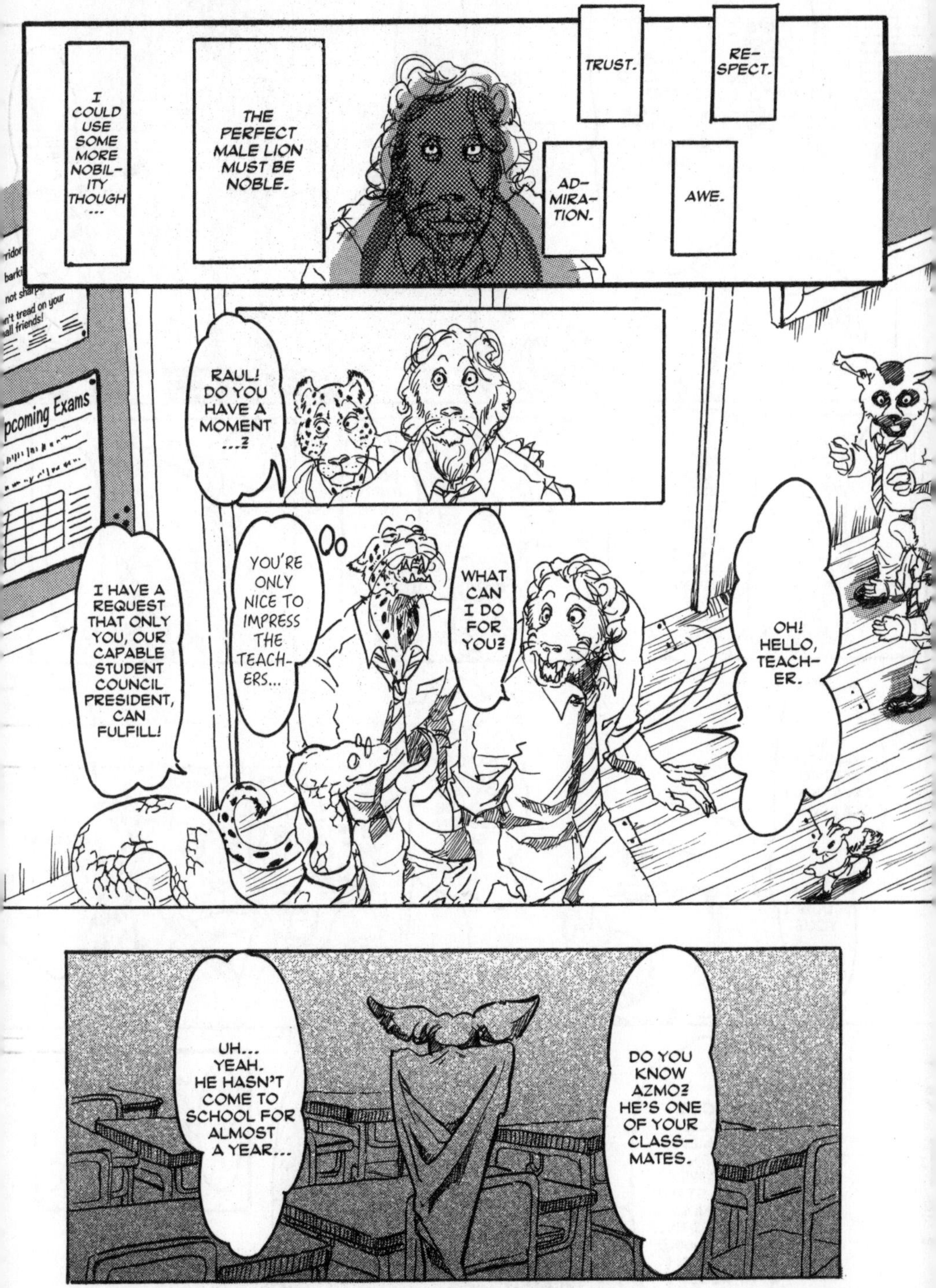
RE-SPECT.
TRUST.
AWE.
ADMIRATION.
THE PERFECT MALE LION MUST BE NOBLE.
I COULD USE SOME MORE NOBILITY THOUGH...
RAUL! DO YOU HAVE A MOMENT...?
OH! HELLO, TEACHER.
WHAT CAN I DO FOR YOU?
YOU'RE ONLY NICE TO IMPRESS THE TEACHERS...
I HAVE A REQUEST THAT ONLY YOU, OUR CAPABLE STUDENT COUNCIL PRESIDENT, CAN FULFILL!
DO YOU KNOW AZMO? HE'S ONE OF YOUR CLASSMATES.
UH... YEAH. HE HASN'T COME TO SCHOOL FOR ALMOST A YEAR...

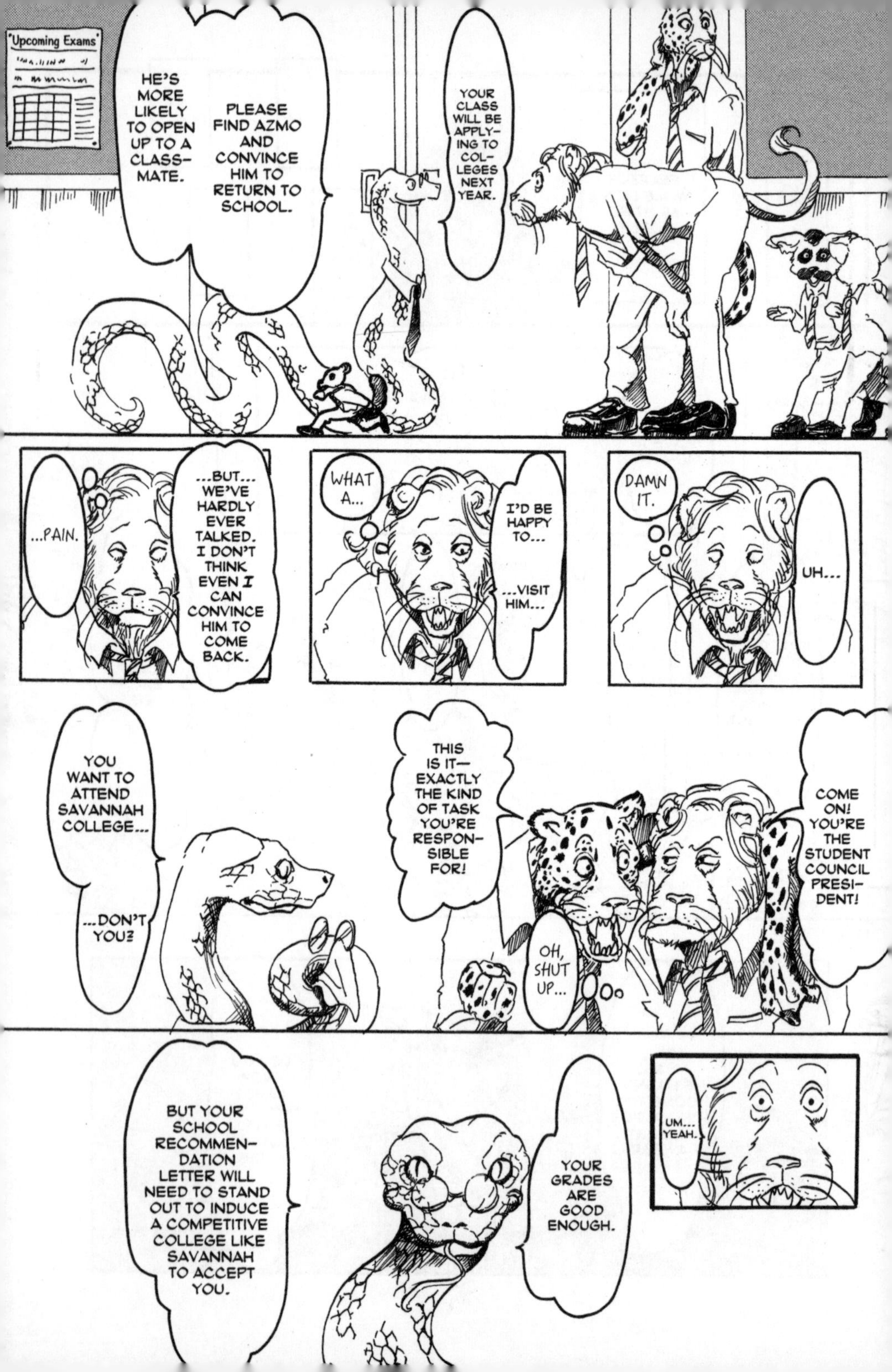
YOUR CLASS WILL BE APPLYING TO COLLEGES NEXT YEAR.
PLEASE FIND AZMO AND CONVINCE HIM TO RETURN TO SCHOOL.
HE'S MORE LIKELY TO OPEN UP TO A CLASSMATE.
"Upcoming Exams"
UH...
DAMN IT.
I'D BE HAPPY TO...
...VISIT HIM...
WHAT A...
...BUT... WE'VE HARDLY EVER TALKED. I DON'T THINK EVEN I CAN CONVINCE HIM TO COME BACK.
...PAIN.
COME ON! YOU'RE THE STUDENT COUNCIL PRESIDENT!
THIS IS IT—EXACTLY THE KIND OF TASK YOU'RE RESPONSIBLE FOR!
OH, SHUT UP...
YOU WANT TO ATTEND SAVANNAH COLLEGE...
...DON'T YOU?
UM... YEAH.
YOUR GRADES ARE GOOD ENOUGH.
BUT YOUR SCHOOL RECOMMENDATION LETTER WILL NEED TO STAND OUT TO INDUCE A COMPETITIVE COLLEGE LIKE SAVANNAH TO ACCEPT YOU.

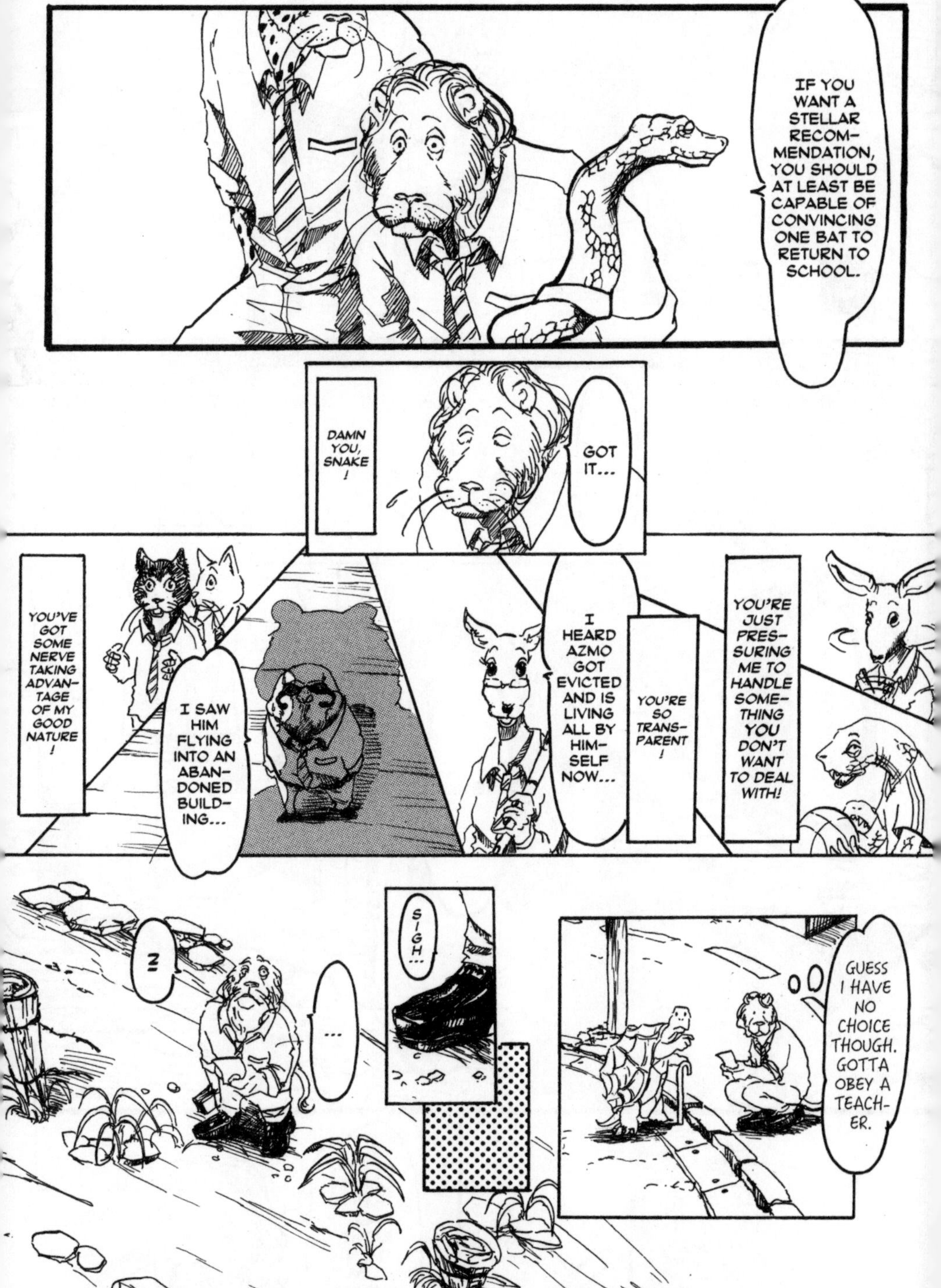
IF YOU WANT A STELLAR RECOMMENDATION, YOU SHOULD AT LEAST BE CAPABLE OF CONVINCING ONE BAT TO RETURN TO SCHOOL.
GOT IT...
DAMN YOU, SNAKE!
YOU'RE JUST PRESSURING ME TO HANDLE SOMETHING YOU DON'T WANT TO DEAL WITH!
YOU'RE SO TRANSPARENT!
I HEARD AZMO GOT EVICTED AND IS LIVING ALL BY HIMSELF NOW...
I SAW HIM FLYING INTO AN ABANDONED BUILDING...
YOU'VE GOT SOME NERVE TAKING ADVANTAGE OF MY GOOD NATURE!
GUESS I HAVE NO CHOICE THOUGH. GOTTA OBEY A TEACHER.
SIGH...
...
!?

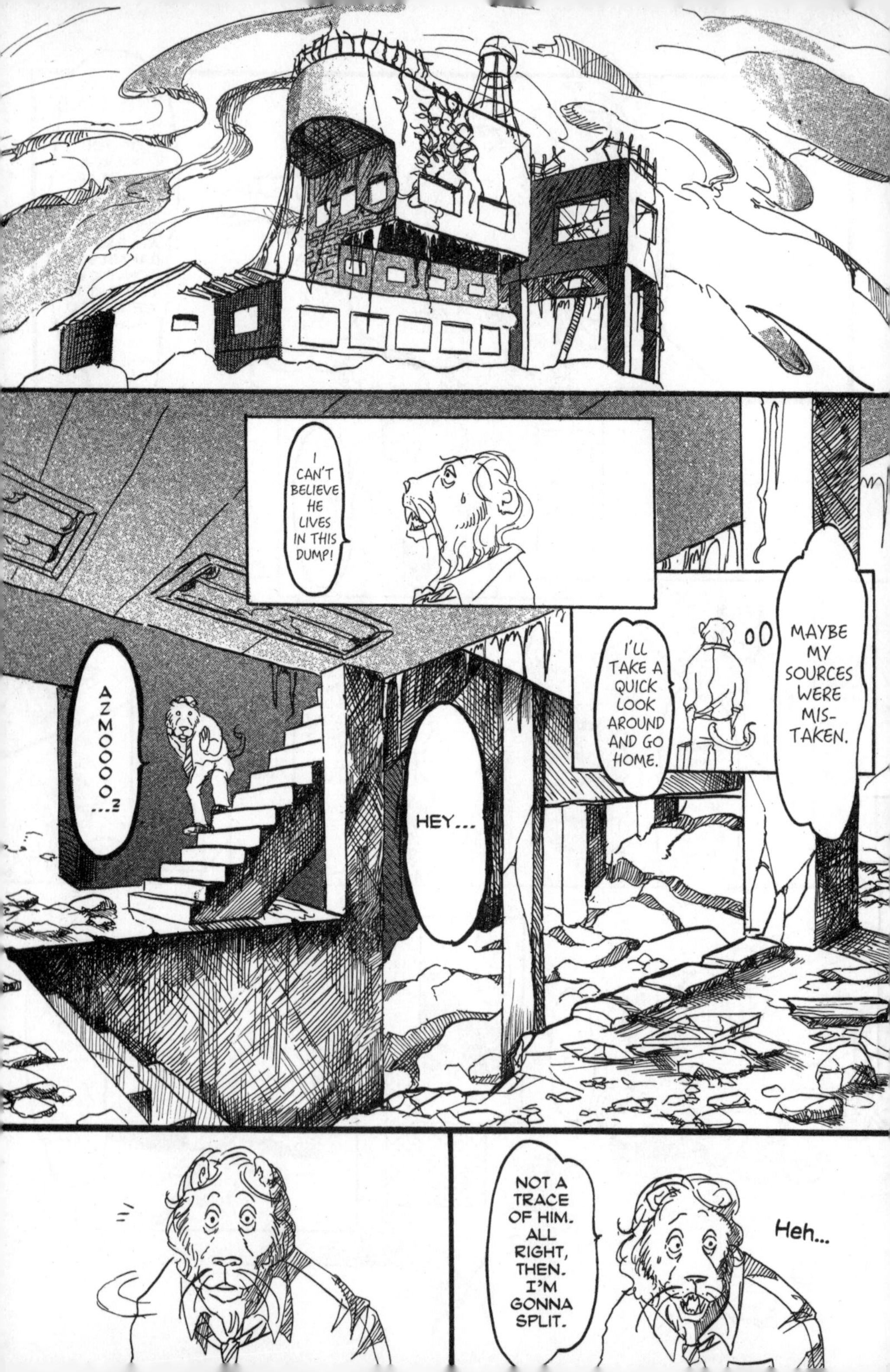
I CAN'T BELIEVE HE LIVES IN THIS DUMP!
MAYBE MY SOURCES WERE MIS-TAKEN.
I'LL TAKE A QUICK LOOK AROUND AND GO HOME.
HEY...
AZMOOOOO...?
Heh...
NOT A TRACE OF HIM. ALL RIGHT, THEN. I'M GONNA SPLIT.

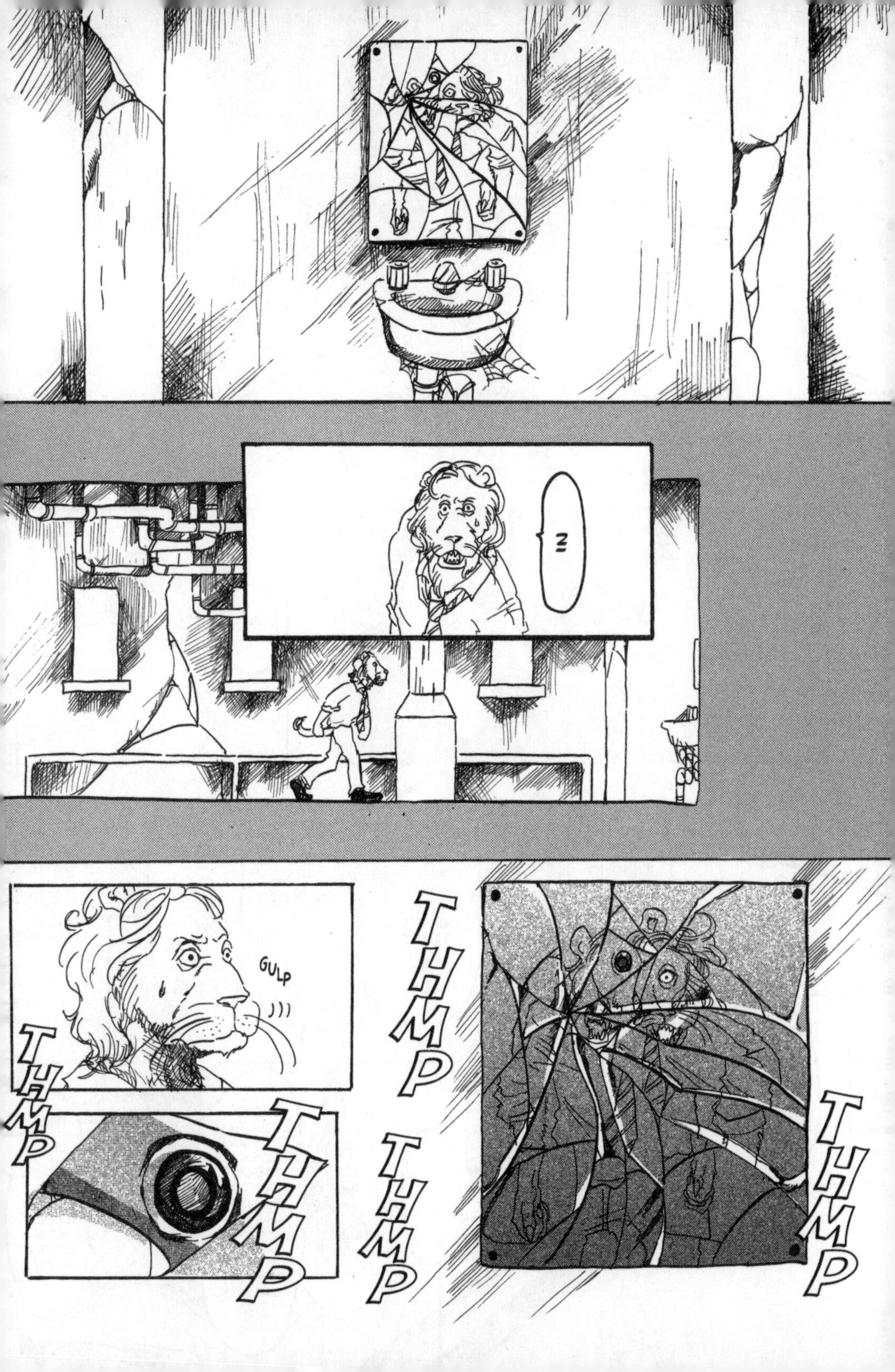
...!!
THMP
THMP
THMP
GULP
THMP
THMP

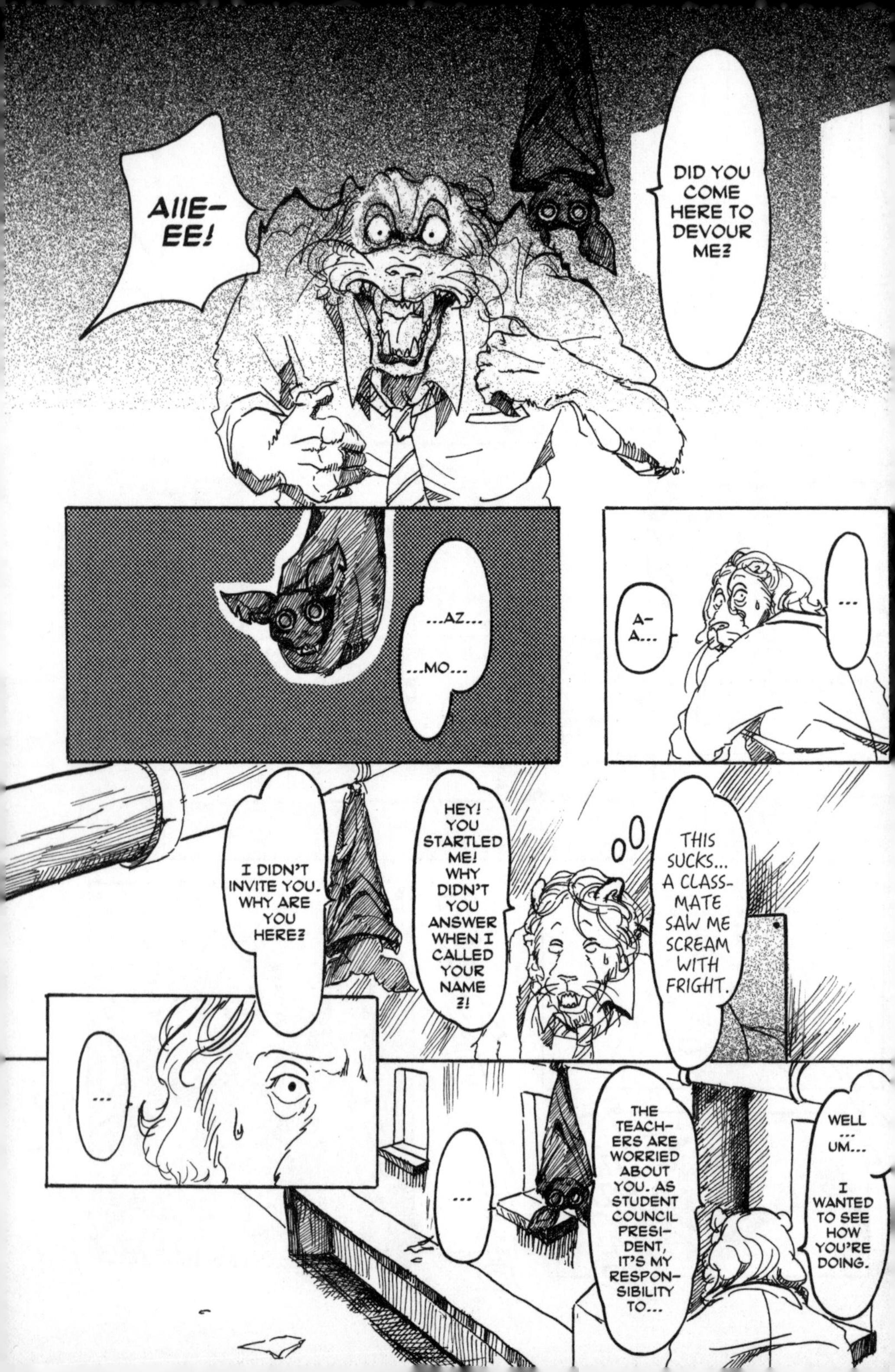
DID YOU COME HERE TO DEVOUR ME?
AIIE-EE!
...
A-A...
...AZ... ...MO...
THIS SUCKS... A CLASSMATE SAW ME SCREAM WITH FRIGHT.
HEY! YOU STARTLED ME! WHY DIDN'T YOU ANSWER WHEN I CALLED YOUR NAME?!
I DIDN'T INVITE YOU. WHY ARE YOU HERE?
WELL... UM... I WANTED TO SEE HOW YOU'RE DOING.
THE TEACHERS ARE WORRIED ABOUT YOU. AS STUDENT COUNCIL PRESIDENT, IT'S MY RESPONSIBILITY TO...
...
...

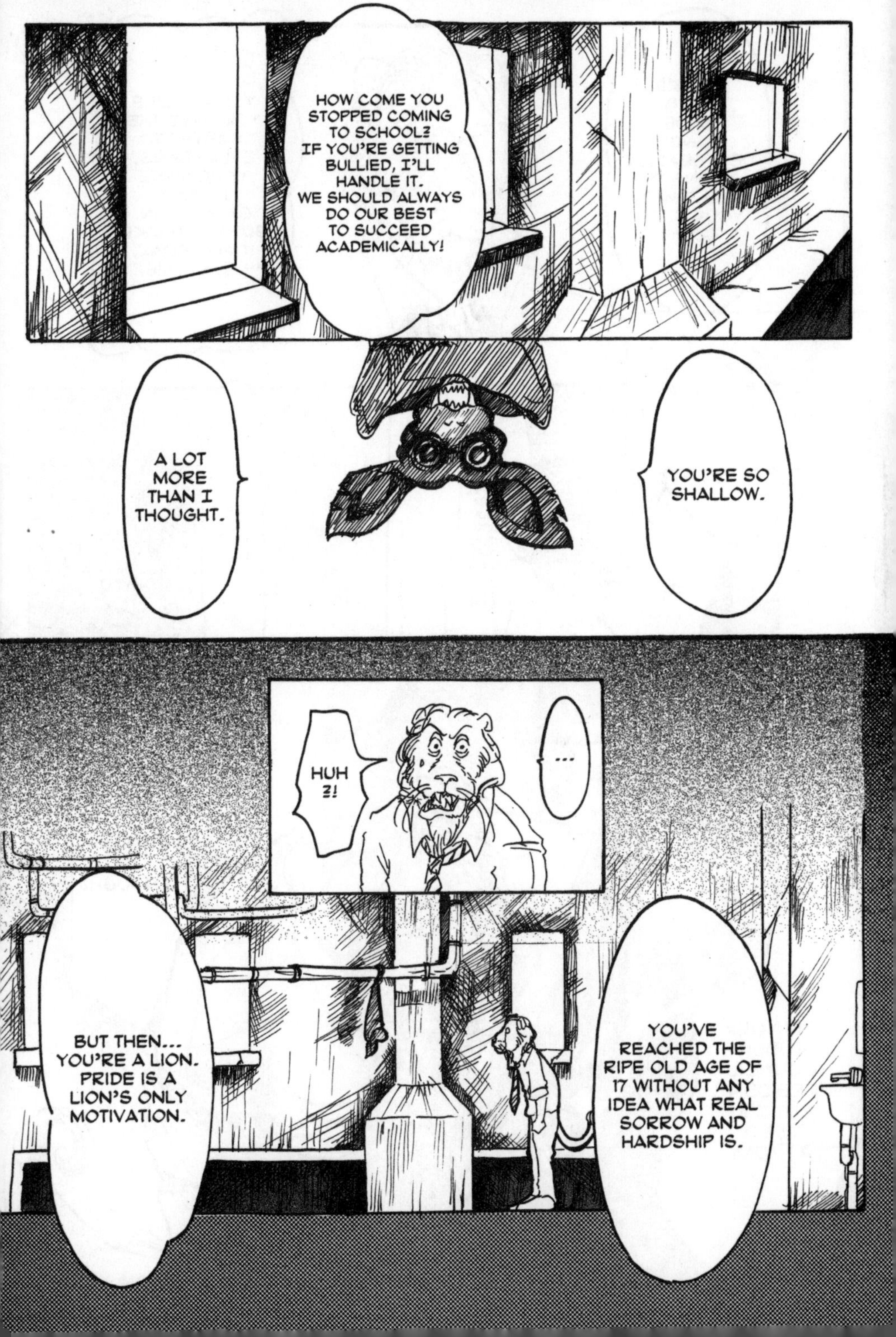
HOW COME YOU STOPPED COMING TO SCHOOL? IF YOU'RE GETTING BULLIED, I'LL HANDLE IT. WE SHOULD ALWAYS DO OUR BEST TO SUCCEED ACADEMICALLY!
YOU'RE SO SHALLOW.
A LOT MORE THAN I THOUGHT.
YOU'VE REACHED THE RIPE OLD AGE OF 17 WITHOUT ANY IDEA WHAT REAL SORROW AND HARDSHIP IS.
BUT THEN... YOU'RE A LION. PRIDE IS A LION'S ONLY MOTIVATION.
...
HUH ?!

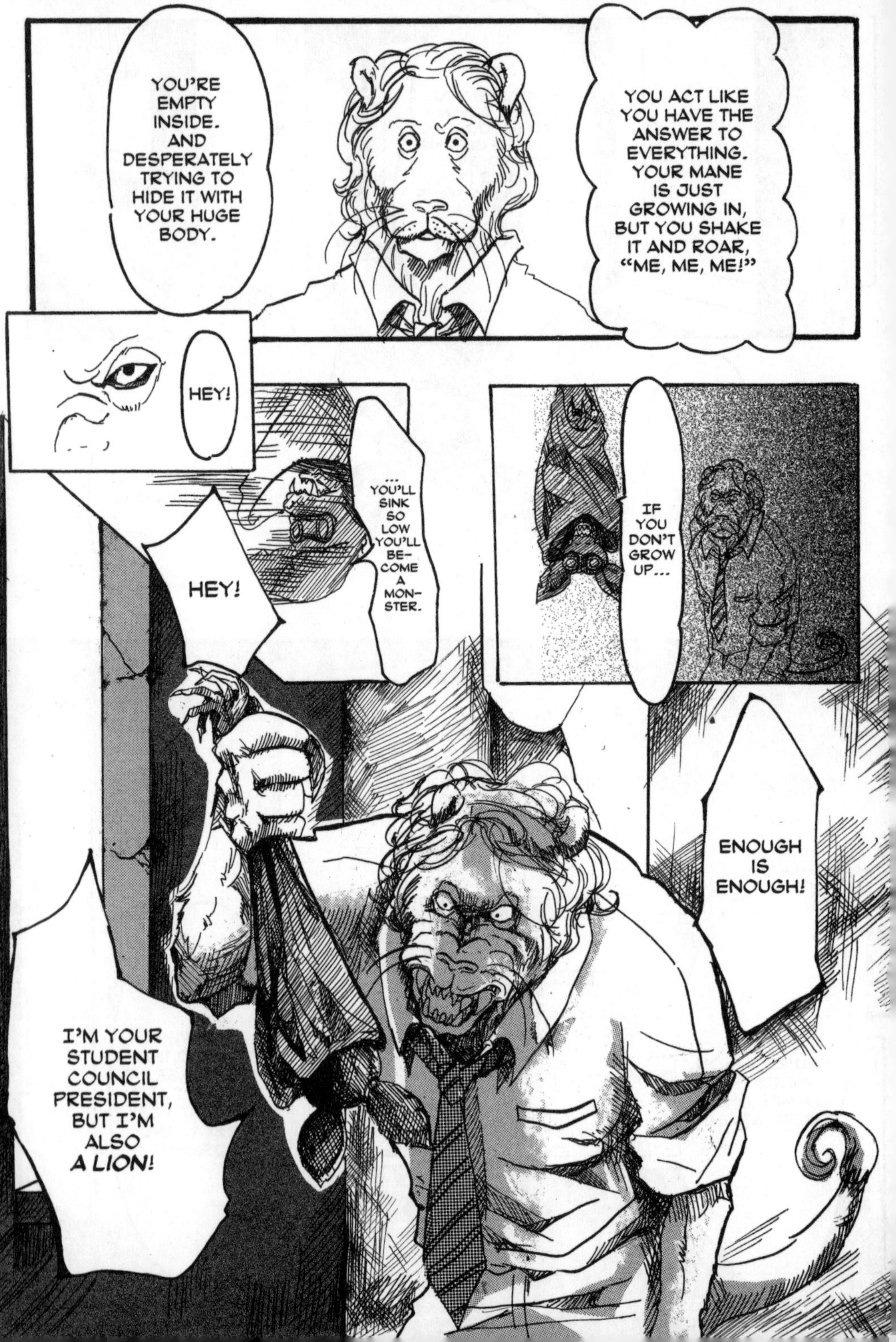
YOU ACT LIKE YOU HAVE THE ANSWER TO EVERYTHING. YOUR MANE IS JUST GROWING IN, BUT YOU SHAKE IT AND ROAR, "ME, ME, ME!"
YOU'RE EMPTY INSIDE. AND DESPERATELY TRYING TO HIDE IT WITH YOUR HUGE BODY.
IF YOU DON'T GROW UP...
...YOU'LL SINK SO LOW YOU'LL BE-COME A MON-STER.
HEY!
HEY!
ENOUGH IS ENOUGH!
I'M YOUR STUDENT COUNCIL PRESIDENT, BUT I'M ALSO A LION!

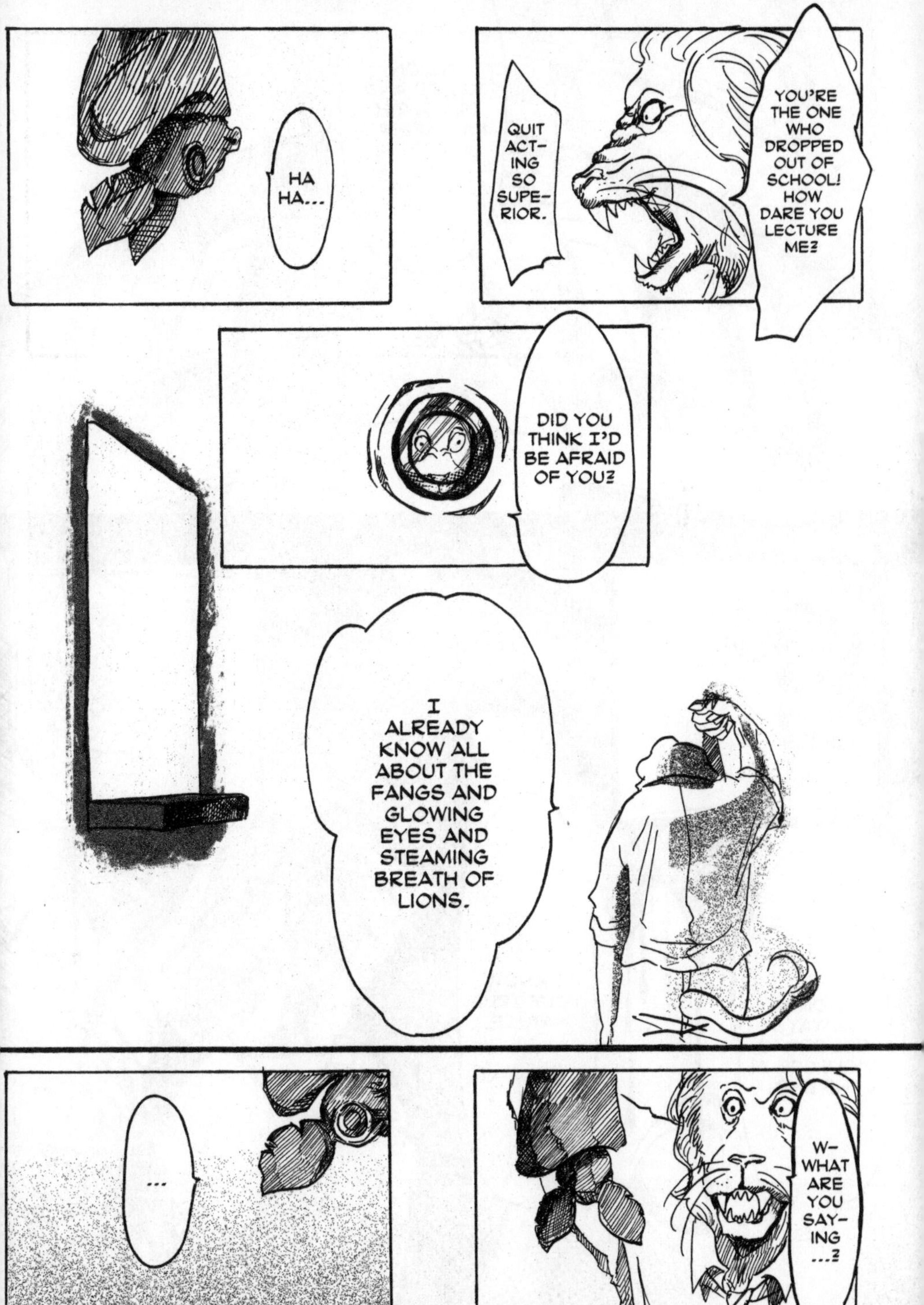
YOU'RE THE ONE WHO DROPPED OUT OF SCHOOL! HOW DARE YOU LECTURE ME?
QUIT ACT-ING SO SUPE-RIOR.
HA HA...
DID YOU THINK I'D BE AFRAID OF YOU?
I ALREADY KNOW ALL ABOUT THE FANGS AND GLOWING EYES AND STEAMING BREATH OF LIONS.
W-WHAT ARE YOU SAY-ING...?
...

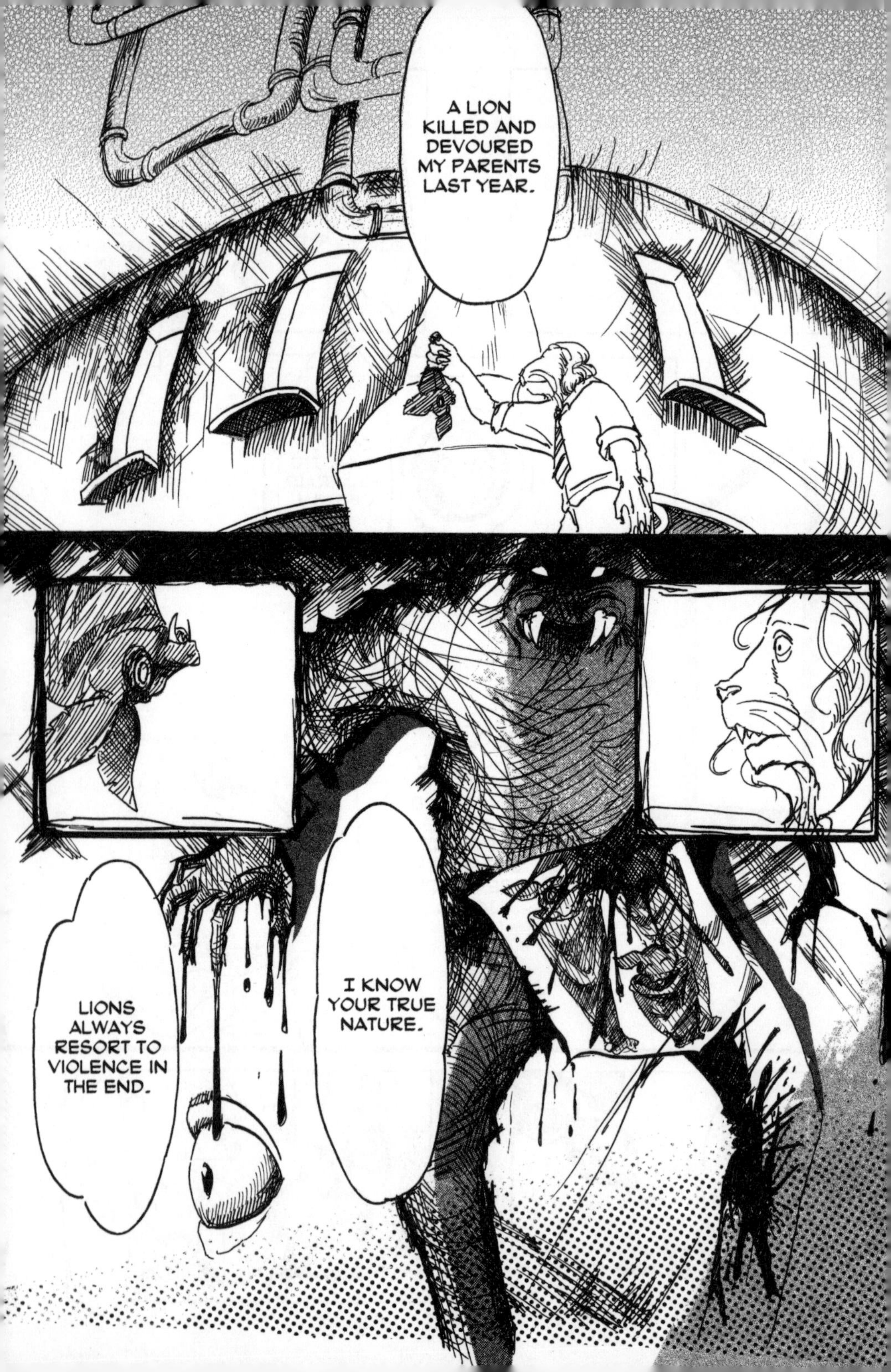
A LION KILLED AND DEVOURED MY PARENTS LAST YEAR.
I KNOW YOUR TRUE NATURE.
LIONS ALWAYS RESORT TO VIOLENCE IN THE END.

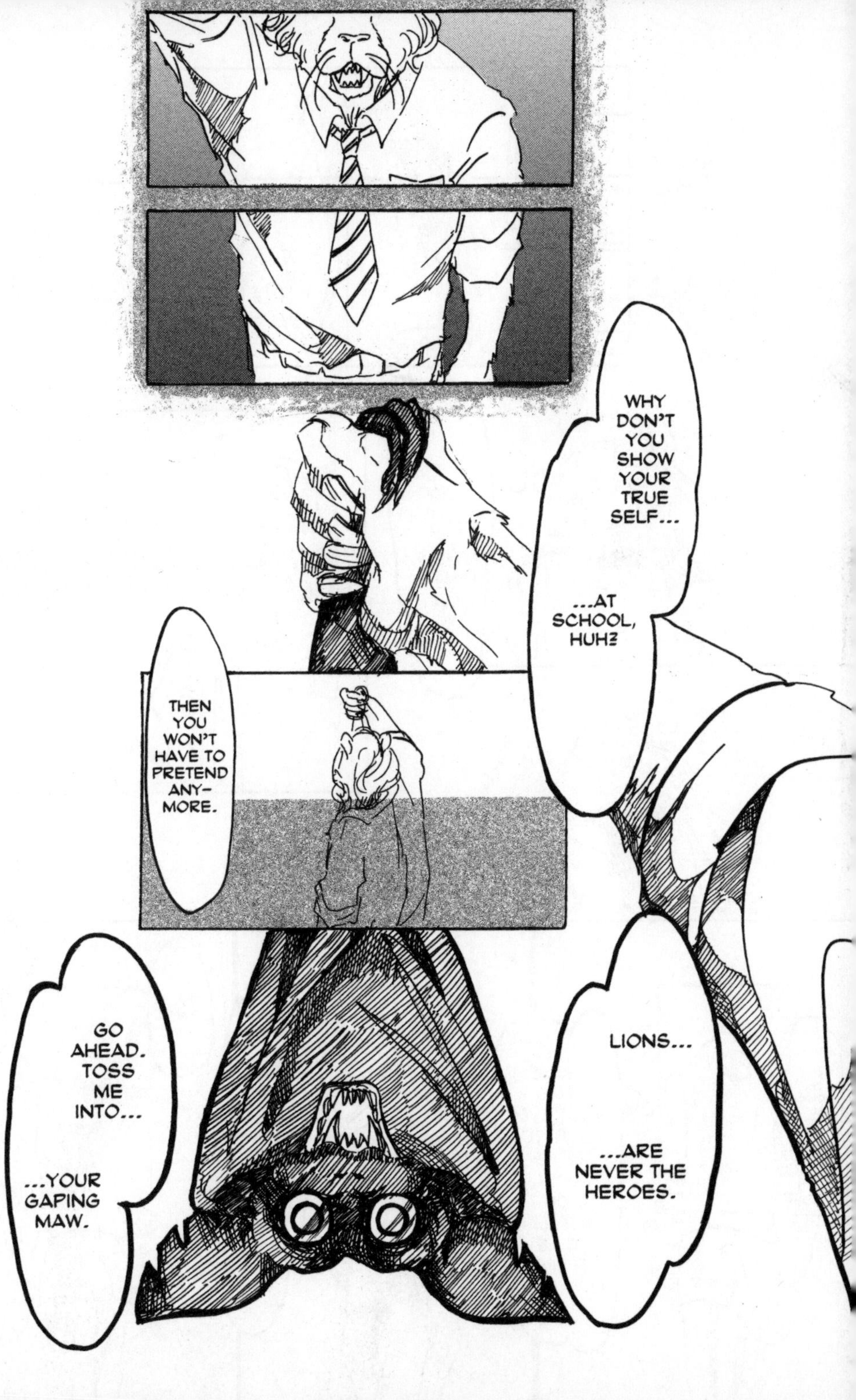
WHY DON'T YOU SHOW YOUR TRUE SELF...
...AT SCHOOL, HUH?
THEN YOU WON'T HAVE TO PRETEND ANY-MORE.
LIONS...
...ARE NEVER THE HEROES.
GO AHEAD. TOSS ME INTO...
...YOUR GAPING MAW.

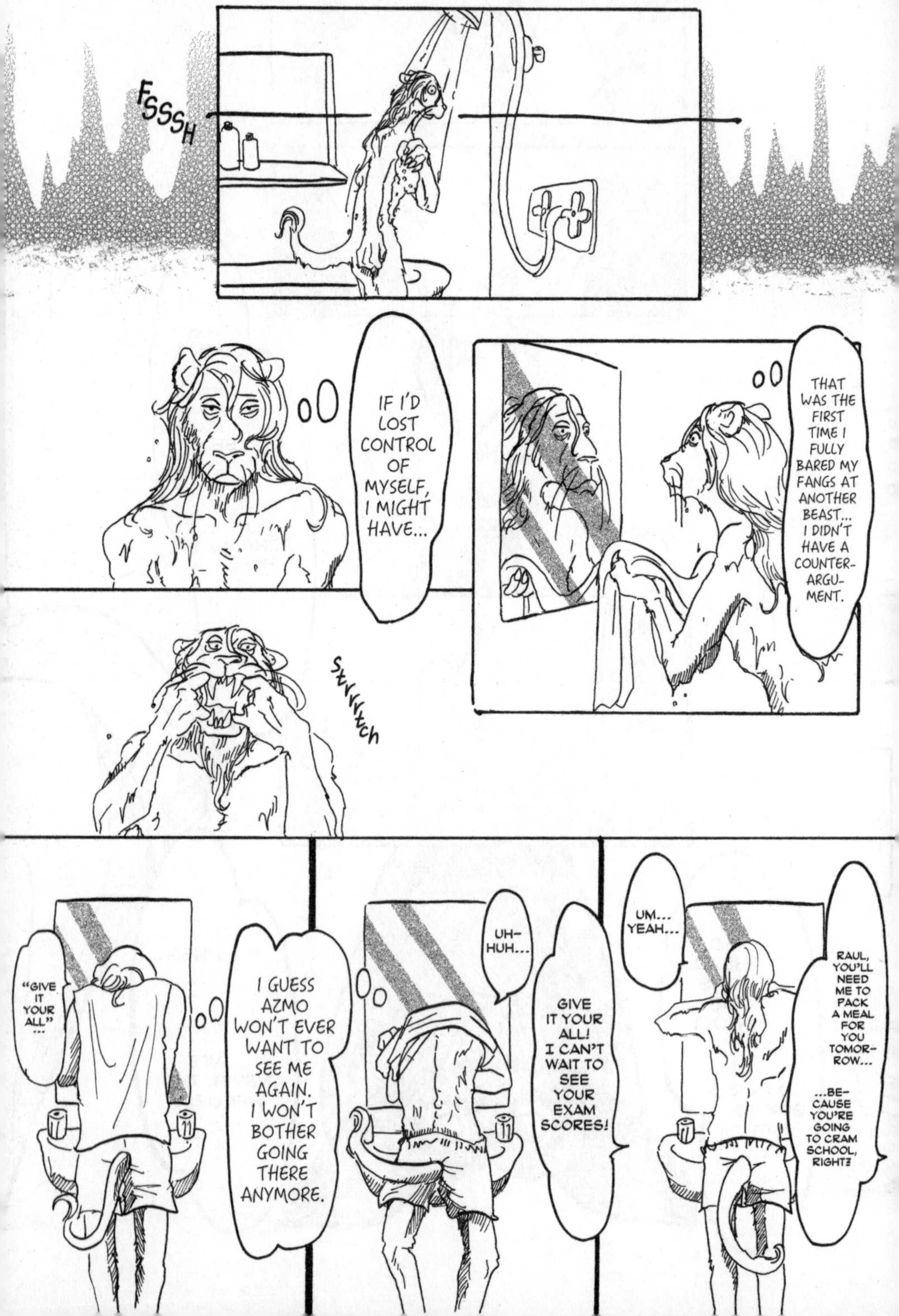
FSSSH
THAT WAS THE FIRST TIME I FULLY BARED MY FANGS AT ANOTHER BEAST... I DIDN'T HAVE A COUNTER-ARGUMENT.
IF I'D LOST CONTROL OF MYSELF, I MIGHT HAVE...
Strrrtch
RAUL, YOU'LL NEED ME TO PACK A MEAL FOR YOU TOMORROW...
...BECAUSE YOU'RE GOING TO CRAM SCHOOL, RIGHT?
UM... YEAH...
GIVE IT YOUR ALL! I CAN'T WAIT TO SEE YOUR EXAM SCORES!
UH-HUH...
I GUESS AZMO WON'T EVER WANT TO SEE ME AGAIN. I WON'T BOTHER GOING THERE ANYMORE.
"GIVE IT YOUR ALL"...

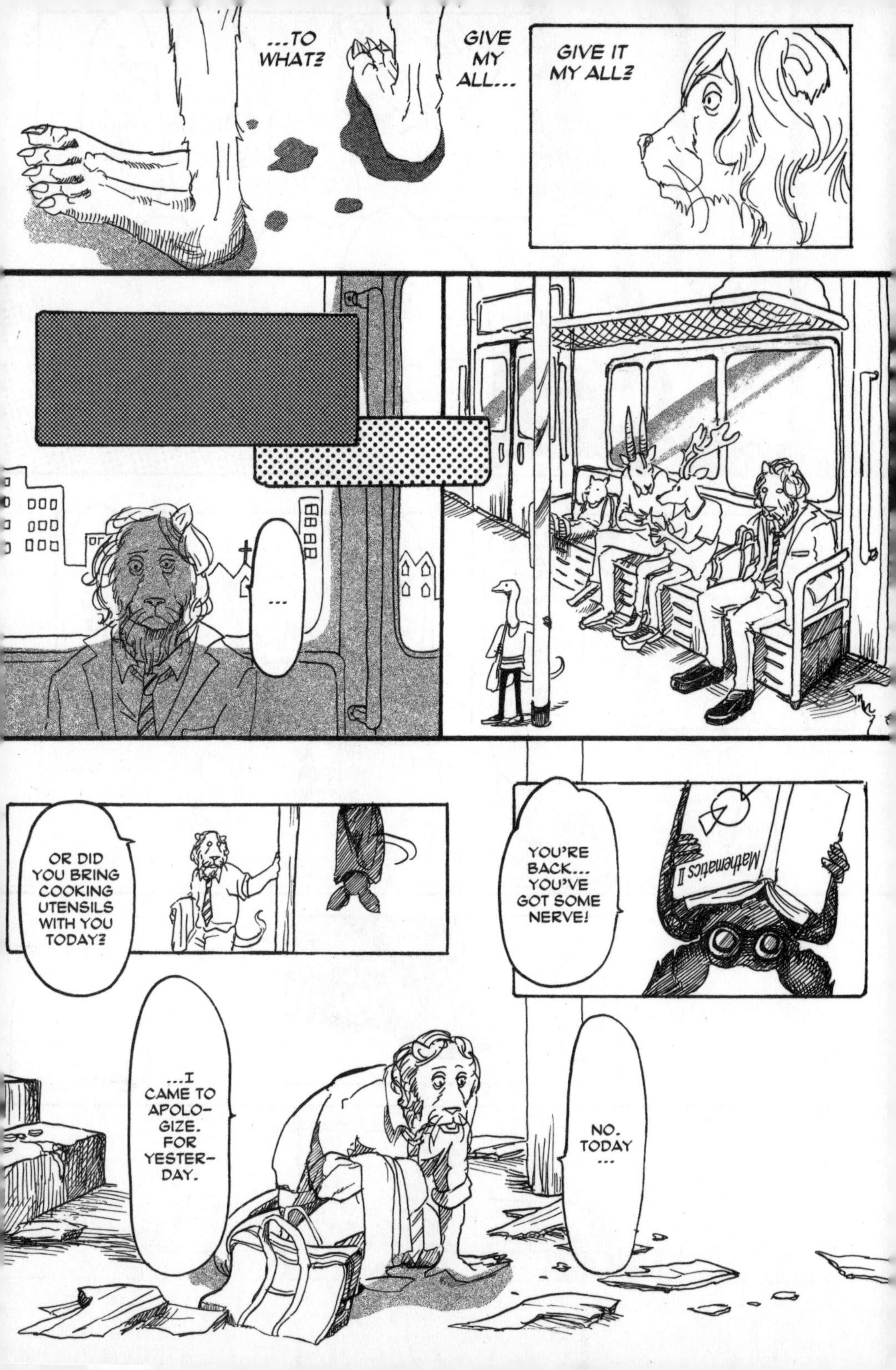
GIVE IT MY ALL?
GIVE MY ALL...
...TO WHAT?
...
YOU'RE BACK... YOU'VE GOT SOME NERVE!
OR DID YOU BRING COOKING UTENSILS WITH YOU TODAY?
NO. TODAY ...
...I CAME TO APOLO-GIZE. FOR YESTER-DAY.

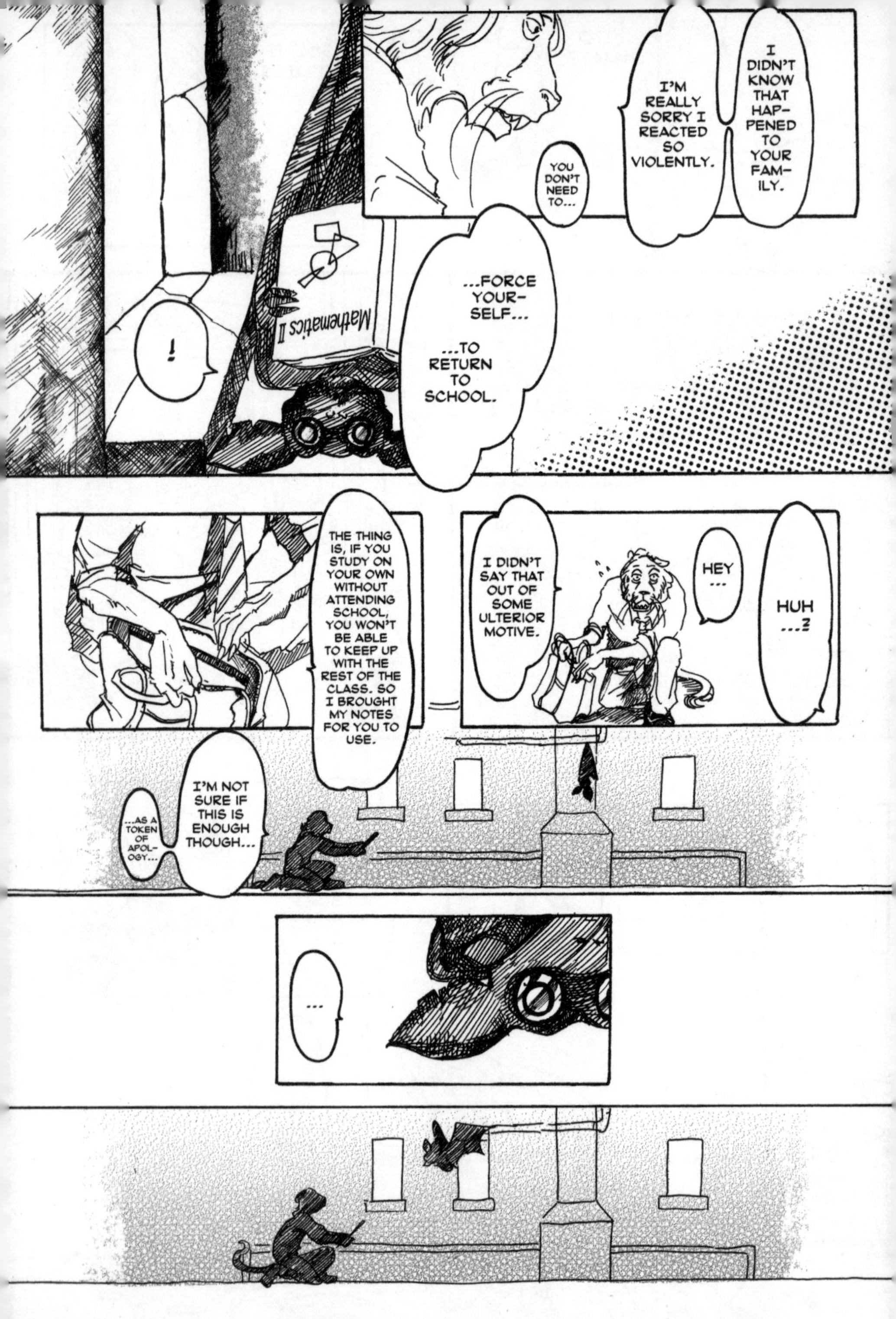
I DIDN'T KNOW THAT HAPPENED TO YOUR FAMILY.
I'M REALLY SORRY I REACTED SO VIOLENTLY.
YOU DON'T NEED TO...
...FORCE YOURSELF...
...TO RETURN TO SCHOOL.
Mathematics II
!
HUH...?
HEY...
I DIDN'T SAY THAT OUT OF SOME ULTERIOR MOTIVE.
THE THING IS, IF YOU STUDY ON YOUR OWN WITHOUT ATTENDING SCHOOL, YOU WON'T BE ABLE TO KEEP UP WITH THE REST OF THE CLASS. SO I BROUGHT MY NOTES FOR YOU TO USE.
I'M NOT SURE IF THIS IS ENOUGH THOUGH...
...AS A TOKEN OF APOLOGY...
...

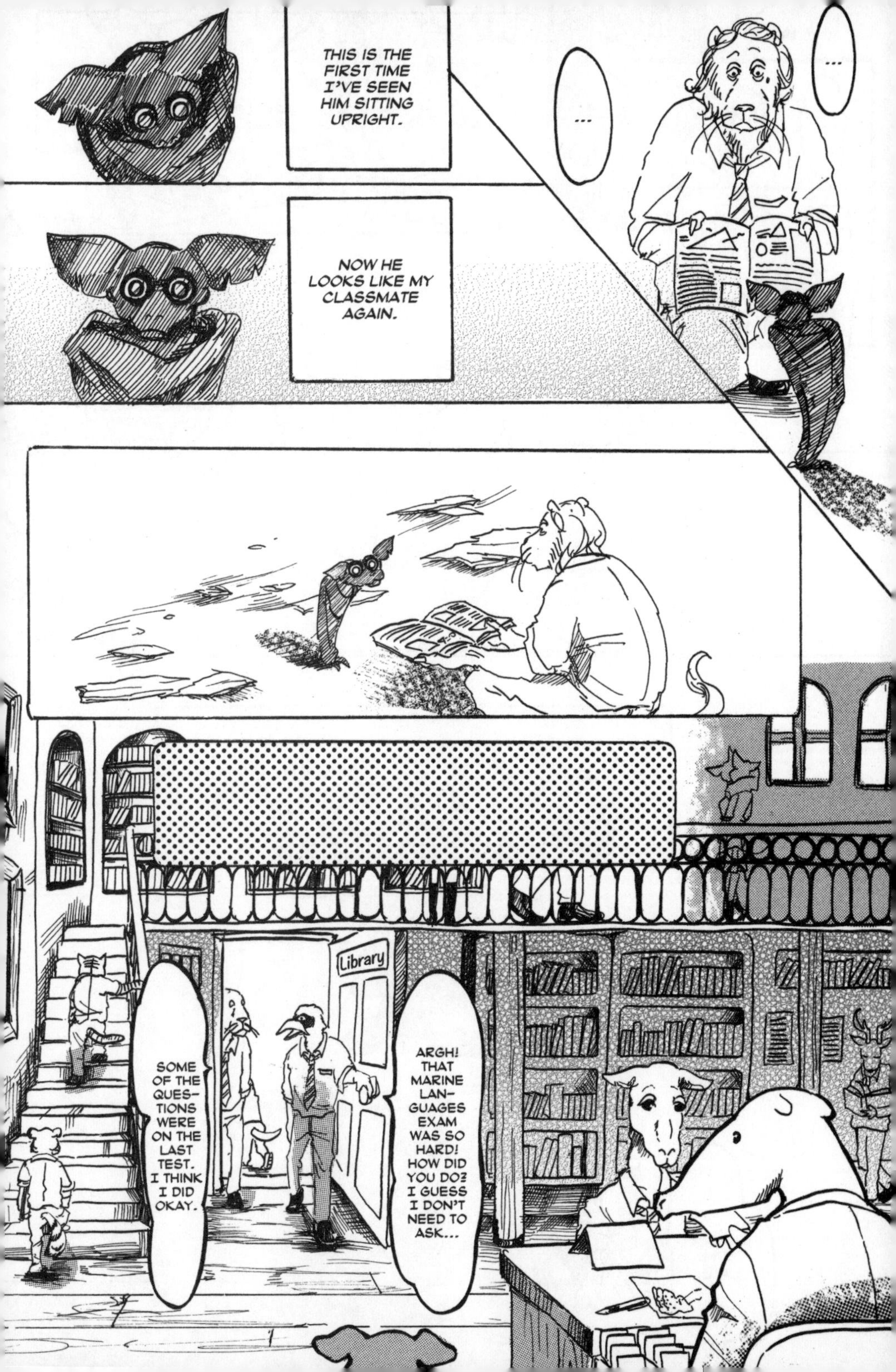
...
...
THIS IS THE FIRST TIME I'VE SEEN HIM SITTING UPRIGHT.
NOW HE LOOKS LIKE MY CLASSMATE AGAIN.
Library
ARGH! THAT MARINE LAN-GUAGES EXAM WAS SO HARD! HOW DID YOU DO? I GUESS I DON'T NEED TO ASK...
SOME OF THE QUES-TIONS WERE ON THE LAST TEST. I THINK I DID OKAY.

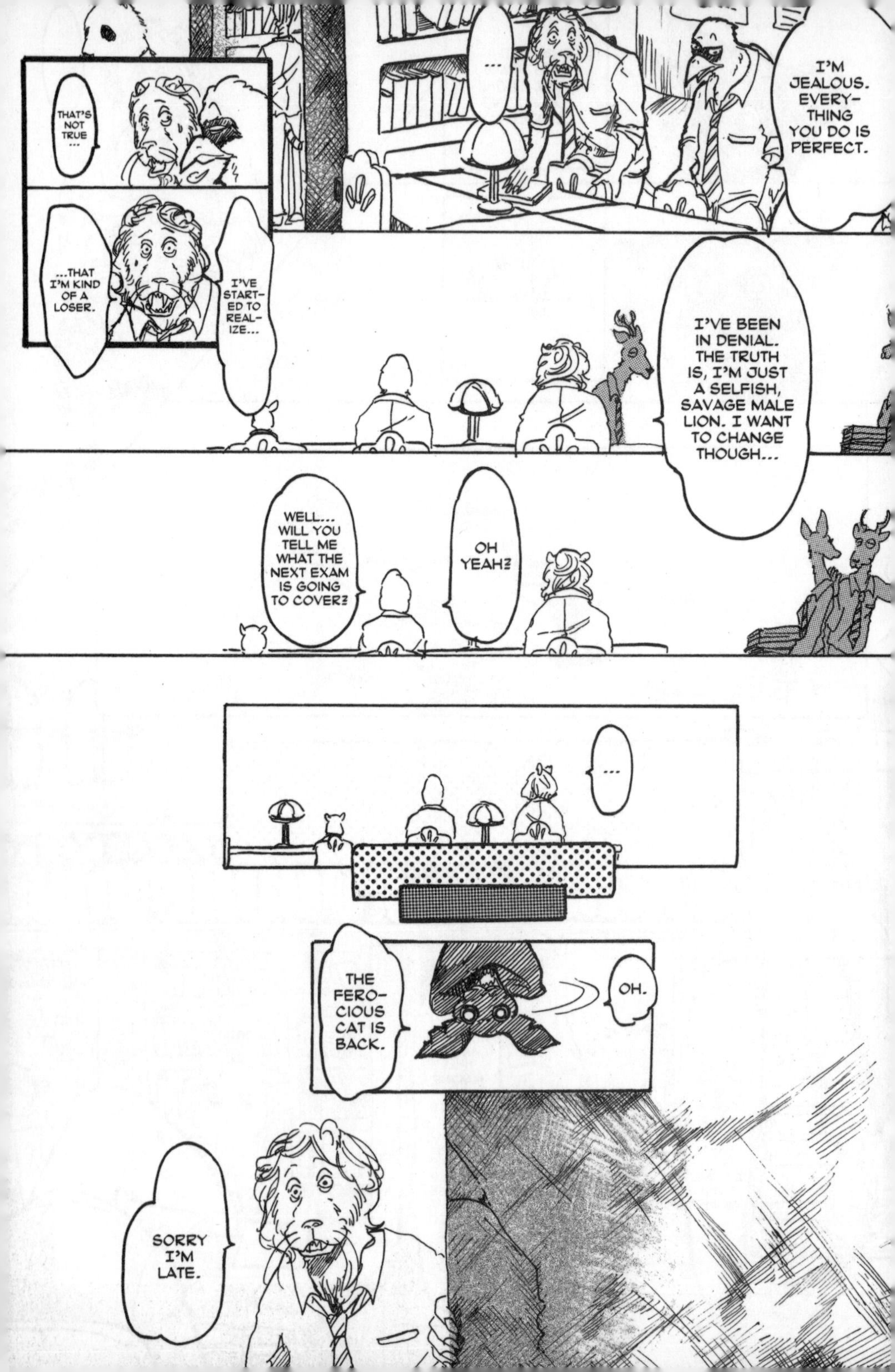
I'M JEALOUS. EVERYTHING YOU DO IS PERFECT.
...
THAT'S NOT TRUE ...
I'VE STARTED TO REALIZE...
...THAT I'M KIND OF A LOSER.
I'VE BEEN IN DENIAL. THE TRUTH IS, I'M JUST A SELFISH, SAVAGE MALE LION. I WANT TO CHANGE THOUGH...
OH YEAH?
WELL... WILL YOU TELL ME WHAT THE NEXT EXAM IS GOING TO COVER?
...
OH.
THE FEROCIOUS CAT IS BACK.
SORRY I'M LATE.

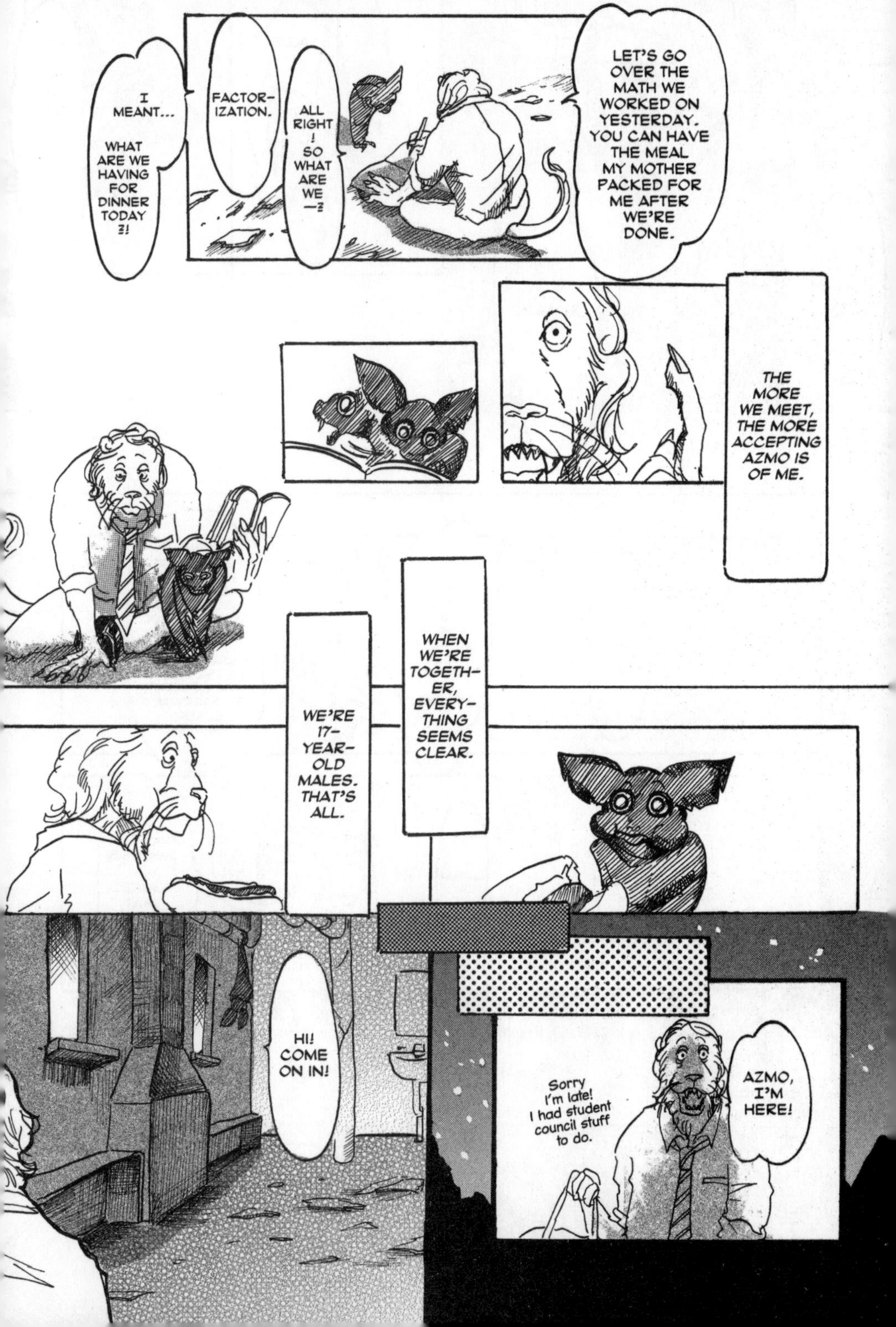

LET'S GO OVER THE MATH WE WORKED ON YESTERDAY. YOU CAN HAVE THE MEAL MY MOTHER PACKED FOR ME AFTER WE'RE DONE.
ALL RIGHT! SO WHAT ARE WE—?
FACTORIZATION.
I MEANT... WHAT ARE WE HAVING FOR DINNER TODAY?!
THE MORE WE MEET, THE MORE ACCEPTING AZMO IS OF ME.
WHEN WE'RE TOGETHER, EVERYTHING SEEMS CLEAR.
WE'RE 17-YEAR-OLD MALES. THAT'S ALL.
AZMO, I'M HERE!
Sorry I'm late! I had student council stuff to do.
HI! COME ON IN!

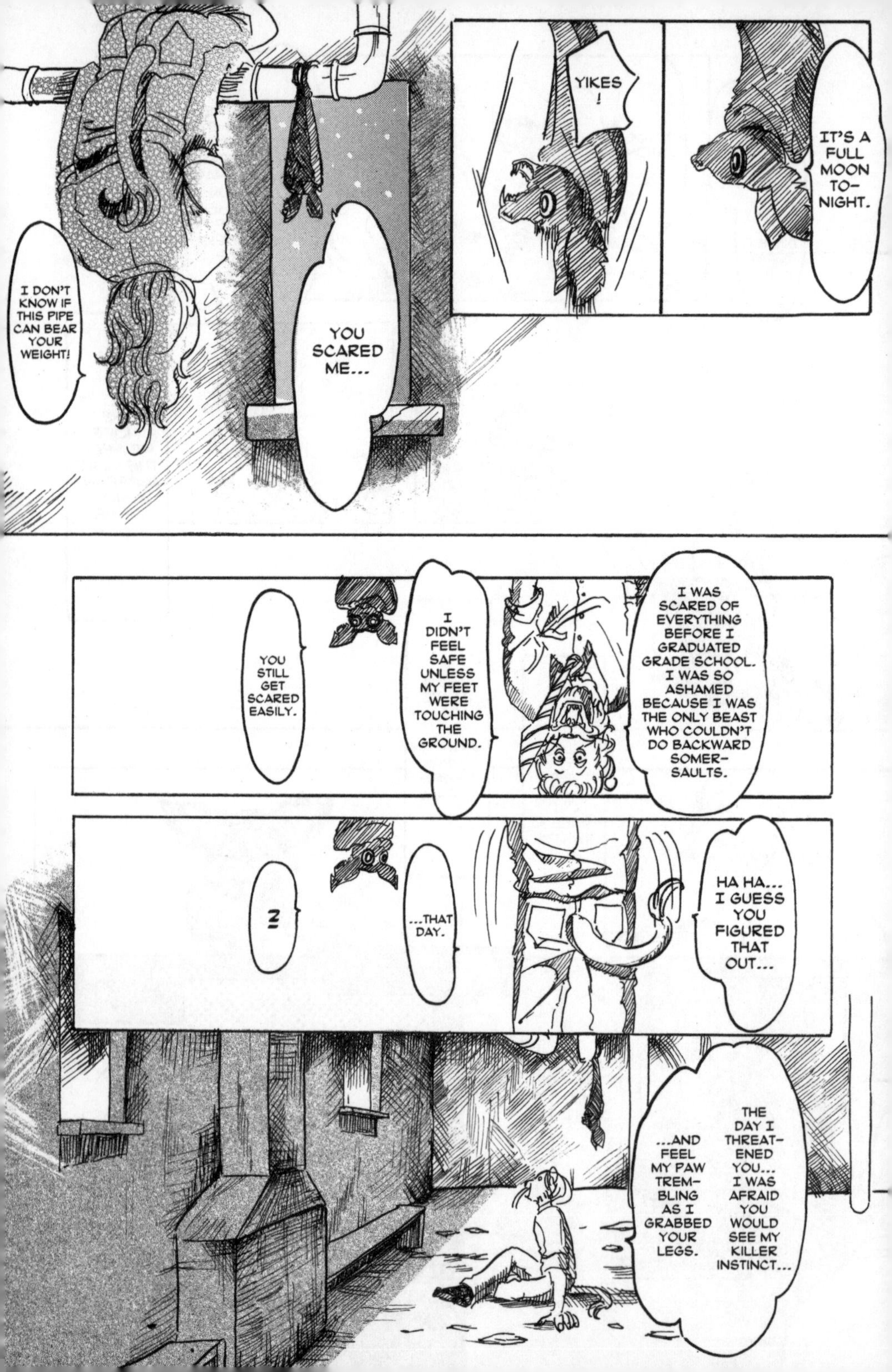

IT'S A FULL MOON TONIGHT.
YIKES!
YOU SCARED ME...
I DON'T KNOW IF THIS PIPE CAN BEAR YOUR WEIGHT!
I WAS SCARED OF EVERYTHING BEFORE I GRADUATED GRADE SCHOOL. I WAS SO ASHAMED BECAUSE I WAS THE ONLY BEAST WHO COULDN'T DO BACKWARD SOMERSAULTS.
I DIDN'T FEEL SAFE UNLESS MY FEET WERE TOUCHING THE GROUND.
YOU STILL GET SCARED EASILY.
HA HA... I GUESS YOU FIGURED THAT OUT...
...THAT DAY.
THE DAY I THREATENED YOU... I WAS AFRAID YOU WOULD SEE MY KILLER INSTINCT...
...AND FEEL MY PAW TREMBLING AS I GRABBED YOUR LEGS.

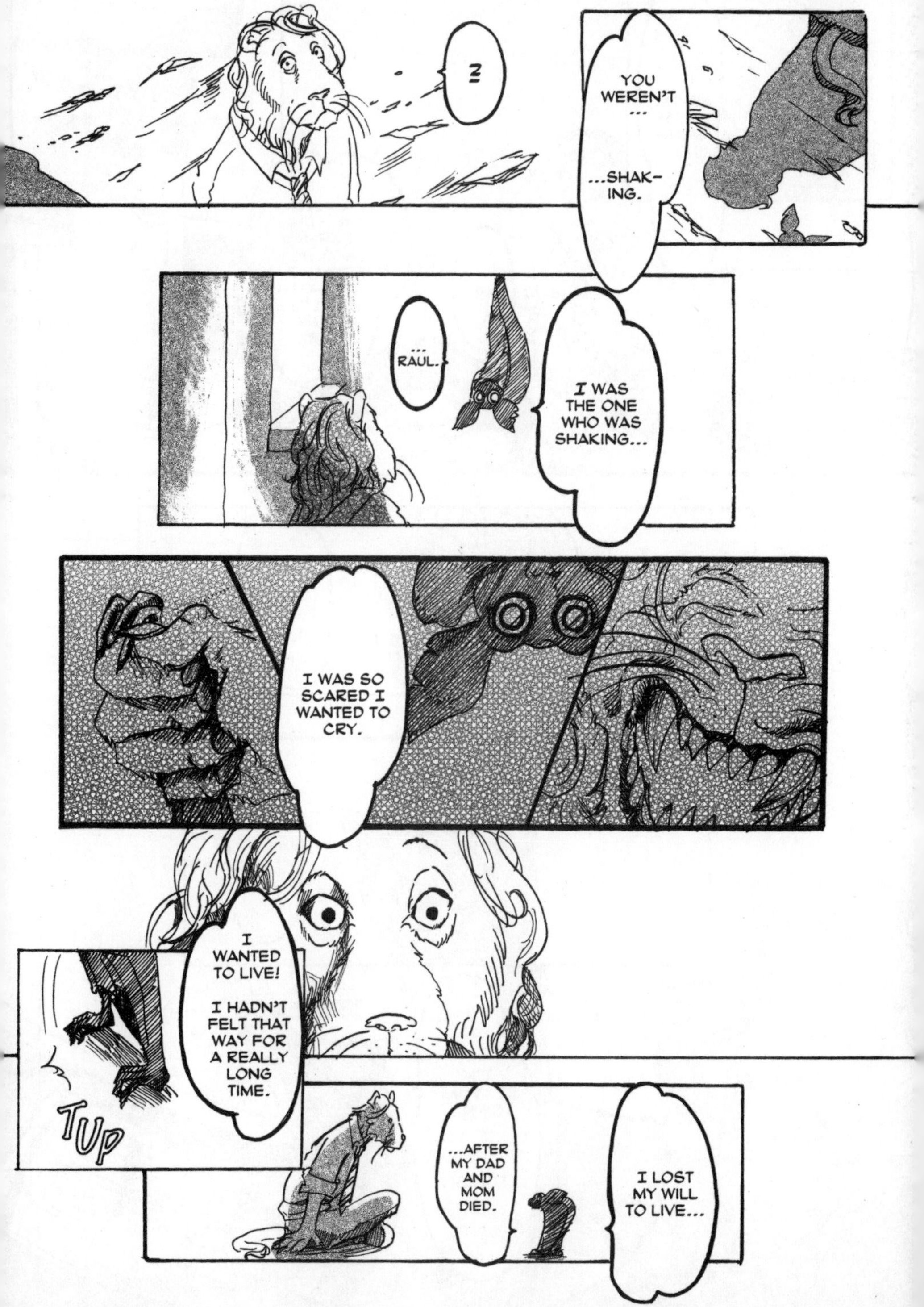
YOU WEREN'T ... ...SHAK-ING.
?!
... RAUL.
I WAS THE ONE WHO WAS SHAKING...
I WAS SO SCARED I WANTED TO CRY.
I WANTED TO LIVE!
I HADN'T FELT THAT WAY FOR A REALLY LONG TIME.
TUP
I LOST MY WILL TO LIVE...
...AFTER MY DAD AND MOM DIED.

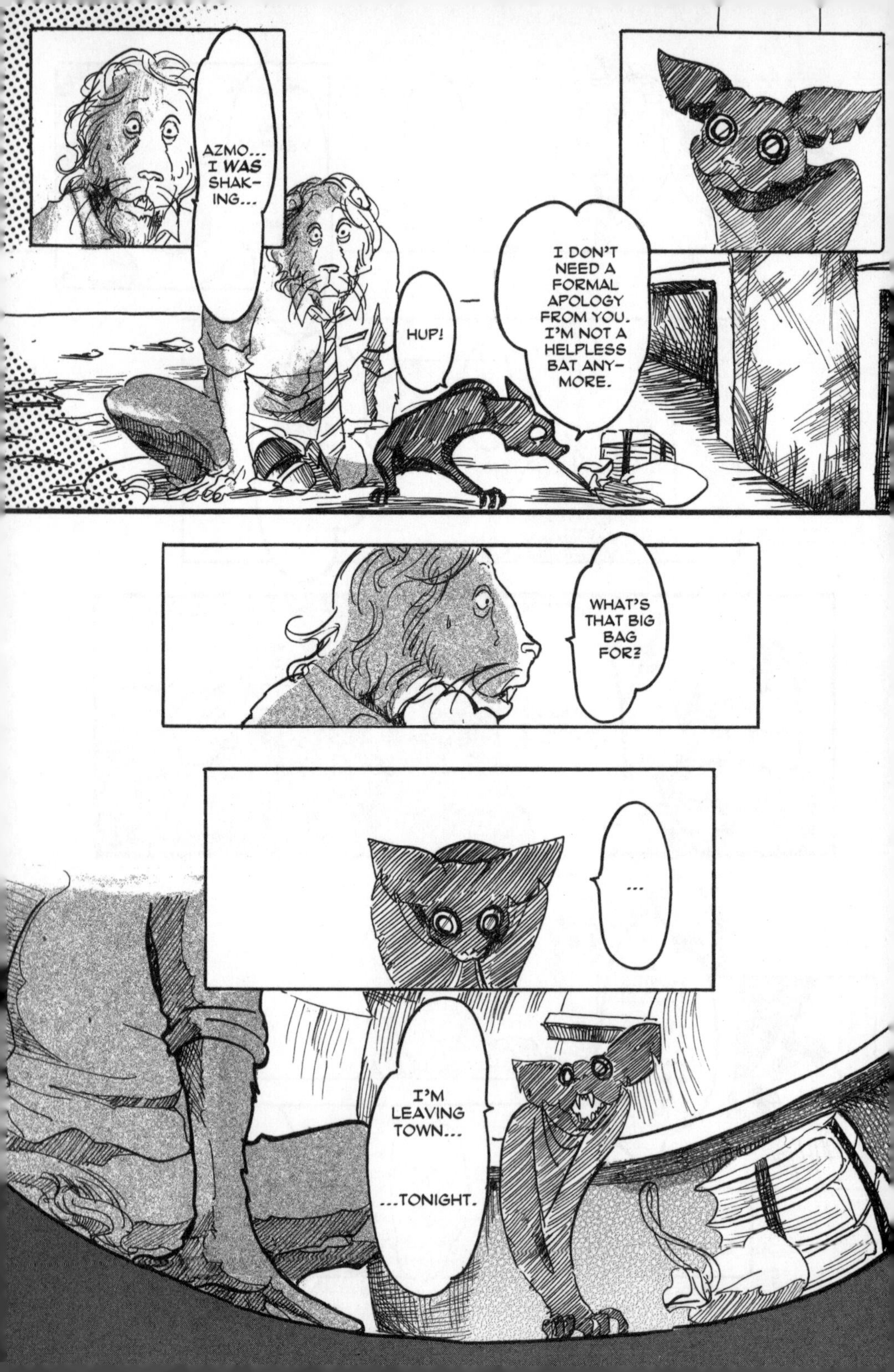
AZMO... I *WAS* SHAKING...
HUP!
I DON'T NEED A FORMAL APOLOGY FROM YOU. I'M NOT A HELPLESS BAT ANYMORE.
WHAT'S THAT BIG BAG FOR?
...
I'M LEAVING TOWN...
...TONIGHT.

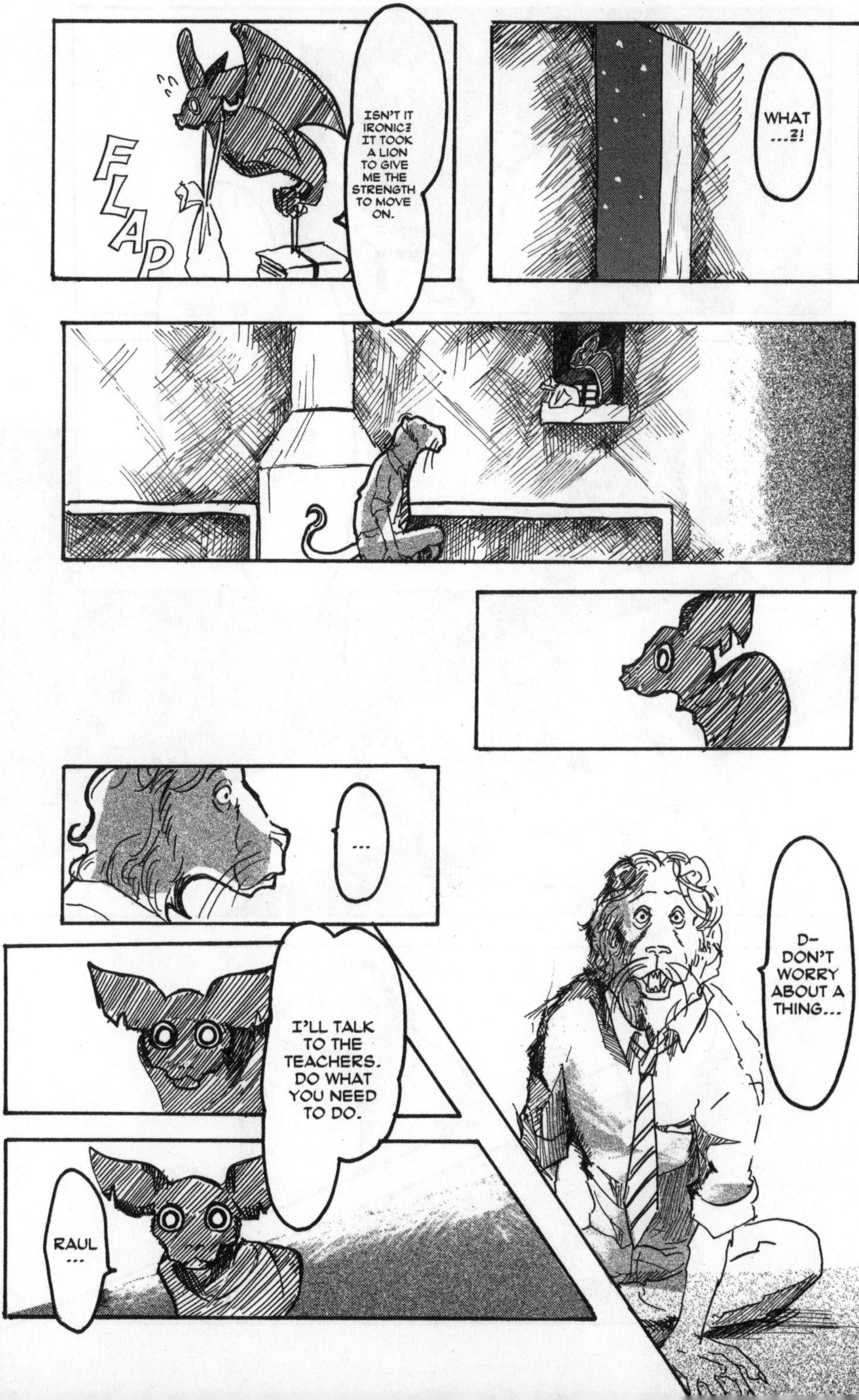
WHAT ...?!
FLAP
ISN'T IT IRONIC? IT TOOK A LION TO GIVE ME THE STRENGTH TO MOVE ON.
D-DON'T WORRY ABOUT A THING...
...
I'LL TALK TO THE TEACHERS. DO WHAT YOU NEED TO DO.
RAUL ...

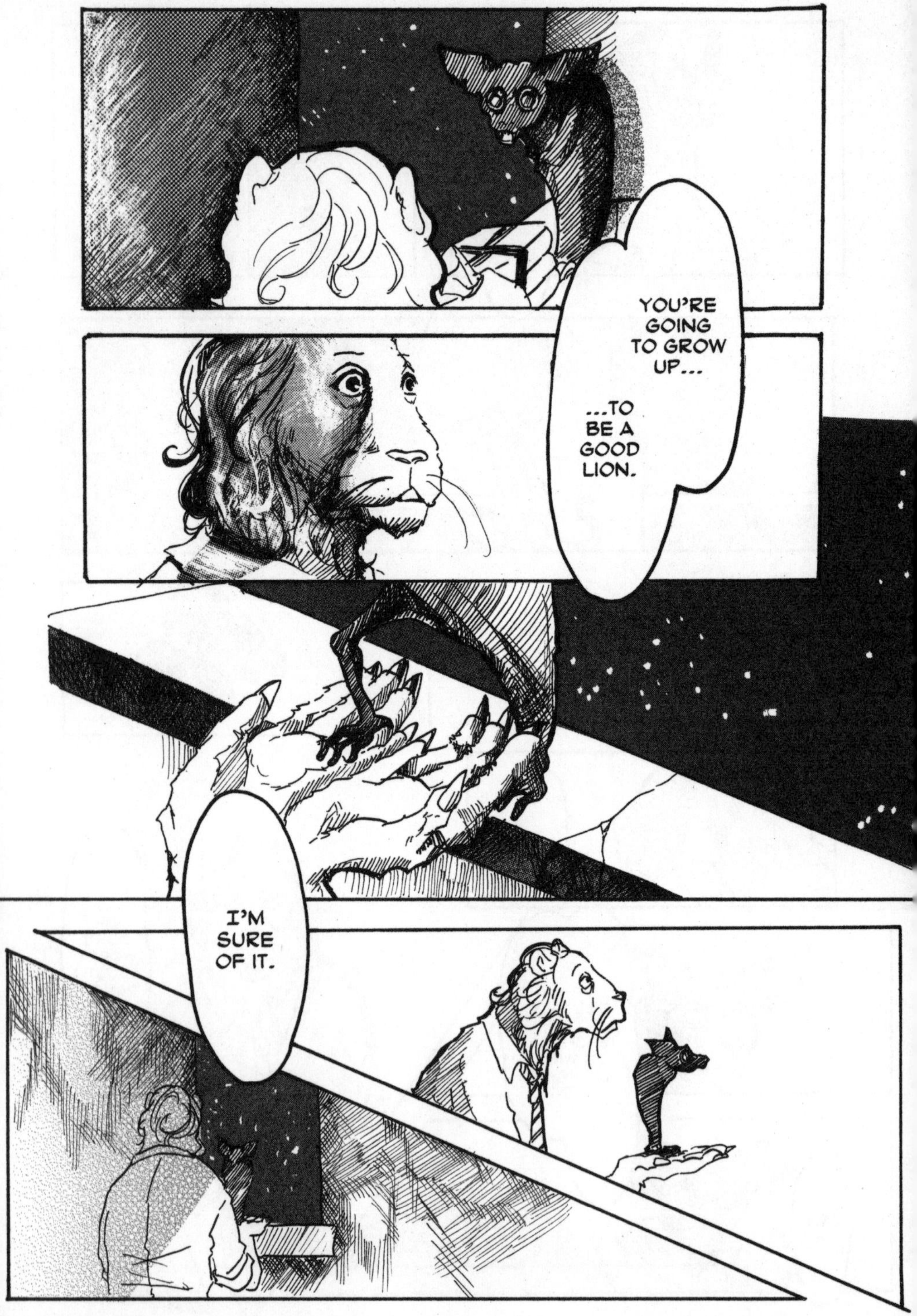
YOU'RE GOING TO GROW UP...
...TO BE A GOOD LION.
I'M SURE OF IT.

SEE YOU.

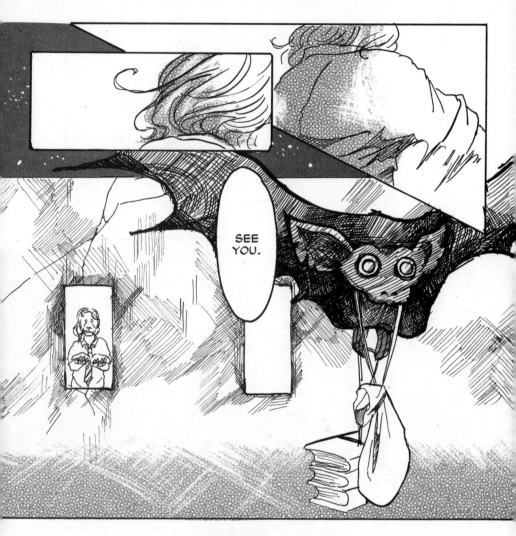

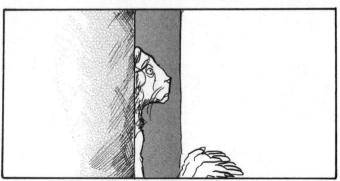

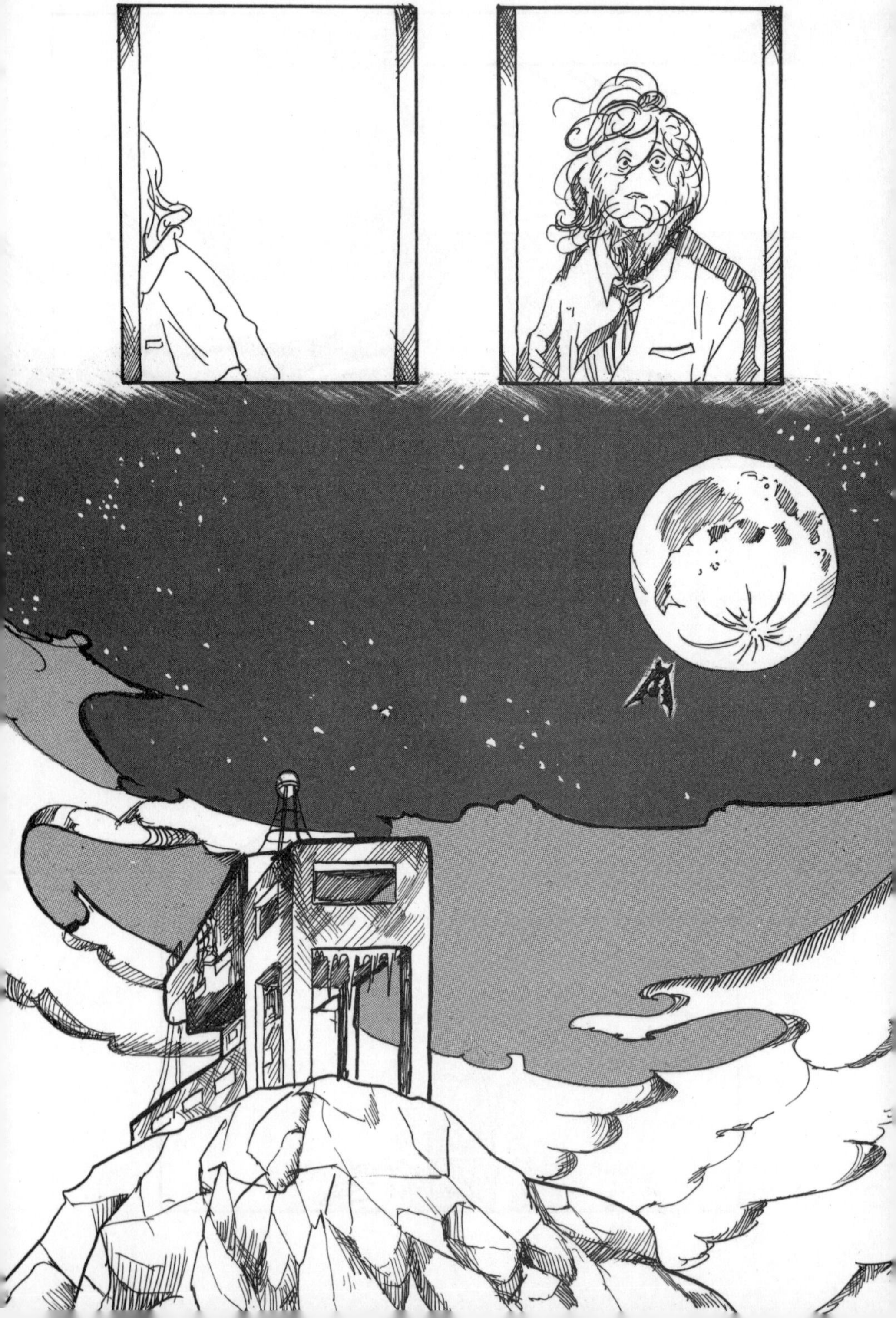

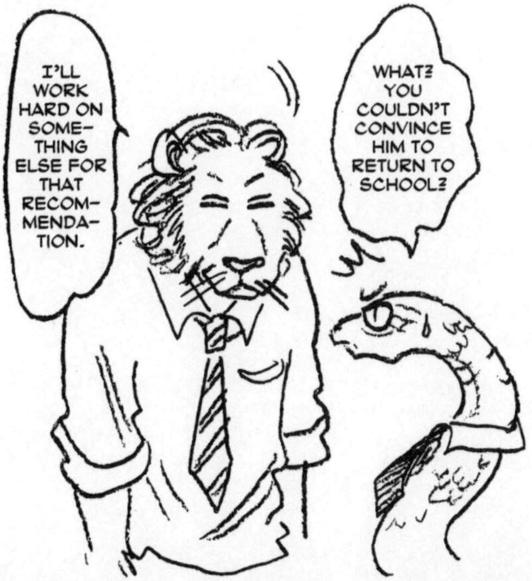
WHAT? YOU COULDN'T CONVINCE HIM TO RETURN TO SCHOOL?
I'LL WORK HARD ON SOMETHING ELSE FOR THAT RECOMMENDATION.

Story 2
The Tiger and the Beaver

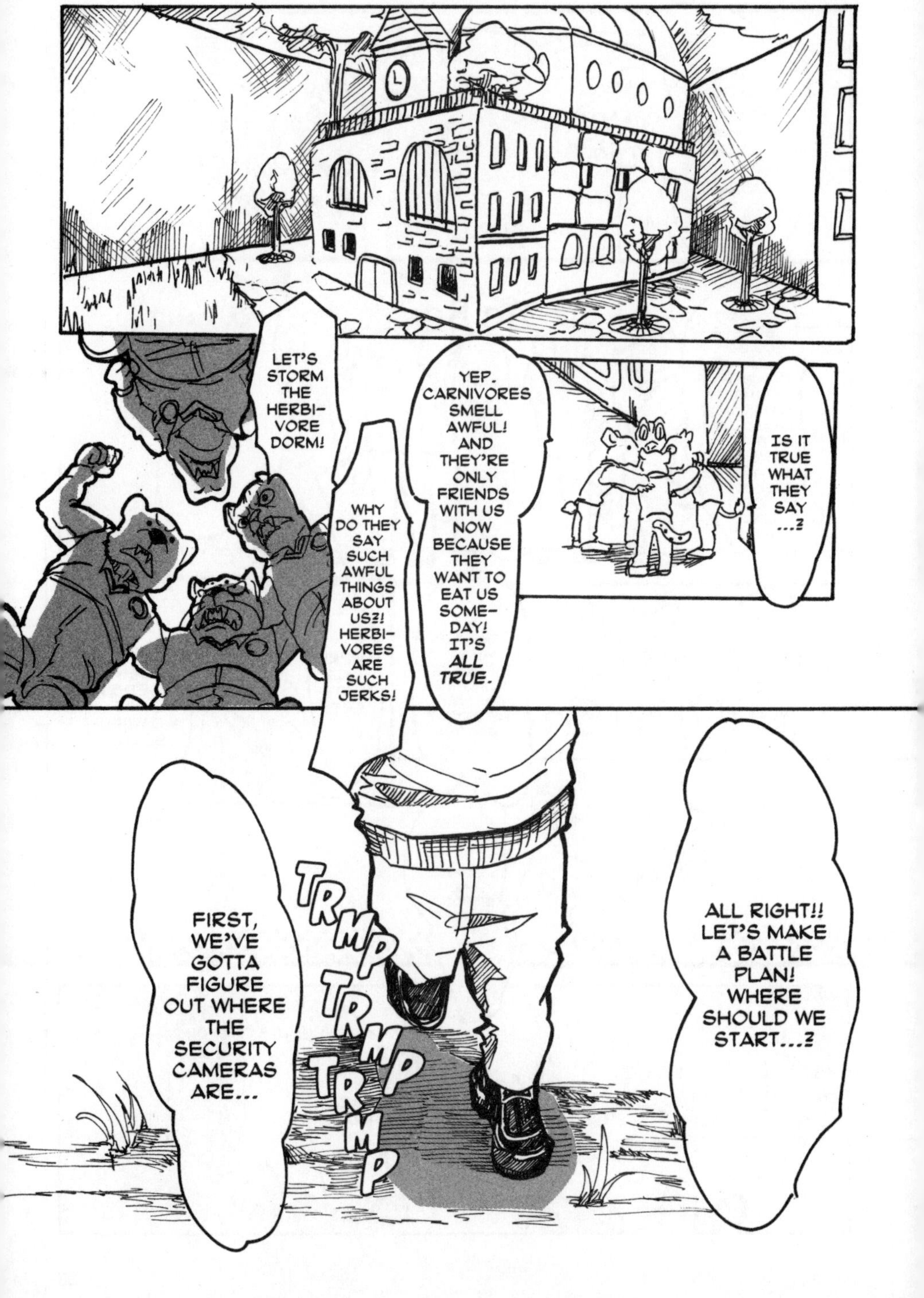
IS IT TRUE WHAT THEY SAY...?
YEP. CARNIVORES SMELL AWFUL! AND THEY'RE ONLY FRIENDS WITH US NOW BECAUSE THEY WANT TO EAT US SOME-DAY! IT'S *ALL TRUE*.
WHY DO THEY SAY SUCH AWFUL THINGS ABOUT US?! HERBI-VORES ARE SUCH JERKS!
LET'S STORM THE HERBI-VORE DORM!
ALL RIGHT!! LET'S MAKE A BATTLE PLAN! WHERE SHOULD WE START...?
TRMP TRMP TRMP TRMP
FIRST, WE'VE GOTTA FIGURE OUT WHERE THE SECURITY CAMERAS ARE...

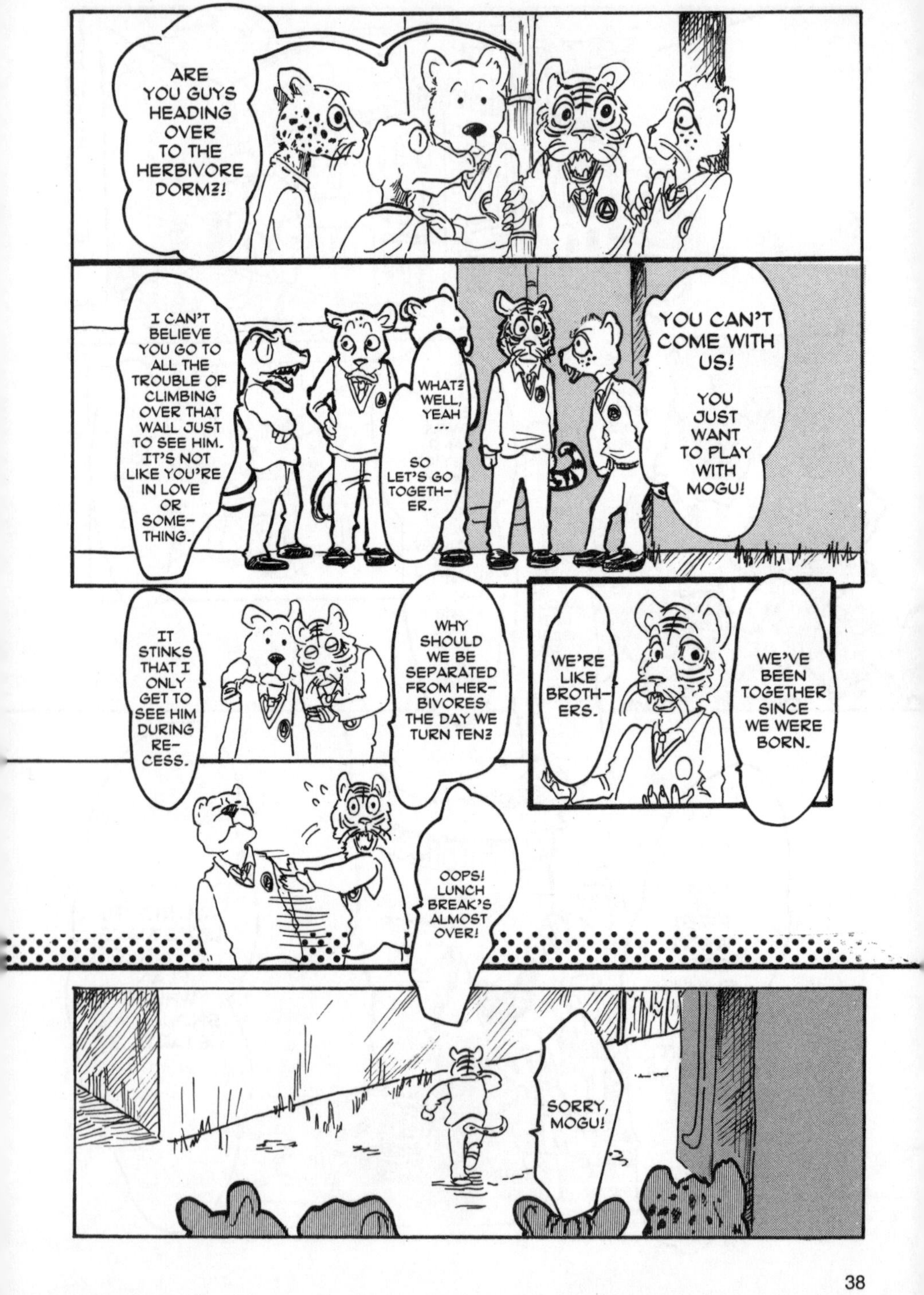
ARE YOU GUYS HEADING OVER TO THE HERBIVORE DORM?!
YOU CAN'T COME WITH US!
YOU JUST WANT TO PLAY WITH MOGU!
WHAT? WELL, YEAH...
SO LET'S GO TOGETH-ER.
I CAN'T BELIEVE YOU GO TO ALL THE TROUBLE OF CLIMBING OVER THAT WALL JUST TO SEE HIM. IT'S NOT LIKE YOU'RE IN LOVE OR SOME-THING.
WE'VE BEEN TOGETHER SINCE WE WERE BORN.
WE'RE LIKE BROTH-ERS.
WHY SHOULD WE BE SEPARATED FROM HER-BIVORES THE DAY WE TURN TEN?
IT STINKS THAT I ONLY GET TO SEE HIM DURING RE-CESS.
OOPS! LUNCH BREAK'S ALMOST OVER!
SORRY, MOGU!

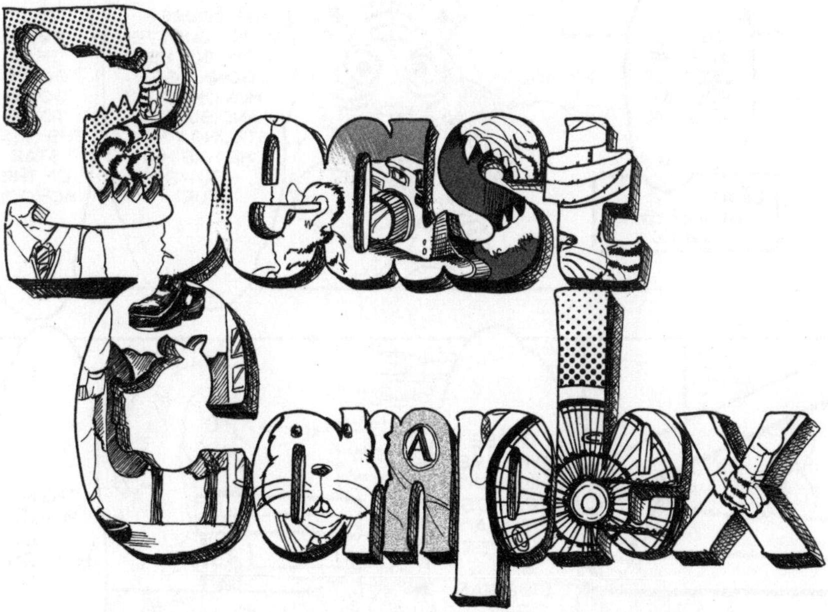
Beast
Complex

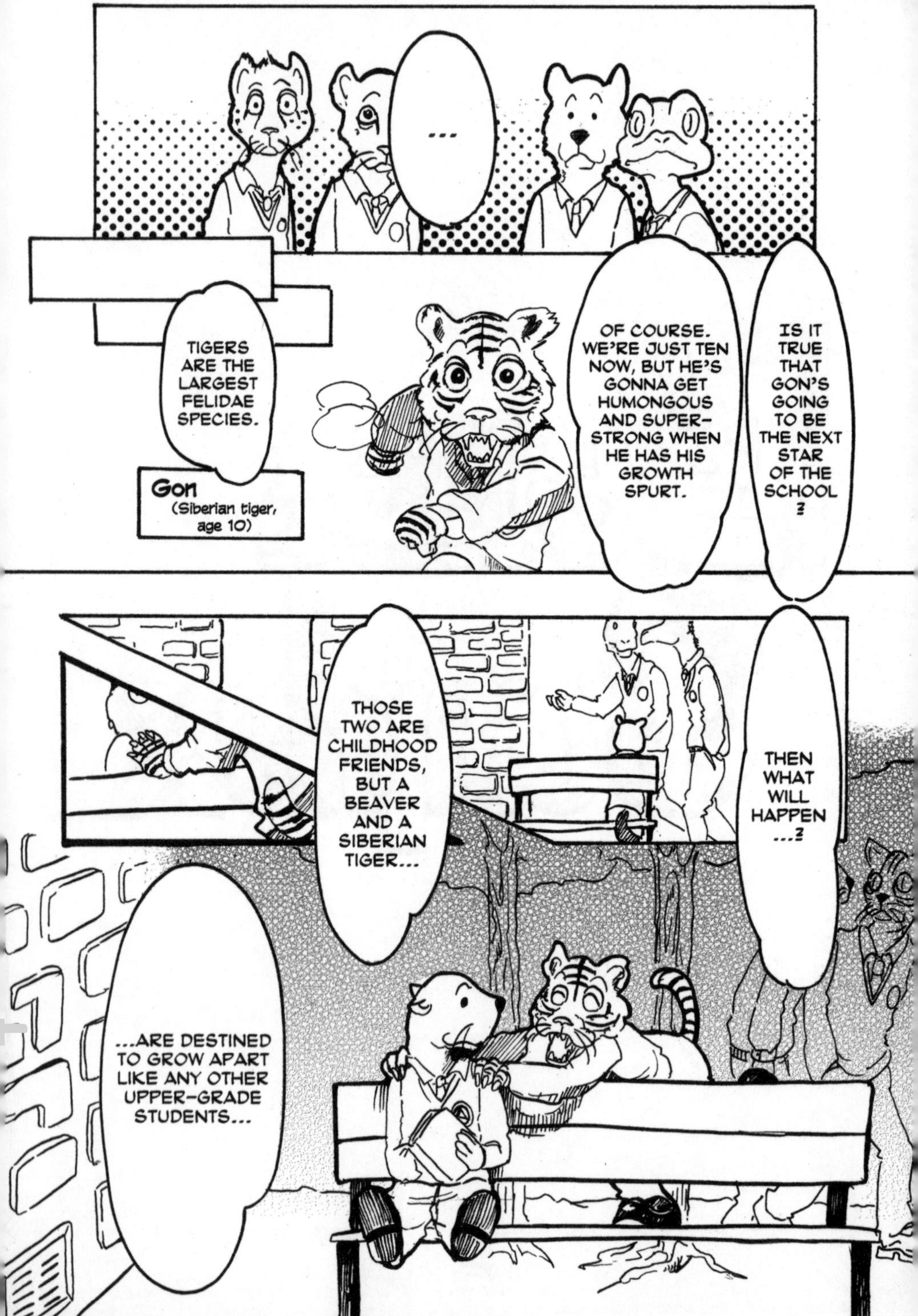
...
IS IT TRUE THAT GON'S GOING TO BE THE NEXT STAR OF THE SCHOOL?
OF COURSE. WE'RE JUST TEN NOW, BUT HE'S GONNA GET HUMONGOUS AND SUPER-STRONG WHEN HE HAS HIS GROWTH SPURT.
TIGERS ARE THE LARGEST FELIDAE SPECIES.
Gon (Siberian tiger, age 10)
THEN WHAT WILL HAPPEN...?
THOSE TWO ARE CHILDHOOD FRIENDS, BUT A BEAVER AND A SIBERIAN TIGER...
...ARE DESTINED TO GROW APART LIKE ANY OTHER UPPER-GRADE STUDENTS...

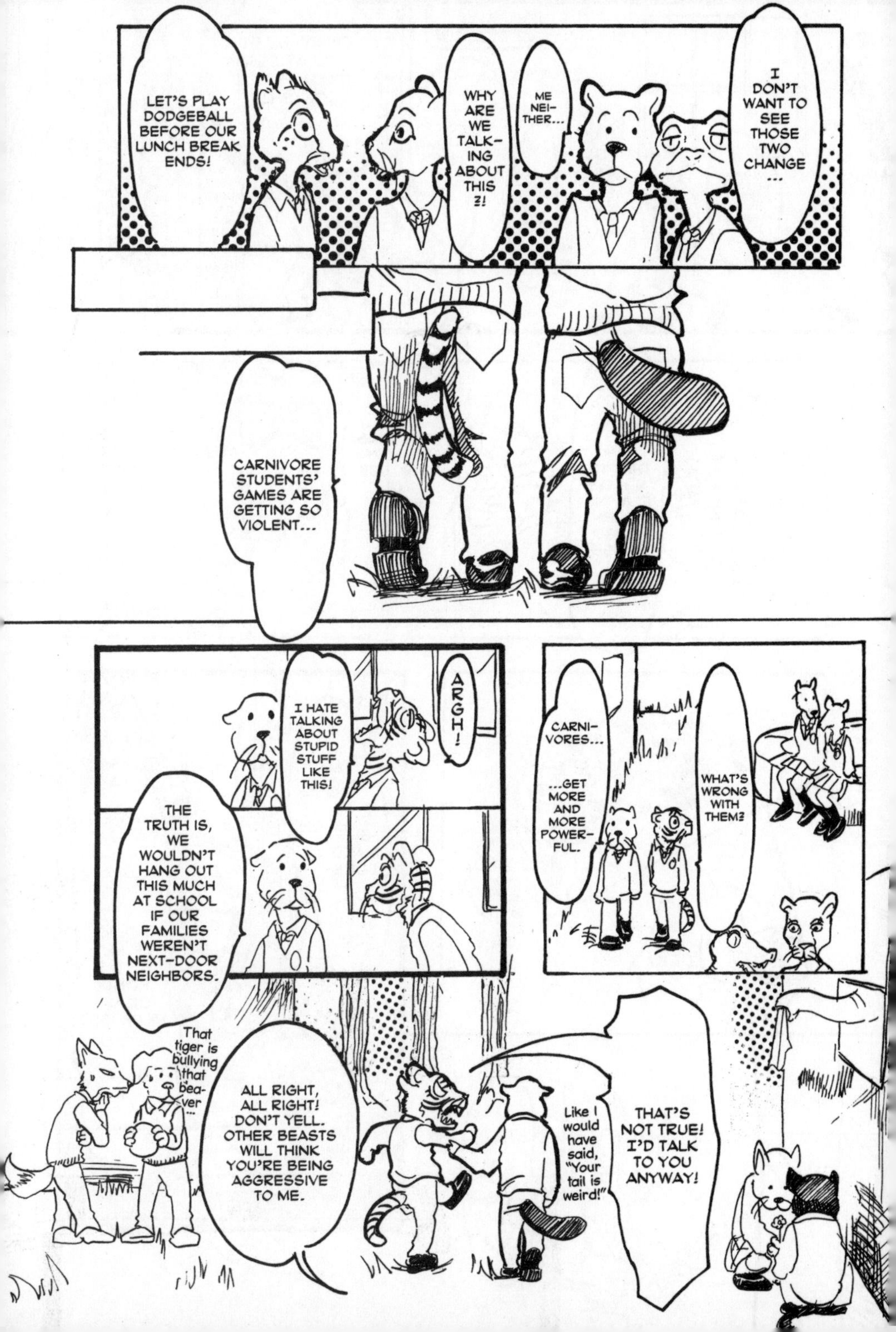
I DON'T WANT TO SEE THOSE TWO CHANGE...
ME NEITHER...
WHY ARE WE TALKING ABOUT THIS?!
LET'S PLAY DODGEBALL BEFORE OUR LUNCH BREAK ENDS!
CARNIVORE STUDENTS' GAMES ARE GETTING SO VIOLENT...
WHAT'S WRONG WITH THEM?
CARNIVORES...
...GET MORE AND MORE POWERFUL.
ARGH!
I HATE TALKING ABOUT STUPID STUFF LIKE THIS!
THE TRUTH IS, WE WOULDN'T HANG OUT THIS MUCH AT SCHOOL IF OUR FAMILIES WEREN'T NEXT-DOOR NEIGHBORS.
THAT'S NOT TRUE! I'D TALK TO YOU ANYWAY!
Like I would have said, "Your tail is weird!"
ALL RIGHT, ALL RIGHT! DON'T YELL. OTHER BEASTS WILL THINK YOU'RE BEING AGGRESSIVE TO ME.
That tiger is bullying that beaver...

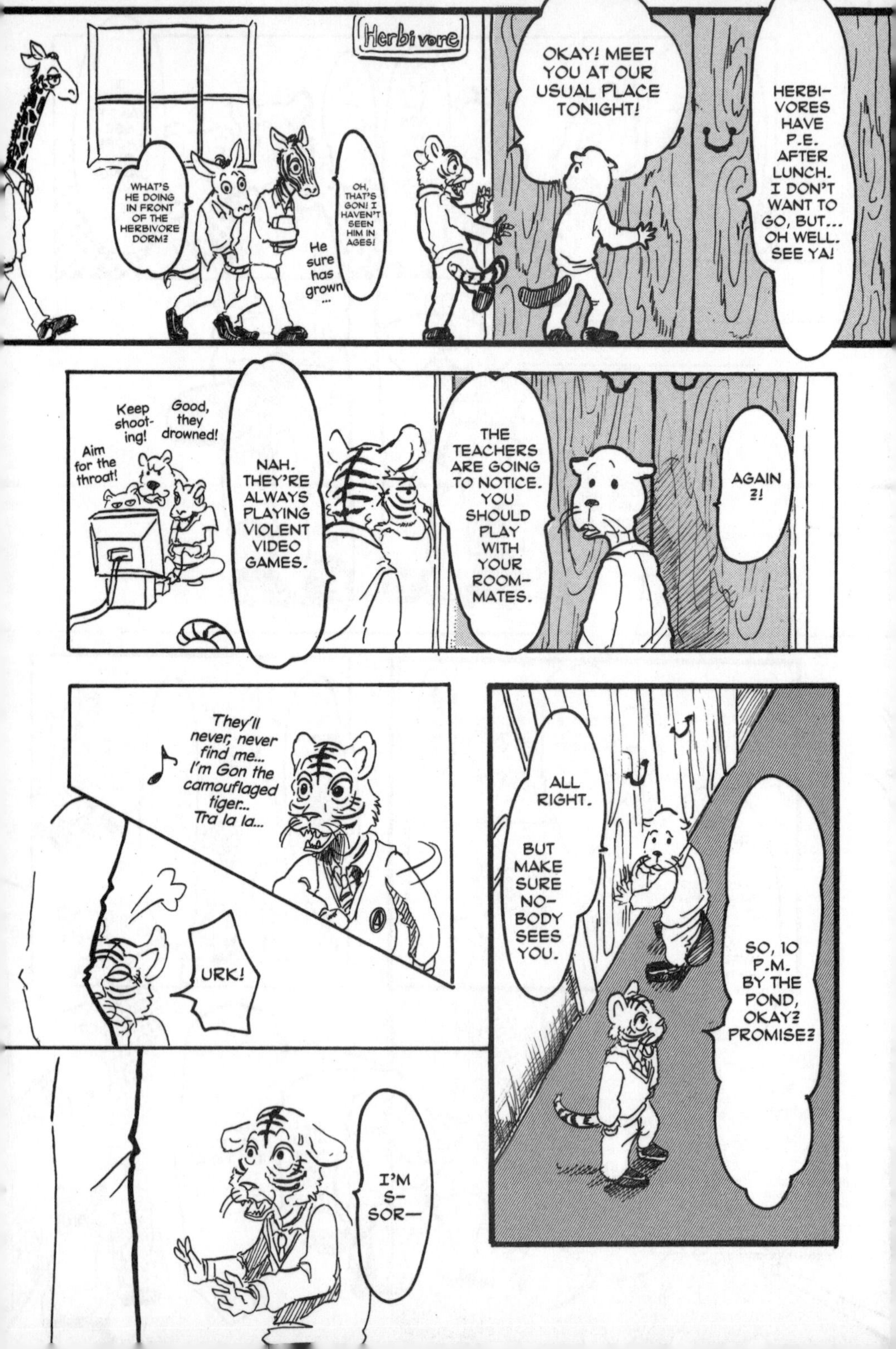
HERBIVORES HAVE P.E. AFTER LUNCH. I DON'T WANT TO GO, BUT... OH WELL. SEE YA!
OKAY! MEET YOU AT OUR USUAL PLACE TONIGHT!
Herbivore
OH, THAT'S GON! I HAVEN'T SEEN HIM IN AGES!
He sure has grown...
WHAT'S HE DOING IN FRONT OF THE HERBIVORE DORM?
AGAIN?!
THE TEACHERS ARE GOING TO NOTICE. YOU SHOULD PLAY WITH YOUR ROOMMATES.
NAH. THEY'RE ALWAYS PLAYING VIOLENT VIDEO GAMES.
Good, they drowned!
Keep shooting!
Aim for the throat!
SO, 10 P.M. BY THE POND, OKAY? PROMISE?
ALL RIGHT.
BUT MAKE SURE NOBODY SEES YOU.
They'll never, never find me... I'm Gon the camouflaged tiger... Tra la la...
URK!
I'M S-SOR—

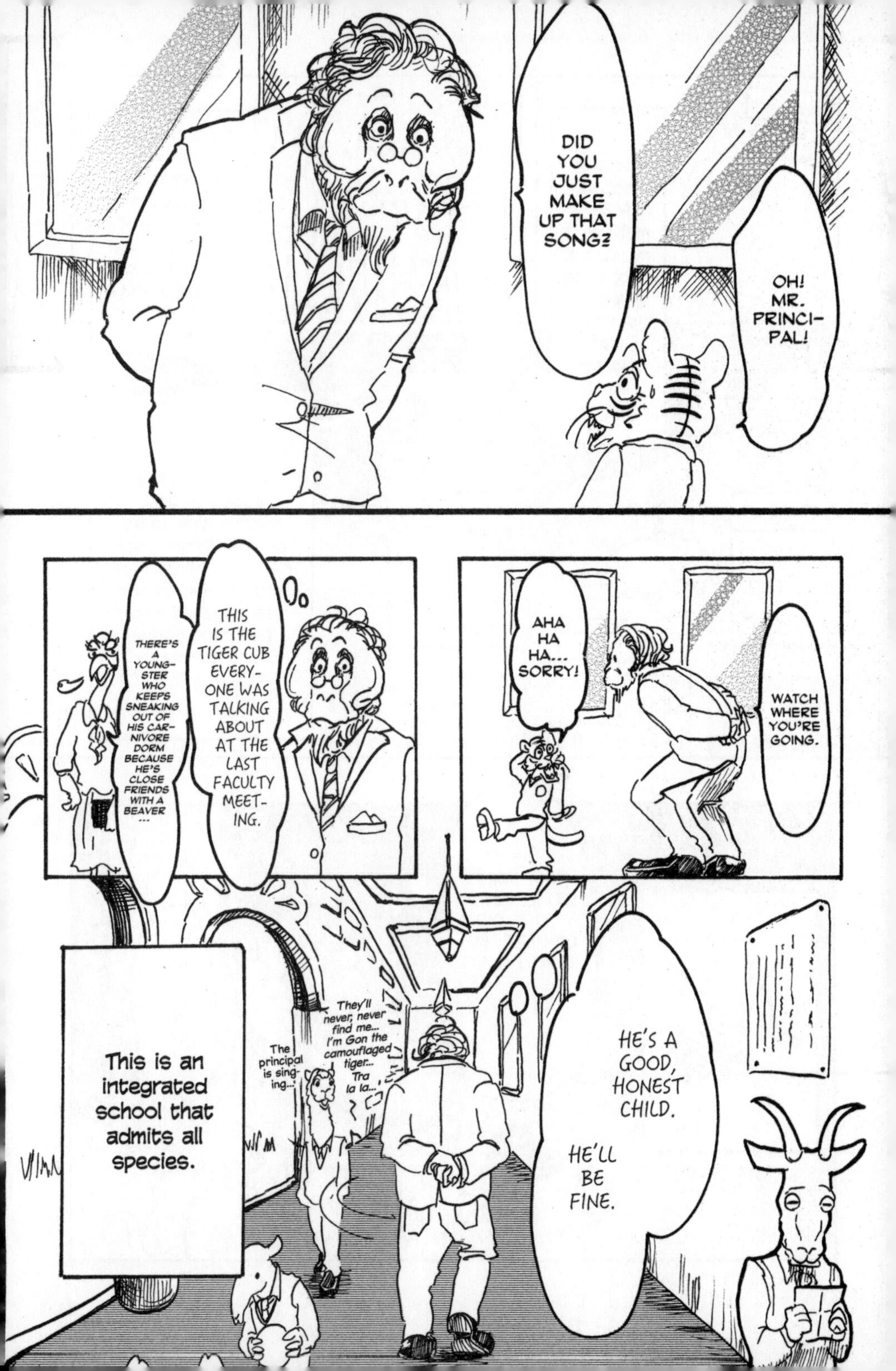
OH! MR. PRINCIPAL!
DID YOU JUST MAKE UP THAT SONG?
WATCH WHERE YOU'RE GOING.
AHA HA HA... SORRY!
THIS IS THE TIGER CUB EVERYONE WAS TALKING ABOUT AT THE LAST FACULTY MEETING.
THERE'S A YOUNGSTER WHO KEEPS SNEAKING OUT OF HIS CARNIVORE DORM BECAUSE HE'S CLOSE FRIENDS WITH A BEAVER...
HE'S A GOOD, HONEST CHILD.
HE'LL BE FINE.
They'll never, never find me... I'm Gon the camouflaged tiger... Tra la la...
The principal is singing...
This is an integrated school that admits all species.

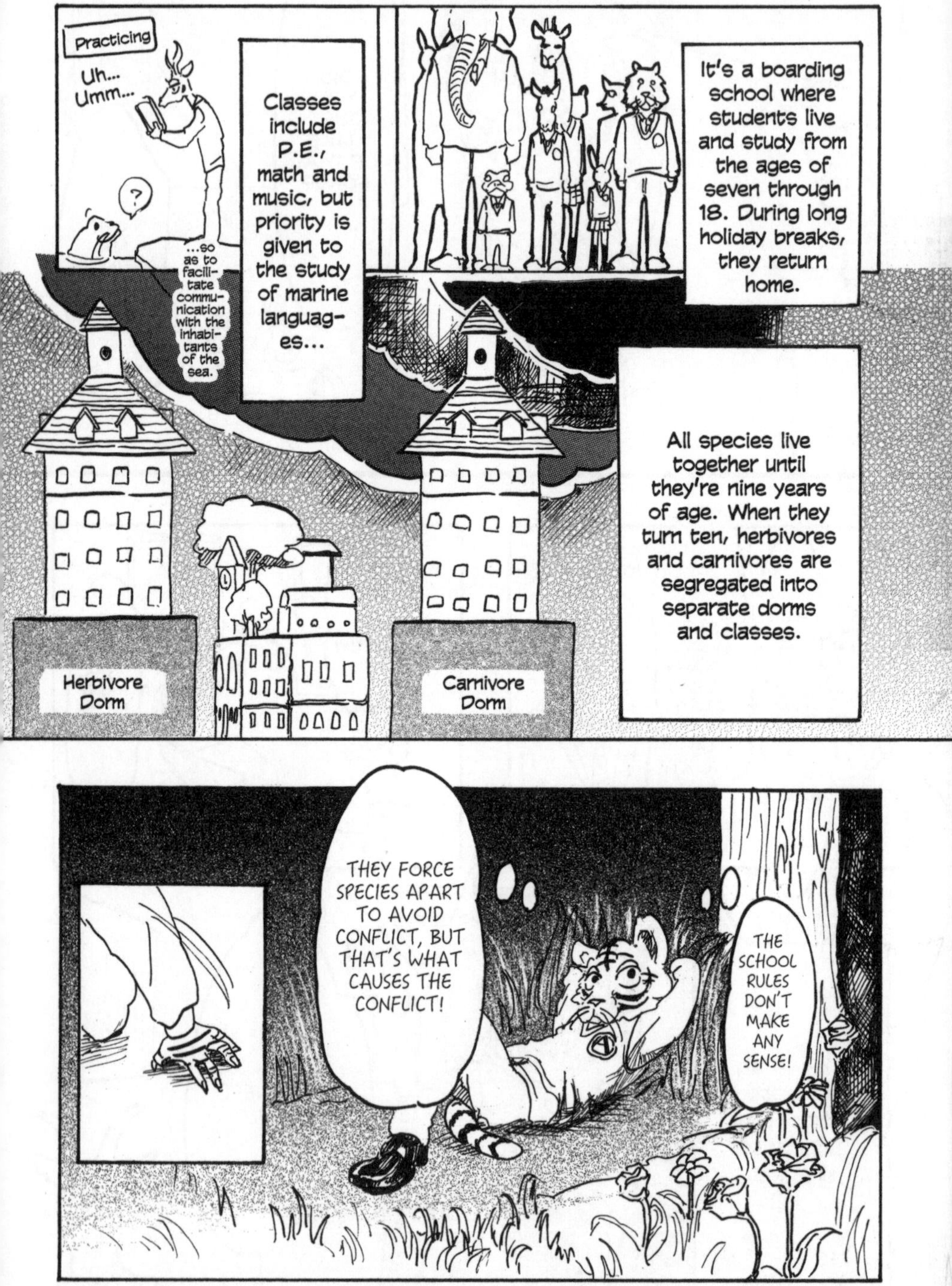
It's a boarding school where students live and study from the ages of seven through 18. During long holiday breaks, they return home.
Classes include P.E., math and music, but priority is given to the study of marine languages...
Practicing
Uh... Umm...
?
...so as to facilitate communication with the inhabitants of the sea.
All species live together until they're nine years of age. When they turn ten, herbivores and carnivores are segregated into separate dorms and classes.
Carnivore Dorm
Herbivore Dorm
THE SCHOOL RULES DON'T MAKE ANY SENSE!
THEY FORCE SPECIES APART TO AVOID CONFLICT, BUT THAT'S WHAT CAUSES THE CONFLICT!

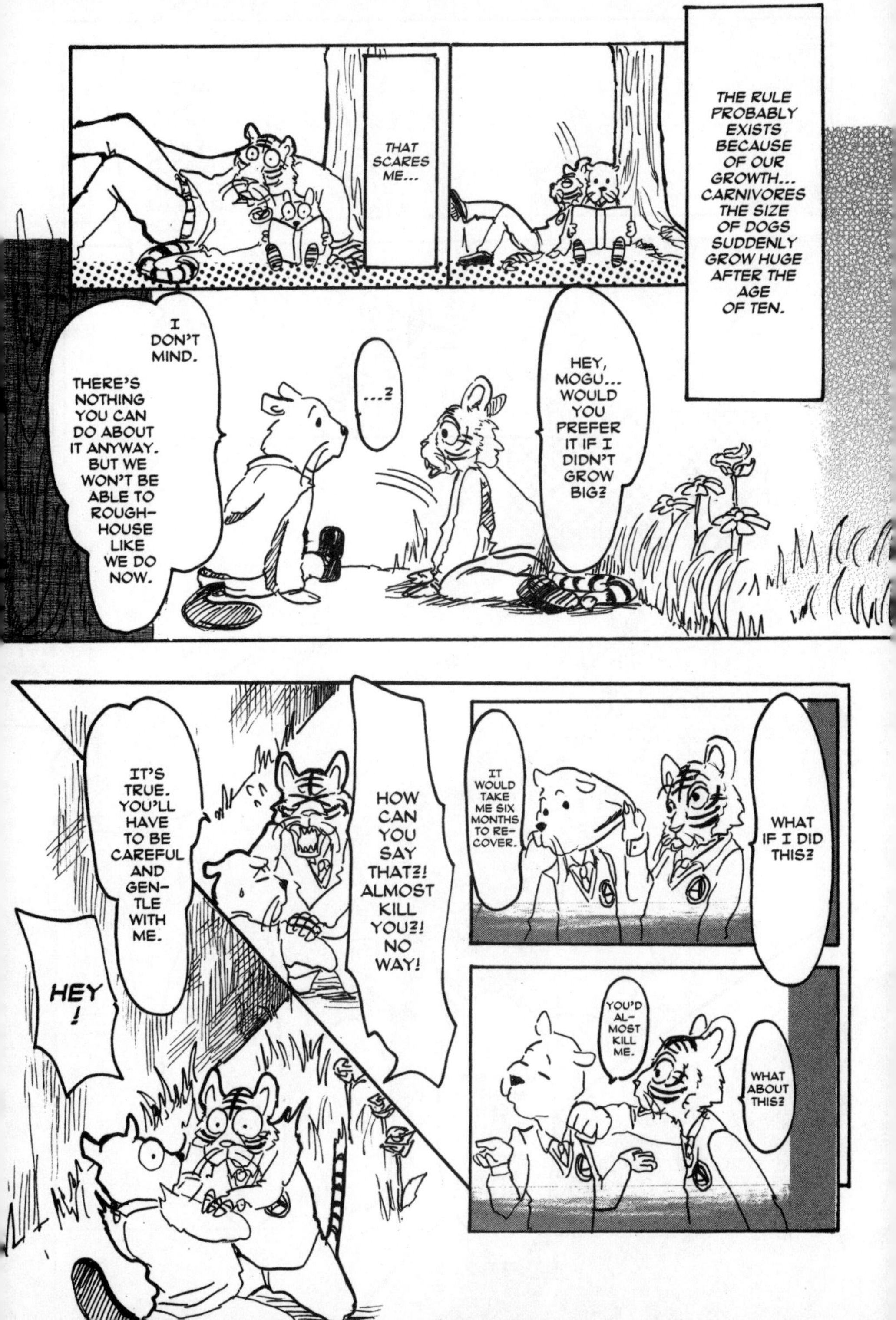
THE RULE PROBABLY EXISTS BECAUSE OF OUR GROWTH... CARNIVORES THE SIZE OF DOGS SUDDENLY GROW HUGE AFTER THE AGE OF TEN.
THAT SCARES ME...
HEY, MOGU... WOULD YOU PREFER IT IF I DIDN'T GROW BIG?
...?
I DON'T MIND.
THERE'S NOTHING YOU CAN DO ABOUT IT ANYWAY. BUT WE WON'T BE ABLE TO ROUGH-HOUSE LIKE WE DO NOW.
WHAT IF I DID THIS?
IT WOULD TAKE ME SIX MONTHS TO RE-COVER.
WHAT ABOUT THIS?
YOU'D AL-MOST KILL ME.
HOW CAN YOU SAY THAT?! ALMOST KILL YOU?! NO WAY!
IT'S TRUE. YOU'LL HAVE TO BE CAREFUL AND GEN-TLE WITH ME.
HEY!

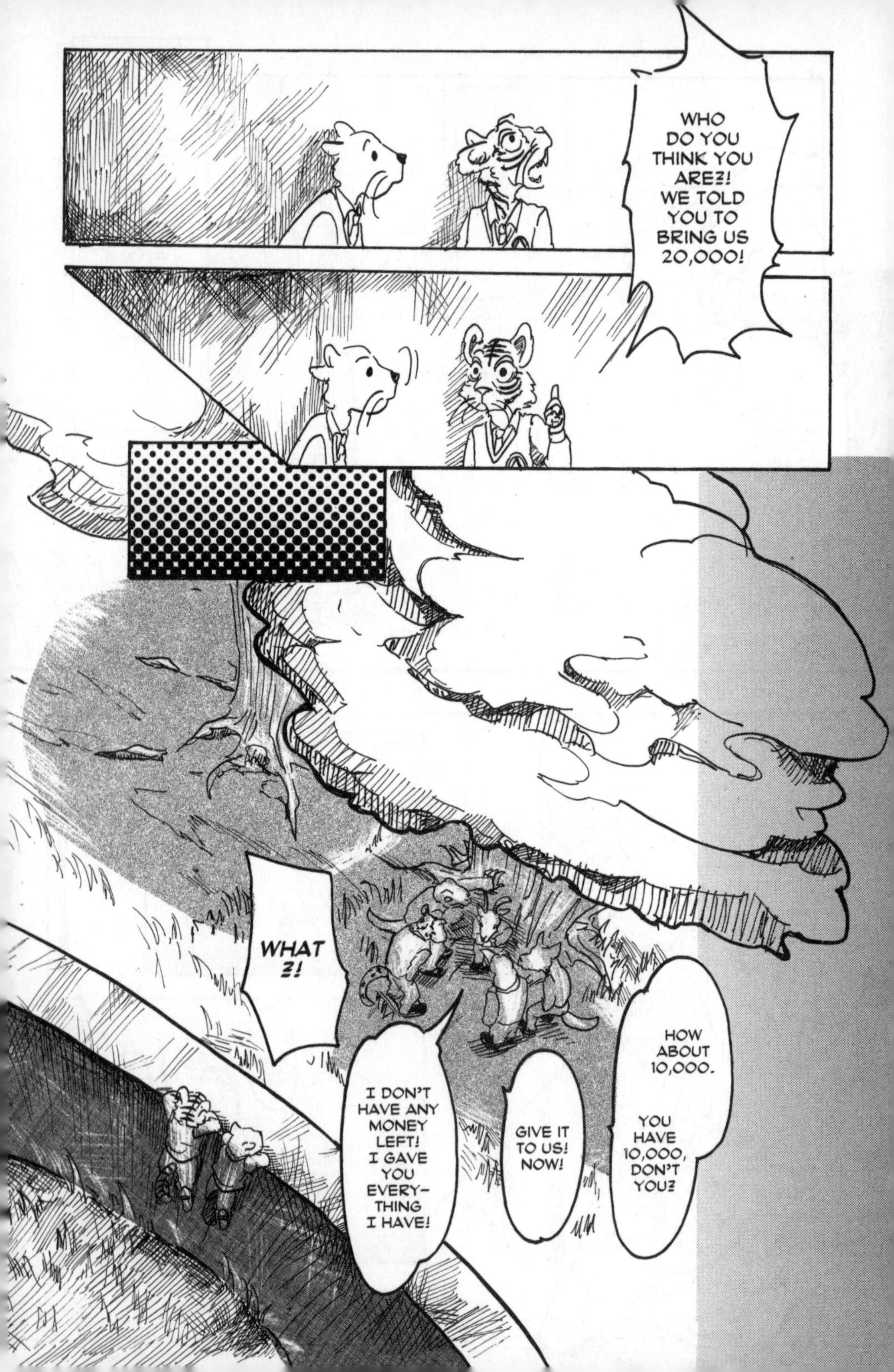

WHO DO YOU THINK YOU ARE?! WE TOLD YOU TO BRING US 20,000!
HOW ABOUT 10,000.
YOU HAVE 10,000, DON'T YOU?
GIVE IT TO US! NOW!
WHAT?!
I DON'T HAVE ANY MONEY LEFT! I GAVE YOU EVERYTHING I HAVE!

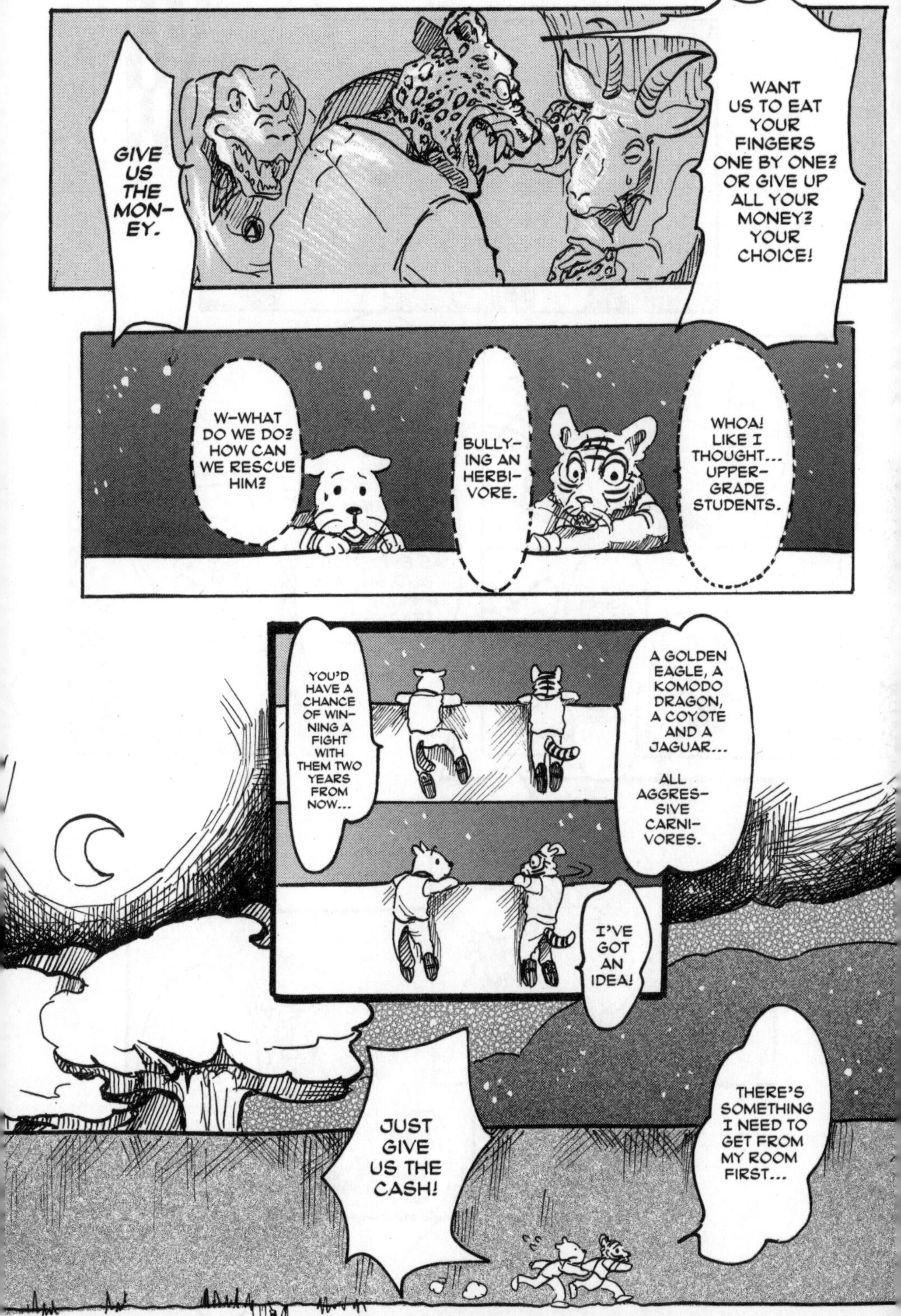
WANT US TO EAT YOUR FINGERS ONE BY ONE? OR GIVE UP ALL YOUR MONEY? YOUR CHOICE!
GIVE US THE MON-EY.
WHOA! LIKE I THOUGHT... UPPER-GRADE STUDENTS.
BULLY-ING AN HERBI-VORE.
W-WHAT DO WE DO? HOW CAN WE RESCUE HIM?
A GOLDEN EAGLE, A KOMODO DRAGON, A COYOTE AND A JAGUAR...
ALL AGGRES-SIVE CARNI-VORES.
YOU'D HAVE A CHANCE OF WIN-NING A FIGHT WITH THEM TWO YEARS FROM NOW...
I'VE GOT AN IDEA!
THERE'S SOMETHING I NEED TO GET FROM MY ROOM FIRST...
JUST GIVE US THE CASH!

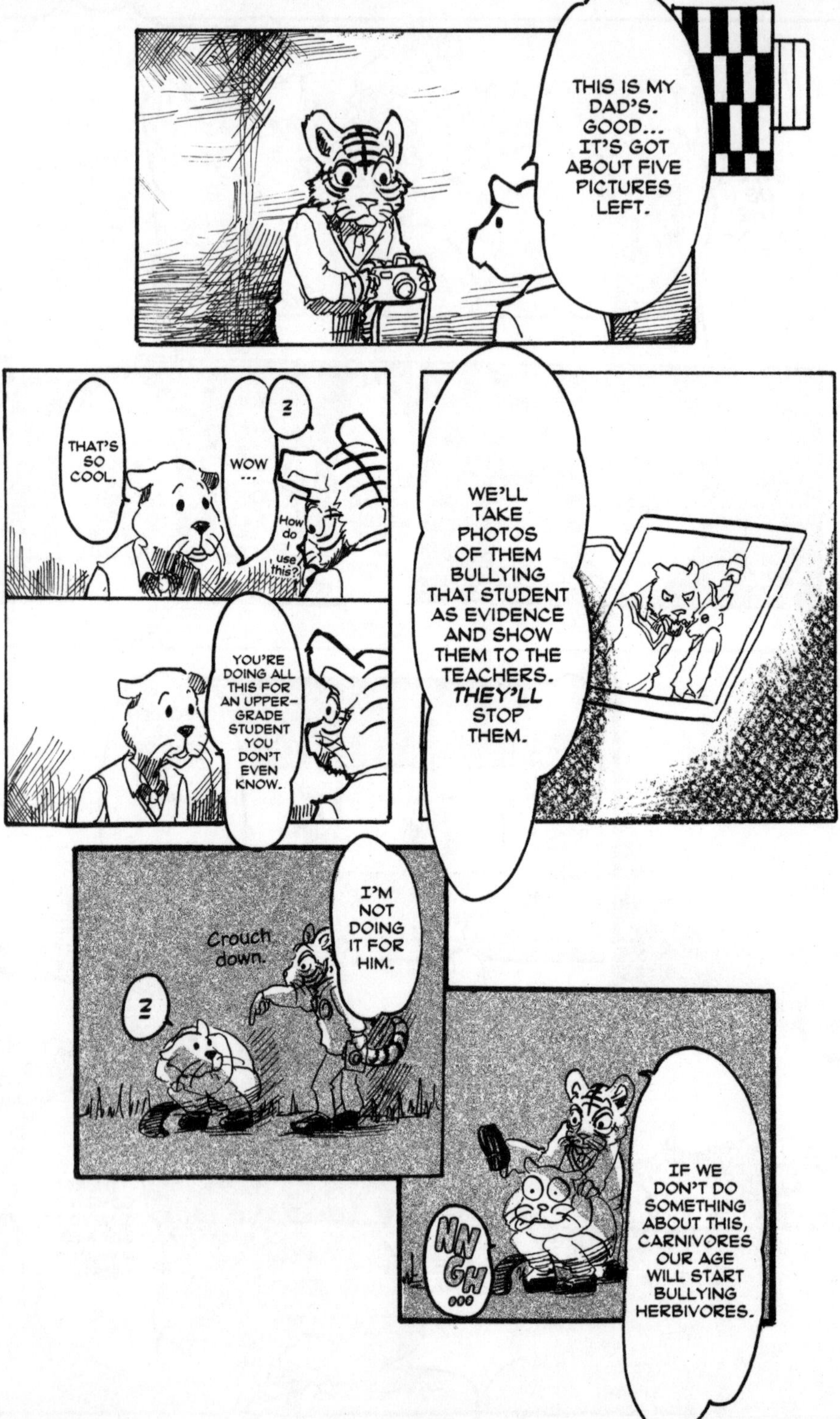
THIS IS MY DAD'S. GOOD... IT'S GOT ABOUT FIVE PICTURES LEFT.
WE'LL TAKE PHOTOS OF THEM BULLYING THAT STUDENT AS EVIDENCE AND SHOW THEM TO THE TEACHERS. *THEY'LL* STOP THEM.
?
WOW...
How do I use this?
THAT'S SO COOL.
YOU'RE DOING ALL THIS FOR AN UPPER-GRADE STUDENT YOU DON'T EVEN KNOW.
I'M NOT DOING IT FOR HIM.
Crouch down.
?
IF WE DON'T DO SOMETHING ABOUT THIS, CARNIVORES OUR AGE WILL START BULLYING HERBIVORES.
NNGH...

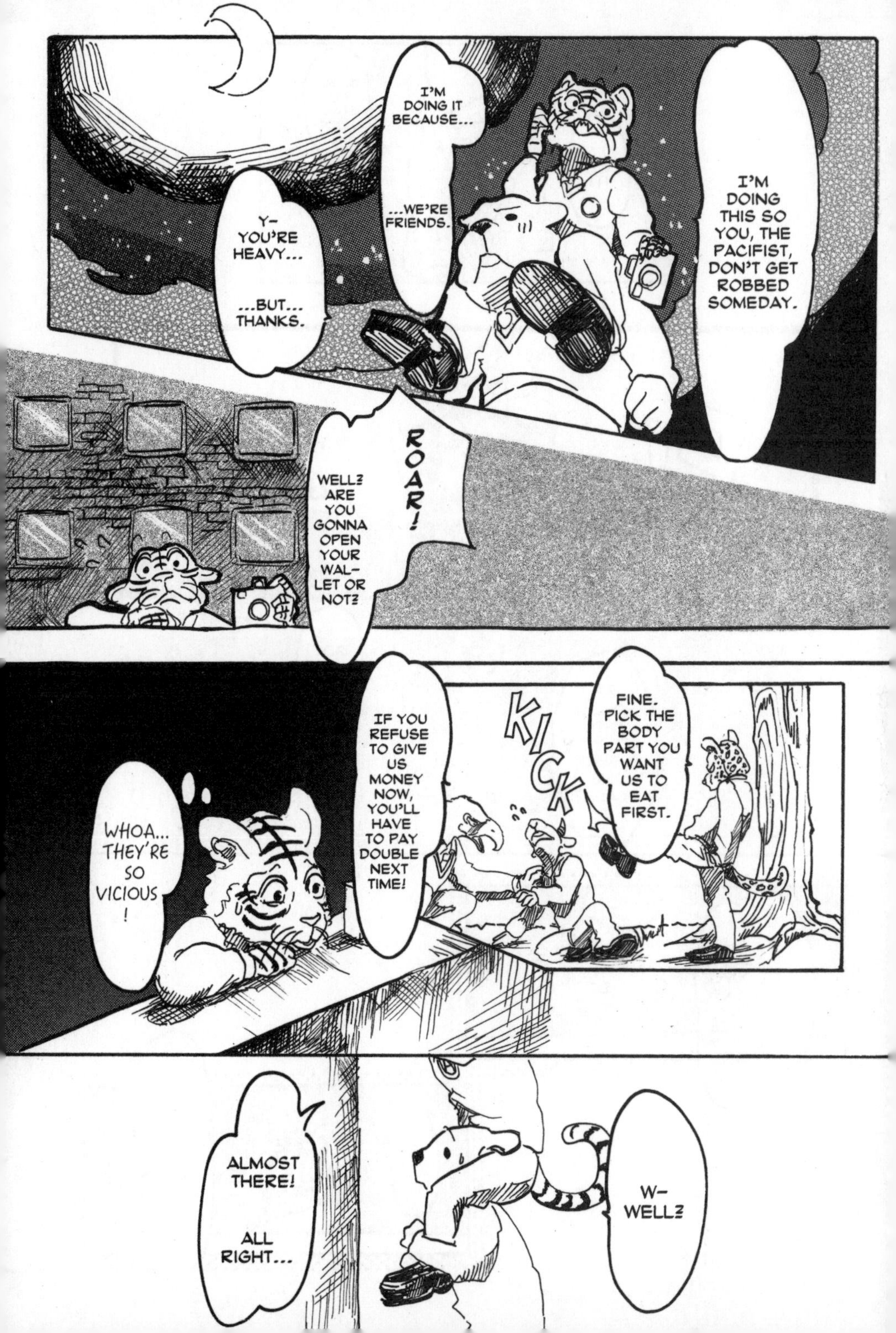
I'M DOING THIS SO YOU, THE PACIFIST, DON'T GET ROBBED SOMEDAY.
I'M DOING IT BECAUSE...
...WE'RE FRIENDS.
Y- YOU'RE HEAVY...
...BUT... THANKS.
ROAR!
WELL? ARE YOU GONNA OPEN YOUR WAL- LET OR NOT?
FINE. PICK THE BODY PART YOU WANT US TO EAT FIRST.
KICK
IF YOU REFUSE TO GIVE US MONEY NOW, YOU'LL HAVE TO PAY DOUBLE NEXT TIME!
WHOA... THEY'RE SO VICIOUS!
W- WELL?
ALMOST THERE!
ALL RIGHT...

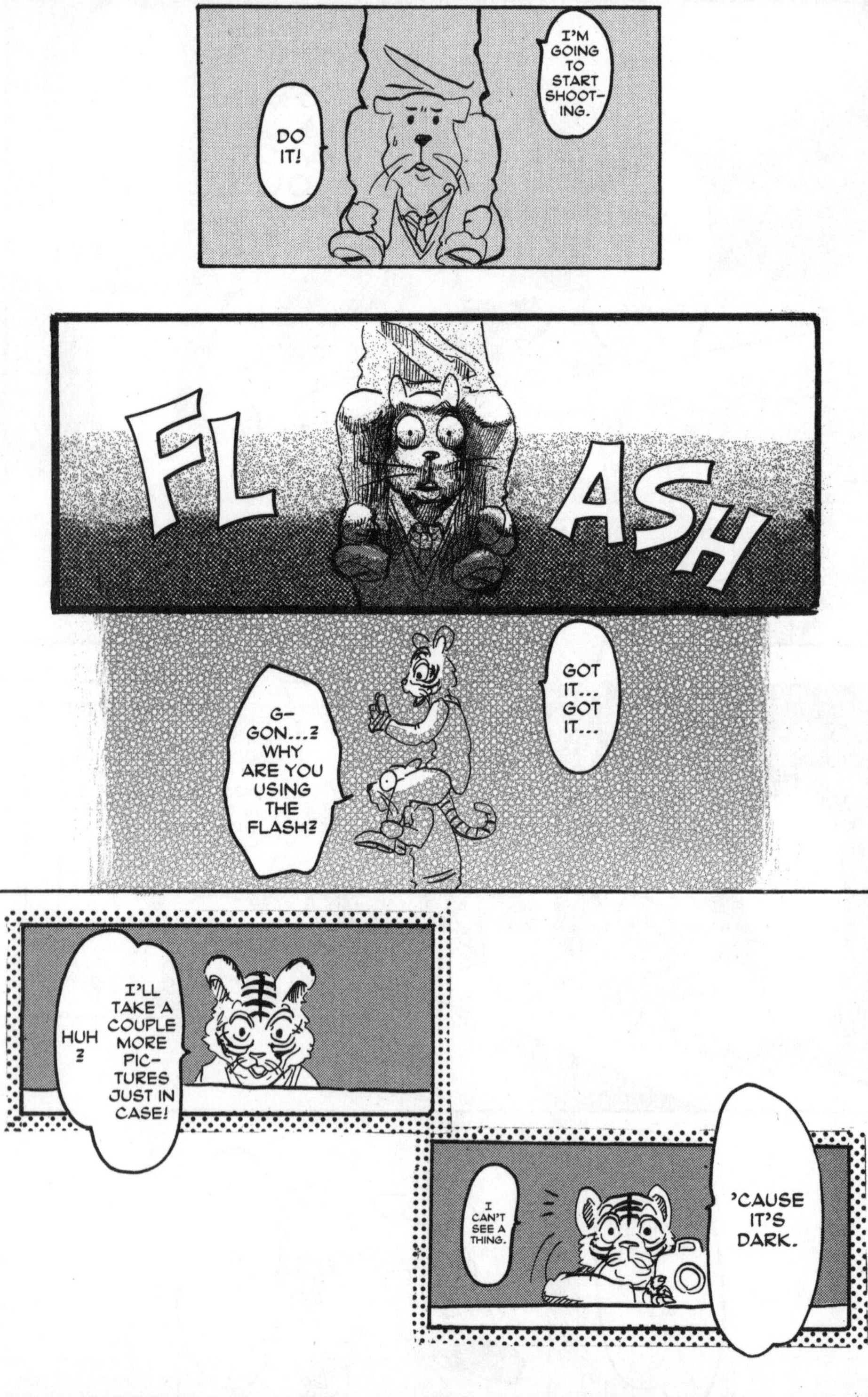
I'M GOING TO START SHOOTING.
DO IT!
FLASH
GOT IT... GOT IT...
G-GON...? WHY ARE YOU USING THE FLASH?
HUH?
I'LL TAKE A COUPLE MORE PICTURES JUST IN CASE!
'CAUSE IT'S DARK.
I CAN'T SEE A THING.

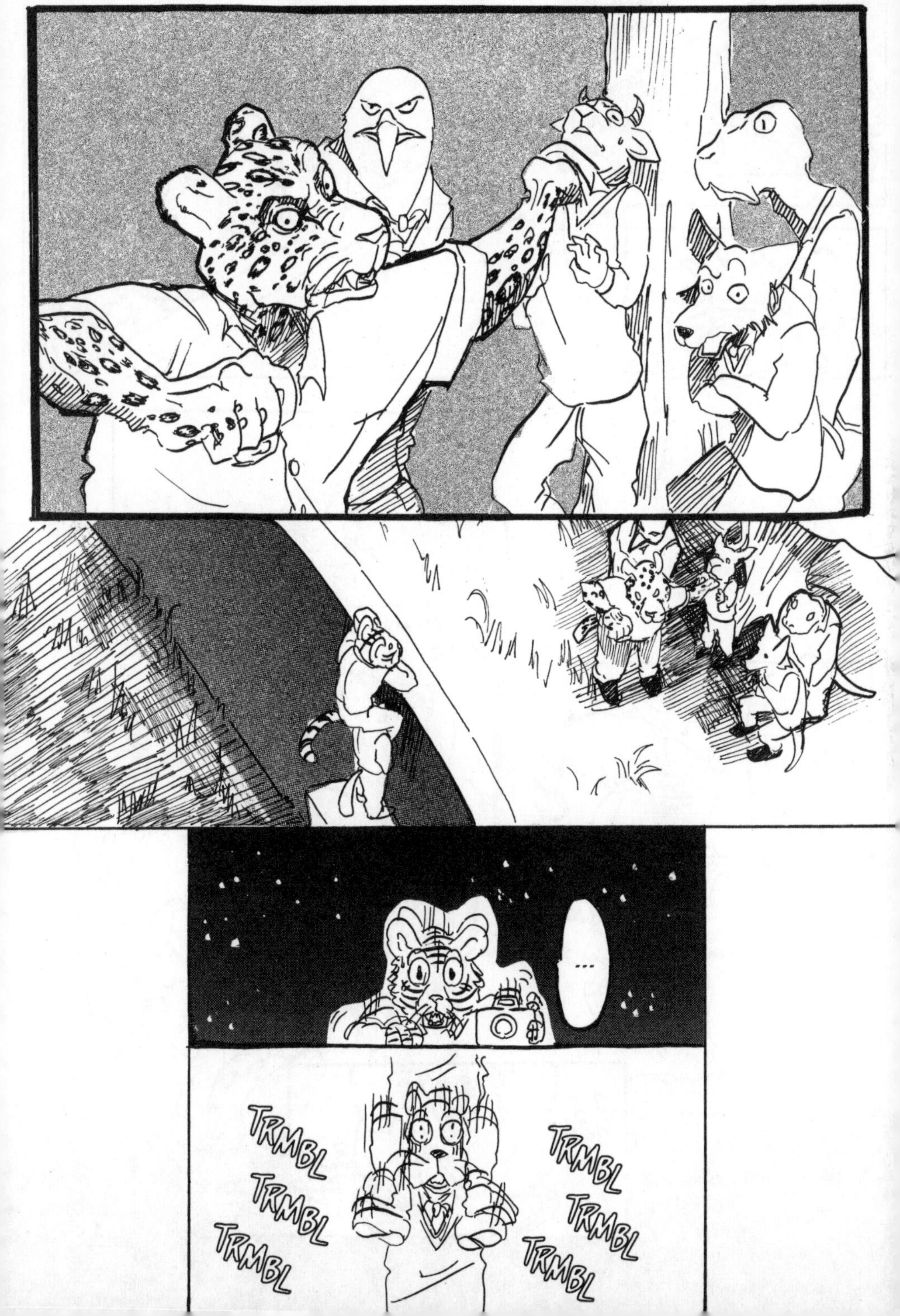
...
TRMBL
TRMBL
TRMBL
TRMBL
TRMBL
TRMBL

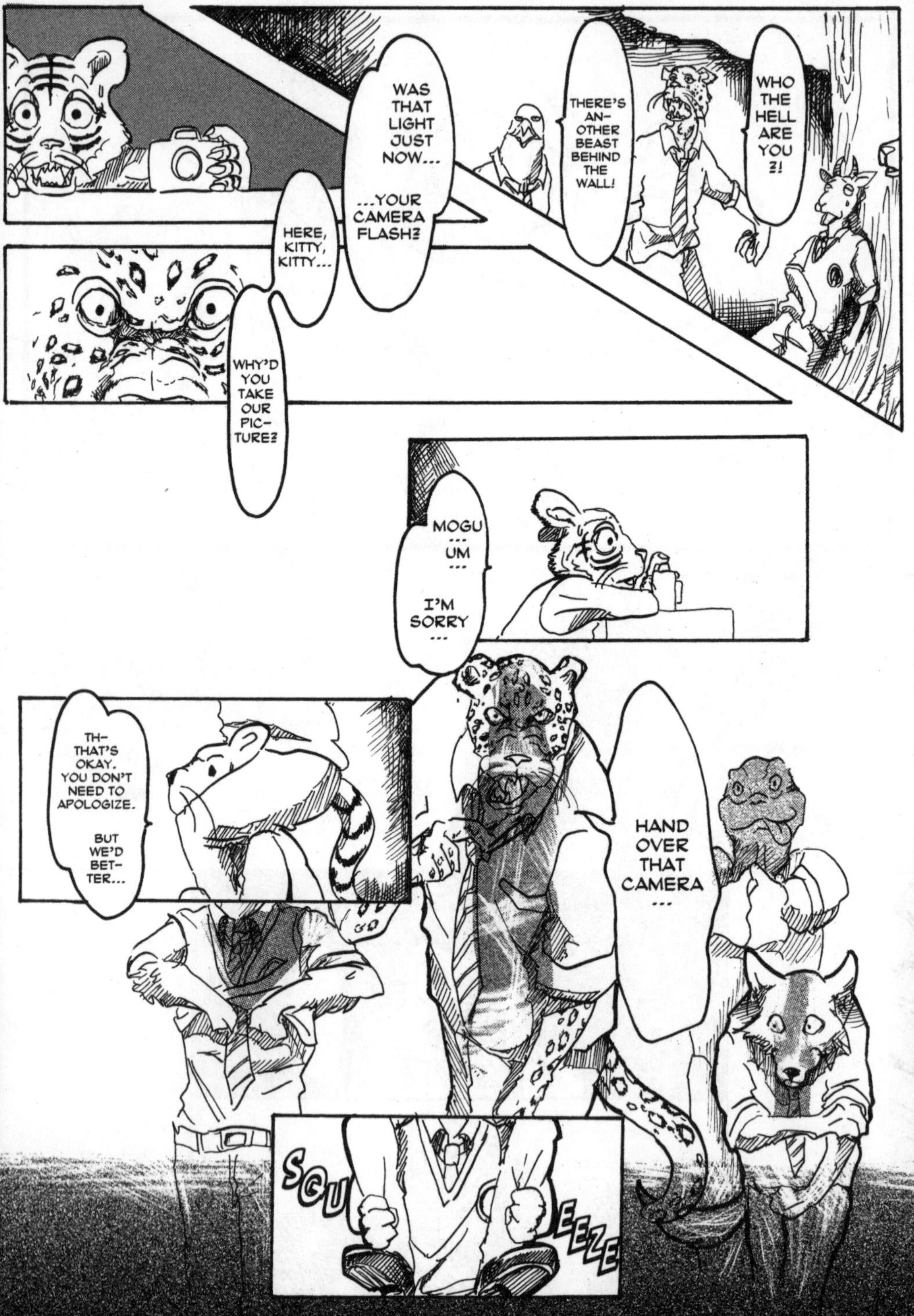

WHO THE HELL ARE YOU?!
THERE'S AN-OTHER BEAST BEHIND THE WALL!
WAS THAT LIGHT JUST NOW...
...YOUR CAMERA FLASH?
HERE, KITTY, KITTY...
WHY'D YOU TAKE OUR PIC-TURE?
MOGU... UM... I'M SORRY...
HAND OVER THAT CAMERA...
TH-THAT'S OKAY. YOU DON'T NEED TO APOLOGIZE. BUT WE'D BET-TER...
SQUEEZE

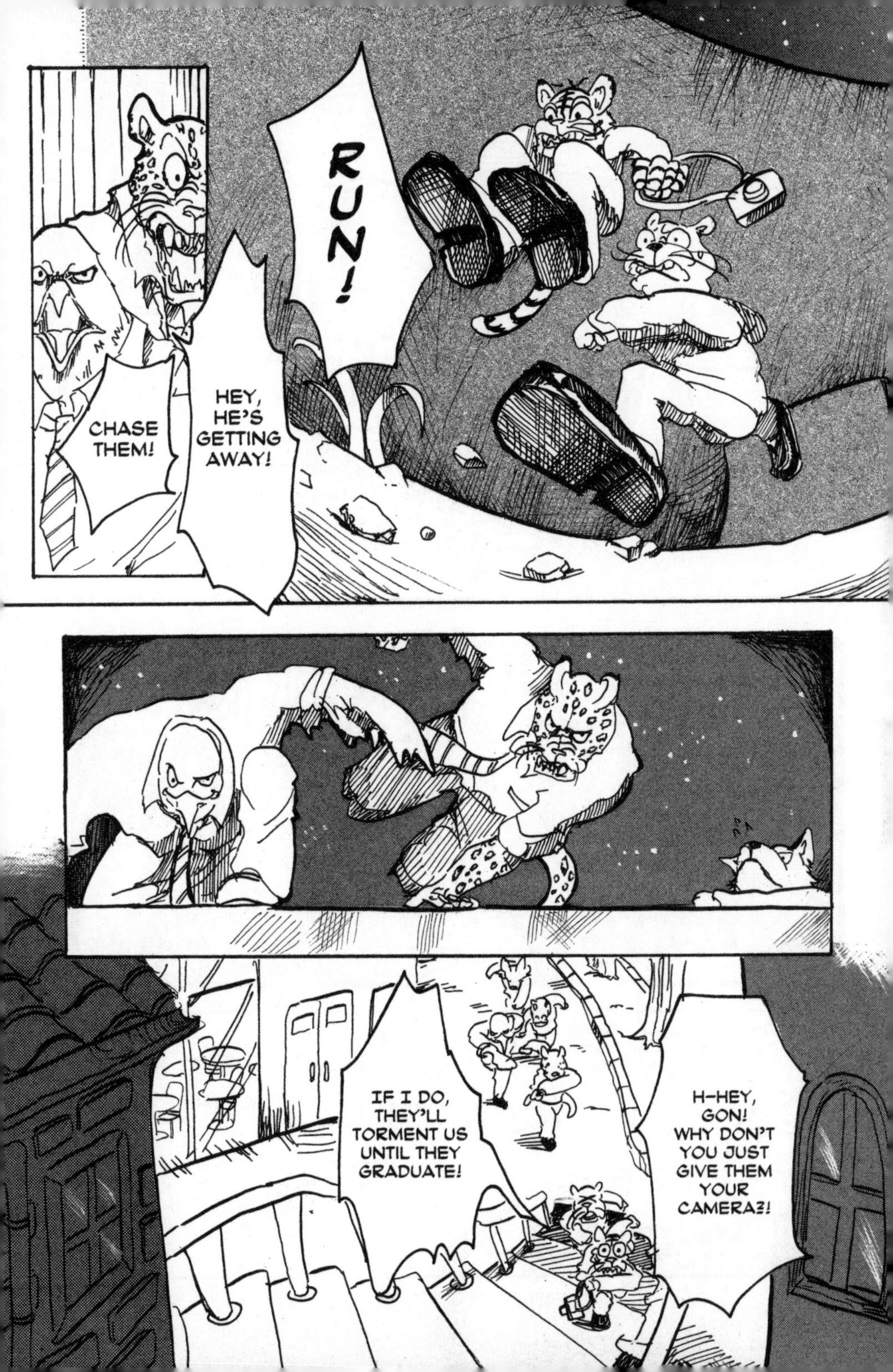
RUN!
HEY, HE'S GETTING AWAY!
CHASE THEM!
H-HEY, GON! WHY DON'T YOU JUST GIVE THEM YOUR CAMERA?!
IF I DO, THEY'LL TORMENT US UNTIL THEY GRADUATE!

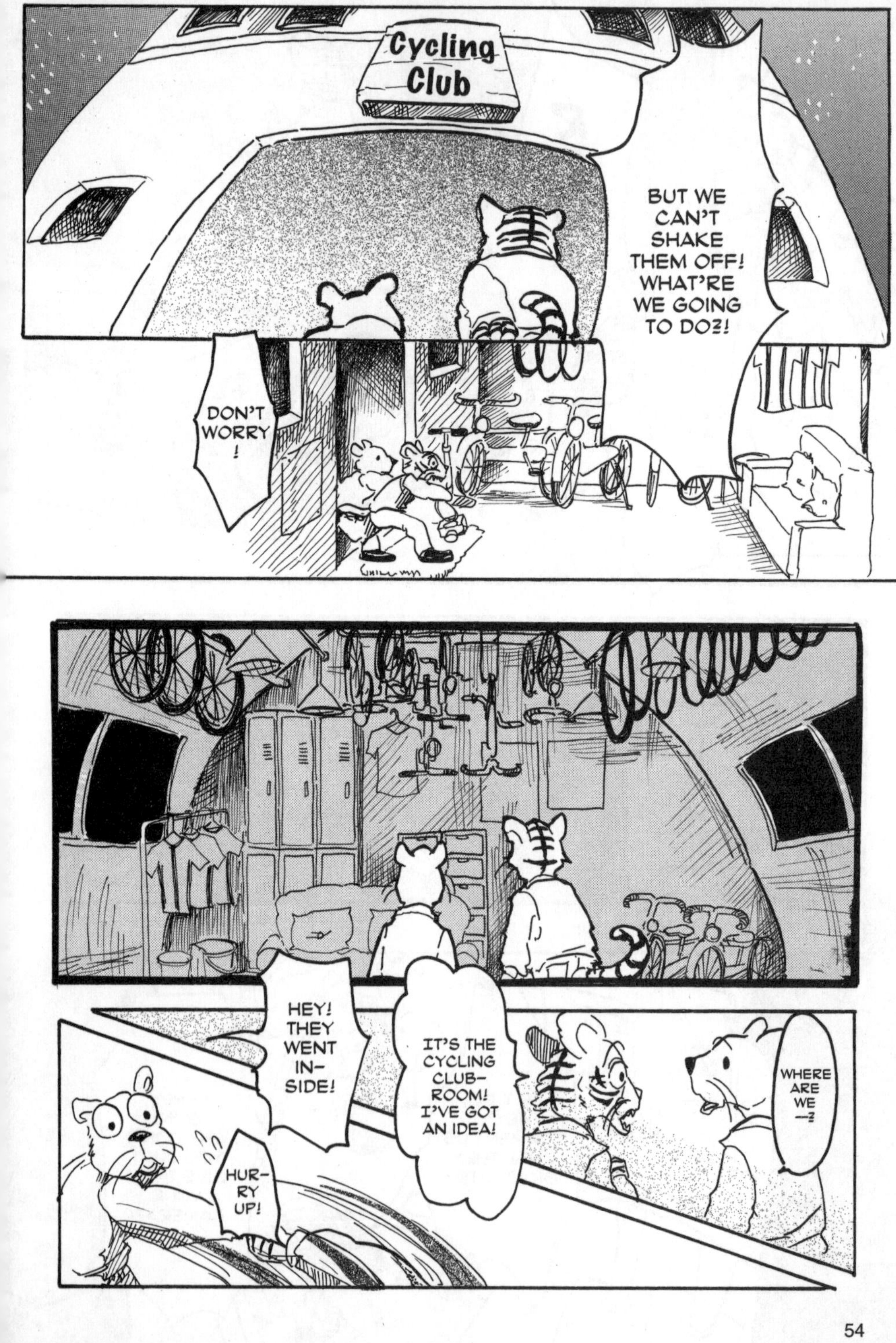
Cycling Club
BUT WE CAN'T SHAKE THEM OFF! WHAT'RE WE GOING TO DO?!
DON'T WORRY!
WHERE ARE WE—?
IT'S THE CYCLING CLUB-ROOM! I'VE GOT AN IDEA!
HEY! THEY WENT IN-SIDE!
HUR-RY UP!

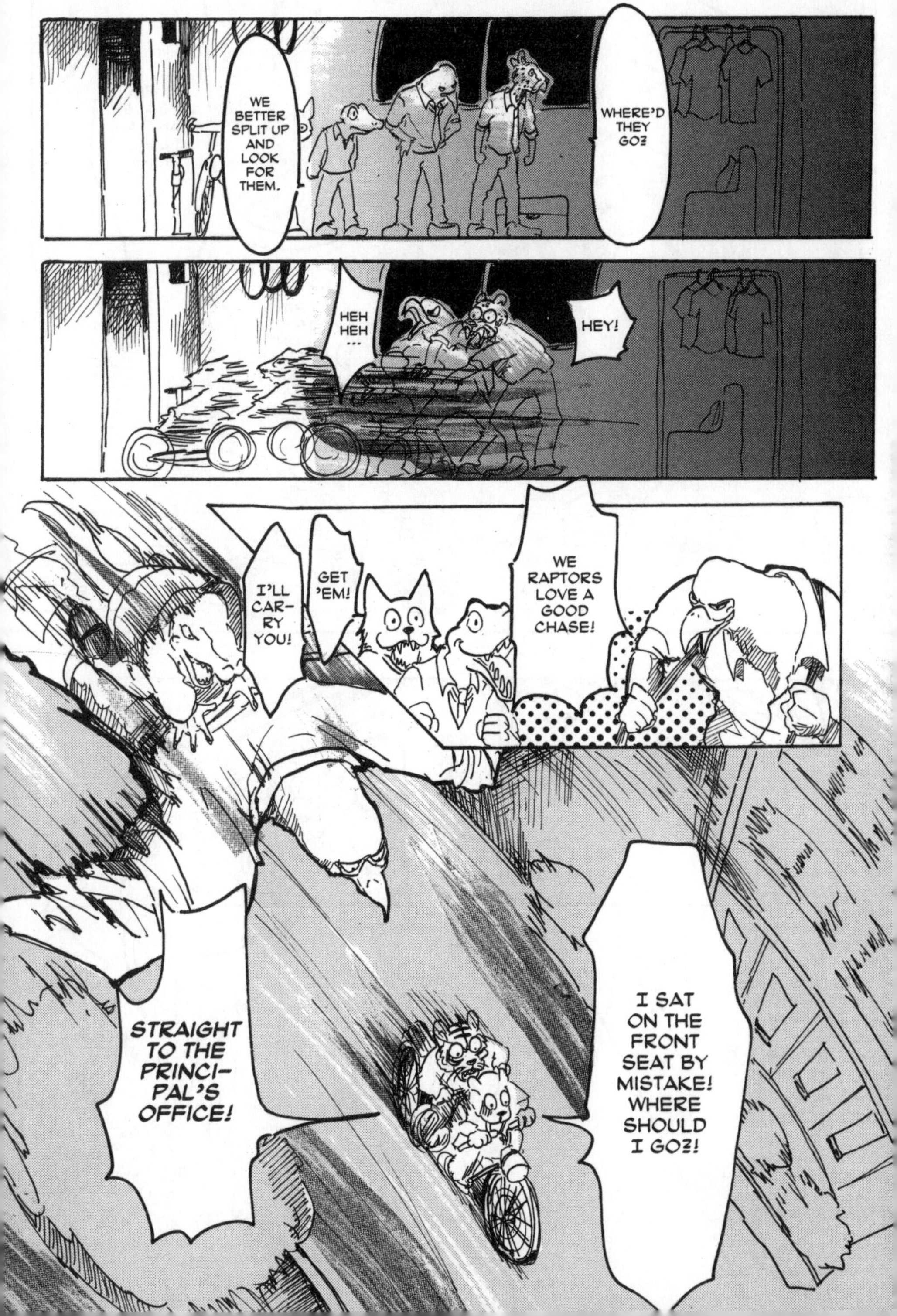
WHERE'D THEY GO?
WE BETTER SPLIT UP AND LOOK FOR THEM.
HEY!
HEH HEH ...
WE RAPTORS LOVE A GOOD CHASE!
GET 'EM!
I'LL CARRY YOU!
I SAT ON THE FRONT SEAT BY MISTAKE! WHERE SHOULD I GO?!
STRAIGHT TO THE PRINCIPAL'S OFFICE!

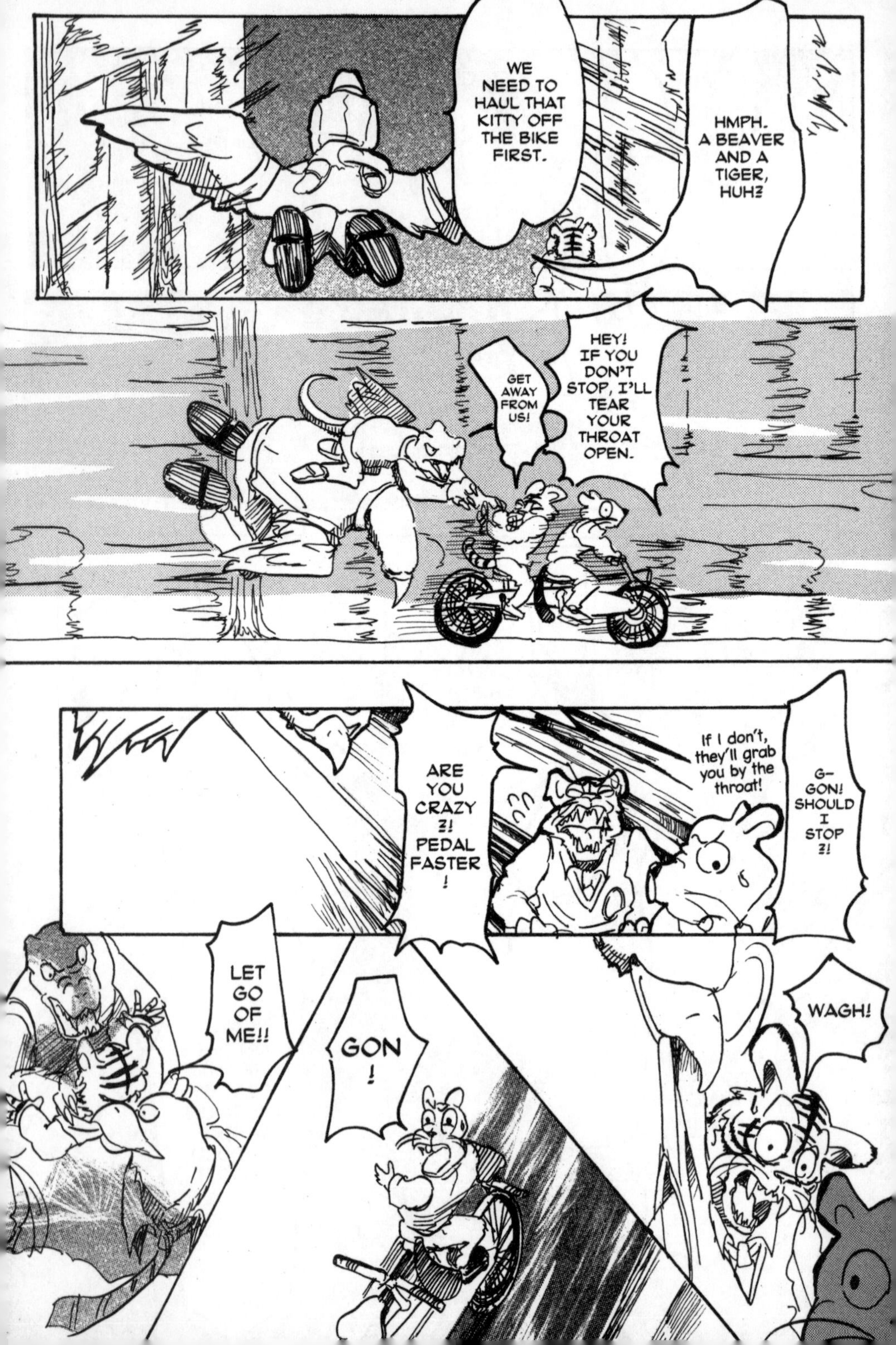
HMPH. A BEAVER AND A TIGER, HUH?!
WE NEED TO HAUL THAT KITTY OFF THE BIKE FIRST.
HEY! IF YOU DON'T STOP, I'LL TEAR YOUR THROAT OPEN.
GET AWAY FROM US!
G-GON! SHOULD I STOP?!
If I don't, they'll grab you by the throat!
ARE YOU CRAZY?! PEDAL FASTER!
WAGH!
GON!
LET GO OF ME!!

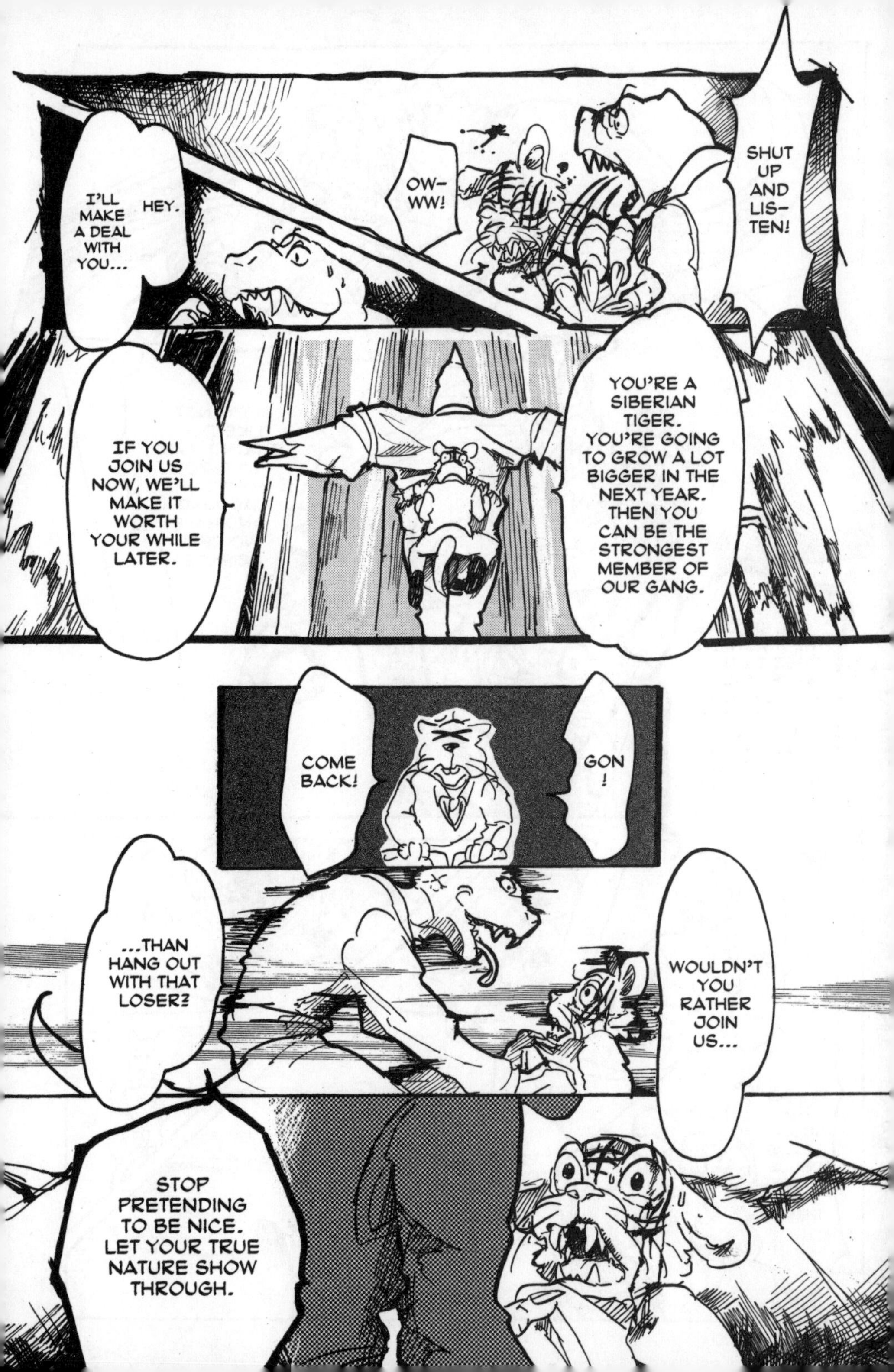
SHUT UP AND LIS-TEN!
OW-WW!
HEY.
I'LL MAKE A DEAL WITH YOU...
YOU'RE A SIBERIAN TIGER. YOU'RE GOING TO GROW A LOT BIGGER IN THE NEXT YEAR. THEN YOU CAN BE THE STRONGEST MEMBER OF OUR GANG.
IF YOU JOIN US NOW, WE'LL MAKE IT WORTH YOUR WHILE LATER.
GON!
COME BACK!
WOULDN'T YOU RATHER JOIN US...
...THAN HANG OUT WITH THAT LOSER?
STOP PRETENDING TO BE NICE. LET YOUR TRUE NATURE SHOW THROUGH.

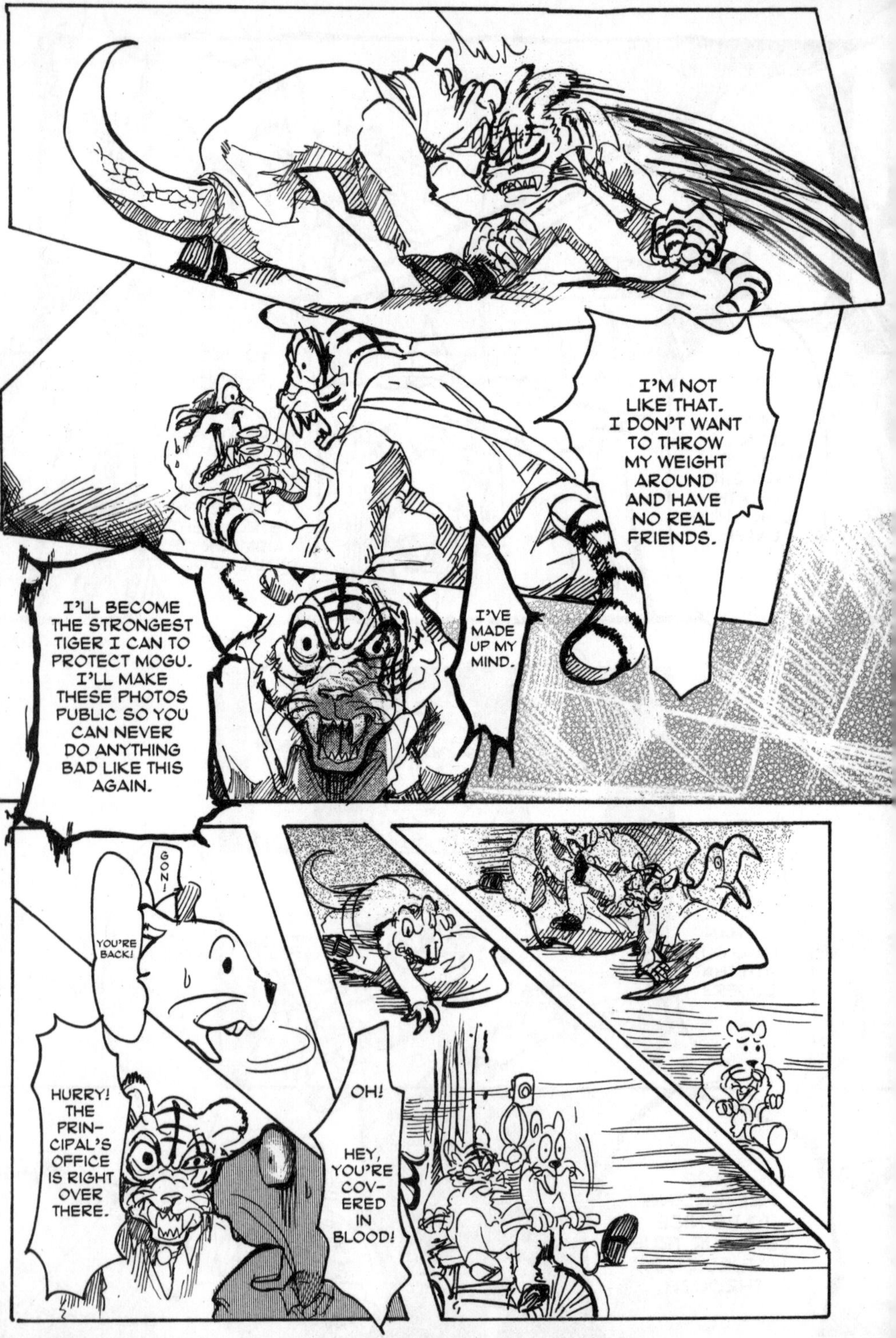
I'M NOT LIKE THAT. I DON'T WANT TO THROW MY WEIGHT AROUND AND HAVE NO REAL FRIENDS.
I'VE MADE UP MY MIND.
I'LL BECOME THE STRONGEST TIGER I CAN TO PROTECT MOGU. I'LL MAKE THESE PHOTOS PUBLIC SO YOU CAN NEVER DO ANYTHING BAD LIKE THIS AGAIN.
OH!
HEY, YOU'RE COV-ERED IN BLOOD!
GON!
YOU'RE BACK!
HURRY! THE PRIN-CIPAL'S OFFICE IS RIGHT OVER THERE.

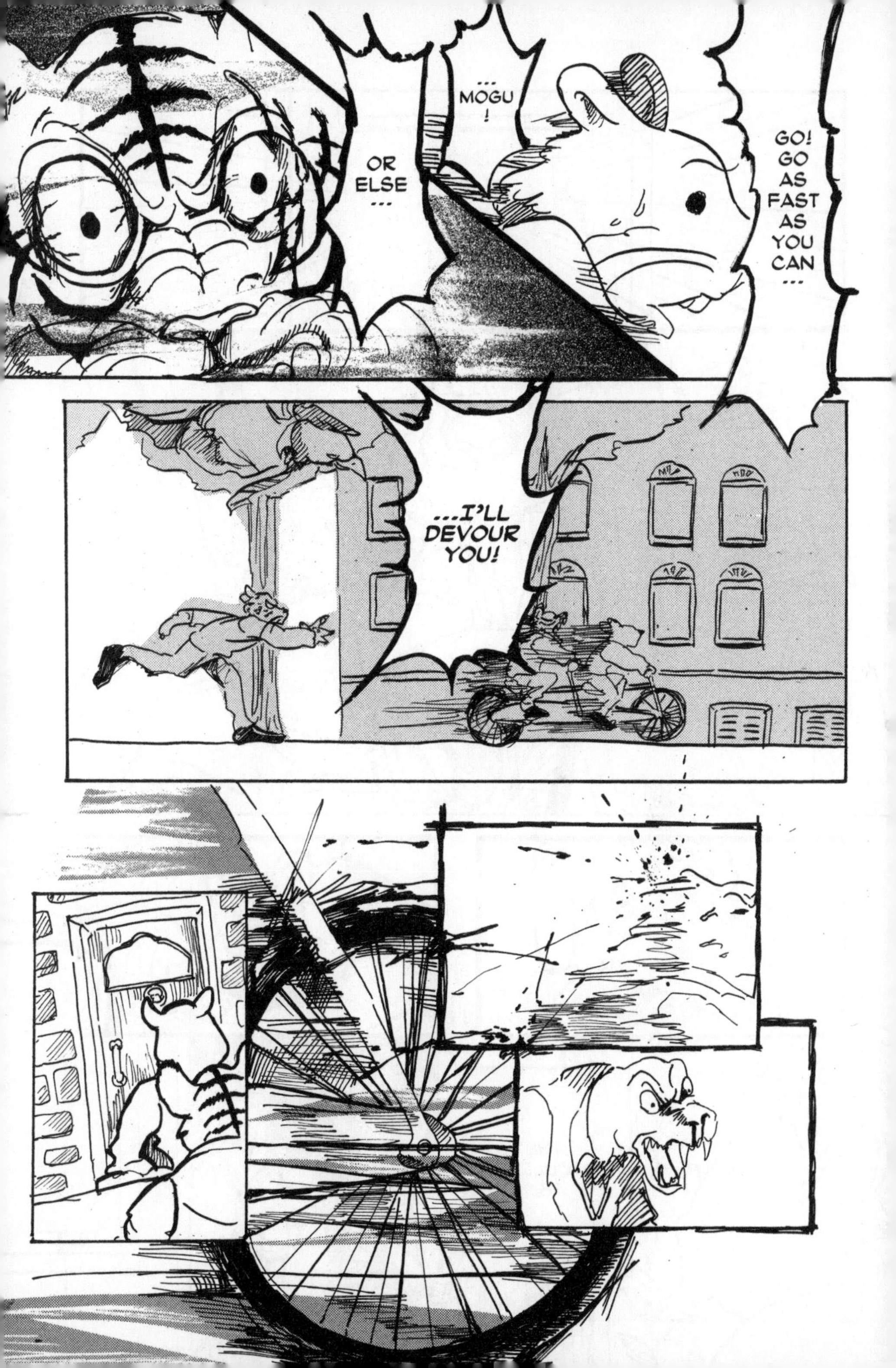
GO! GO AS FAST AS YOU CAN...
...MOGU!
OR ELSE...
...I'LL DEVOUR YOU!

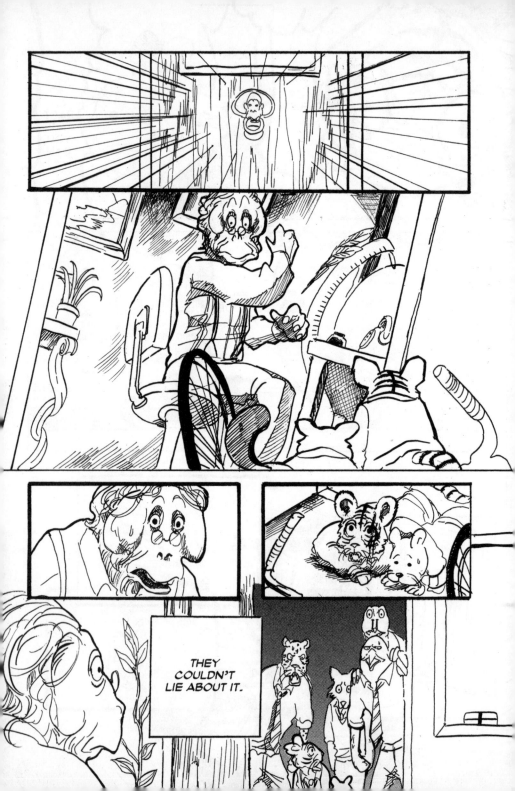

THEY COULDN'T LIE ABOUT IT.

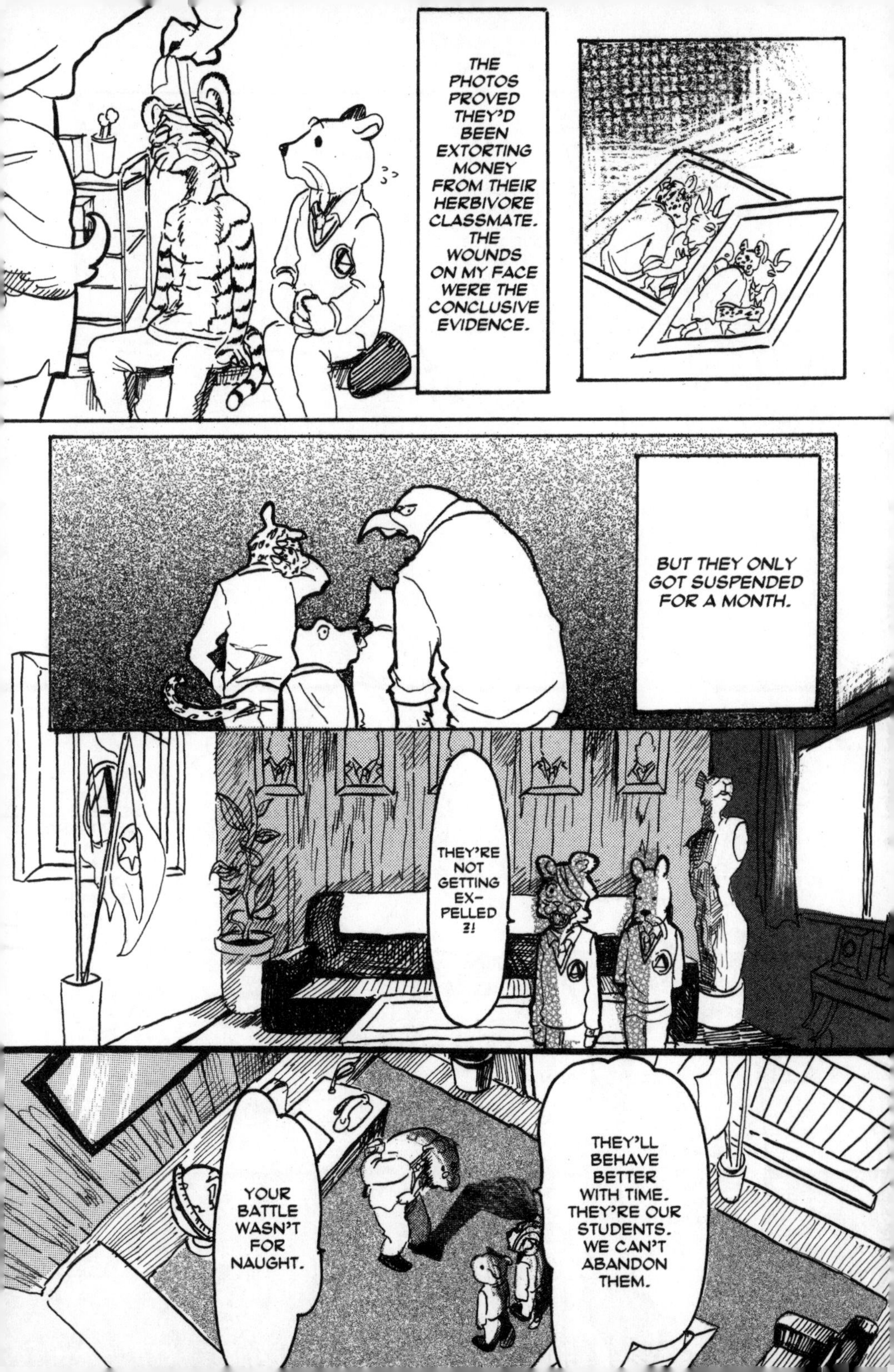
THE PHOTOS PROVED THEY'D BEEN EXTORTING MONEY FROM THEIR HERBIVORE CLASSMATE. THE WOUNDS ON MY FACE WERE THE CONCLUSIVE EVIDENCE.
BUT THEY ONLY GOT SUSPENDED FOR A MONTH.
THEY'RE NOT GETTING EX-PELLED?!
THEY'LL BEHAVE BETTER WITH TIME. THEY'RE OUR STUDENTS. WE CAN'T ABANDON THEM.
YOUR BATTLE WASN'T FOR NAUGHT.

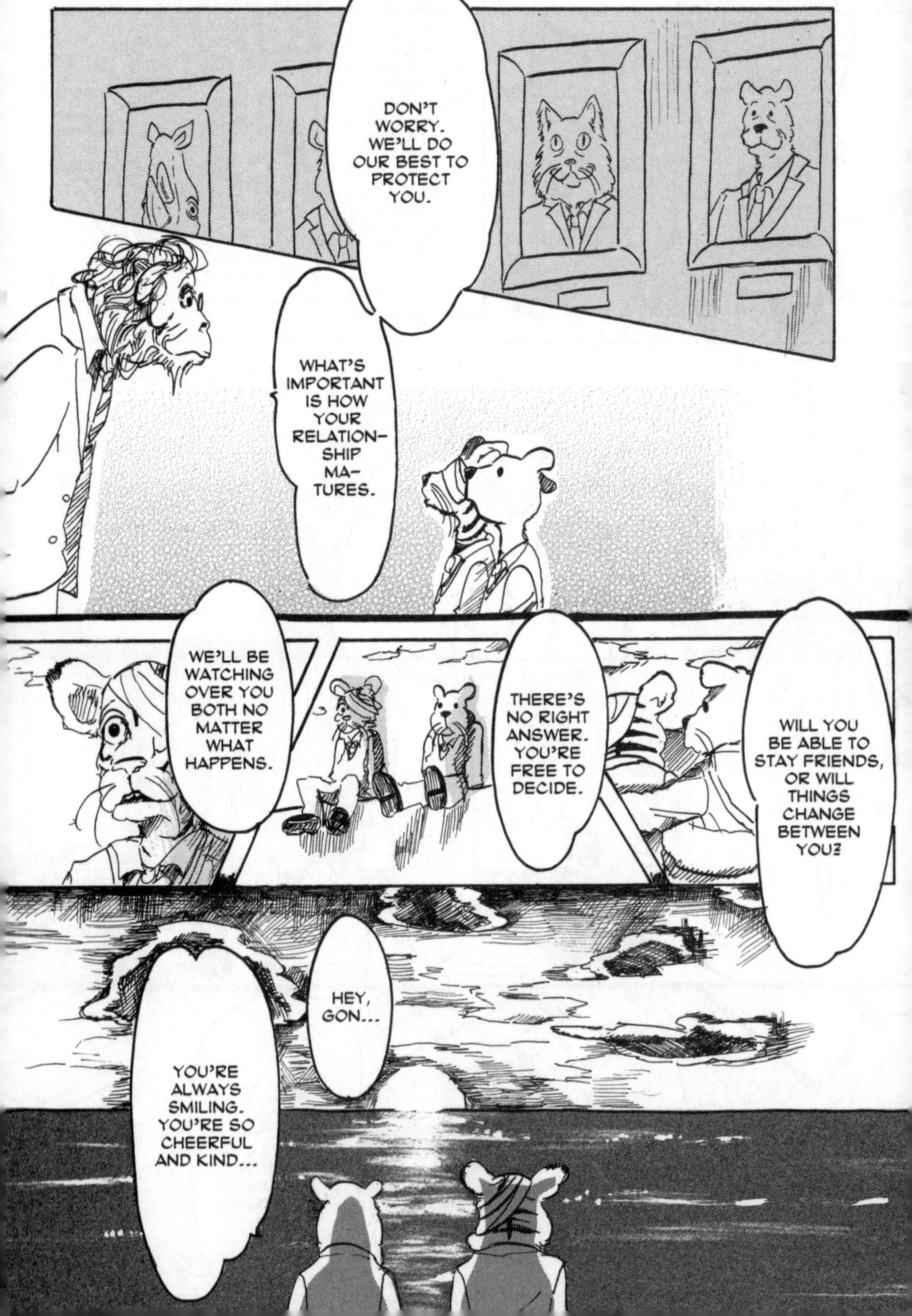
DON'T WORRY. WE'LL DO OUR BEST TO PROTECT YOU.
WHAT'S IMPORTANT IS HOW YOUR RELATIONSHIP MATURES.
WILL YOU BE ABLE TO STAY FRIENDS, OR WILL THINGS CHANGE BETWEEN YOU?
THERE'S NO RIGHT ANSWER. YOU'RE FREE TO DECIDE.
WE'LL BE WATCHING OVER YOU BOTH NO MATTER WHAT HAPPENS.
HEY, GON...
YOU'RE ALWAYS SMILING. YOU'RE SO CHEERFUL AND KIND...

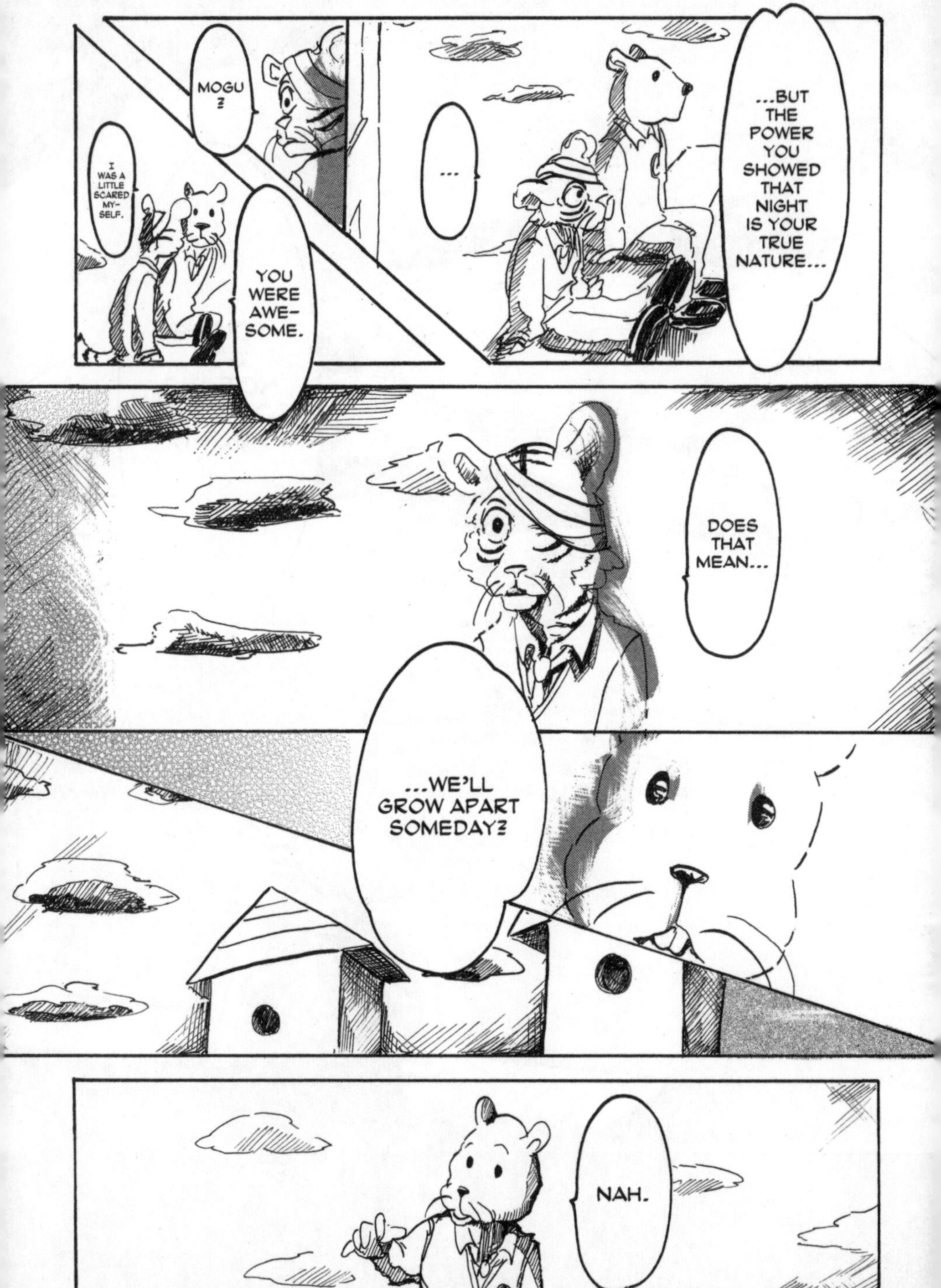
...BUT THE POWER YOU SHOWED THAT NIGHT IS YOUR TRUE NATURE...
...
MOGU?
YOU WERE AWESOME.
I WAS A LITTLE SCARED MYSELF.
DOES THAT MEAN...
...WE'LL GROW APART SOMEDAY?
NAH.

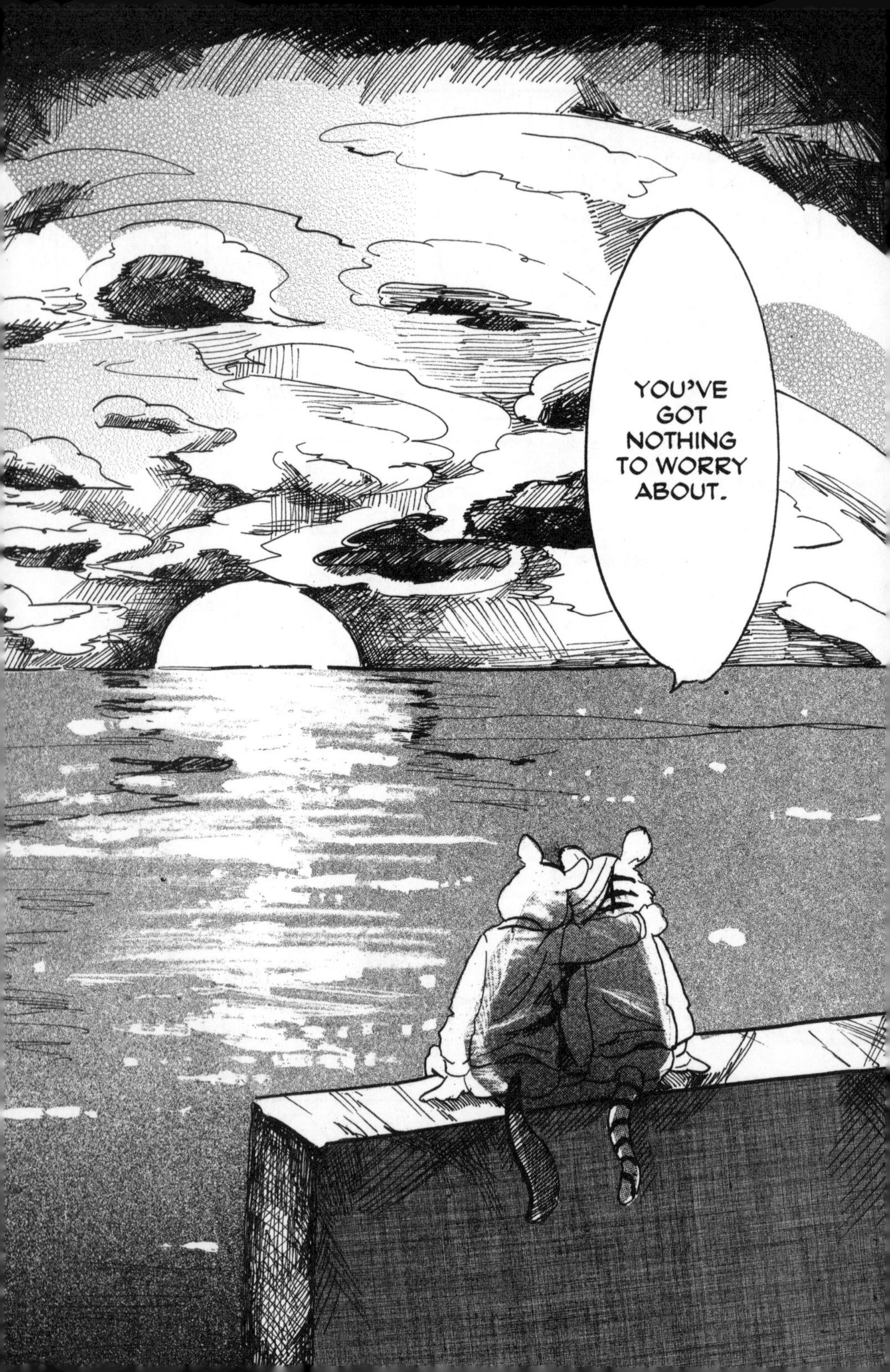
YOU'VE GOT NOTHING TO WORRY ABOUT.

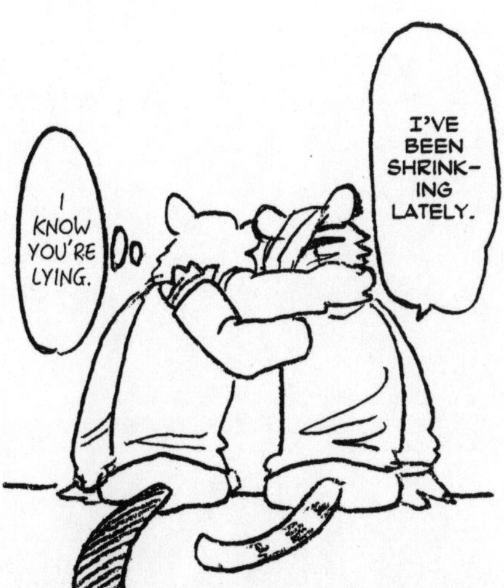
I'VE BEEN SHRINKING-ING LATELY.
I KNOW YOU'RE LYING.

Story 3
The Camel and the Wolf

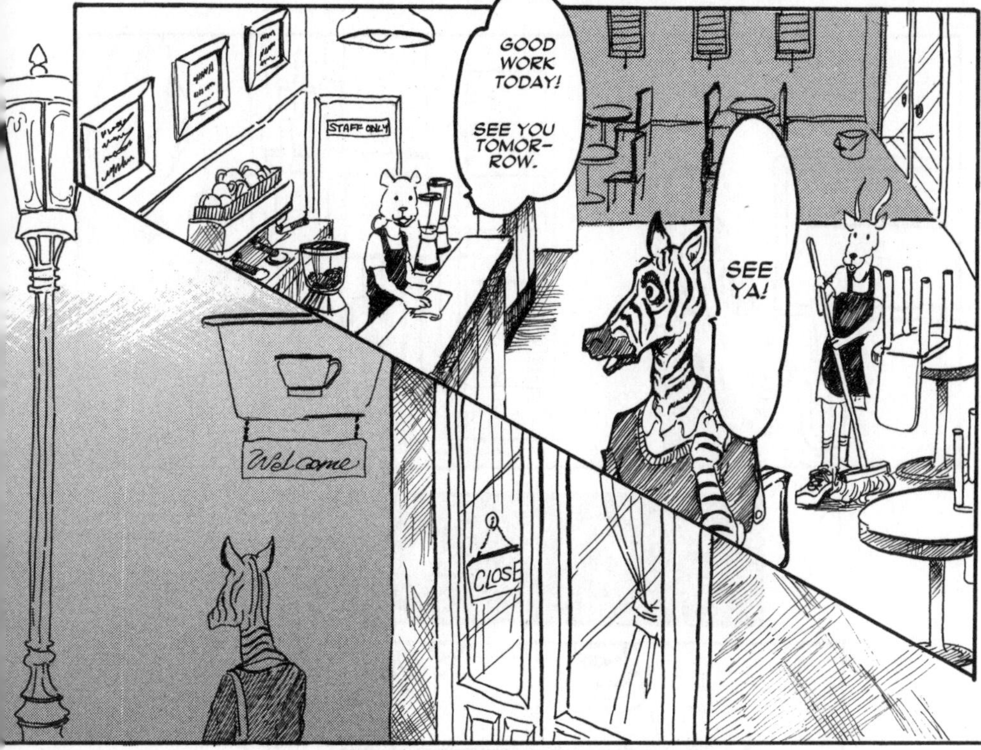
GOOD WORK TODAY!
SEE YOU TOMOR-ROW.
SEE YA!
STAFF ONLY
Welcome
CLOSE

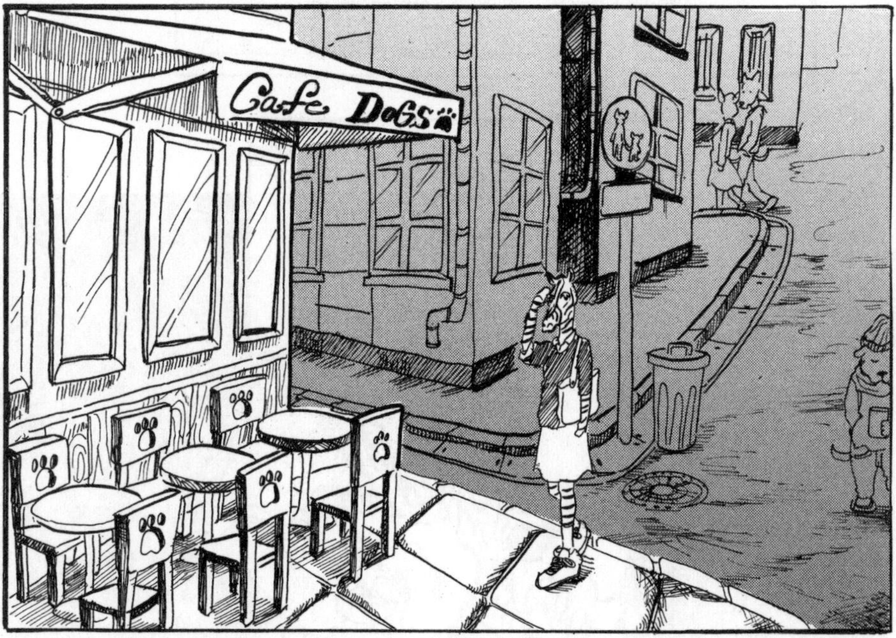
Cafe DoGS

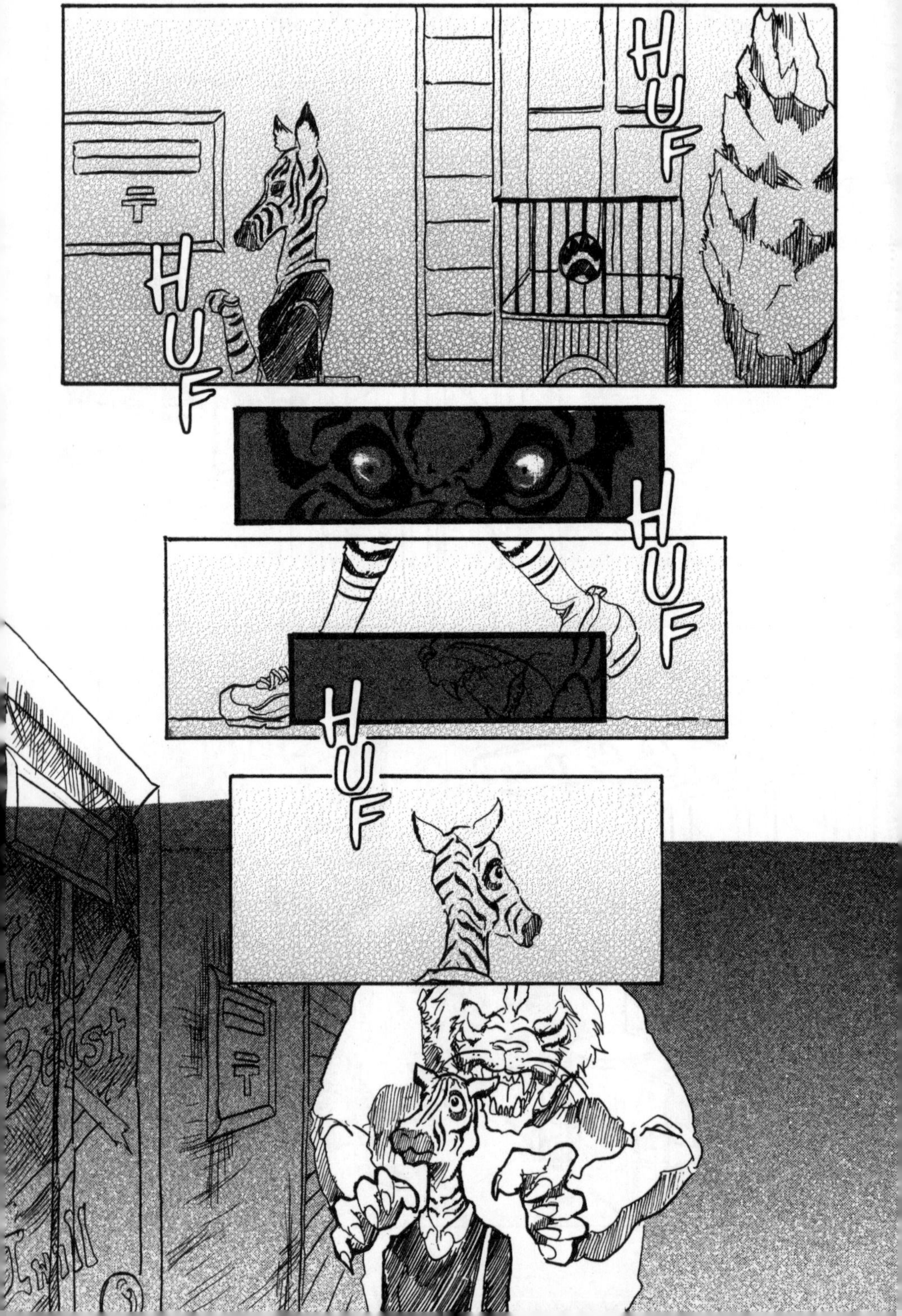
HUF
HUF
HUF
HUF
Beast

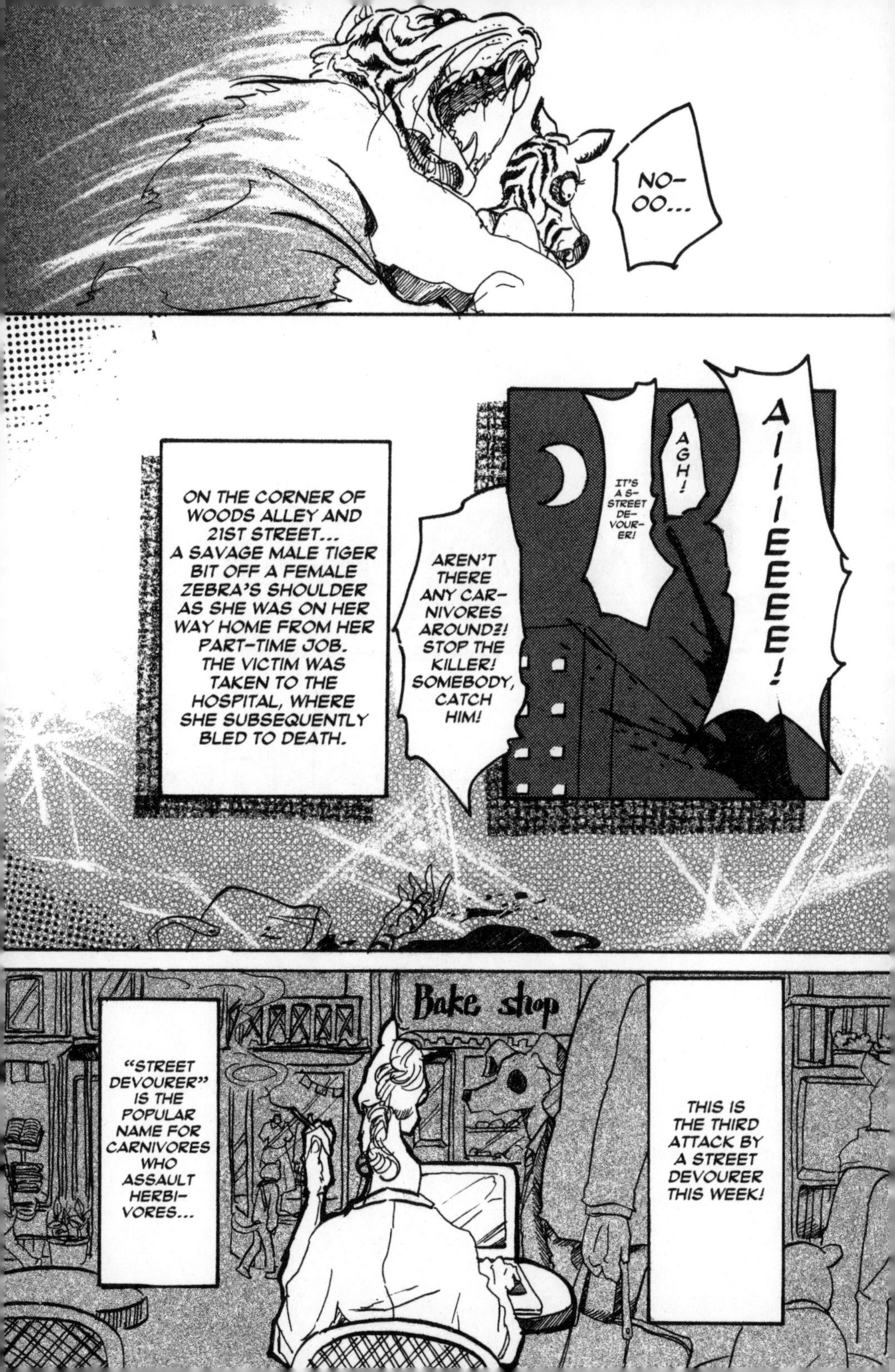
NO-
OO...
AIIIEEEE!
AGH!
IT'S A S-STREET DE-VOUR-ER!
AREN'T THERE ANY CAR-NIVORES AROUND?! STOP THE KILLER! SOMEBODY, CATCH HIM!
ON THE CORNER OF WOODS ALLEY AND 21ST STREET... A SAVAGE MALE TIGER BIT OFF A FEMALE ZEBRA'S SHOULDER AS SHE WAS ON HER WAY HOME FROM HER PART-TIME JOB. THE VICTIM WAS TAKEN TO THE HOSPITAL, WHERE SHE SUBSEQUENTLY BLED TO DEATH.
THIS IS THE THIRD ATTACK BY A STREET DEVOURER THIS WEEK!
Bake shop
"STREET DEVOURER" IS THE POPULAR NAME FOR CARNIVORES WHO ASSAULT HERBI-VORES...

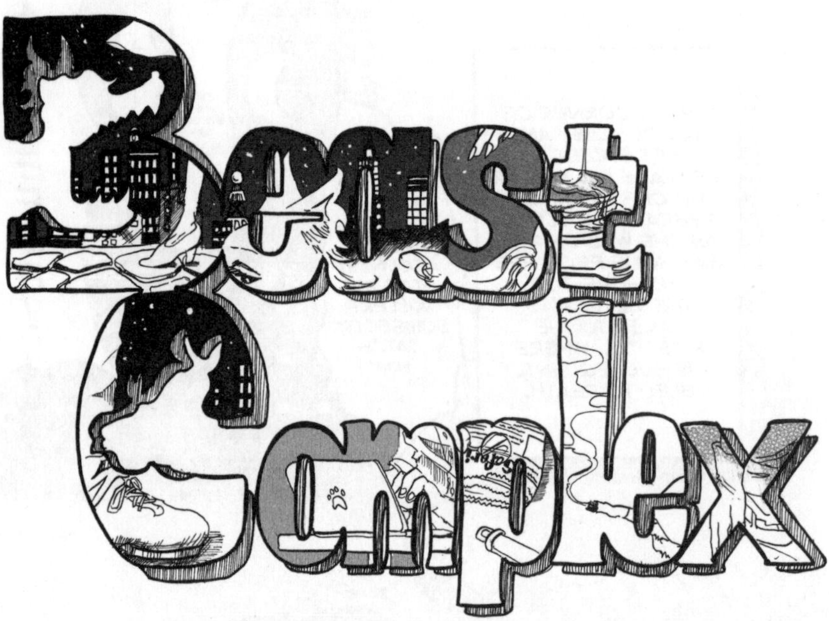
Beast Complex

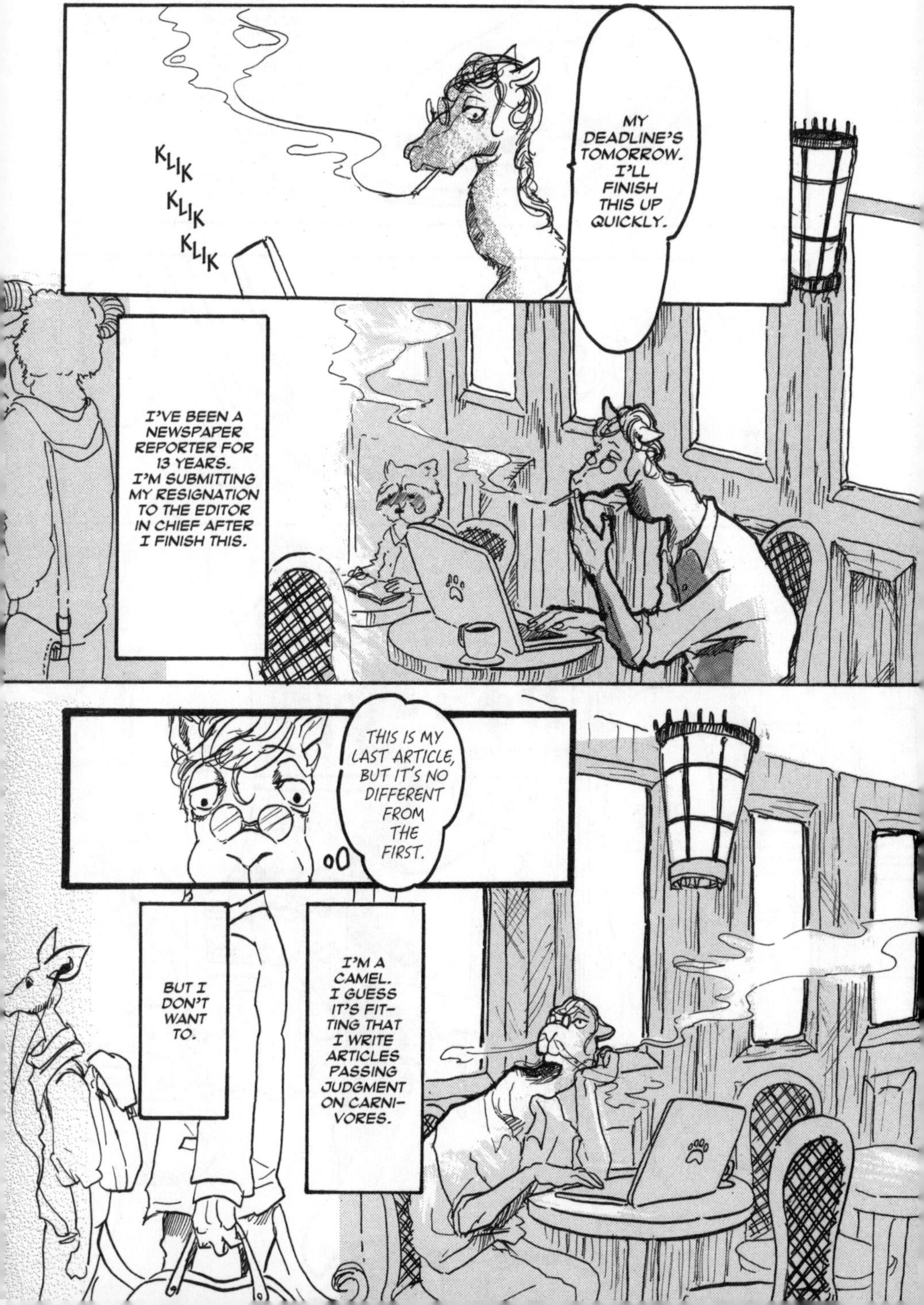
MY DEADLINE'S TOMORROW. I'LL FINISH THIS UP QUICKLY.
KLIK KLIK KLIK
I'VE BEEN A NEWSPAPER REPORTER FOR 13 YEARS. I'M SUBMITTING MY RESIGNATION TO THE EDITOR IN CHIEF AFTER I FINISH THIS.
THIS IS MY LAST ARTICLE, BUT IT'S NO DIFFERENT FROM THE FIRST.
I'M A CAMEL. I GUESS IT'S FIT-TING THAT I WRITE ARTICLES PASSING JUDGMENT ON CARNI-VORES.
BUT I DON'T WANT TO.

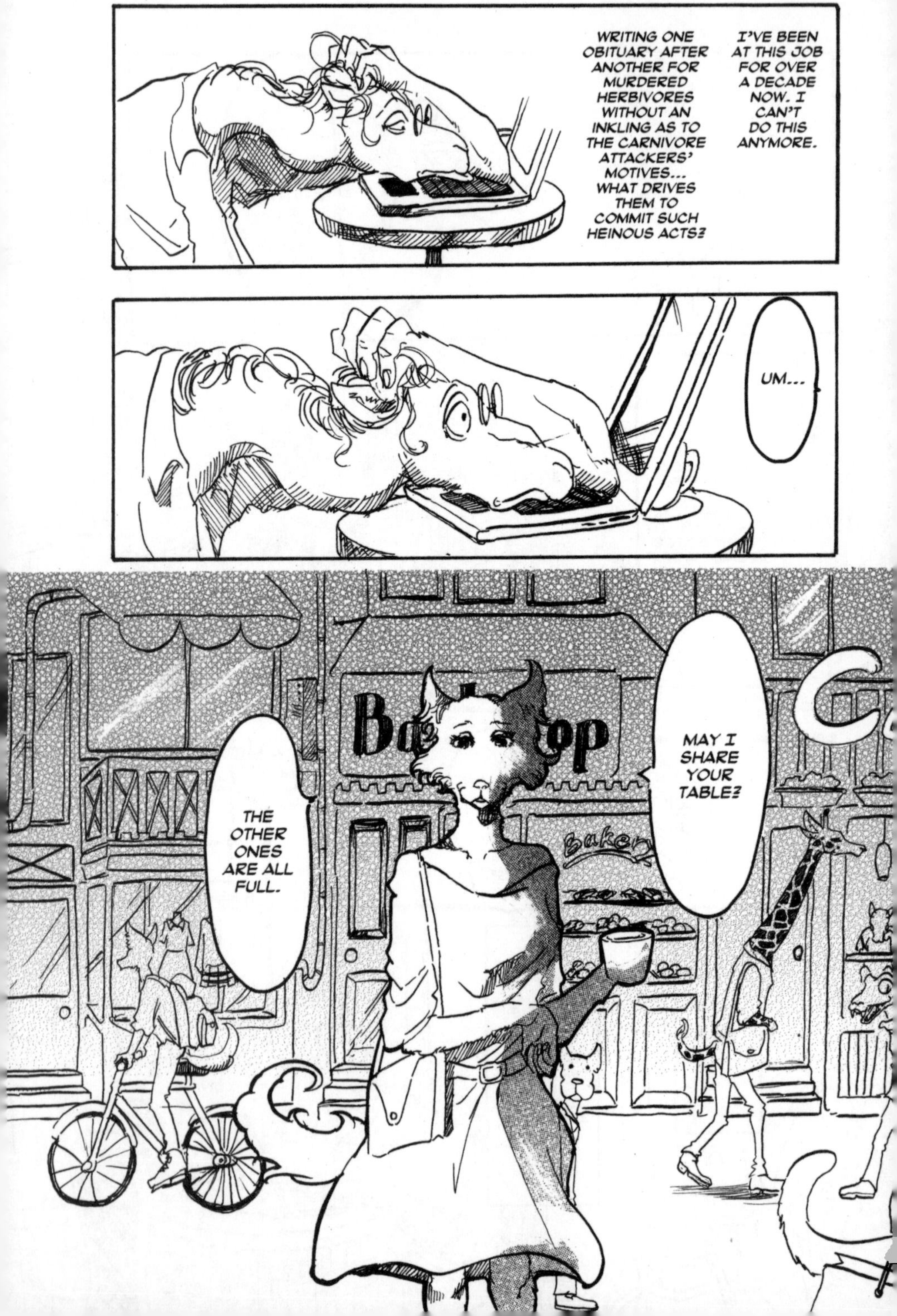

I'VE BEEN AT THIS JOB FOR OVER A DECADE NOW. I CAN'T DO THIS ANYMORE.
WRITING ONE OBITUARY AFTER ANOTHER FOR MURDERED HERBIVORES WITHOUT AN INKLING AS TO THE CARNIVORE ATTACKERS' MOTIVES... WHAT DRIVES THEM TO COMMIT SUCH HEINOUS ACTS?
UM...
MAY I SHARE YOUR TABLE?
THE OTHER ONES ARE ALL FULL.
Bakery

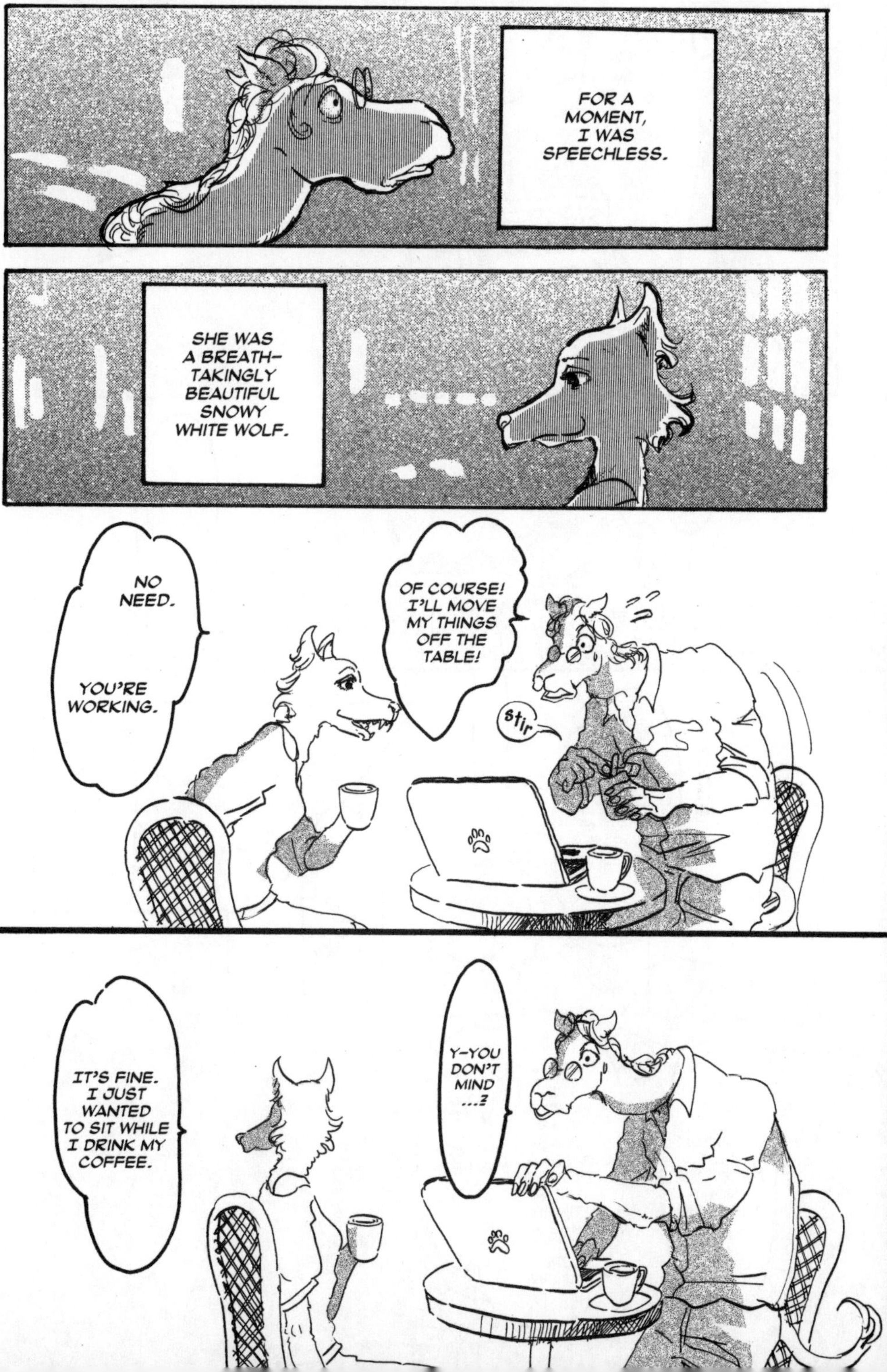
FOR A MOMENT, I WAS SPEECHLESS.
SHE WAS A BREATH-TAKINGLY BEAUTIFUL SNOWY WHITE WOLF.
OF COURSE! I'LL MOVE MY THINGS OFF THE TABLE!
stir
NO NEED.
YOU'RE WORKING.
Y-YOU DON'T MIND ...?
IT'S FINE. I JUST WANTED TO SIT WHILE I DRINK MY COFFEE.

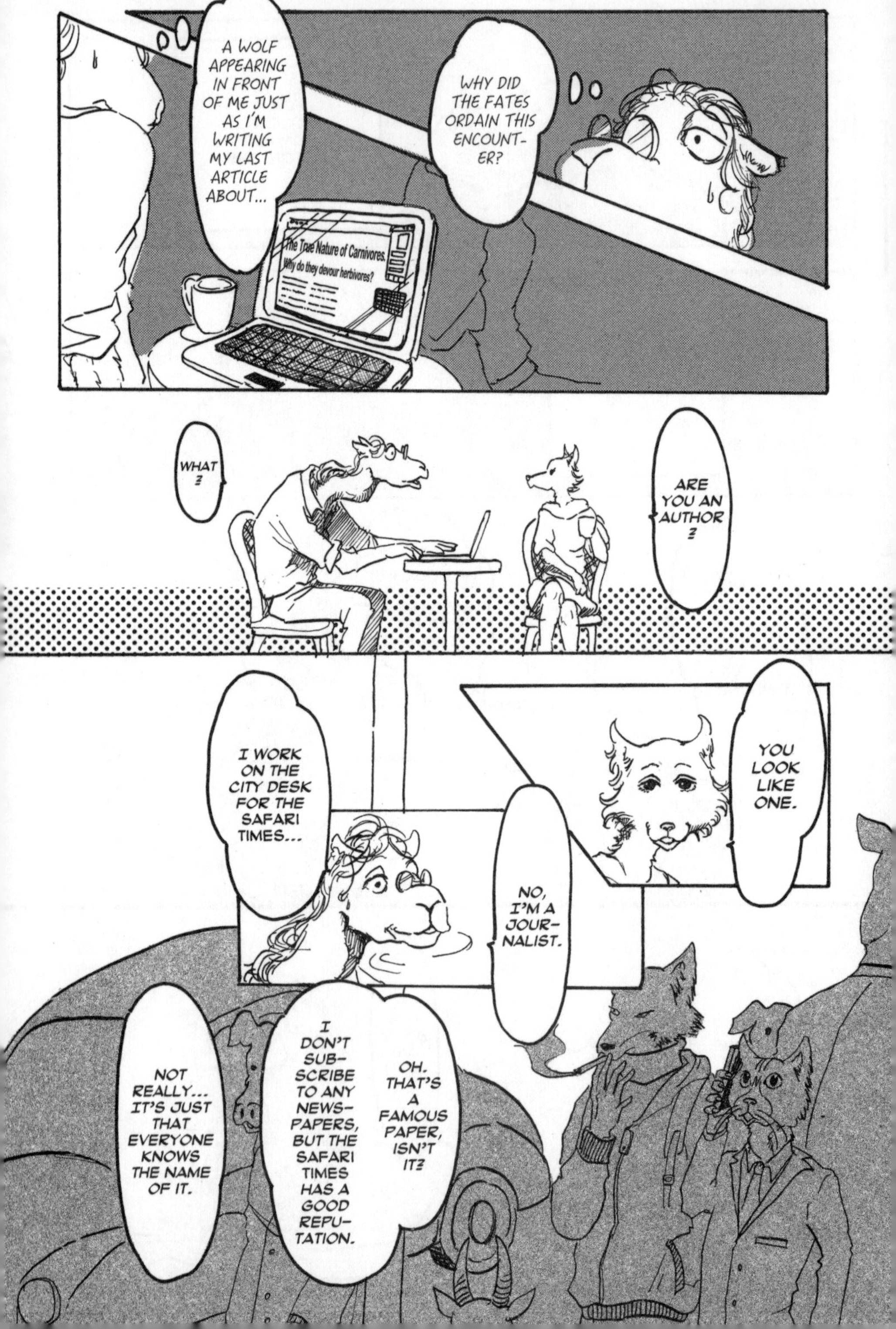
WHY DID THE FATES ORDAIN THIS ENCOUNTER?
A WOLF APPEARING IN FRONT OF ME JUST AS I'M WRITING MY LAST ARTICLE ABOUT...
The True Nature of Carnivores.
Why do they devour herbivores?
ARE YOU AN AUTHOR?
WHAT?
YOU LOOK LIKE ONE.
NO, I'M A JOURNALIST.
I WORK ON THE CITY DESK FOR THE SAFARI TIMES...
OH. THAT'S A FAMOUS PAPER, ISN'T IT?
I DON'T SUBSCRIBE TO ANY NEWSPAPERS, BUT THE SAFARI TIMES HAS A GOOD REPUTATION.
NOT REALLY... IT'S JUST THAT EVERYONE KNOWS THE NAME OF IT.

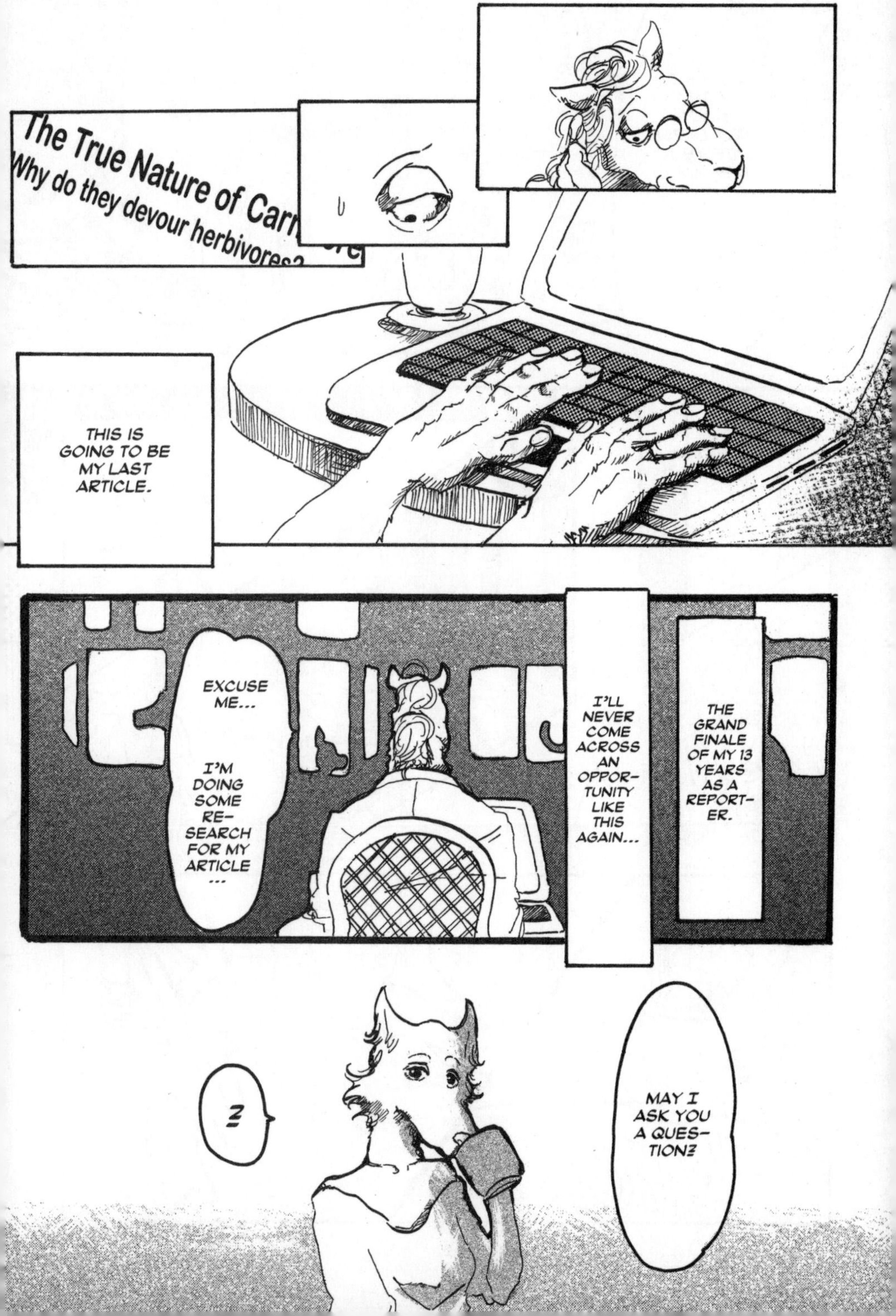
The True Nature of Carn
Why do they devour herbivores?
THIS IS GOING TO BE MY LAST ARTICLE.
THE GRAND FINALE OF MY 13 YEARS AS A REPORTER.
I'LL NEVER COME ACROSS AN OPPORTUNITY LIKE THIS AGAIN...
EXCUSE ME...
I'M DOING SOME RESEARCH FOR MY ARTICLE...
MAY I ASK YOU A QUESTION?
?

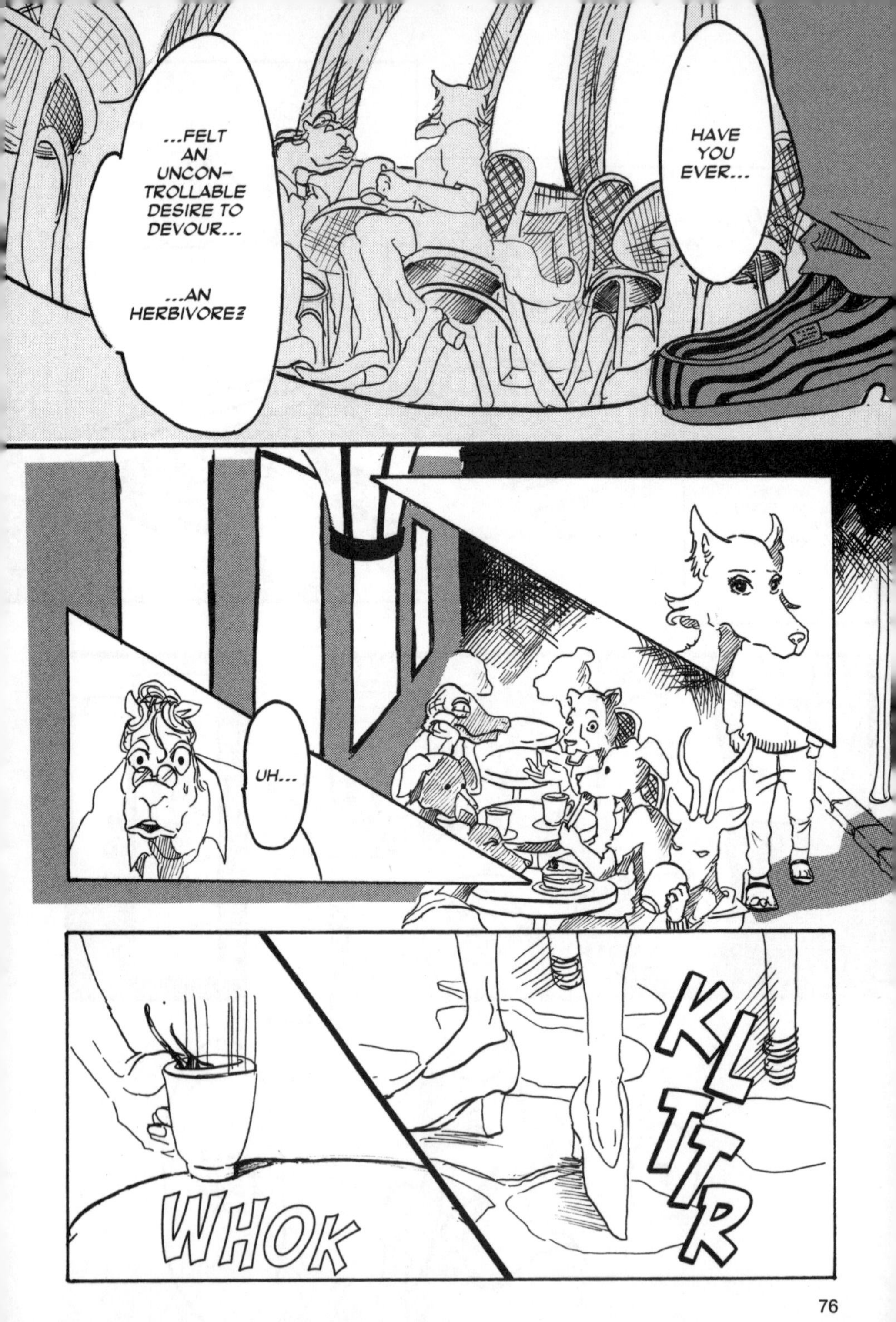
HAVE YOU EVER...
...FELT AN UNCONTROLLABLE DESIRE TO DEVOUR...
...AN HERBIVORE?
UH...
KLTTR
WHOK

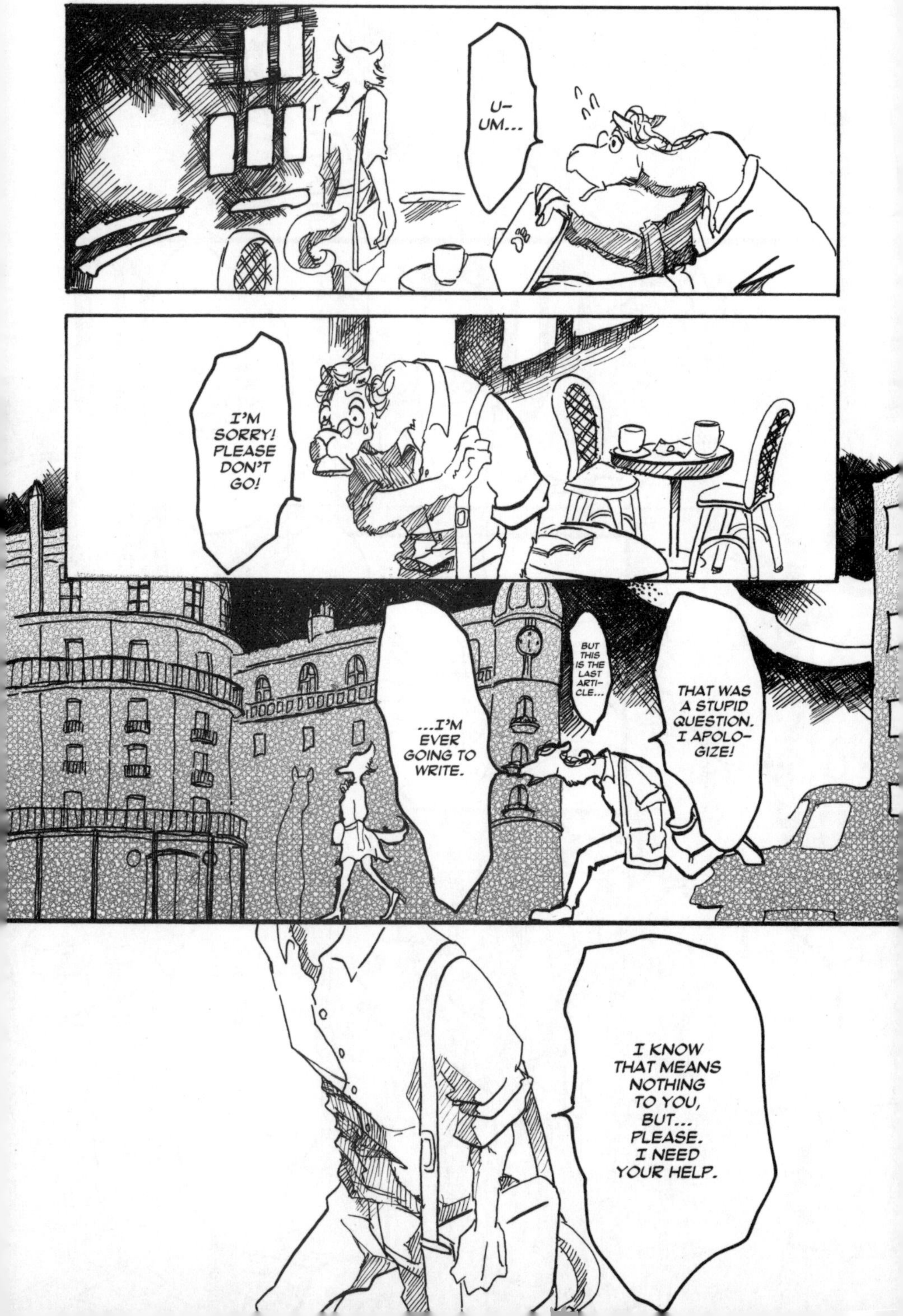
U- UM...
I'M SORRY! PLEASE DON'T GO!
THAT WAS A STUPID QUESTION. I APOLOGIZE!
BUT THIS IS THE LAST ARTI- CLE...
...I'M EVER GOING TO WRITE.
I KNOW THAT MEANS NOTHING TO YOU, BUT... PLEASE. I NEED YOUR HELP.

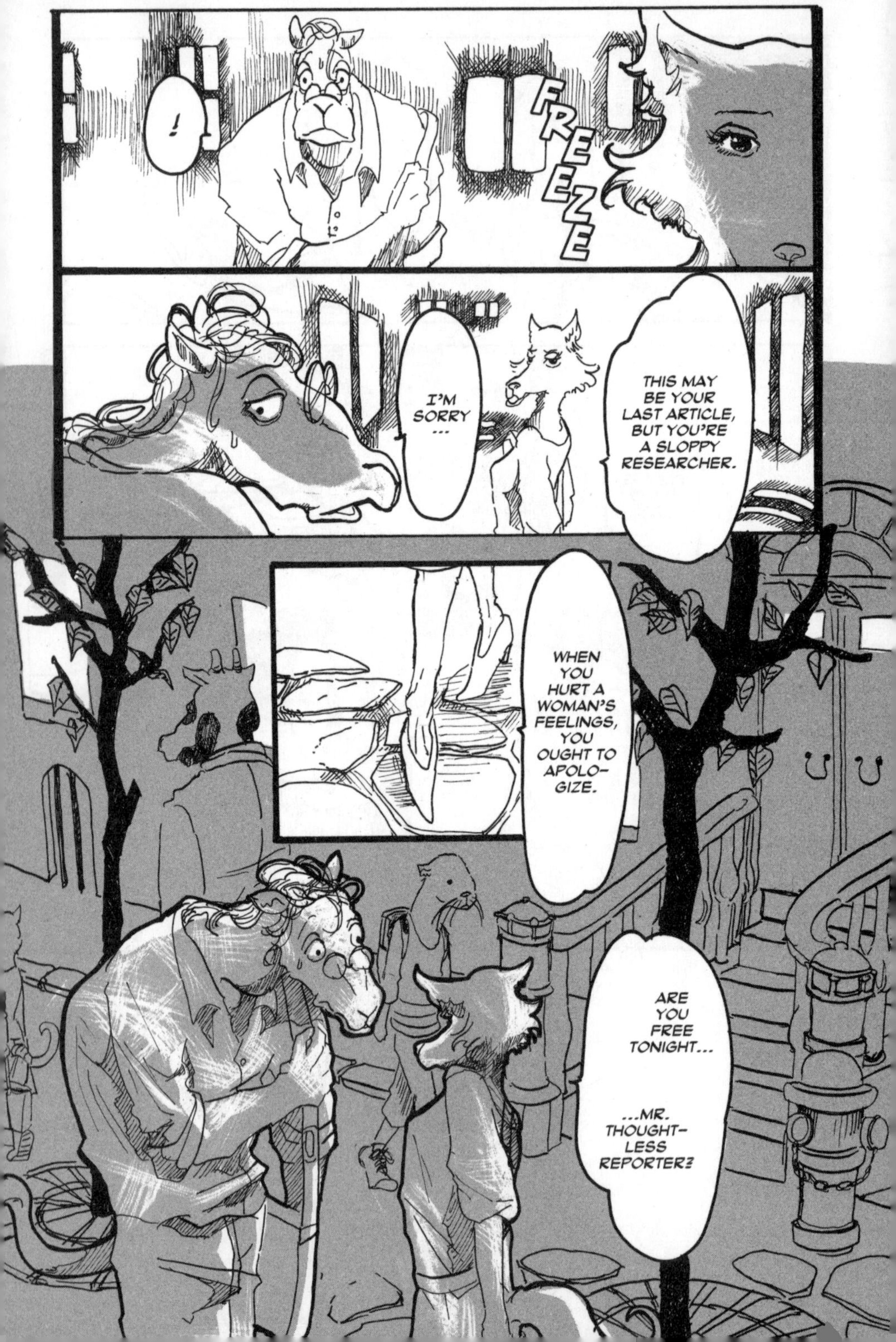
FREEZE
!
THIS MAY BE YOUR LAST ARTICLE, BUT YOU'RE A SLOPPY RESEARCHER.
I'M SORRY...
WHEN YOU HURT A WOMAN'S FEELINGS, YOU OUGHT TO APOLOGIZE.
ARE YOU FREE TONIGHT...
...MR. THOUGHTLESS REPORTER?

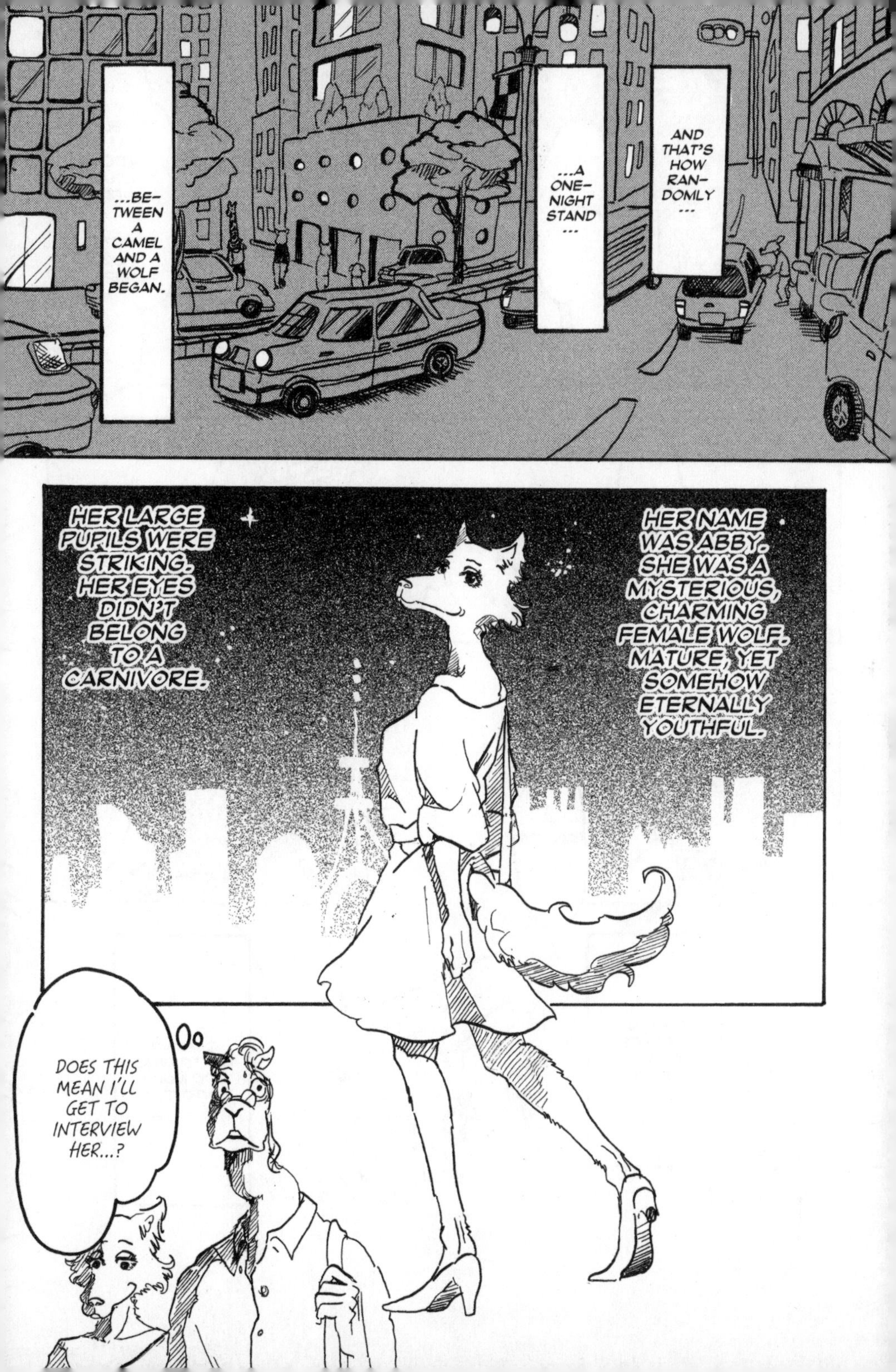
AND THAT'S HOW RAN-DOMLY...
...A ONE-NIGHT STAND...
...BE-TWEEN A CAMEL AND A WOLF BEGAN.
HER NAME WAS ABBY. SHE WAS A MYSTERIOUS, CHARMING FEMALE WOLF. MATURE, YET SOMEHOW ETERNALLY YOUTHFUL.
HER LARGE PUPILS WERE STRIKING. HER EYES DIDN'T BELONG TO A CARNIVORE.
DOES THIS MEAN I'LL GET TO INTERVIEW HER...?

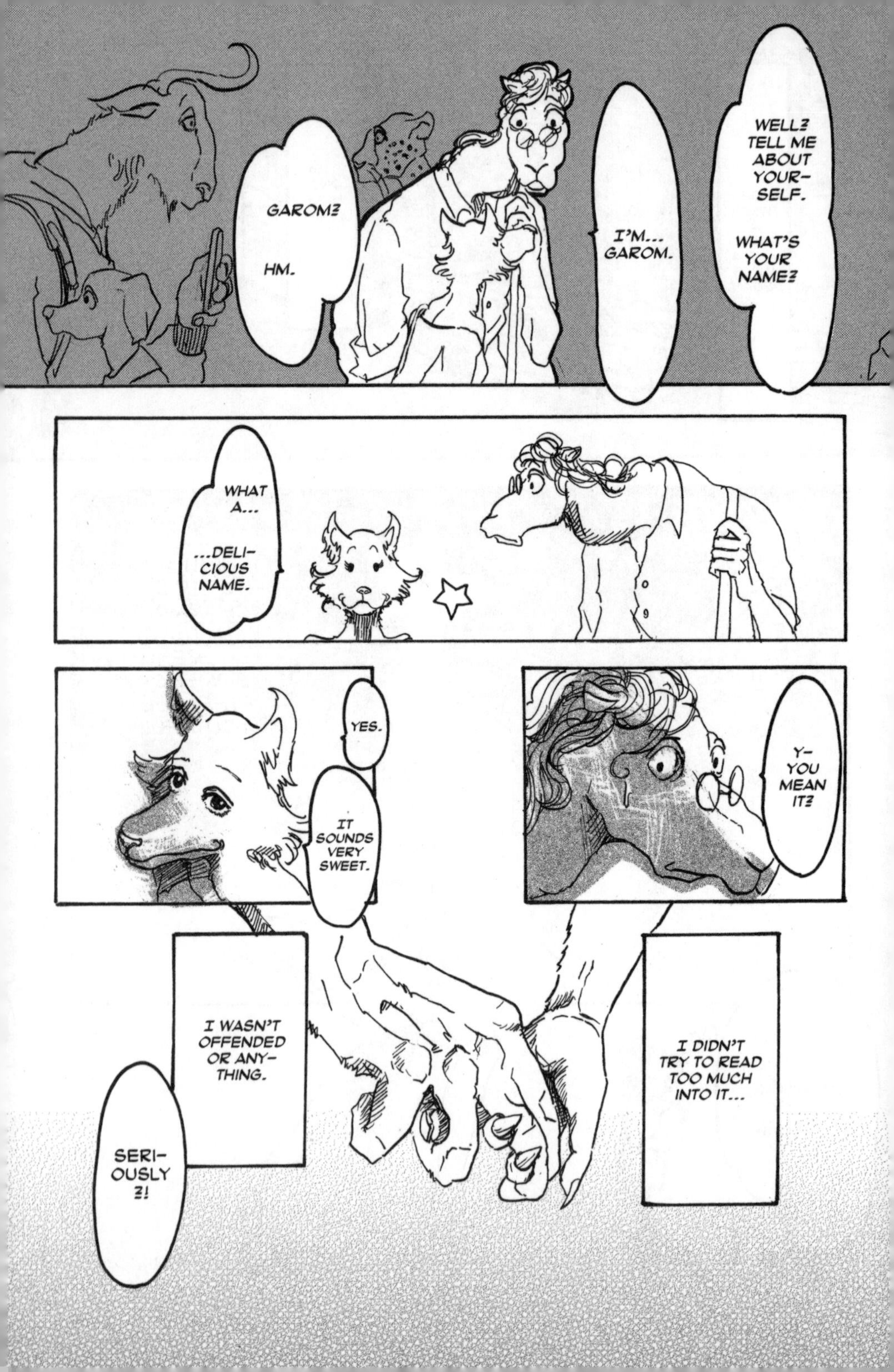
WELL? TELL ME ABOUT YOUR-SELF. WHAT'S YOUR NAME?
I'M... GAROM.
GAROM? HM.
WHAT A... ...DELI-CIOUS NAME.
Y-YOU MEAN IT?
YES.
IT SOUNDS VERY SWEET.
I DIDN'T TRY TO READ TOO MUCH INTO IT...
I WASN'T OFFENDED OR ANY-THING.
SERI-OUSLY?!

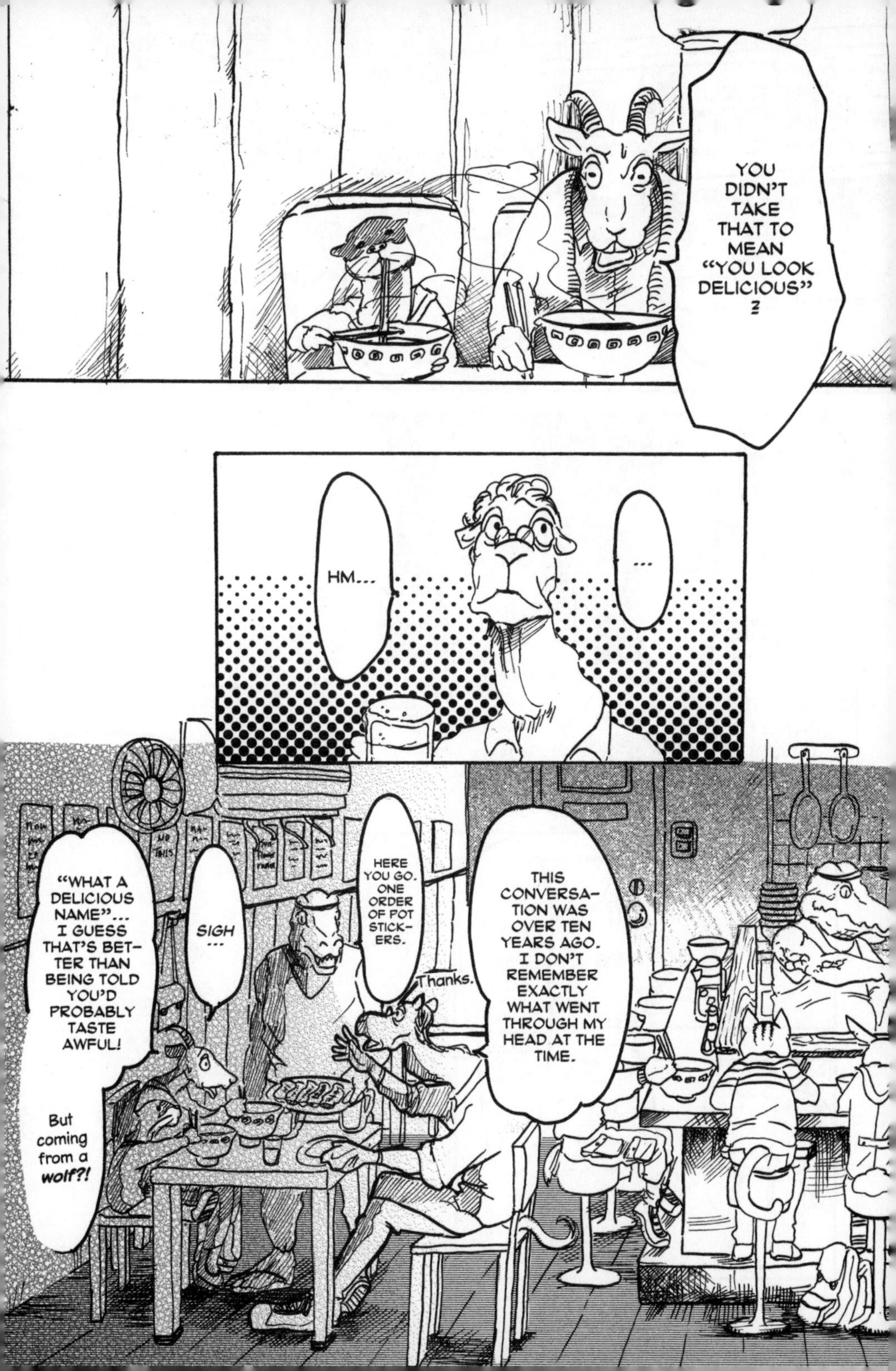
YOU DIDN'T TAKE THAT TO MEAN "YOU LOOK DELICIOUS"?
...
HM...
THIS CONVERSATION WAS OVER TEN YEARS AGO. I DON'T REMEMBER EXACTLY WHAT WENT THROUGH MY HEAD AT THE TIME.
HERE YOU GO. ONE ORDER OF POT STICKERS.
Thanks.
SIGH...
"WHAT A DELICIOUS NAME"... I GUESS THAT'S BETTER THAN BEING TOLD YOU'D PROBABLY TASTE AWFUL!
But coming from a *wolf?!*

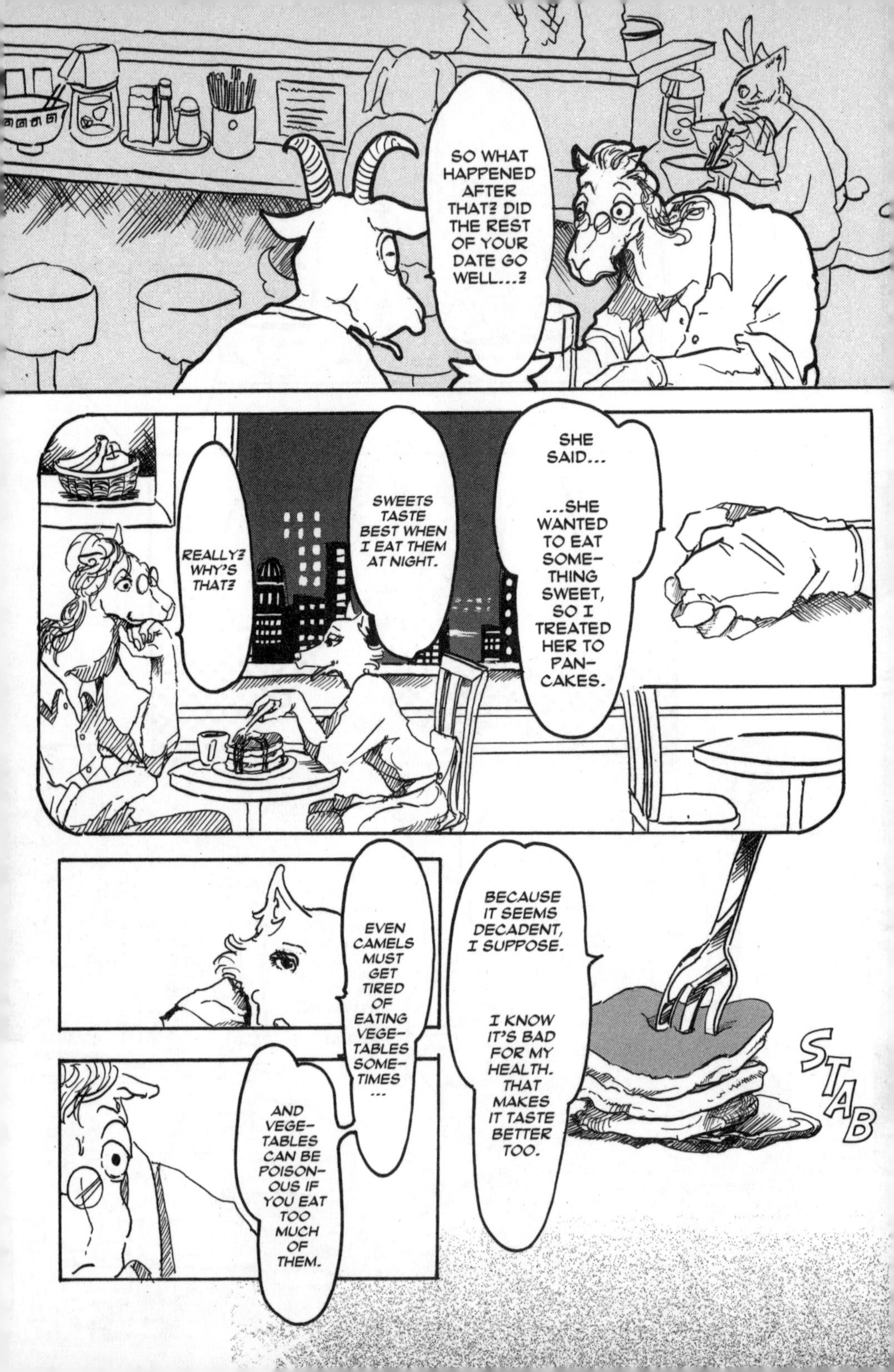
SO WHAT HAPPENED AFTER THAT? DID THE REST OF YOUR DATE GO WELL...?
SHE SAID...
...SHE WANTED TO EAT SOMETHING SWEET, SO I TREATED HER TO PANCAKES.
SWEETS TASTE BEST WHEN I EAT THEM AT NIGHT.
REALLY? WHY'S THAT?
BECAUSE IT SEEMS DECADENT, I SUPPOSE.
I KNOW IT'S BAD FOR MY HEALTH. THAT MAKES IT TASTE BETTER TOO.
STAB
EVEN CAMELS MUST GET TIRED OF EATING VEGETABLES SOMETIMES...
AND VEGETABLES CAN BE POISONOUS IF YOU EAT TOO MUCH OF THEM.

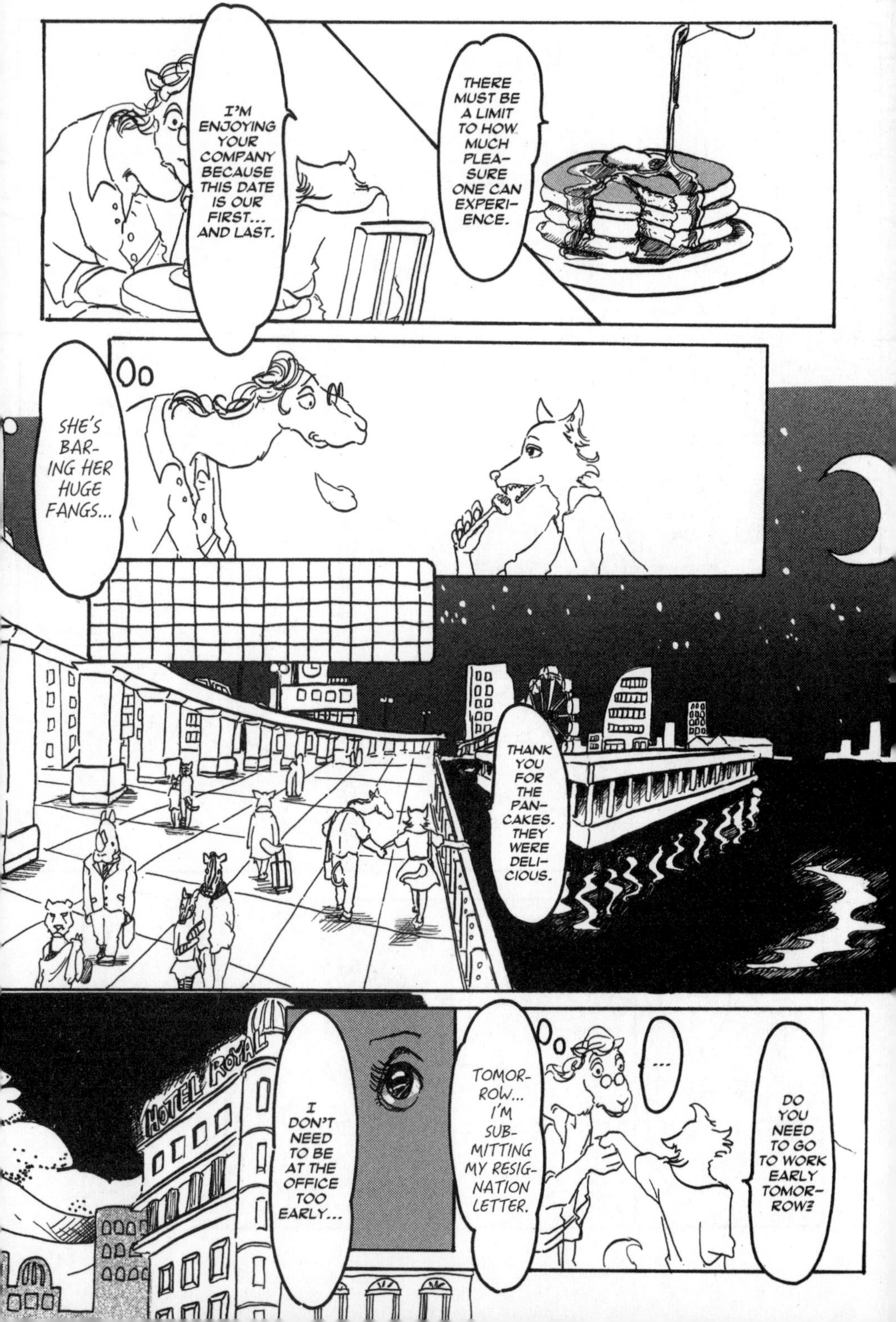

THERE MUST BE A LIMIT TO HOW MUCH PLEASURE ONE CAN EXPERIENCE.
I'M ENJOYING YOUR COMPANY BECAUSE THIS DATE IS OUR FIRST... AND LAST.
Oo
SHE'S BARING HER HUGE FANGS...
THANK YOU FOR THE PANCAKES. THEY WERE DELICIOUS.
DO YOU NEED TO GO TO WORK EARLY TOMORROW?
...
Oo
TOMORROW... I'M SUBMITTING MY RESIGNATION LETTER.
I DON'T NEED TO BE AT THE OFFICE TOO EARLY...
HOTEL ROYAL

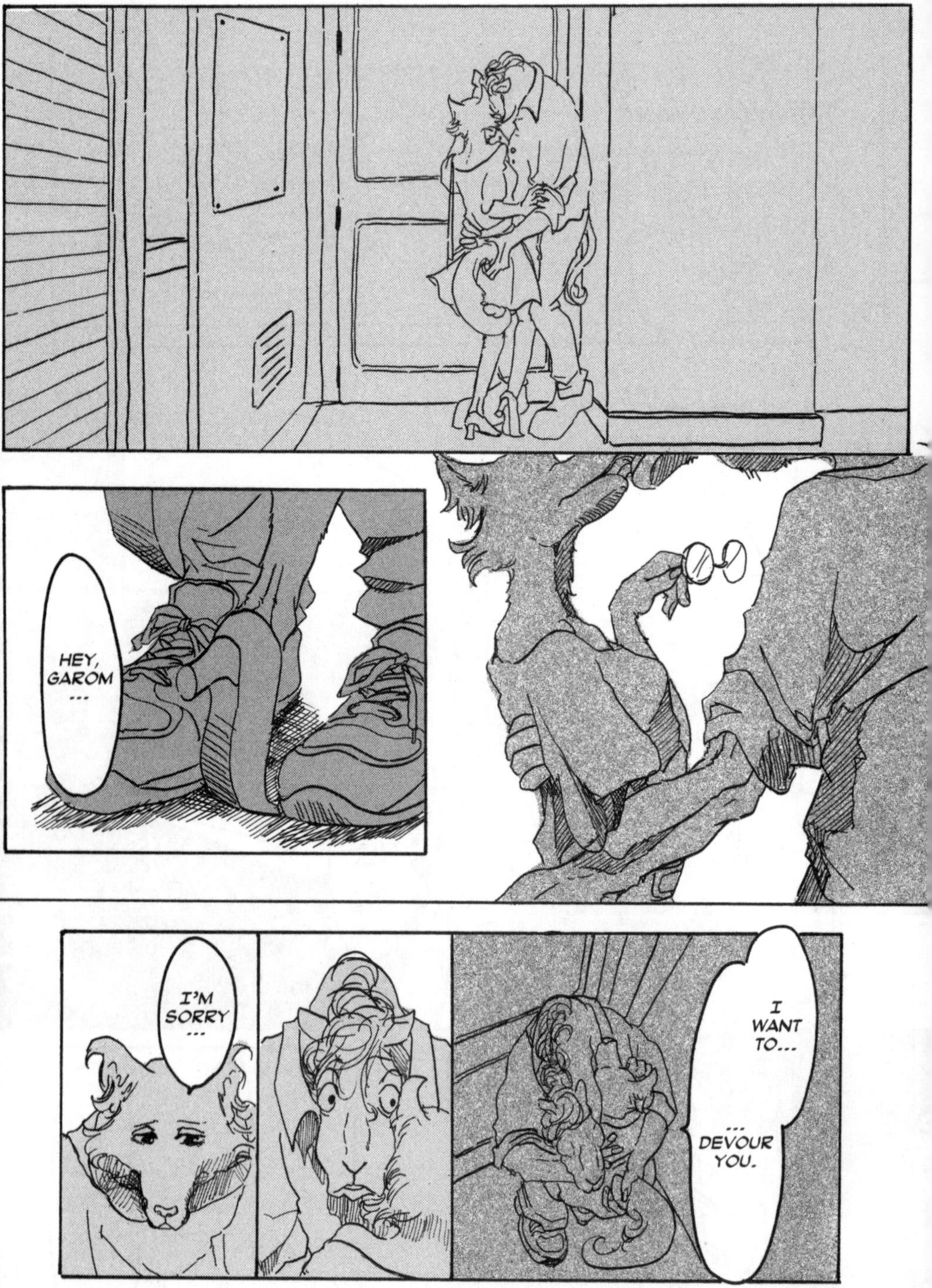
HEY, GAROM ...
I WANT TO...
... DEVOUR YOU.
I'M SORRY ...

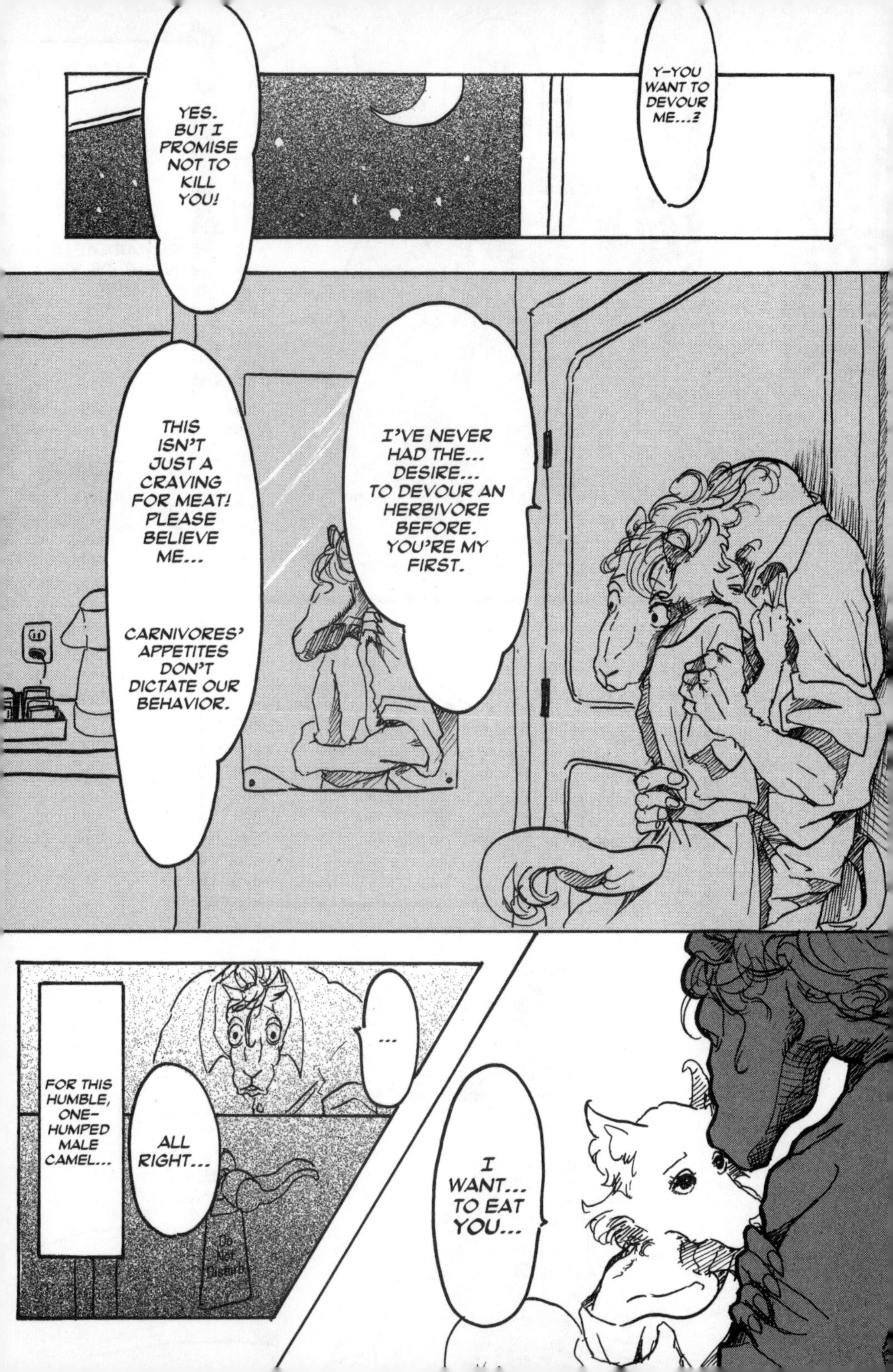
Y-YOU WANT TO DEVOUR ME...?
YES. BUT I PROMISE NOT TO KILL YOU!
I'VE NEVER HAD THE... DESIRE... TO DEVOUR AN HERBIVORE BEFORE. YOU'RE MY FIRST.
THIS ISN'T JUST A CRAVING FOR MEAT! PLEASE BELIEVE ME...
CARNIVORES' APPETITES DON'T DICTATE OUR BEHAVIOR.
I WANT... TO EAT YOU...
...
ALL RIGHT...
FOR THIS HUMBLE, ONE-HUMPED MALE CAMEL...
Do Not Disturb

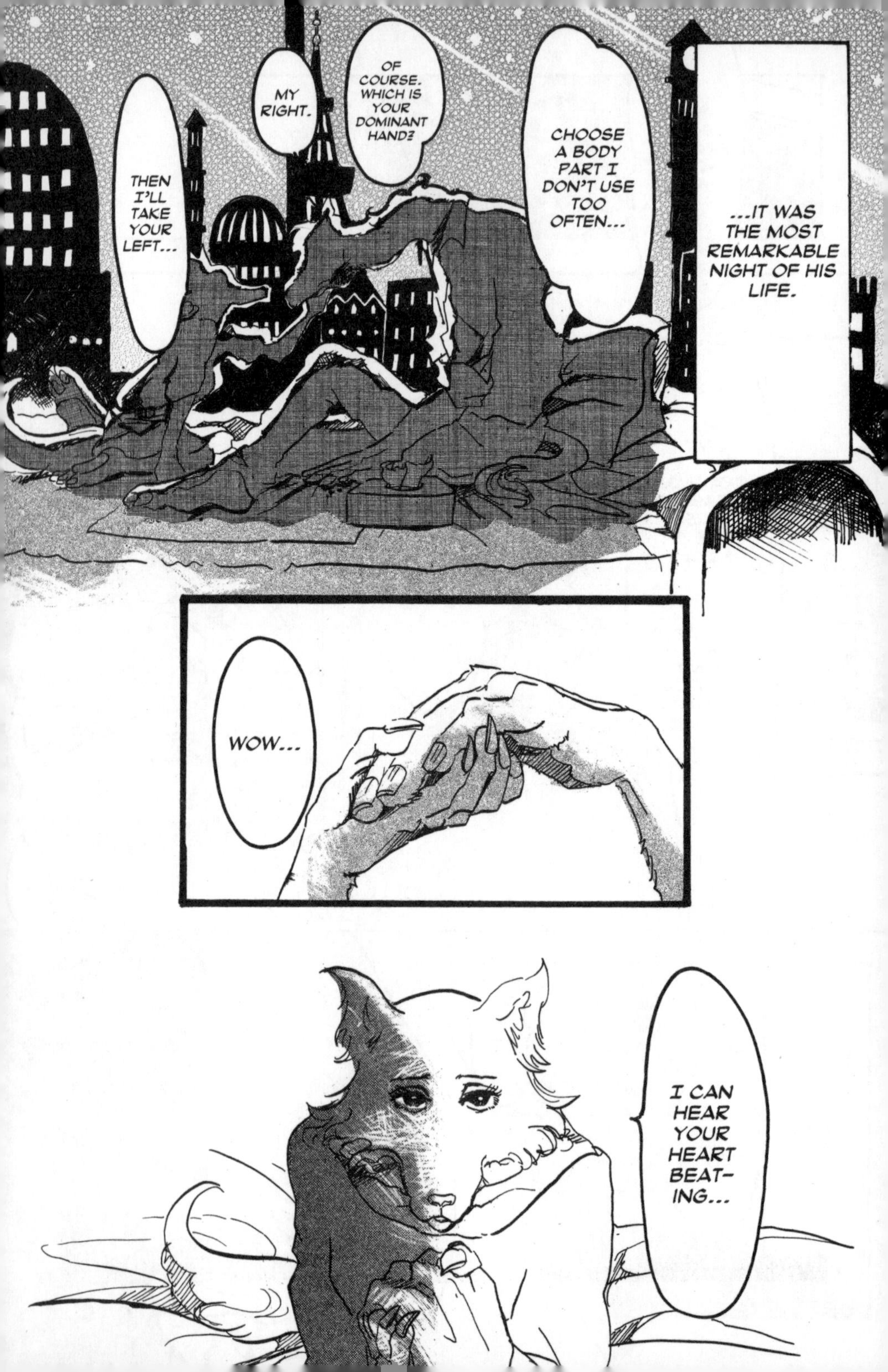
...IT WAS THE MOST REMARKABLE NIGHT OF HIS LIFE.
CHOOSE A BODY PART I DON'T USE TOO OFTEN...
OF COURSE. WHICH IS YOUR DOMINANT HAND?
MY RIGHT.
THEN I'LL TAKE YOUR LEFT...
WOW...
I CAN HEAR YOUR HEART BEAT-ING...

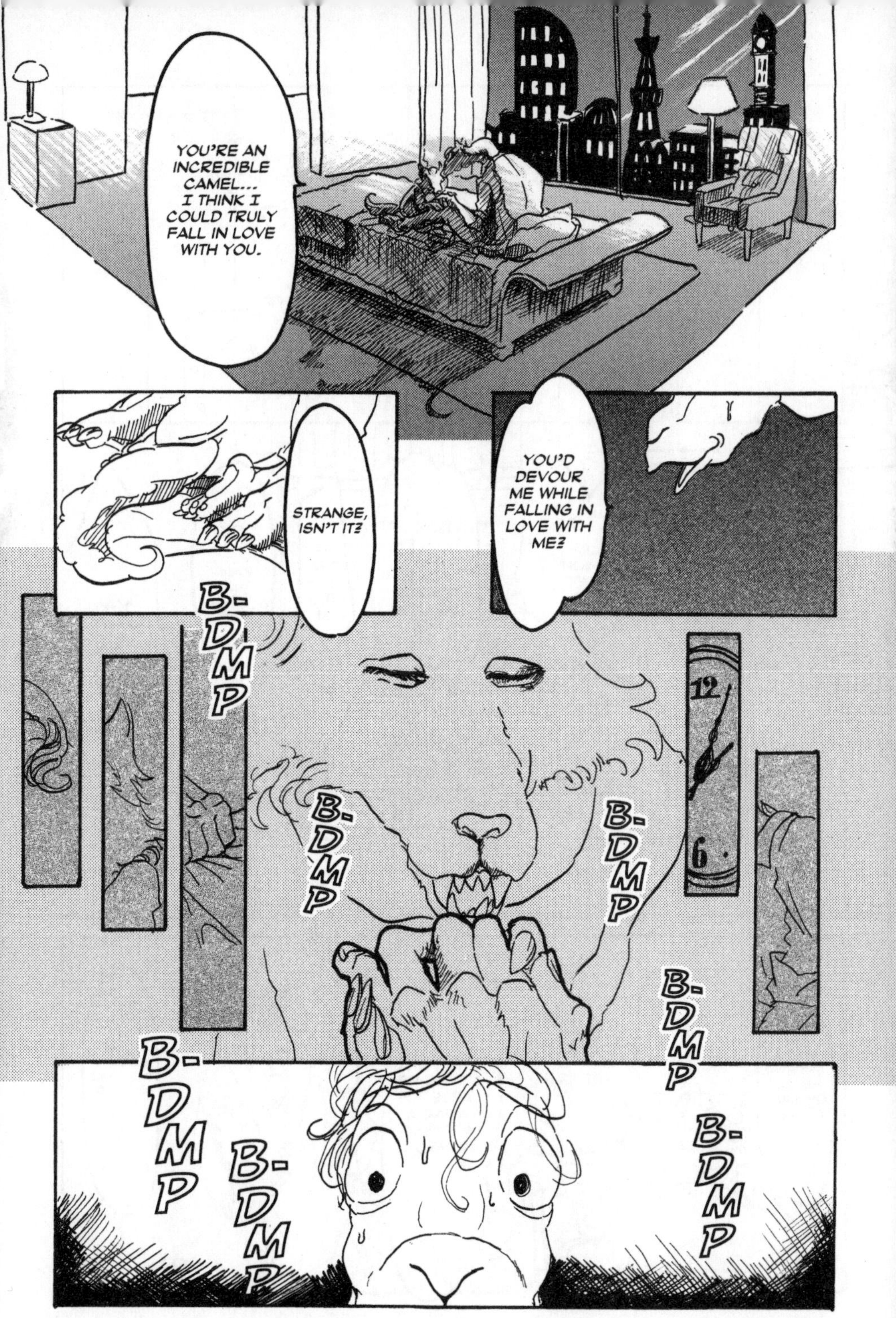
YOU'RE AN INCREDIBLE CAMEL... I THINK I COULD TRULY FALL IN LOVE WITH YOU.
YOU'D DEVOUR ME WHILE FALLING IN LOVE WITH ME?
STRANGE, ISN'T IT?
B-DMP
B-DMP
B-DMP
B-DMP
B-DMP
B-DMP
B-DMP

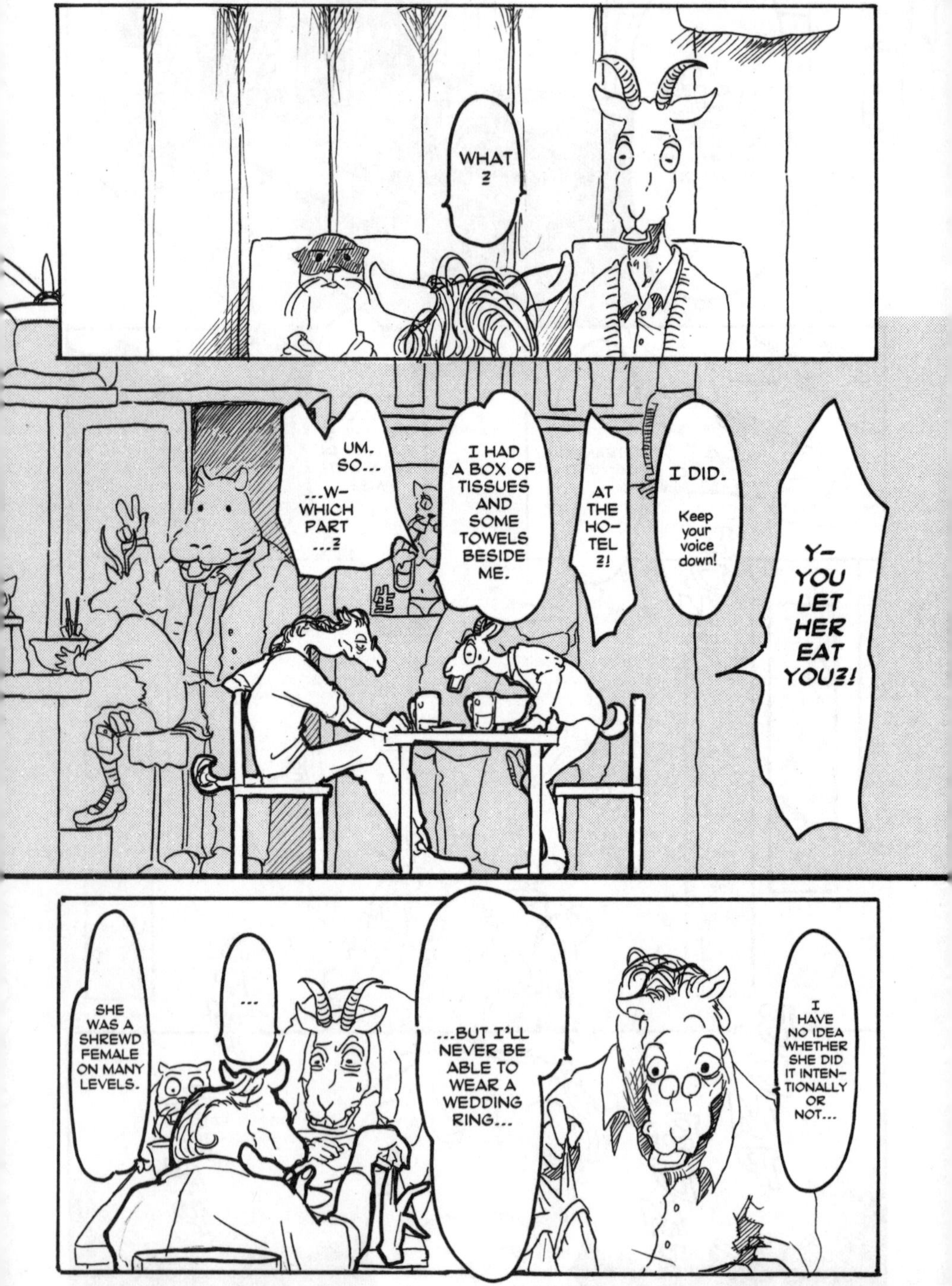
WHAT?
Y-YOU LET HER EAT YOU?!
I DID. Keep your voice down!
AT THE HOTEL?!
I HAD A BOX OF TISSUES AND SOME TOWELS BESIDE ME.
UM. SO... ...W-WHICH PART...?
I HAVE NO IDEA WHETHER SHE DID IT INTENTIONALLY OR NOT...
...BUT I'LL NEVER BE ABLE TO WEAR A WEDDING RING...
...
SHE WAS A SHREWD FEMALE ON MANY LEVELS.

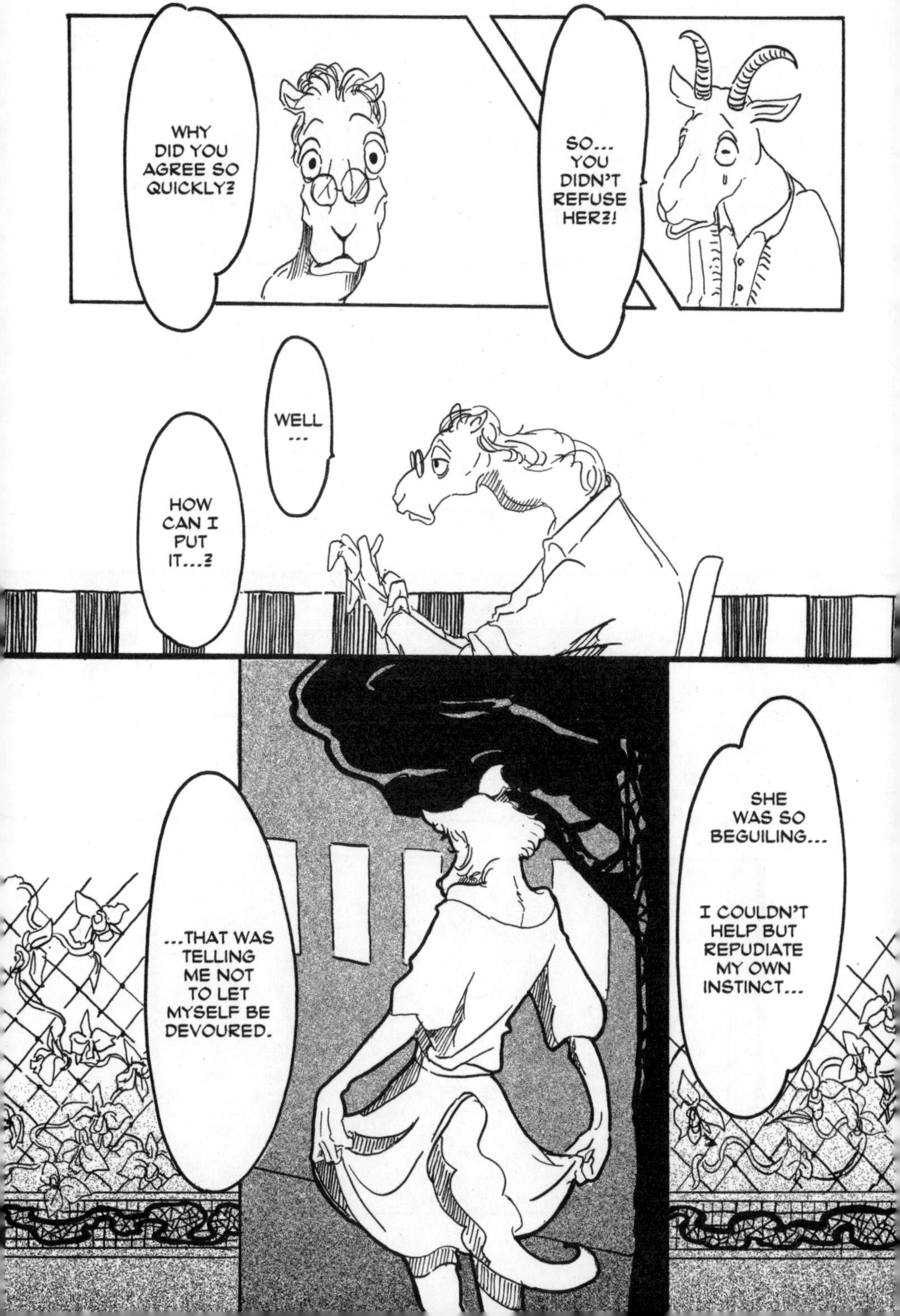
SO... YOU DIDN'T REFUSE HER?!
WHY DID YOU AGREE SO QUICKLY?
WELL...
HOW CAN I PUT IT...?
SHE WAS SO BEGUILING...
I COULDN'T HELP BUT REPUDIATE MY OWN INSTINCT...
...THAT WAS TELLING ME NOT TO LET MYSELF BE DEVOURED.

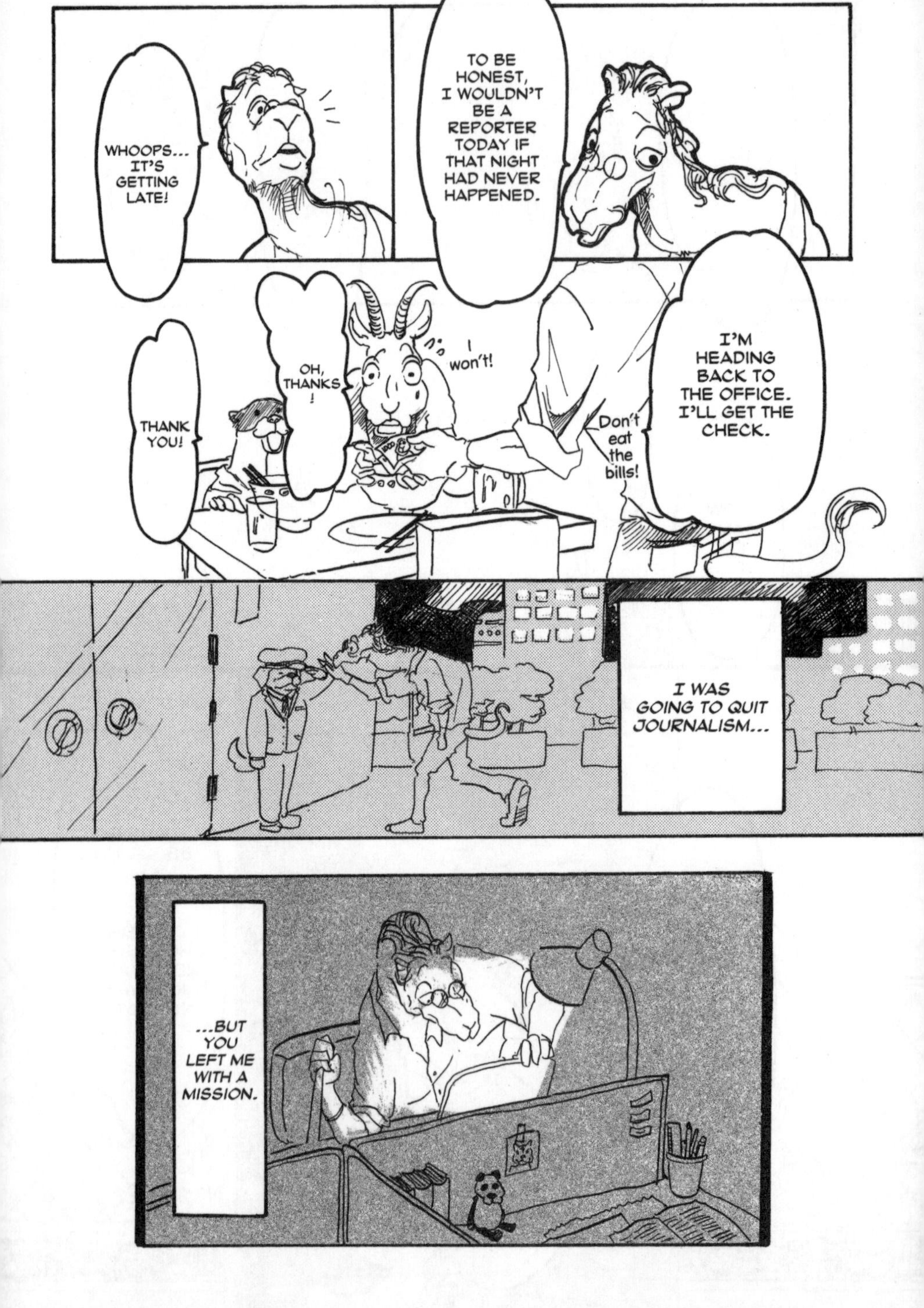
TO BE HONEST, I WOULDN'T BE A REPORTER TODAY IF THAT NIGHT HAD NEVER HAPPENED.
WHOOPS... IT'S GETTING LATE!
I'M HEADING BACK TO THE OFFICE. I'LL GET THE CHECK.
Don't eat the bills!
I won't!
OH, THANKS!
THANK YOU!
I WAS GOING TO QUIT JOURNALISM...
...BUT YOU LEFT ME WITH A MISSION.

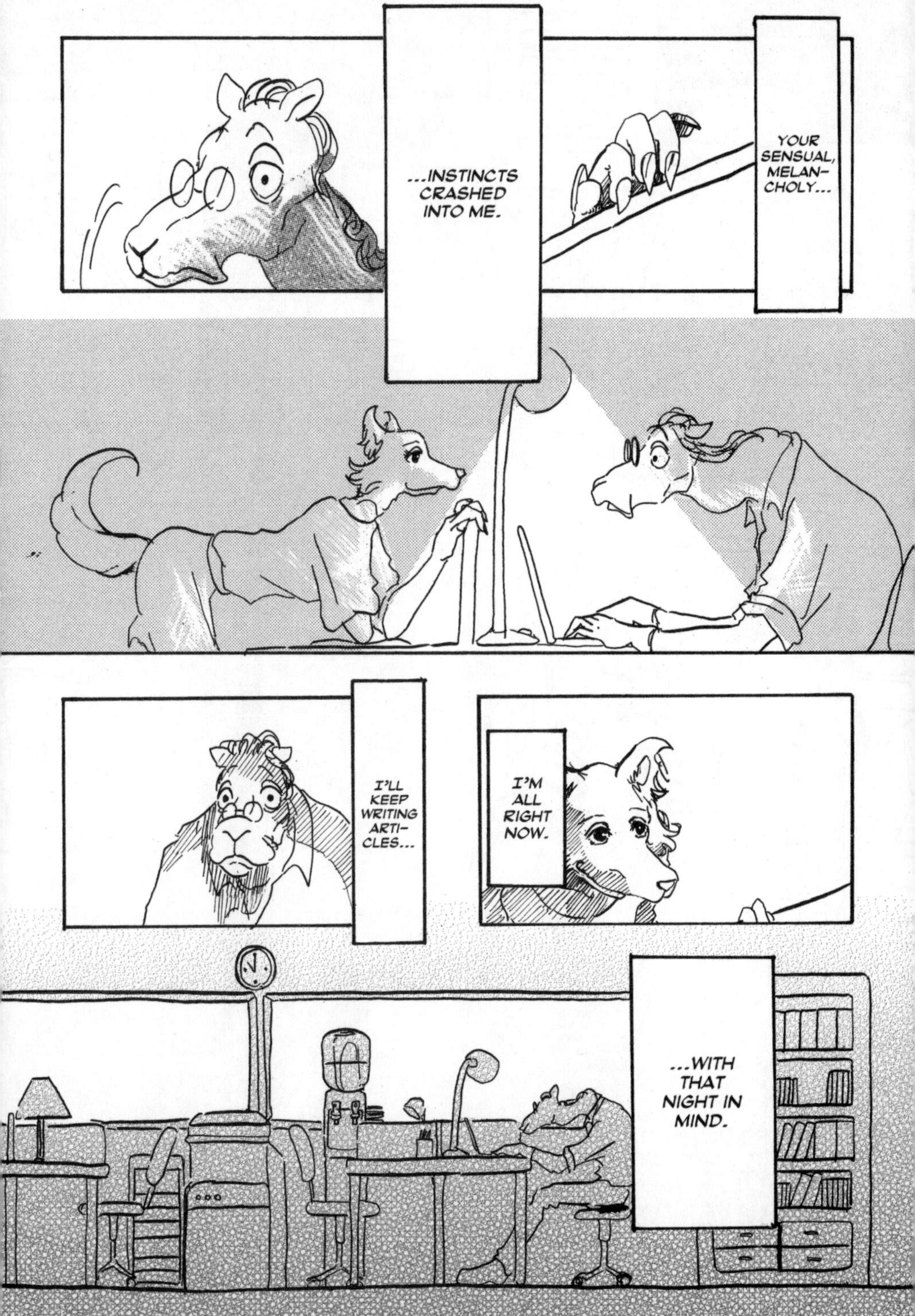
YOUR SENSUAL, MELANCHOLY...
...INSTINCTS CRASHED INTO ME.
I'M ALL RIGHT NOW.
I'LL KEEP WRITING ARTICLES...
...WITH THAT NIGHT IN MIND.

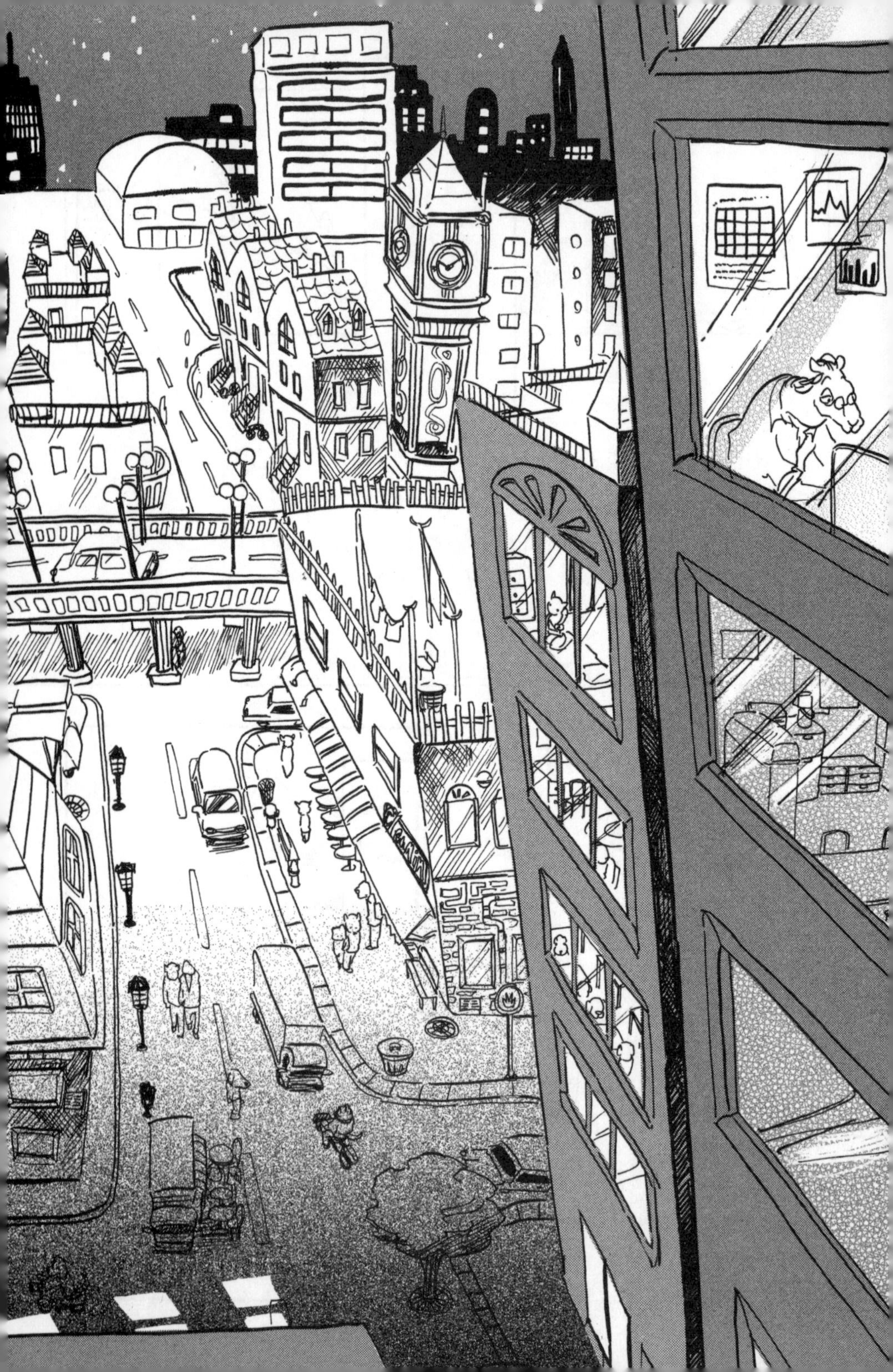

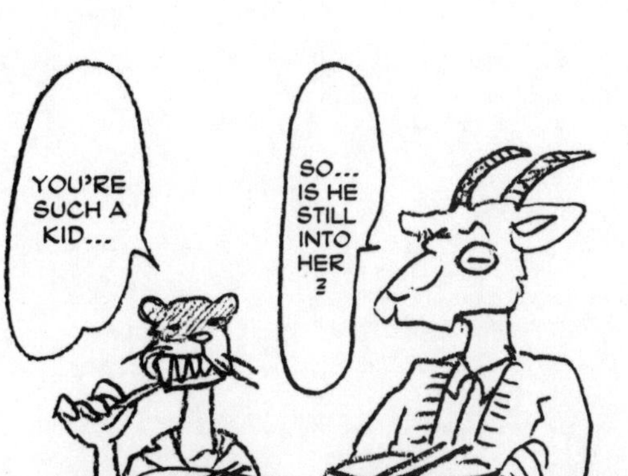
SO... IS HE STILL INTO HER?
YOU'RE SUCH A KID...

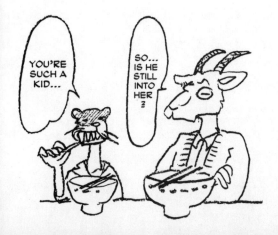

Story 4
The Kangaroo and the Black Panther

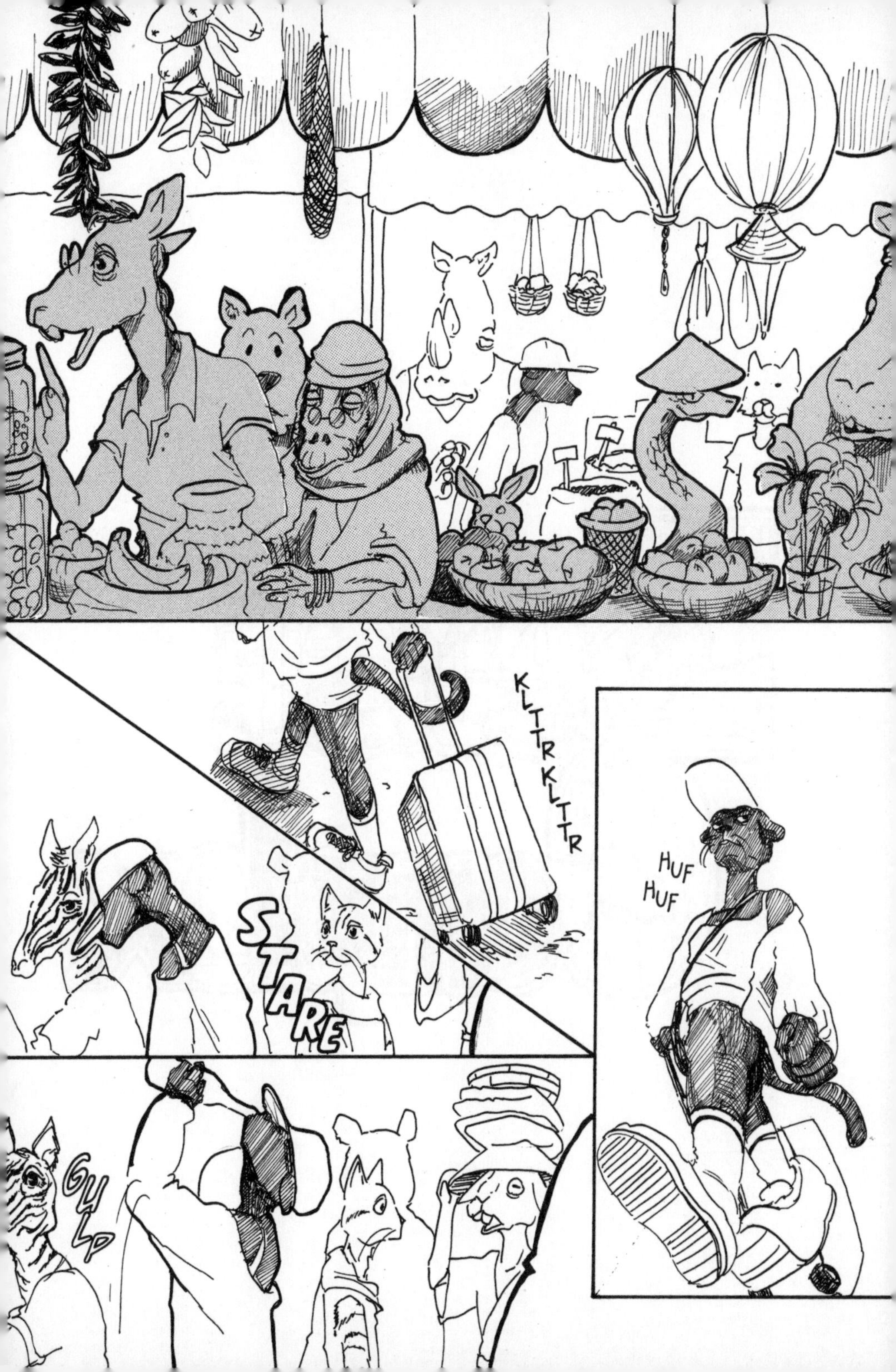
HUF HUF
KLTTR KLTTR
STARE
GULP

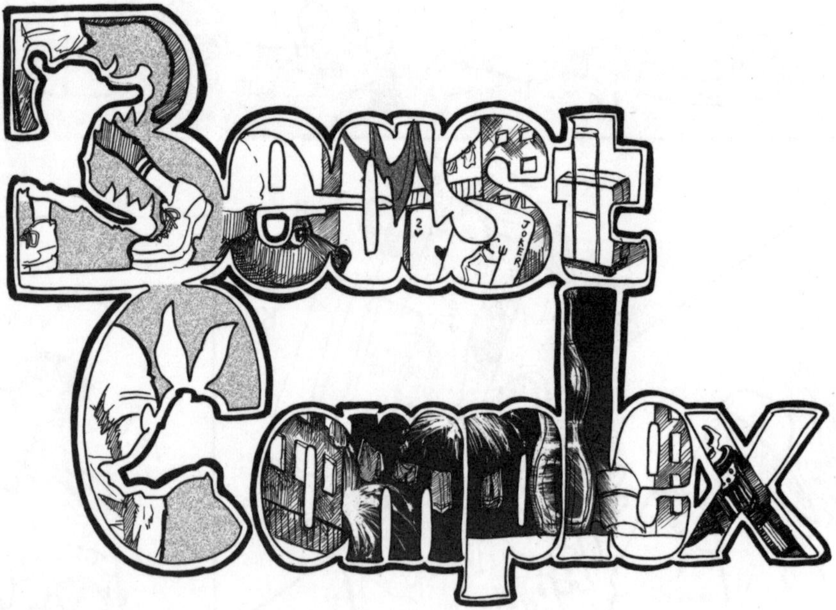
Beast Complex
JOKER

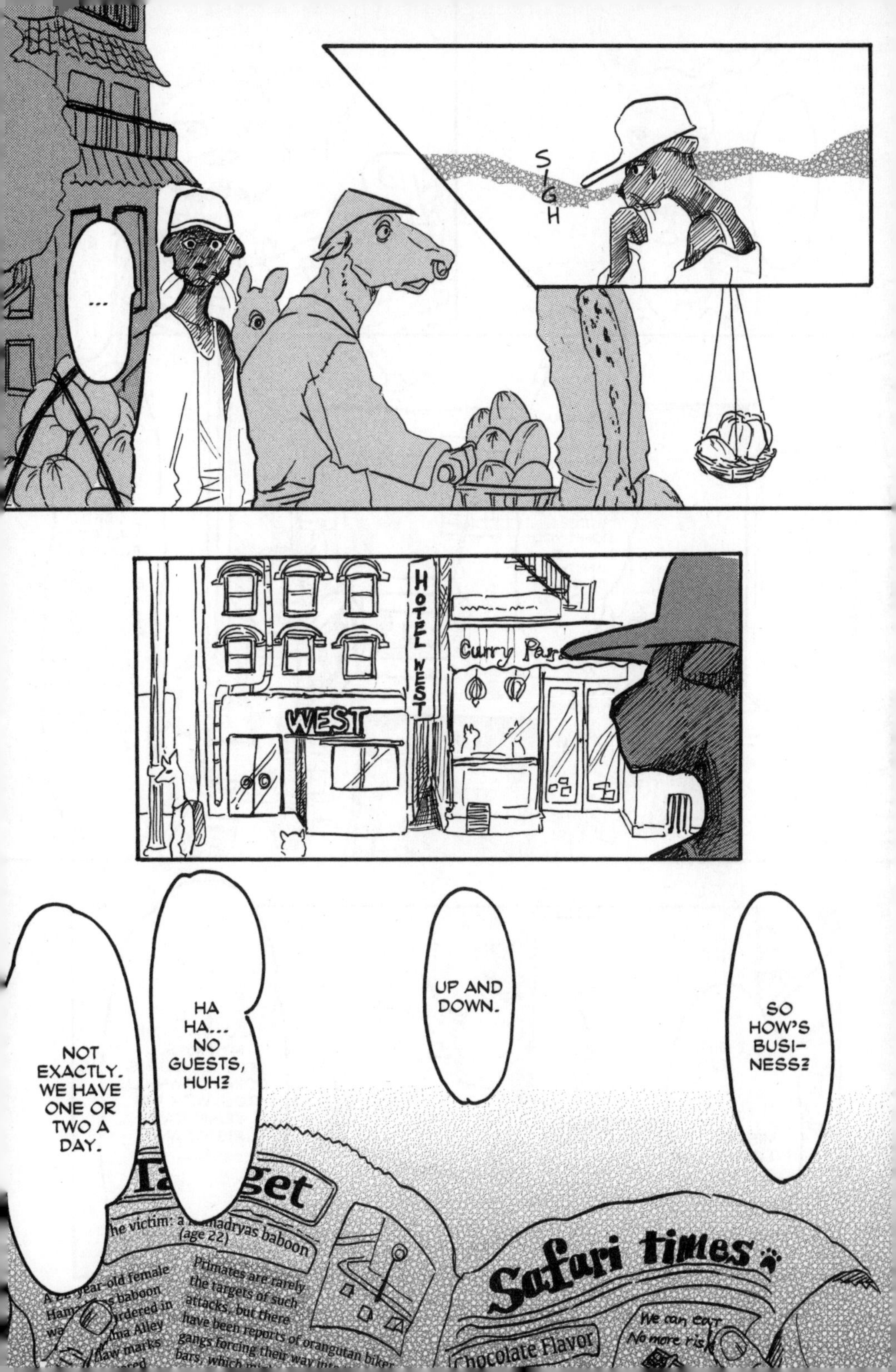
SIGH
...
HOTEL WEST
WEST
SO HOW'S BUSI- NESS?
UP AND DOWN.
HA HA... NO GUESTS, HUH?
NOT EXACTLY. WE HAVE ONE OR TWO A DAY.
Safari times
Chocolate Flavor
(age 22)
Primates are rarely the targets of such attacks, but there have been reports of orangutan biker gangs forcing their way into

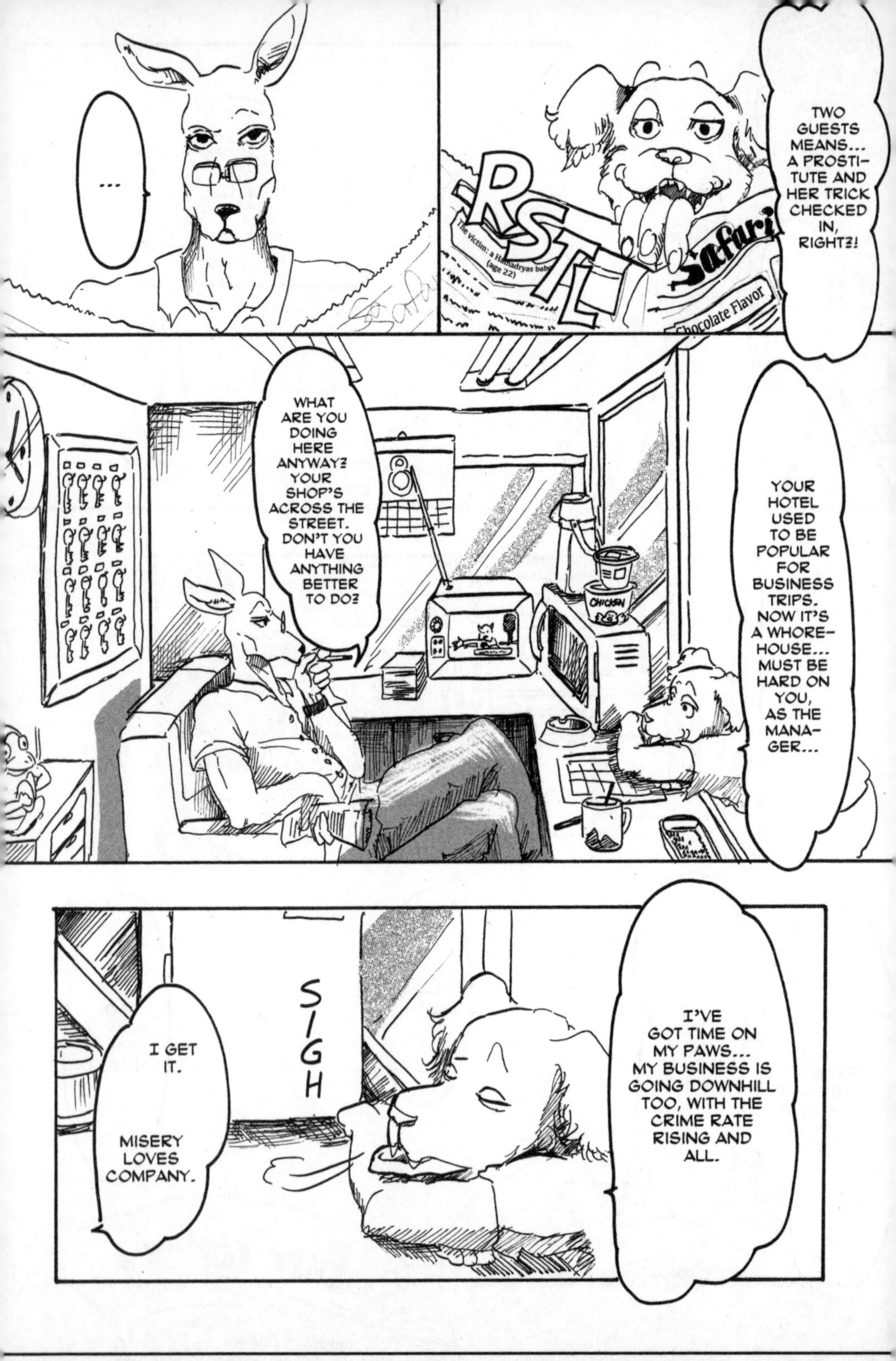
TWO GUESTS MEANS... A PROSTITUTE AND HER TRICK CHECKED IN, RIGHT?!
RSTL
The victim: a Hamadryas babo
(age 22)
Safari
Chocolate Flavor
...
YOUR HOTEL USED TO BE POPULAR FOR BUSINESS TRIPS. NOW IT'S A WHORE-HOUSE... MUST BE HARD ON YOU, AS THE MANA-GER...
WHAT ARE YOU DOING HERE ANYWAY? YOUR SHOP'S ACROSS THE STREET. DON'T YOU HAVE ANYTHING BETTER TO DO?
CHICKEN
I'VE GOT TIME ON MY PAWS... MY BUSINESS IS GOING DOWNHILL TOO, WITH THE CRIME RATE RISING AND ALL.
SIGH
I GET IT.
MISERY LOVES COMPANY.

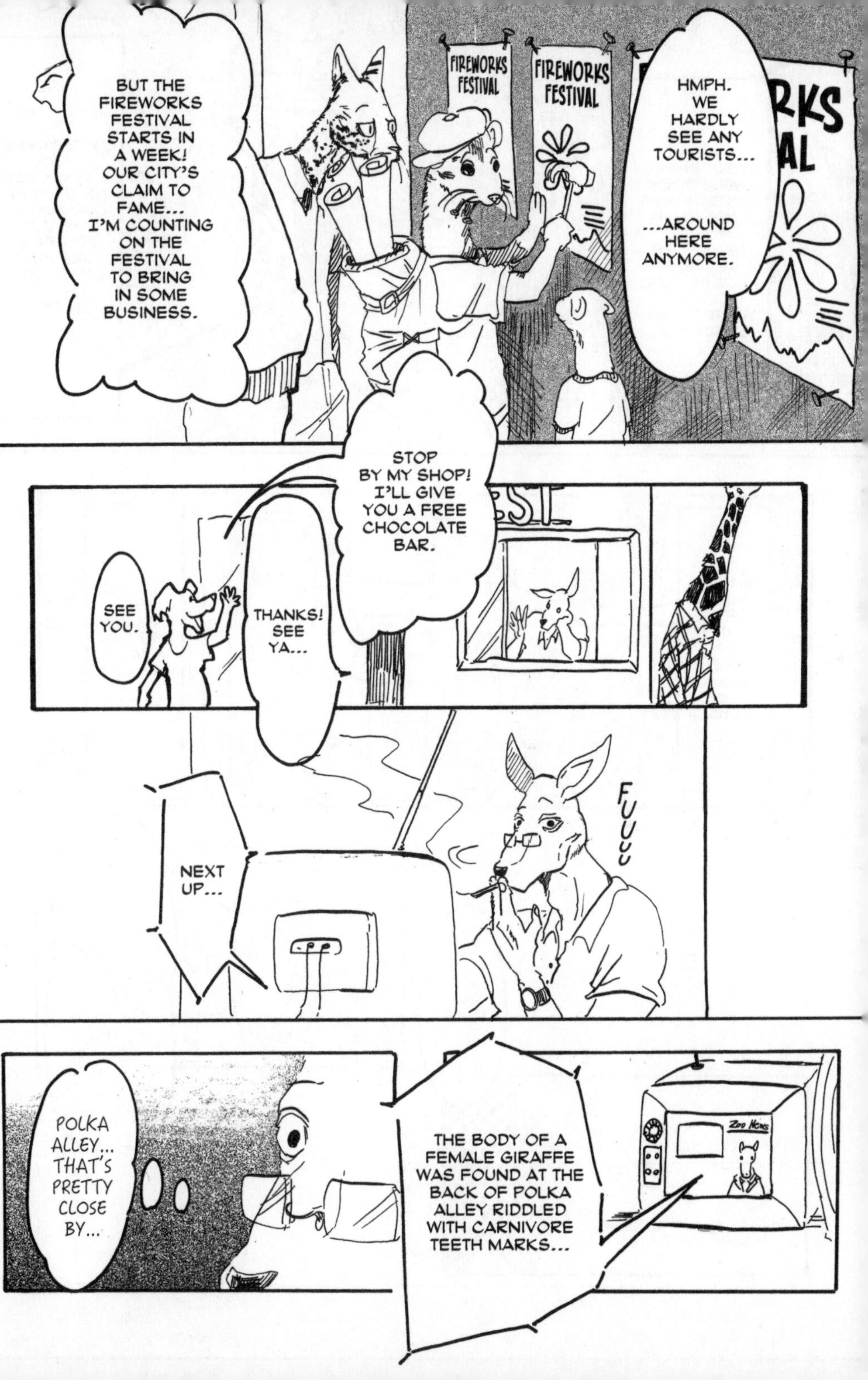
FIREWORKS FESTIVAL
FIREWORKS FESTIVAL
HMPH. WE HARDLY SEE ANY TOURISTS...
...AROUND HERE ANYMORE.
BUT THE FIREWORKS FESTIVAL STARTS IN A WEEK! OUR CITY'S CLAIM TO FAME... I'M COUNTING ON THE FESTIVAL TO BRING IN SOME BUSINESS.
STOP BY MY SHOP! I'LL GIVE YOU A FREE CHOCOLATE BAR.
THANKS! SEE YA...
SEE YOU.
FUUU
NEXT UP...
THE BODY OF A FEMALE GIRAFFE WAS FOUND AT THE BACK OF POLKA ALLEY RIDDLED WITH CARNIVORE TEETH MARKS...
ZOO NEWS
POLKA ALLEY... THAT'S PRETTY CLOSE BY...

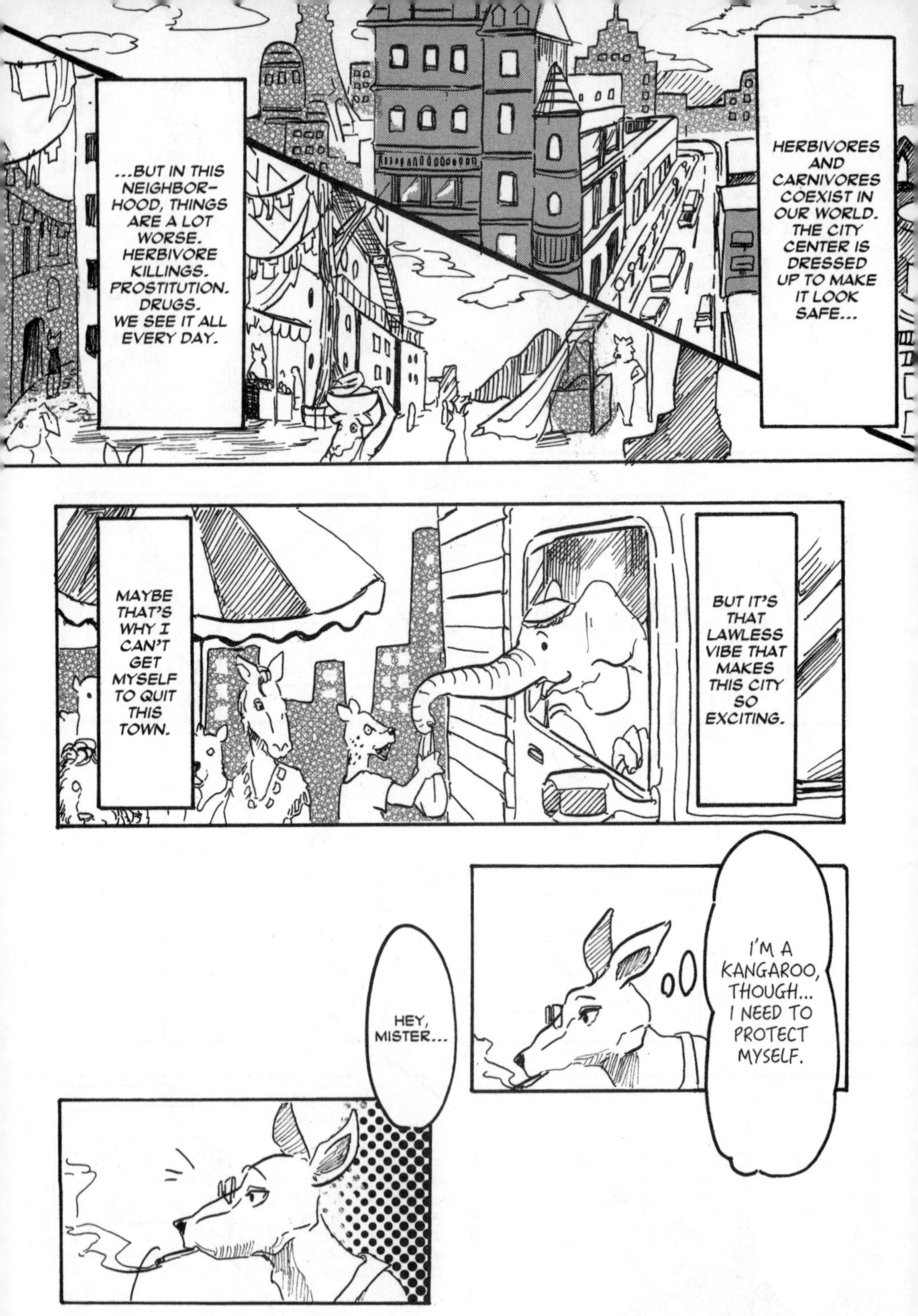
HERBIVORES AND CARNIVORES COEXIST IN OUR WORLD. THE CITY CENTER IS DRESSED UP TO MAKE IT LOOK SAFE...
...BUT IN THIS NEIGHBOR-HOOD, THINGS ARE A LOT WORSE. HERBIVORE KILLINGS. PROSTITUTION. DRUGS. WE SEE IT ALL EVERY DAY.
BUT IT'S THAT LAWLESS VIBE THAT MAKES THIS CITY SO EXCITING.
MAYBE THAT'S WHY I CAN'T GET MYSELF TO QUIT THIS TOWN.
I'M A KANGAROO, THOUGH... I NEED TO PROTECT MYSELF.
HEY, MISTER...

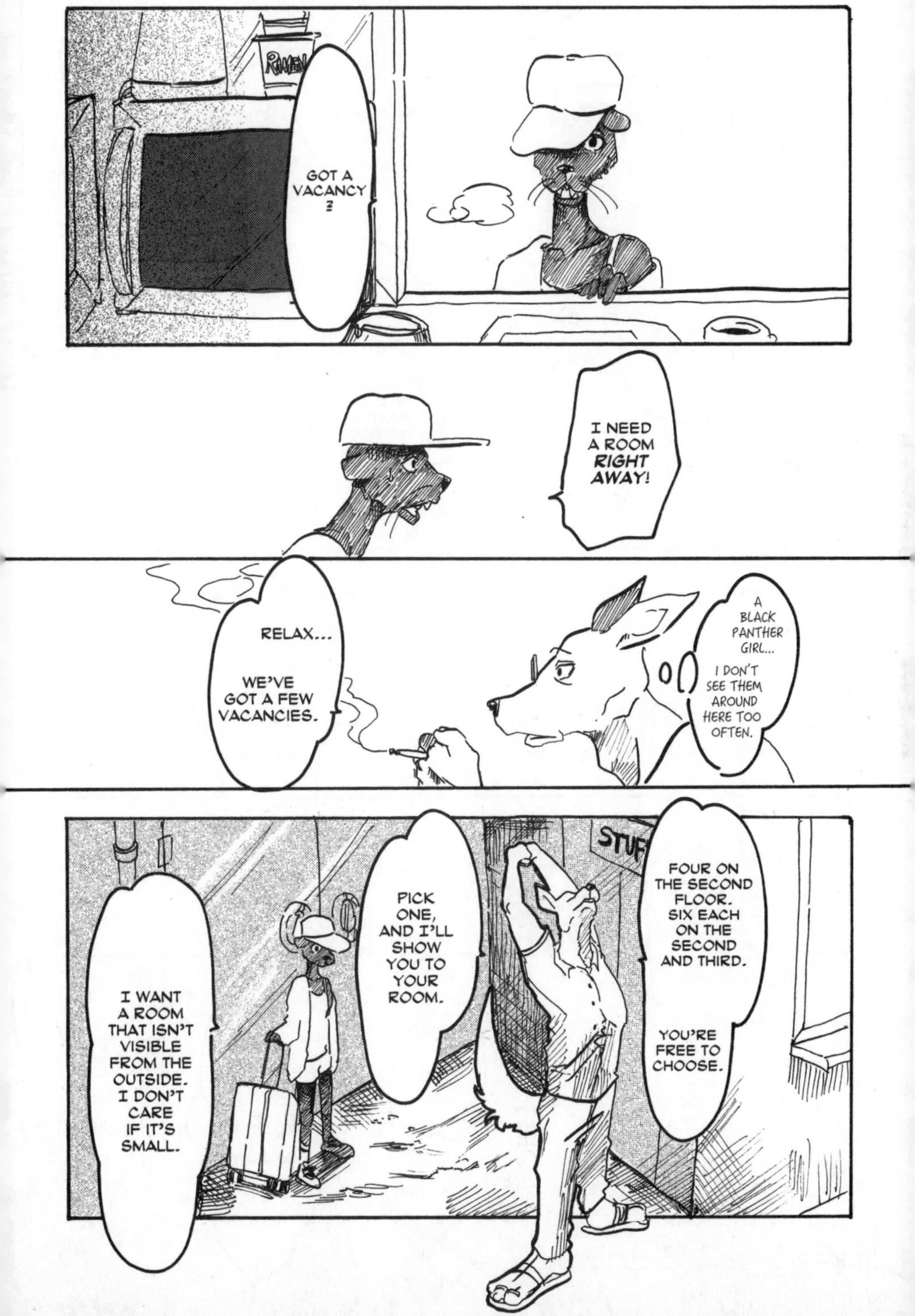
GOT A VACANCY?
I NEED A ROOM RIGHT AWAY!
A BLACK PANTHER GIRL...
I DON'T SEE THEM AROUND HERE TOO OFTEN.
RELAX...
WE'VE GOT A FEW VACANCIES.
FOUR ON THE SECOND FLOOR. SIX EACH ON THE SECOND AND THIRD.
YOU'RE FREE TO CHOOSE.
PICK ONE, AND I'LL SHOW YOU TO YOUR ROOM.
I WANT A ROOM THAT ISN'T VISIBLE FROM THE OUTSIDE. I DON'T CARE IF IT'S SMALL.

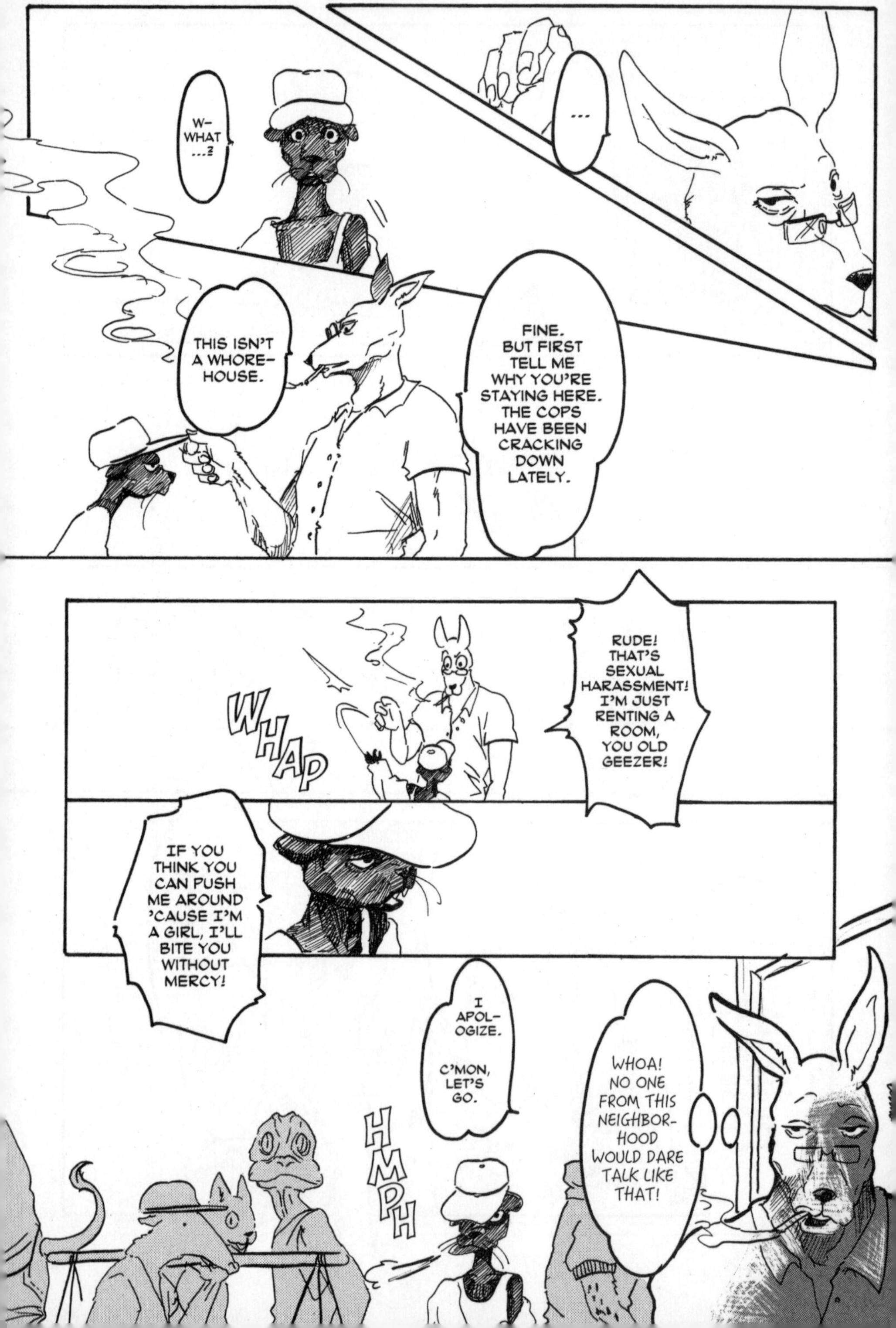
...
W-WHAT...?
FINE. BUT FIRST TELL ME WHY YOU'RE STAYING HERE. THE COPS HAVE BEEN CRACKING DOWN LATELY.
THIS ISN'T A WHORE-HOUSE.
RUDE! THAT'S SEXUAL HARASSMENT! I'M JUST RENTING A ROOM, YOU OLD GEEZER!
WHAP
IF YOU THINK YOU CAN PUSH ME AROUND 'CAUSE I'M A GIRL, I'LL BITE YOU WITHOUT MERCY!
I APOLOGIZE.
C'MON, LET'S GO.
WHOA! NO ONE FROM THIS NEIGHBOR-HOOD WOULD DARE TALK LIKE THAT!
HMPH

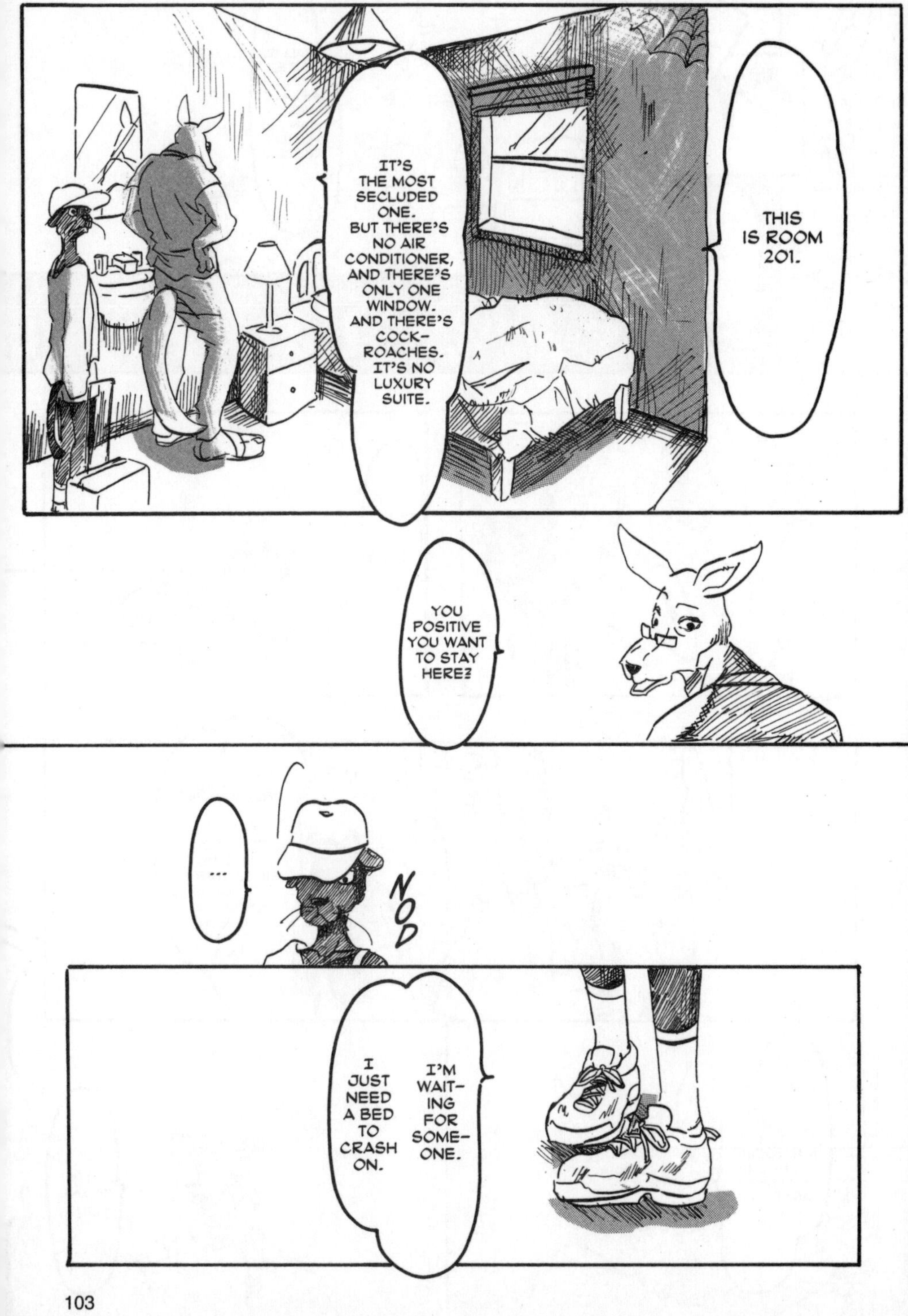
THIS IS ROOM 201.
IT'S THE MOST SECLUDED ONE. BUT THERE'S NO AIR CONDITIONER, AND THERE'S ONLY ONE WINDOW. AND THERE'S COCK-ROACHES. IT'S NO LUXURY SUITE.
YOU POSITIVE YOU WANT TO STAY HERE?
...
NOD
I'M WAIT-ING FOR SOME-ONE.
I JUST NEED A BED TO CRASH ON.

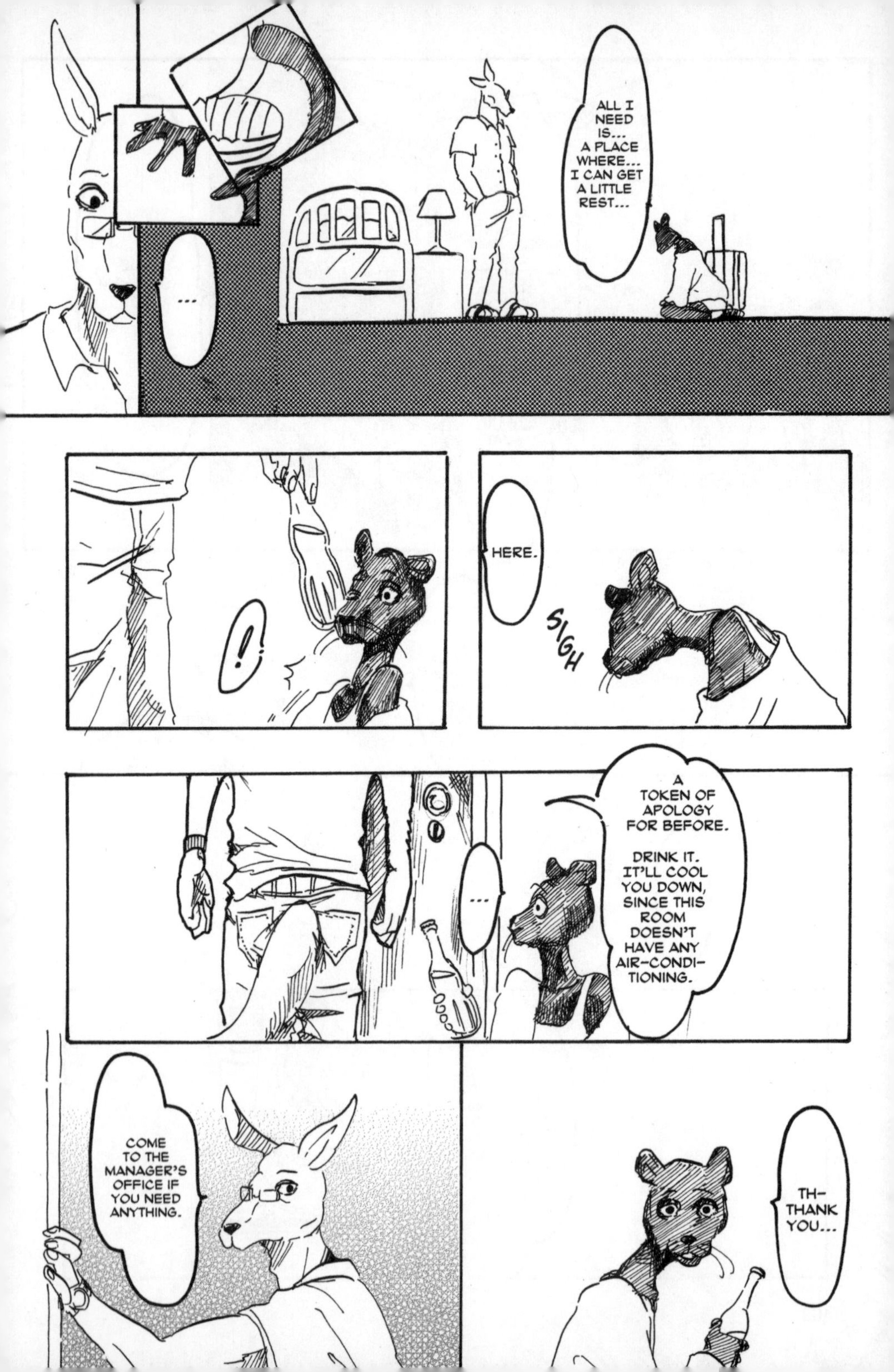
ALL I NEED IS... A PLACE WHERE... I CAN GET A LITTLE REST...
...
HERE.
SIGH
!
A TOKEN OF APOLOGY FOR BEFORE.
DRINK IT. IT'LL COOL YOU DOWN, SINCE THIS ROOM DOESN'T HAVE ANY AIR-CONDITIONING.
...
TH- THANK YOU...
COME TO THE MANAGER'S OFFICE IF YOU NEED ANYTHING.

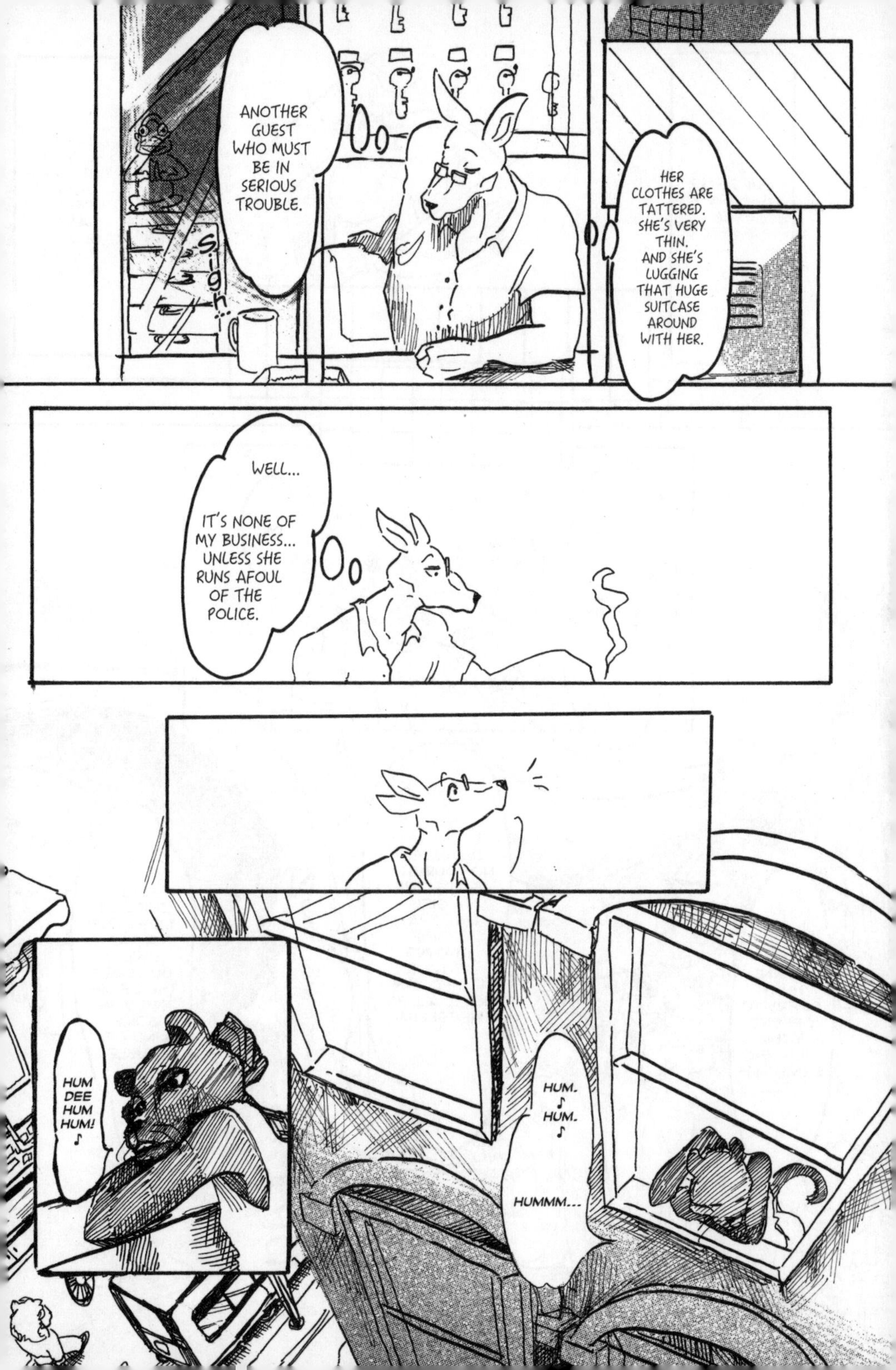
HER CLOTHES ARE TATTERED. SHE'S VERY THIN. AND SHE'S LUGGING THAT HUGE SUITCASE AROUND WITH HER.
ANOTHER GUEST WHO MUST BE IN SERIOUS TROUBLE.
Sigh...
WELL...
IT'S NONE OF MY BUSINESS... UNLESS SHE RUNS AFOUL OF THE POLICE.
HUM. ♪ HUM. ♪
HUMMM...
HUM DEE HUM HUM! ♪

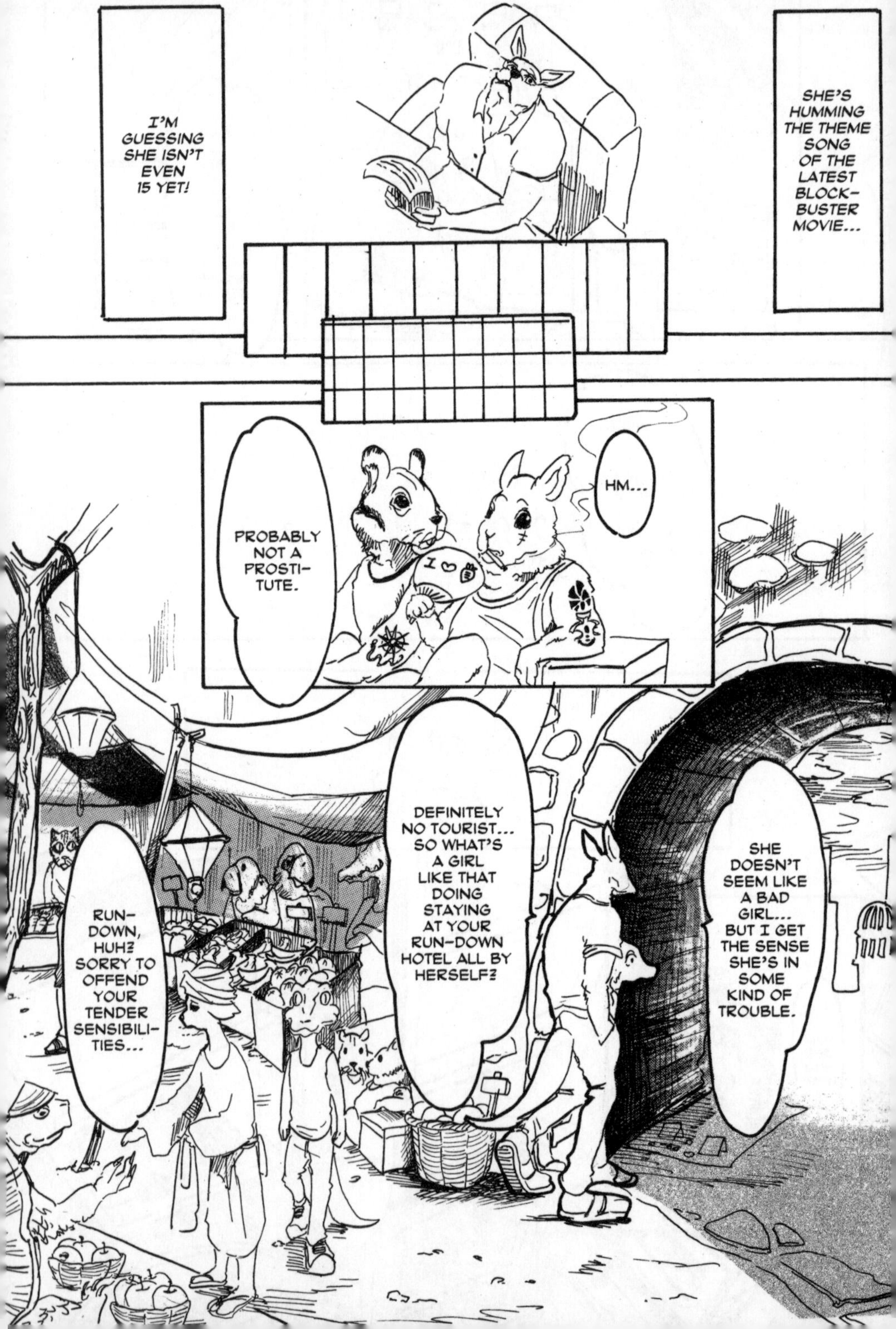
SHE'S HUMMING THE THEME SONG OF THE LATEST BLOCK-BUSTER MOVIE...
I'M GUESSING SHE ISN'T EVEN 15 YET!
HM...
PROBABLY NOT A PROSTI-TUTE.
SHE DOESN'T SEEM LIKE A BAD GIRL... BUT I GET THE SENSE SHE'S IN SOME KIND OF TROUBLE.
DEFINITELY NO TOURIST... SO WHAT'S A GIRL LIKE THAT DOING STAYING AT YOUR RUN-DOWN HOTEL ALL BY HERSELF?
RUN-DOWN, HUH? SORRY TO OFFEND YOUR TENDER SENSIBILI-TIES...

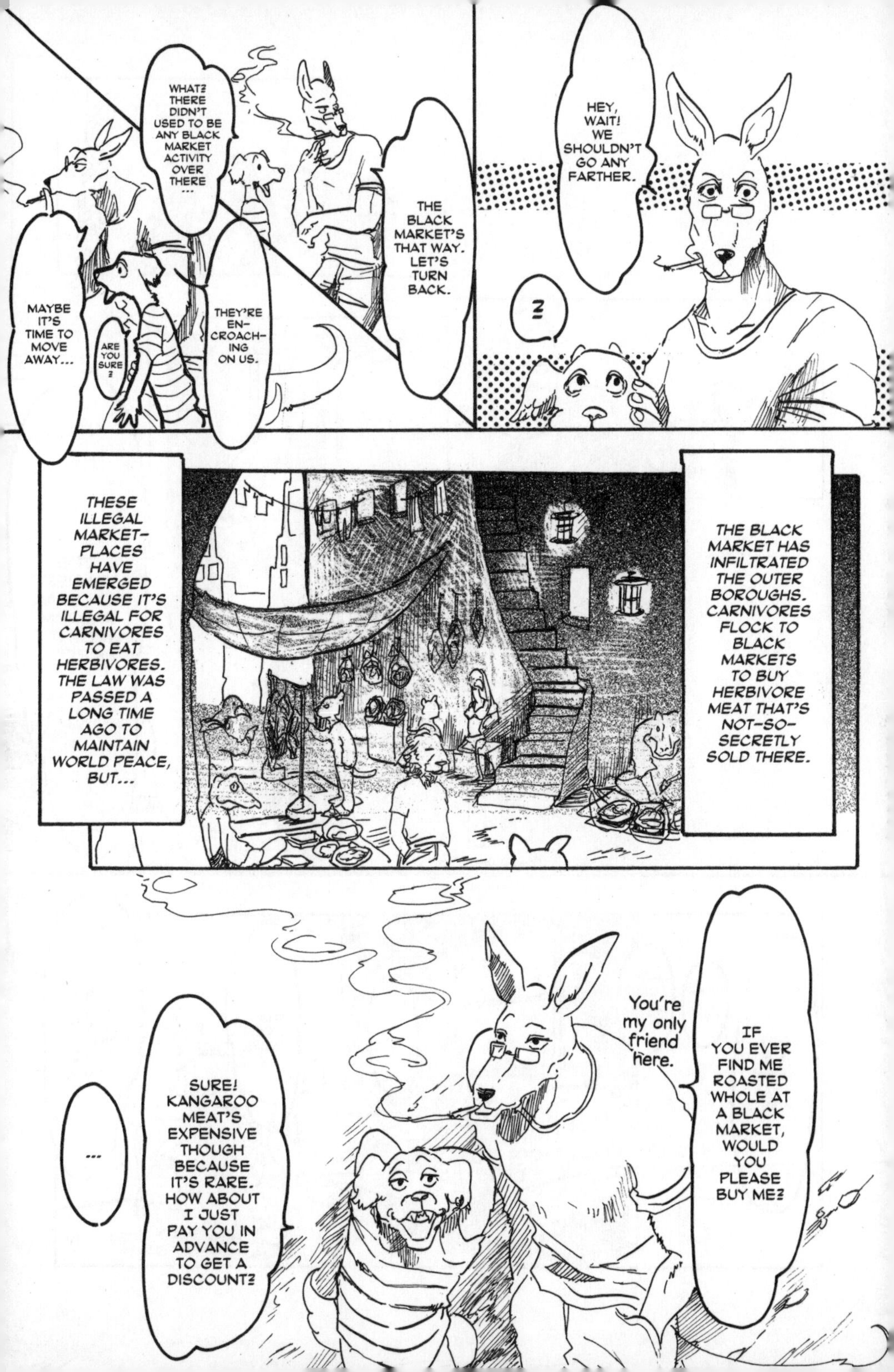
HEY, WAIT! WE SHOULDN'T GO ANY FARTHER.
?
THE BLACK MARKET'S THAT WAY. LET'S TURN BACK.
WHAT? THERE DIDN'T USED TO BE ANY BLACK MARKET ACTIVITY OVER THERE ...
THEY'RE EN-CROACHING ON US.
ARE YOU SURE?
MAYBE IT'S TIME TO MOVE AWAY...
THE BLACK MARKET HAS INFILTRATED THE OUTER BOROUGHS. CARNIVORES FLOCK TO BLACK MARKETS TO BUY HERBIVORE MEAT THAT'S NOT-SO-SECRETLY SOLD THERE.
THESE ILLEGAL MARKET-PLACES HAVE EMERGED BECAUSE IT'S ILLEGAL FOR CARNIVORES TO EAT HERBIVORES. THE LAW WAS PASSED A LONG TIME AGO TO MAINTAIN WORLD PEACE, BUT...
IF YOU EVER FIND ME ROASTED WHOLE AT A BLACK MARKET, WOULD YOU PLEASE BUY ME?
You're my only friend here.
SURE! KANGAROO MEAT'S EXPENSIVE THOUGH BECAUSE IT'S RARE. HOW ABOUT I JUST PAY YOU IN ADVANCE TO GET A DISCOUNT?
...

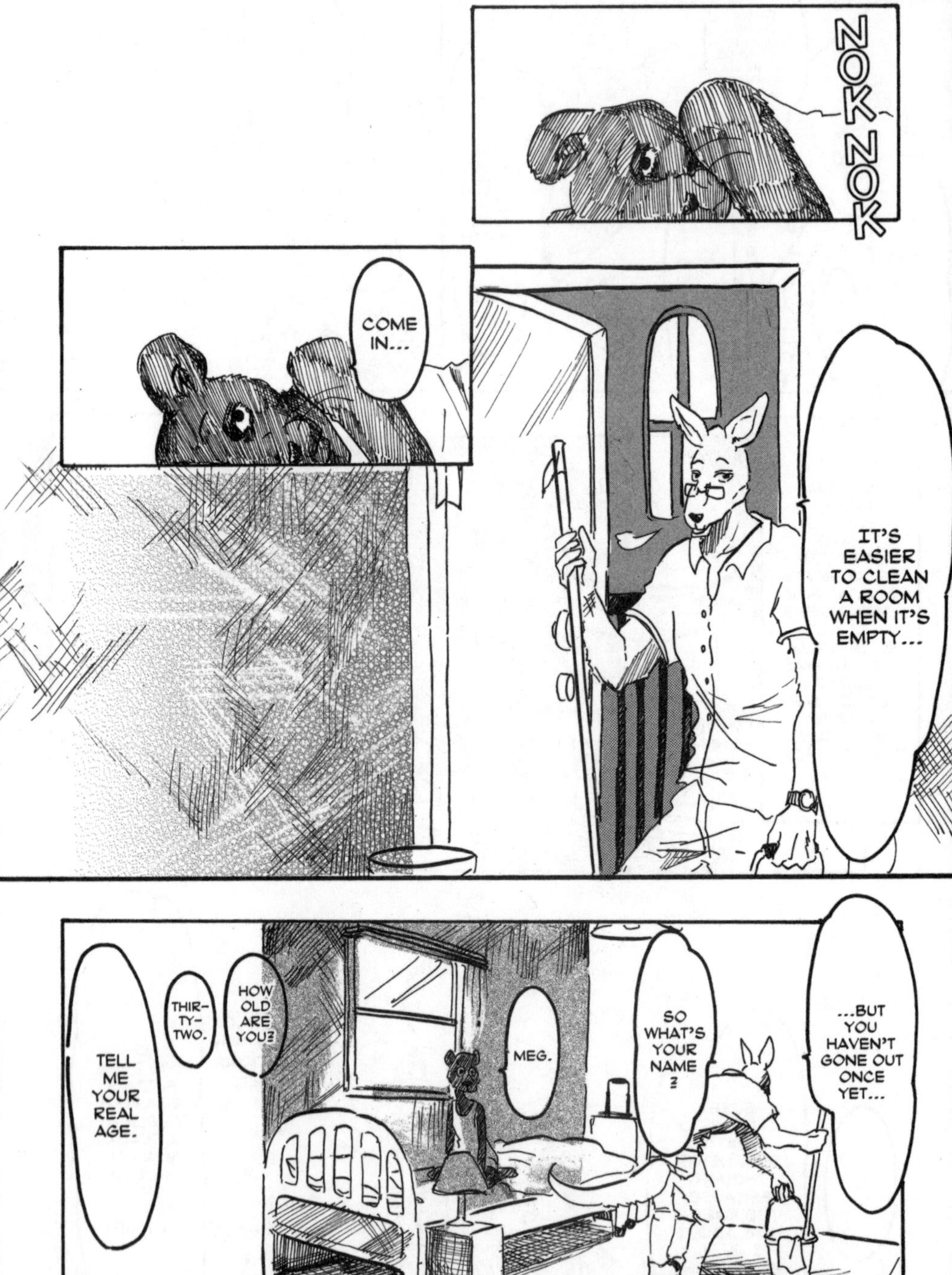
NOK NOK
COME IN...
IT'S EASIER TO CLEAN A ROOM WHEN IT'S EMPTY...
...BUT YOU HAVEN'T GONE OUT ONCE YET...
SO WHAT'S YOUR NAME?
MEG.
HOW OLD ARE YOU?
THIRTY-TWO.
TELL ME YOUR REAL AGE.

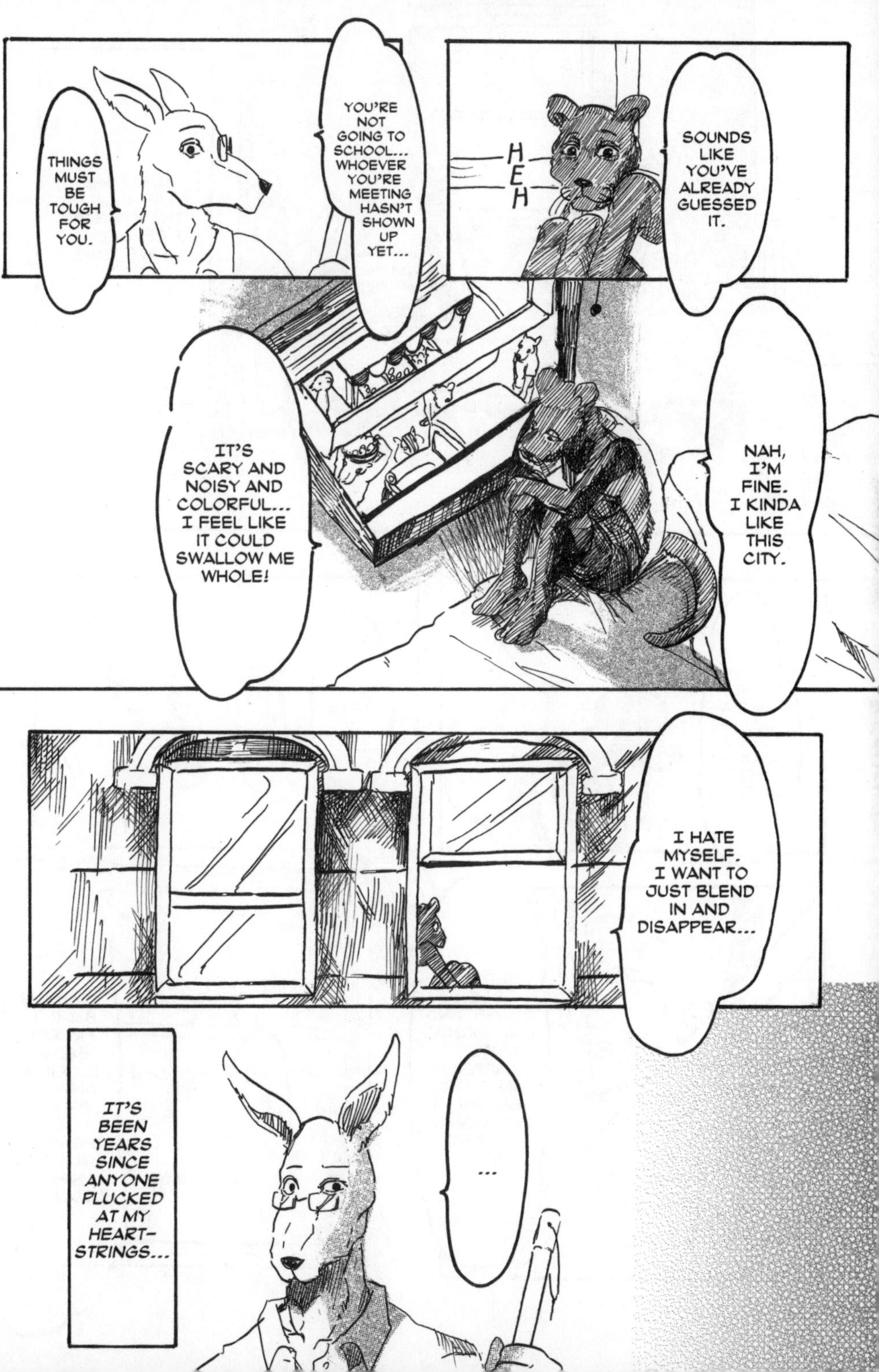
YOU'RE NOT GOING TO SCHOOL... WHOEVER YOU'RE MEETING HASN'T SHOWN UP YET...
HEH HEH
SOUNDS LIKE YOU'VE ALREADY GUESSED IT.
THINGS MUST BE TOUGH FOR YOU.
NAH, I'M FINE. I KINDA LIKE THIS CITY.
IT'S SCARY AND NOISY AND COLORFUL... I FEEL LIKE IT COULD SWALLOW ME WHOLE!
I HATE MYSELF. I WANT TO JUST BLEND IN AND DISAPPEAR...
...
IT'S BEEN YEARS SINCE ANYONE PLUCKED AT MY HEART-STRINGS...

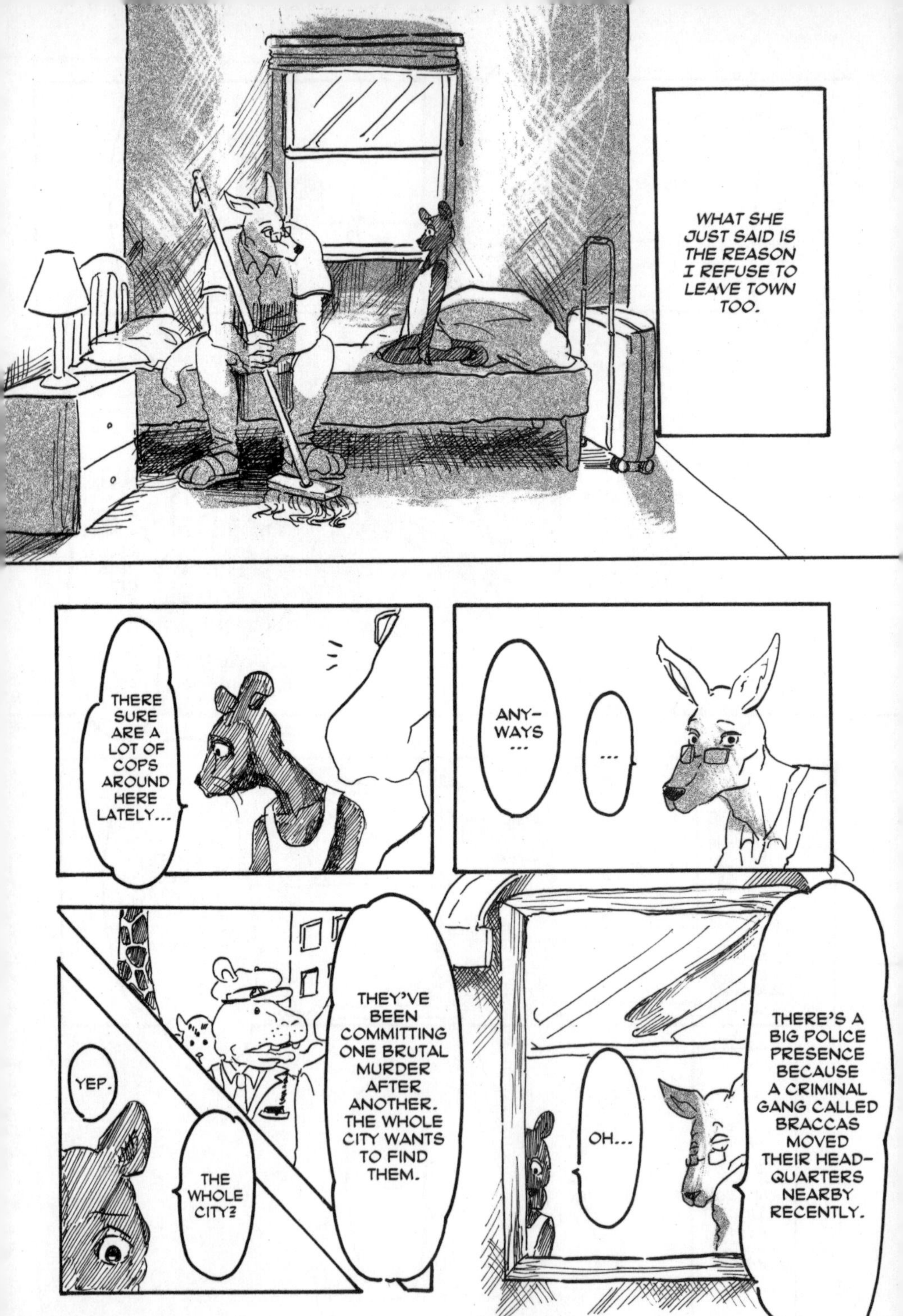
WHAT SHE JUST SAID IS THE REASON I REFUSE TO LEAVE TOWN TOO.
...
ANY-WAYS...
THERE SURE ARE A LOT OF COPS AROUND HERE LATELY...
THERE'S A BIG POLICE PRESENCE BECAUSE A CRIMINAL GANG CALLED BRACCAS MOVED THEIR HEAD-QUARTERS NEARBY RECENTLY.
OH...
THEY'VE BEEN COMMITTING ONE BRUTAL MURDER AFTER ANOTHER. THE WHOLE CITY WANTS TO FIND THEM.
THE WHOLE CITY?
YEP.

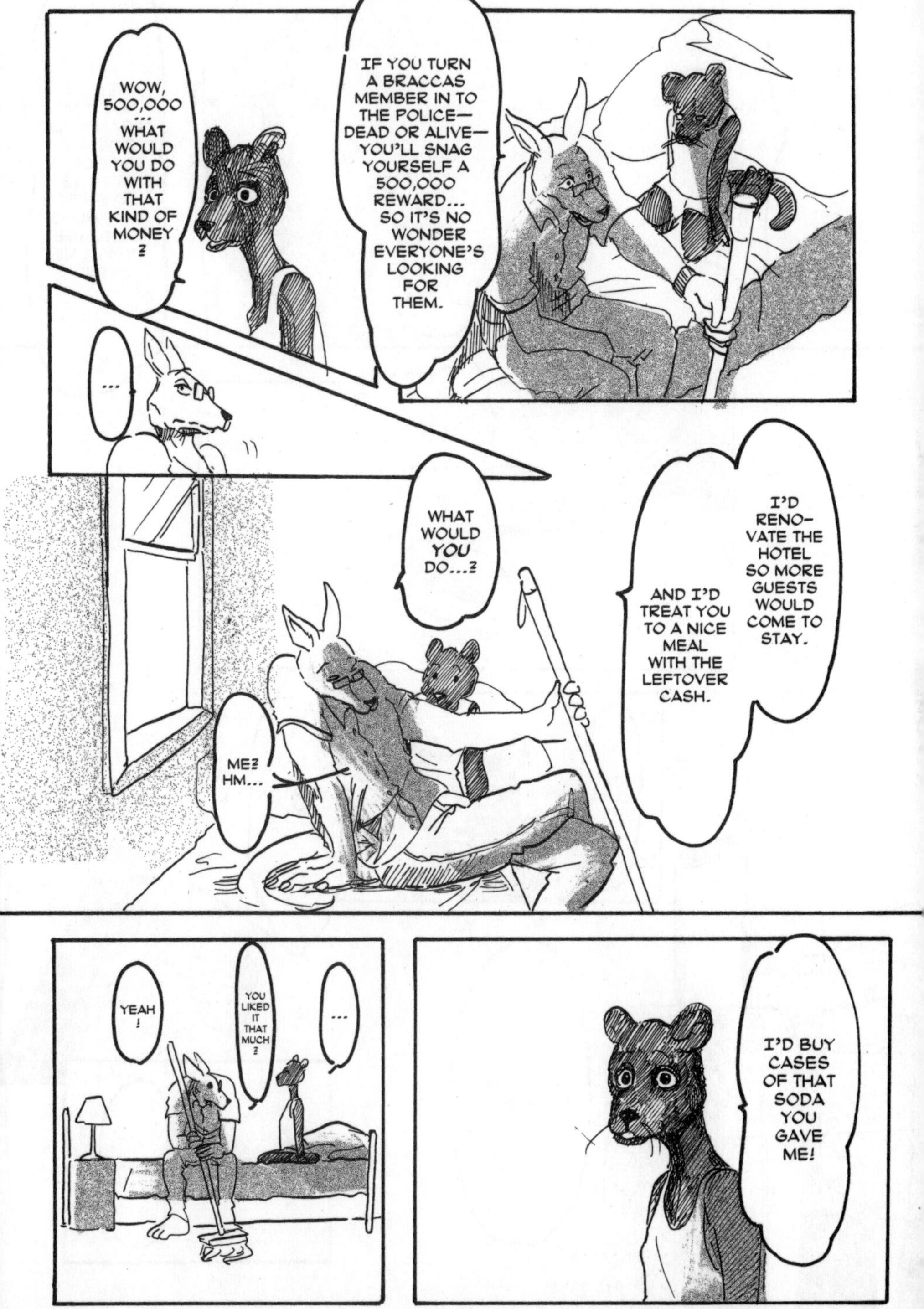
IF YOU TURN A BRACCAS MEMBER IN TO THE POLICE—DEAD OR ALIVE—YOU'LL SNAG YOURSELF A 500,000 REWARD... SO IT'S NO WONDER EVERYONE'S LOOKING FOR THEM.
WOW, 500,000... WHAT WOULD YOU DO WITH THAT KIND OF MONEY?
...
WHAT WOULD *YOU* DO...?
ME? HM...
I'D RENOVATE THE HOTEL SO MORE GUESTS WOULD COME TO STAY.
AND I'D TREAT YOU TO A NICE MEAL WITH THE LEFTOVER CASH.
I'D BUY CASES OF THAT SODA YOU GAVE ME!
...
YOU LIKED IT THAT MUCH?
YEAH!

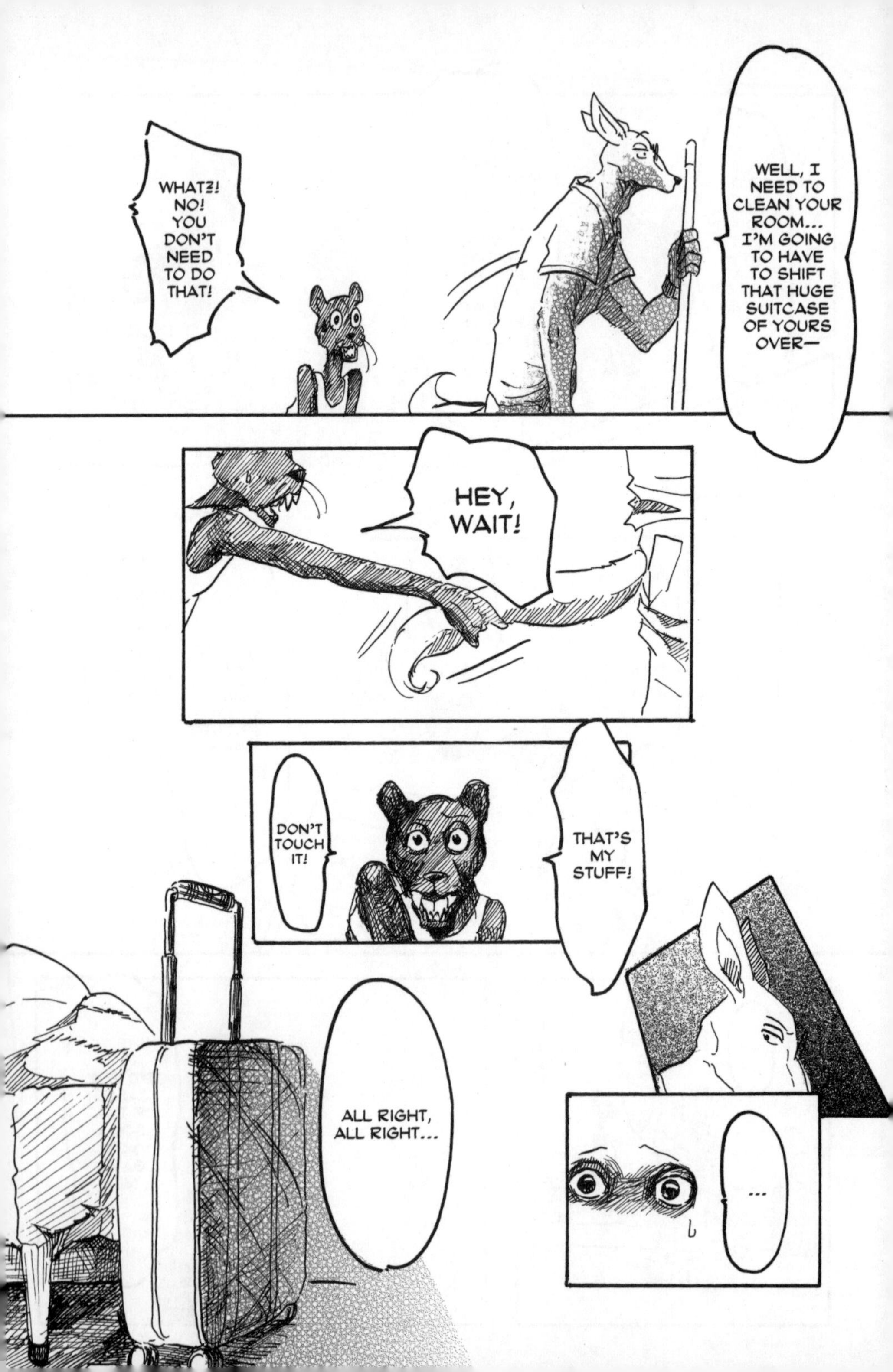
WELL, I NEED TO CLEAN YOUR ROOM... I'M GOING TO HAVE TO SHIFT THAT HUGE SUITCASE OF YOURS OVER—
WHAT?! NO! YOU DON'T NEED TO DO THAT!
HEY, WAIT!
THAT'S MY STUFF!
DON'T TOUCH IT!
ALL RIGHT, ALL RIGHT...
...

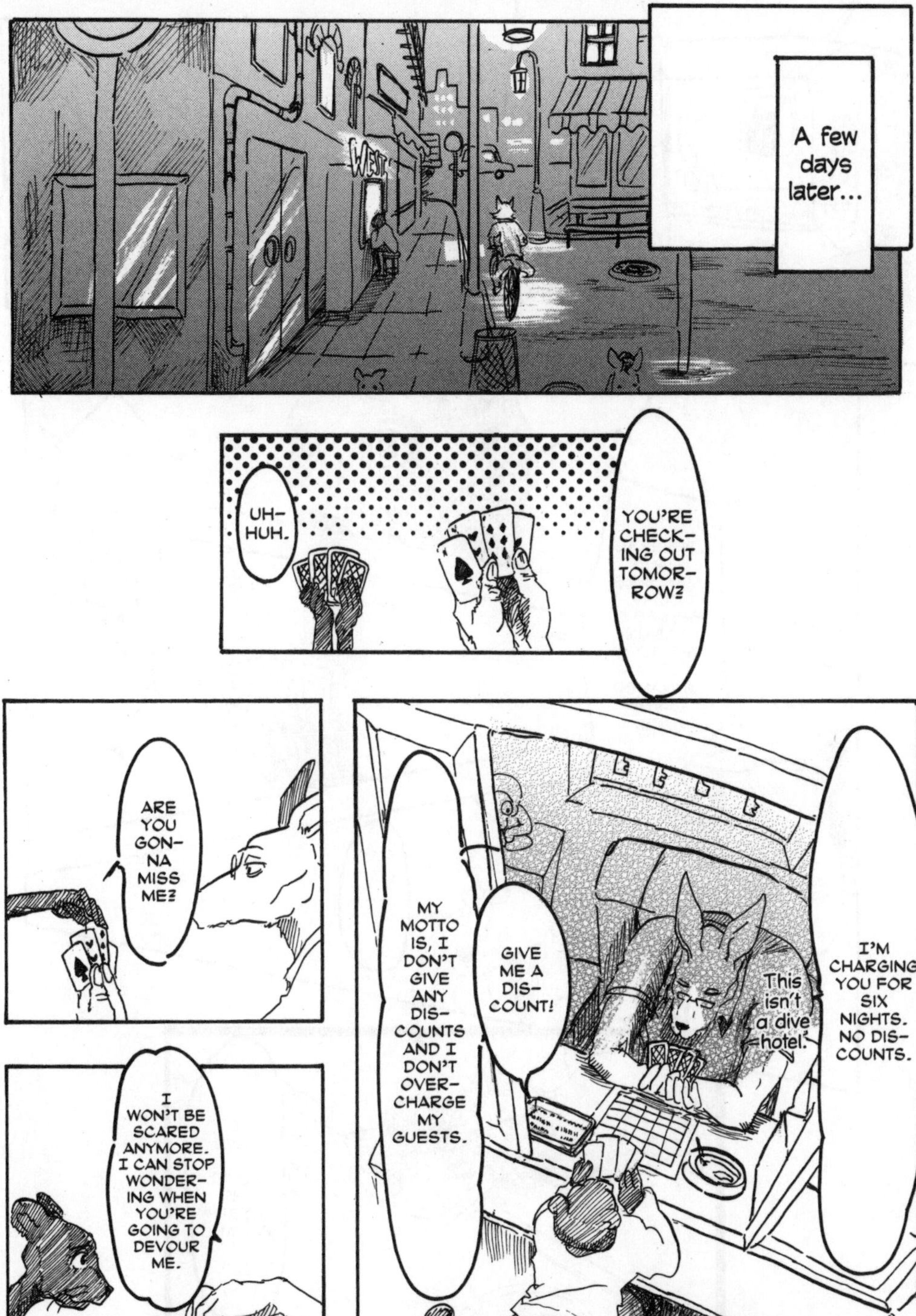
A few days later...
YOU'RE CHECKING-OUT TOMORROW?
UH-HUH.
I'M CHARGING YOU FOR SIX NIGHTS. NO DISCOUNTS.
This isn't a dive hotel.
GIVE ME A DISCOUNT!
MY MOTTO IS, I DON'T GIVE ANY DISCOUNTS AND I DON'T OVERCHARGE MY GUESTS.
ARE YOU GONNA MISS ME?
I WON'T BE SCARED ANYMORE. I CAN STOP WONDERING WHEN YOU'RE GOING TO DEVOUR ME.

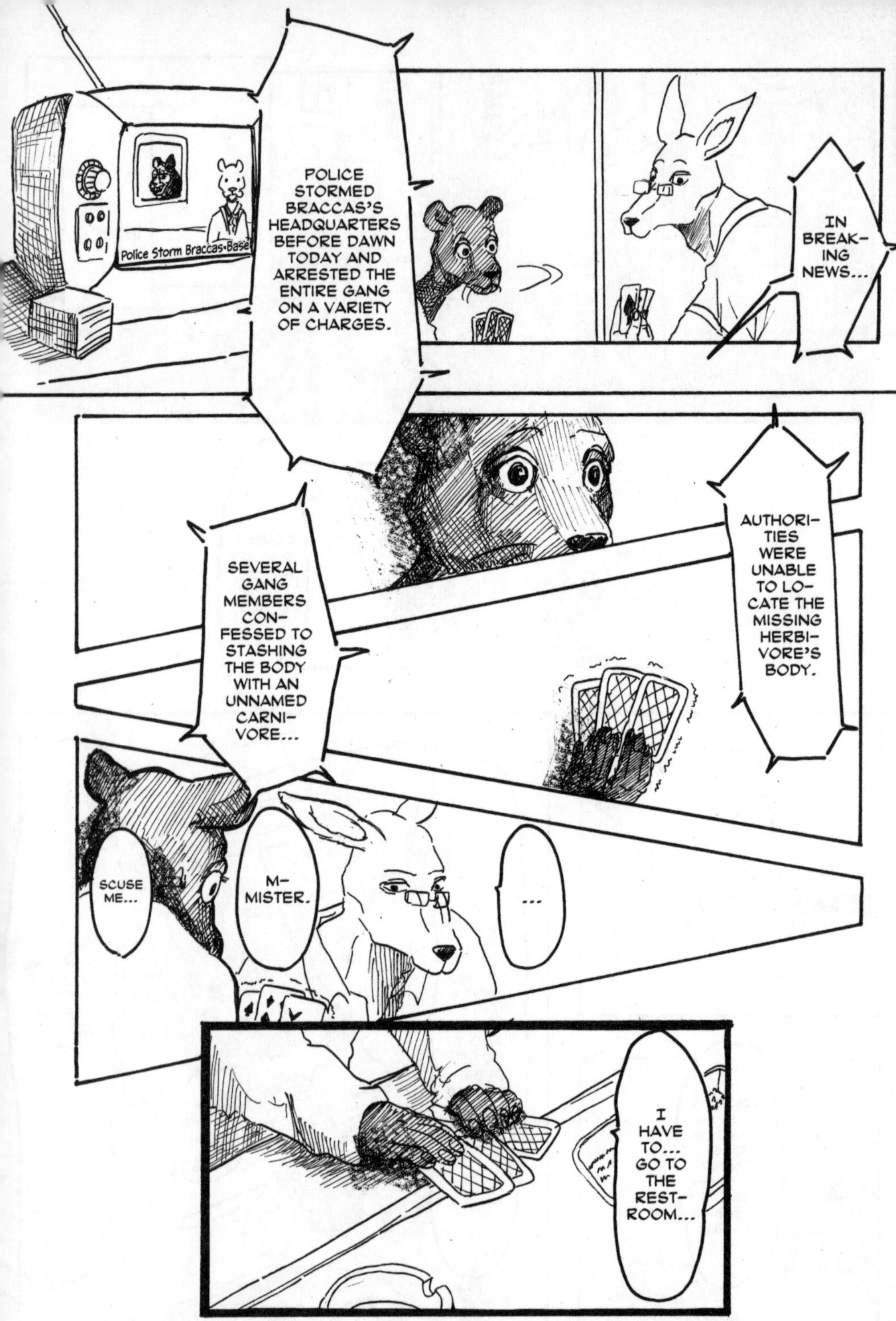
IN BREAKING NEWS...
POLICE STORMED BRACCAS'S HEADQUARTERS BEFORE DAWN TODAY AND ARRESTED THE ENTIRE GANG ON A VARIETY OF CHARGES.
Police Storm Braccas Base
AUTHORITIES WERE UNABLE TO LOCATE THE MISSING HERBIVORE'S BODY.
SEVERAL GANG MEMBERS CONFESSED TO STASHING THE BODY WITH AN UNNAMED CARNIVORE...
...
M-MISTER.
SCUSE ME...
I HAVE TO... GO TO THE RESTROOM...

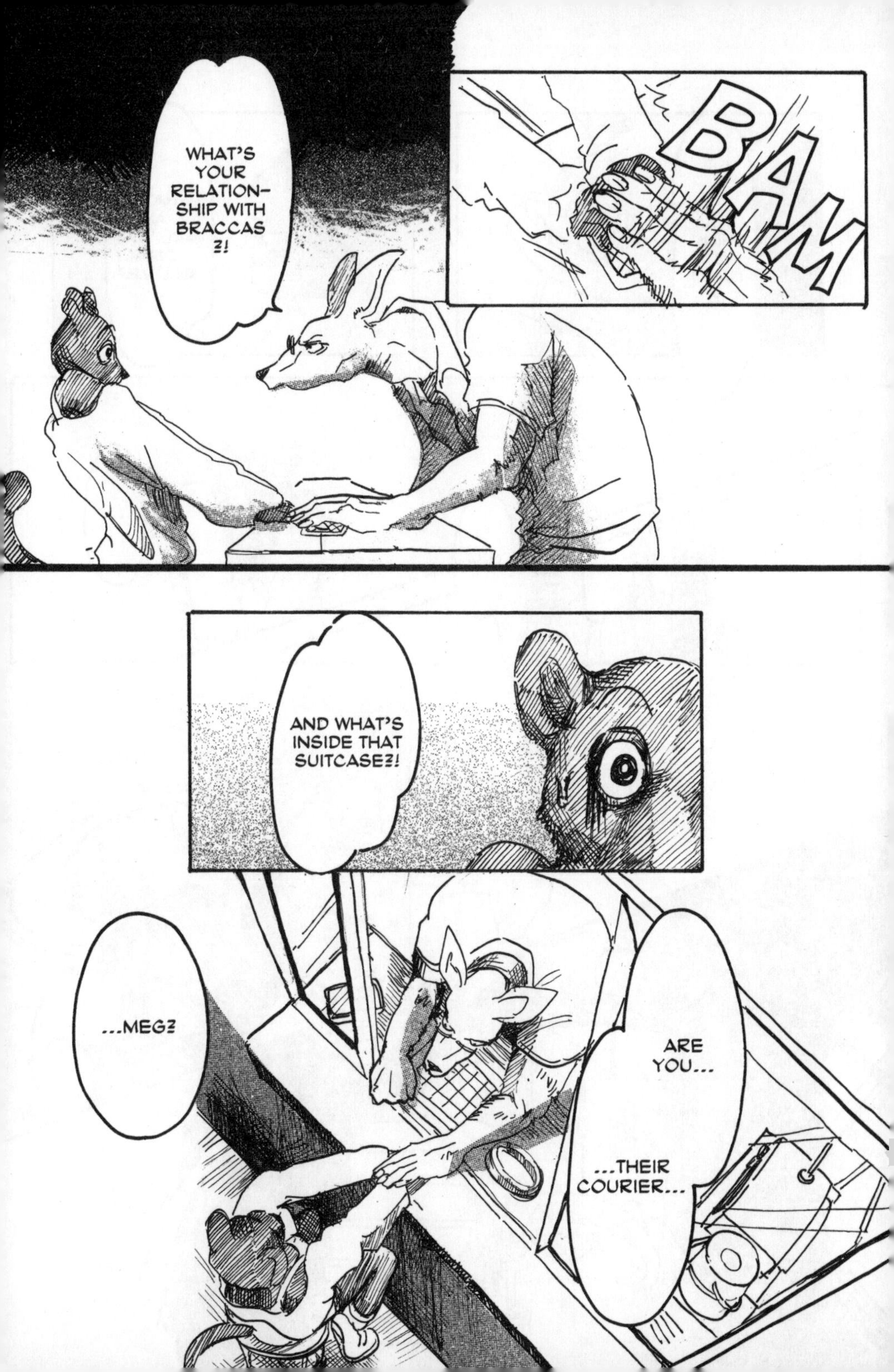

BAM
WHAT'S YOUR RELATION-SHIP WITH BRACCAS?!
AND WHAT'S INSIDE THAT SUITCASE?!
ARE YOU... ...THEIR COURIER...
...MEG?

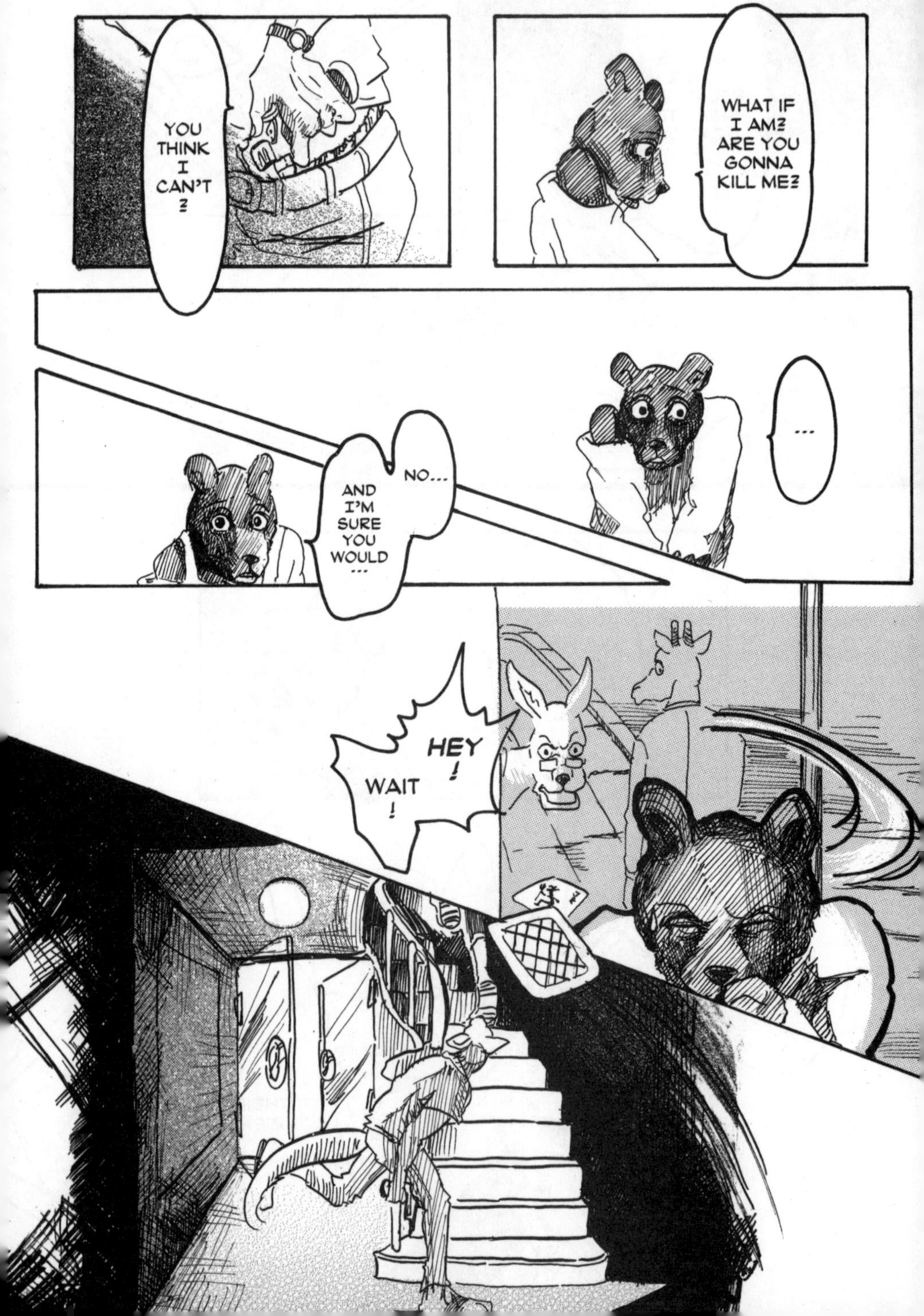

WHAT IF I AM? ARE YOU GONNA KILL ME?
YOU THINK I CAN'T?
...
NO... AND I'M SURE YOU WOULD...
HEY! WAIT!

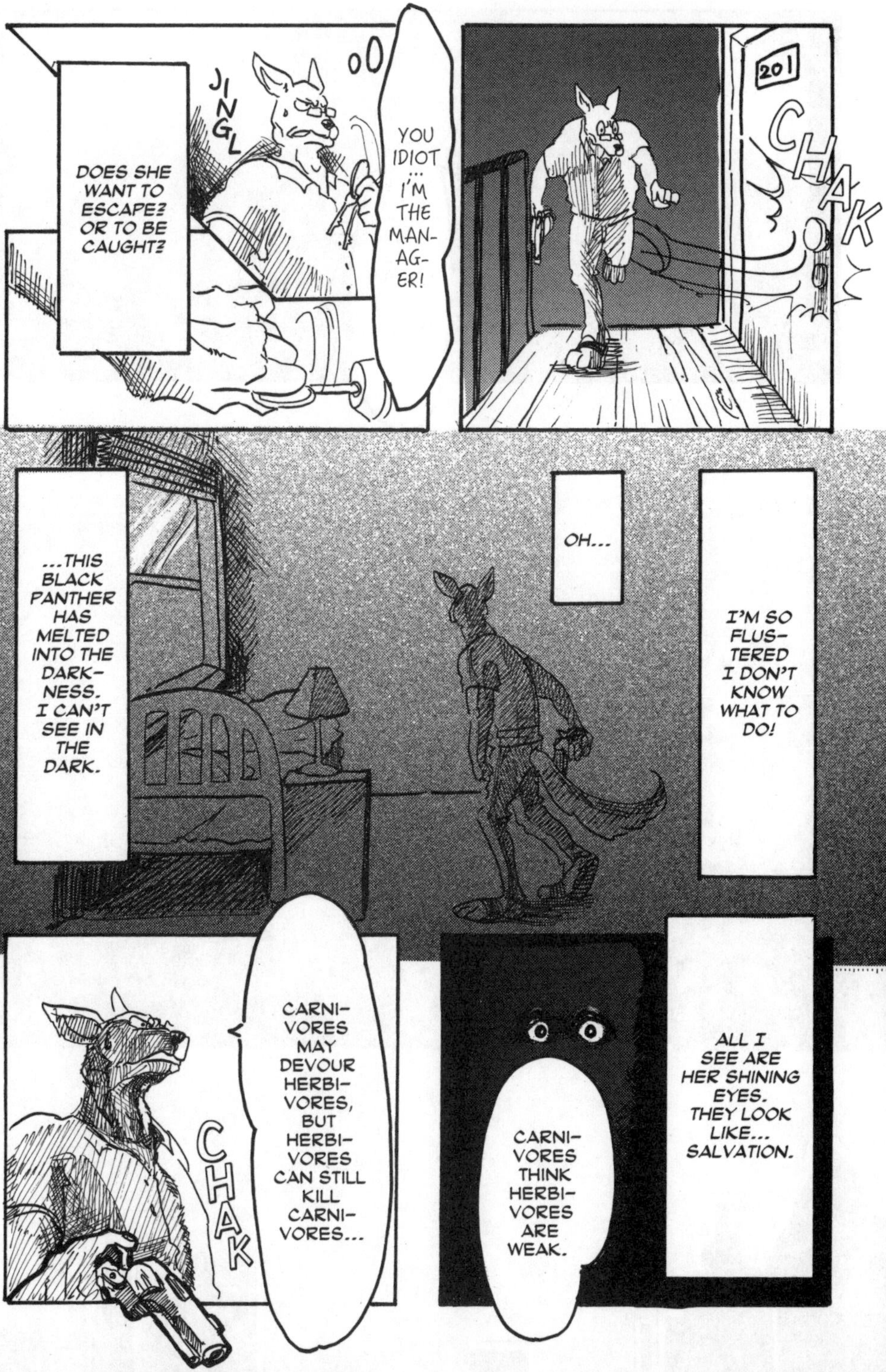
201
CHAK
CHAK
YOU IDIOT... I'M THE MANAGER!
JINGL
DOES SHE WANT TO ESCAPE? OR TO BE CAUGHT?
I'M SO FLUSTERED I DON'T KNOW WHAT TO DO!
OH...
...THIS BLACK PANTHER HAS MELTED INTO THE DARKNESS. I CAN'T SEE IN THE DARK.
ALL I SEE ARE HER SHINING EYES. THEY LOOK LIKE... SALVATION.
CARNIVORES THINK HERBIVORES ARE WEAK.
CARNIVORES MAY DEVOUR HERBIVORES, BUT HERBIVORES CAN STILL KILL CARNIVORES...
CHAK

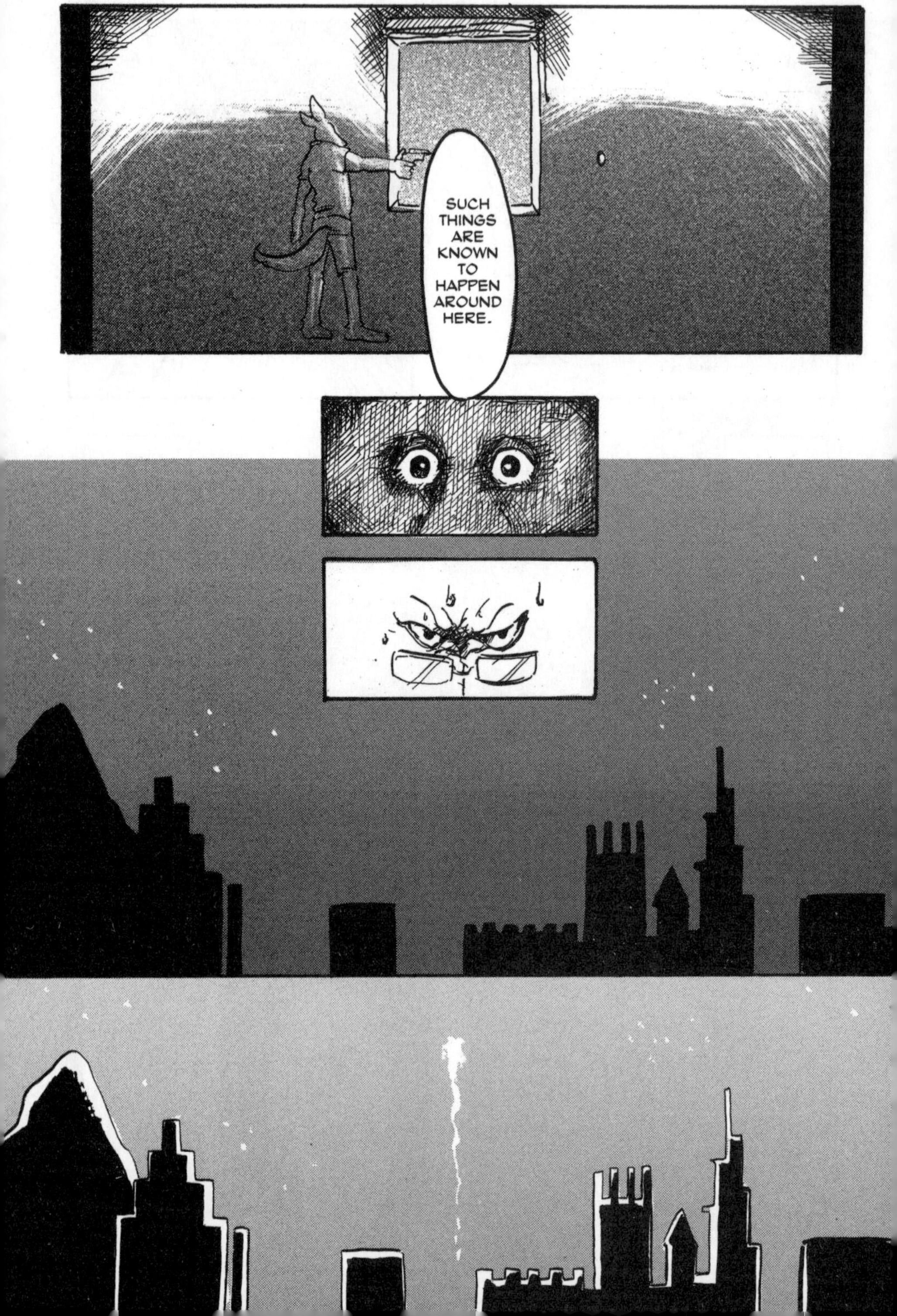
SUCH THINGS ARE KNOWN TO HAPPEN AROUND HERE.

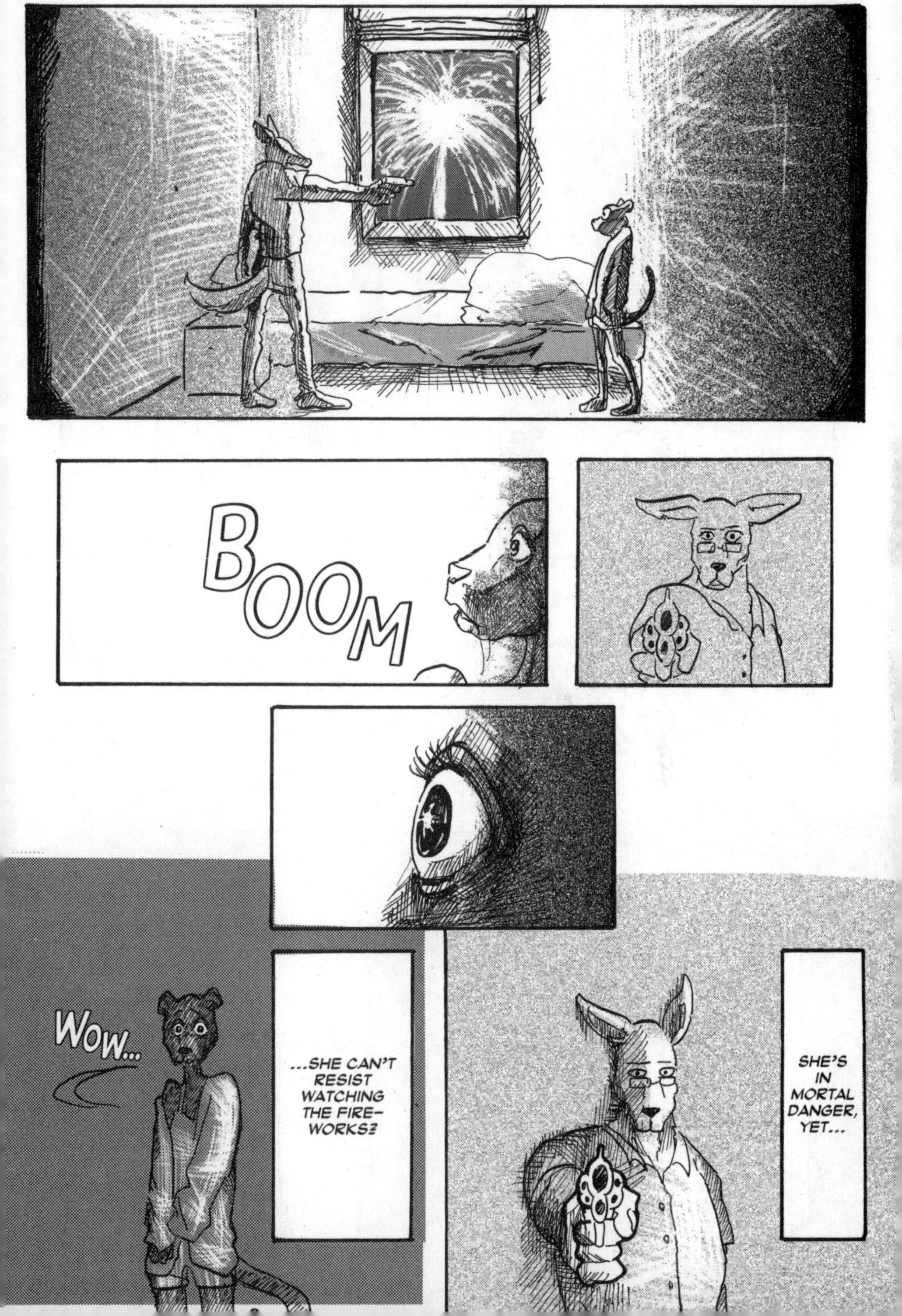
BOOM
SHE'S IN MORTAL DANGER, YET...
...SHE CAN'T RESIST WATCHING THE FIRE-WORKS?
WOW...

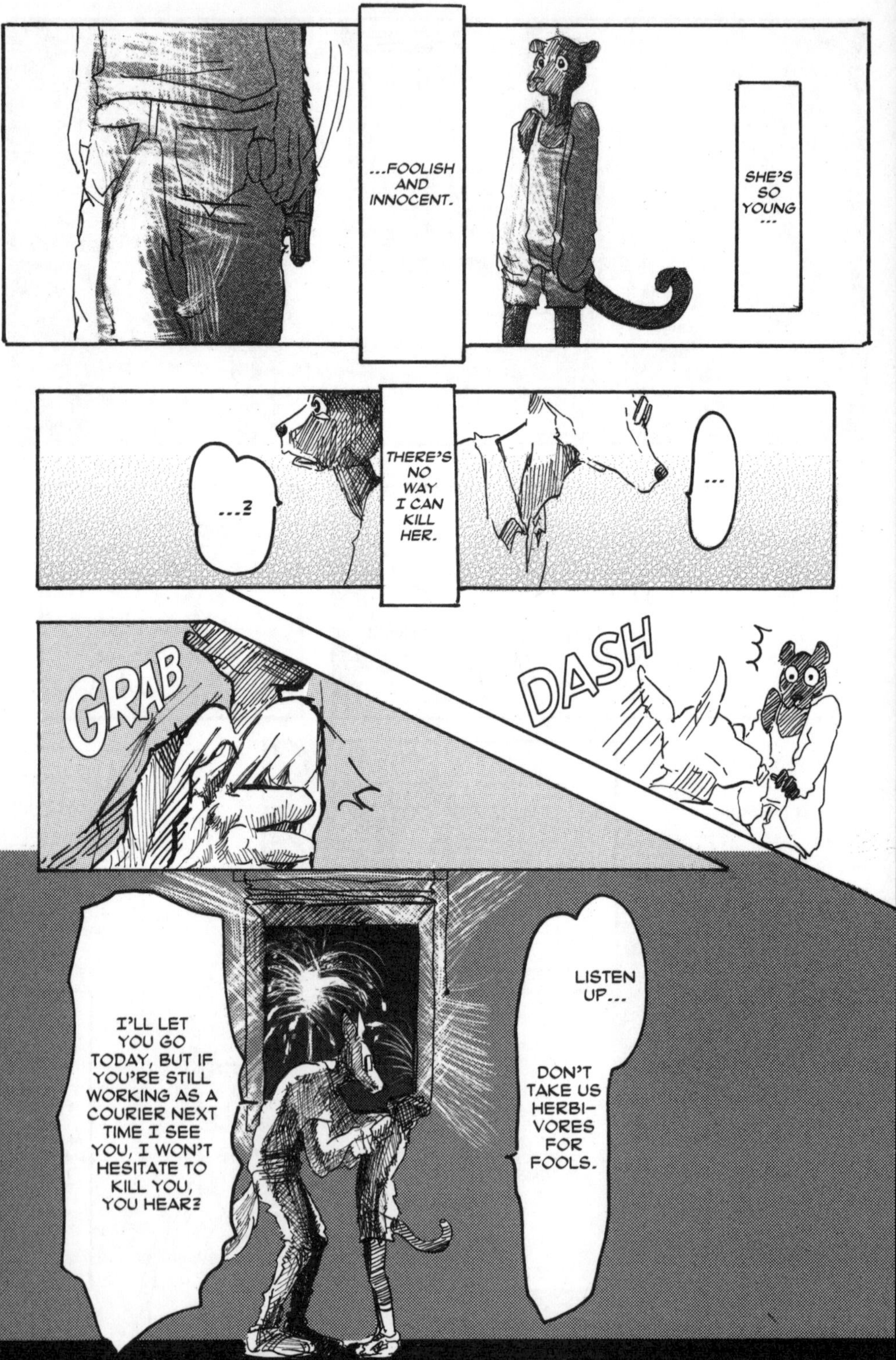
SHE'S SO YOUNG...
...FOOLISH AND INNOCENT.
...
THERE'S NO WAY I CAN KILL HER.
...?
DASH
GRAB
LISTEN UP...
DON'T TAKE US HERBIVORES FOR FOOLS.
I'LL LET YOU GO TODAY, BUT IF YOU'RE STILL WORKING AS A COURIER NEXT TIME I SEE YOU, I WON'T HESITATE TO KILL YOU, YOU HEAR?

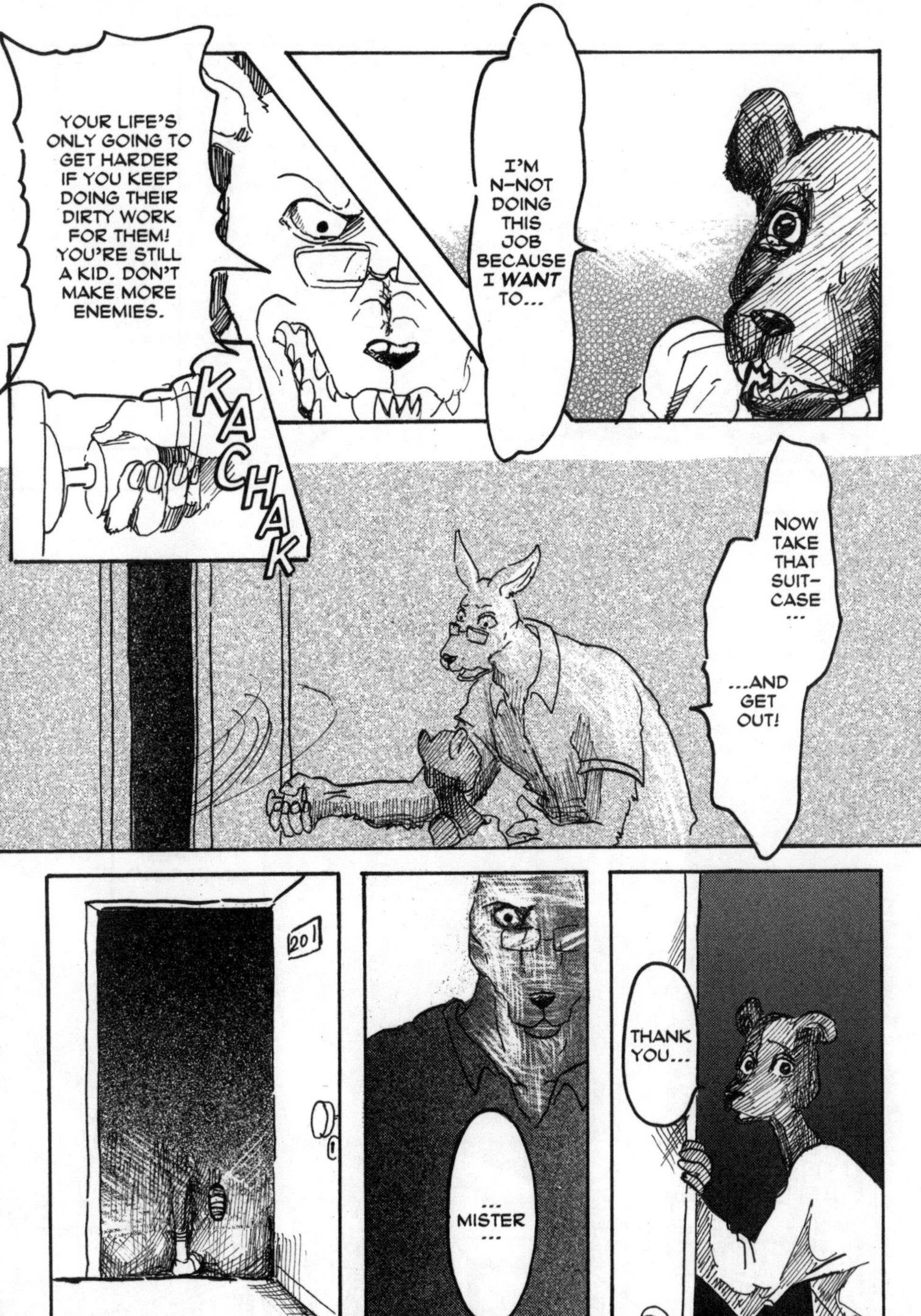
I'M N-NOT DOING THIS JOB BECAUSE I *WANT* TO...
YOUR LIFE'S ONLY GOING TO GET HARDER IF YOU KEEP DOING THEIR DIRTY WORK FOR THEM! YOU'RE STILL A KID. DON'T MAKE MORE ENEMIES.
KACHAK
NOW TAKE THAT SUIT-CASE...
...AND GET OUT!
THANK YOU...
...MISTER...
201

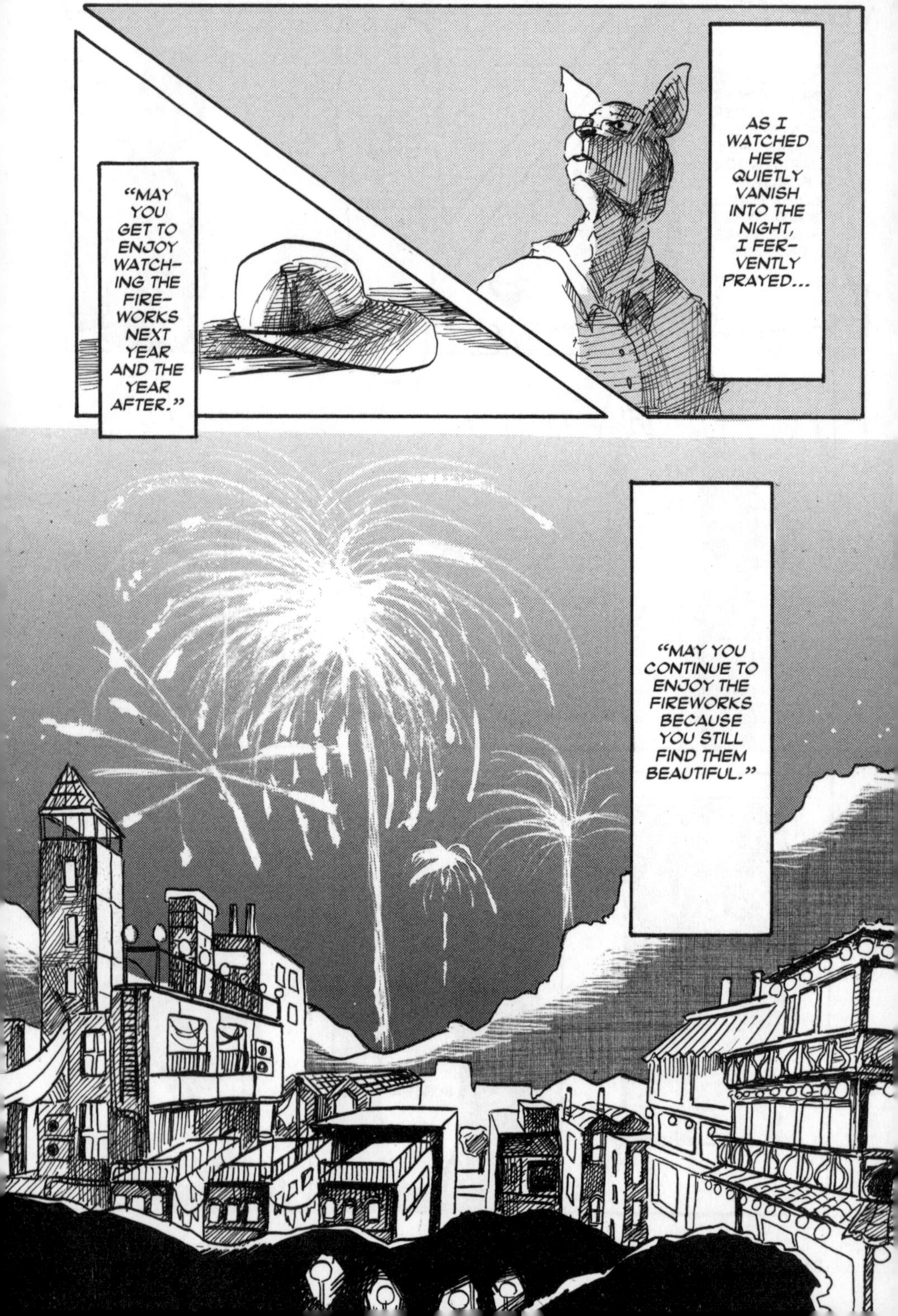
AS I WATCHED HER QUIETLY VANISH INTO THE NIGHT, I FER-VENTLY PRAYED...
"MAY YOU GET TO ENJOY WATCH-ING THE FIRE-WORKS NEXT YEAR AND THE YEAR AFTER."
"MAY YOU CONTINUE TO ENJOY THE FIREWORKS BECAUSE YOU STILL FIND THEM BEAUTIFUL."

Story 5
The Crocodile and the Gazelle

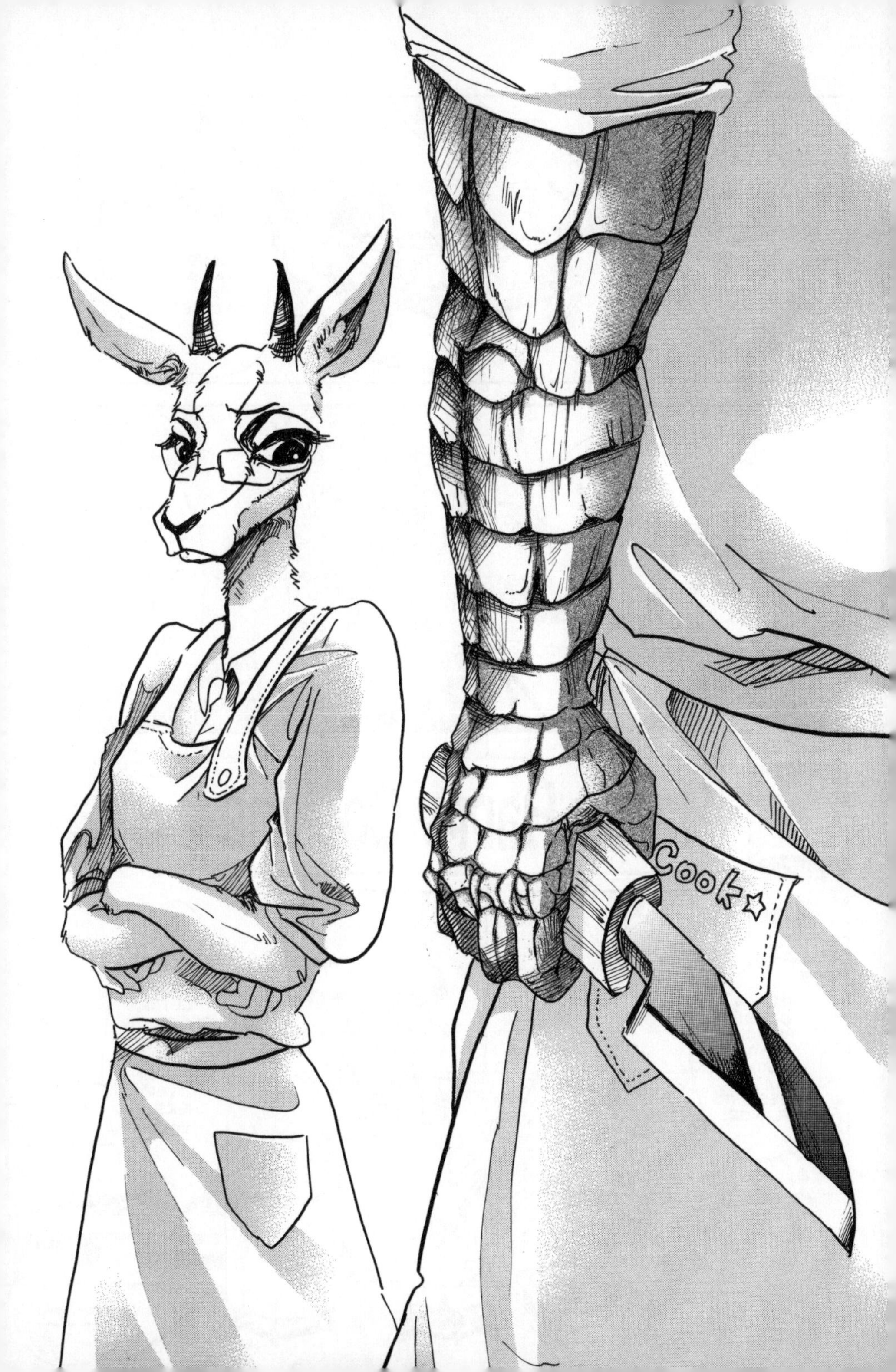
Cook☆

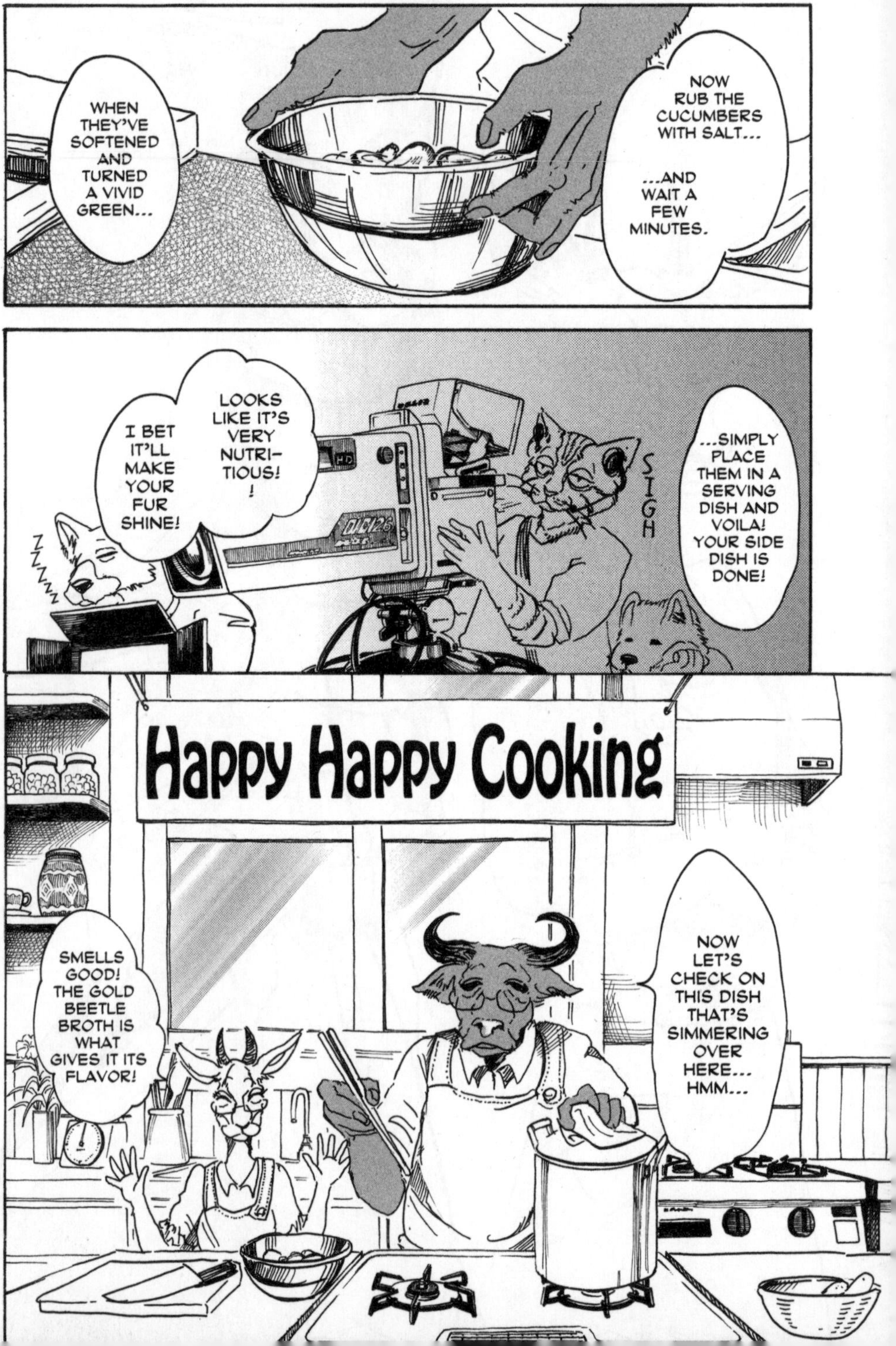
NOW RUB THE CUCUMBERS WITH SALT...
...AND WAIT A FEW MINUTES.
WHEN THEY'VE SOFTENED AND TURNED A VIVID GREEN...
...SIMPLY PLACE THEM IN A SERVING DISH AND VOILA! YOUR SIDE DISH IS DONE!
SIGH
LOOKS LIKE IT'S VERY NUTRITIOUS! !
I BET IT'LL MAKE YOUR FUR SHINE!
Happy Happy Cooking
NOW LET'S CHECK ON THIS DISH THAT'S SIMMERING OVER HERE... HMM...
SMELLS GOOD! THE GOLD BEETLE BROTH IS WHAT GIVES IT ITS FLAVOR!

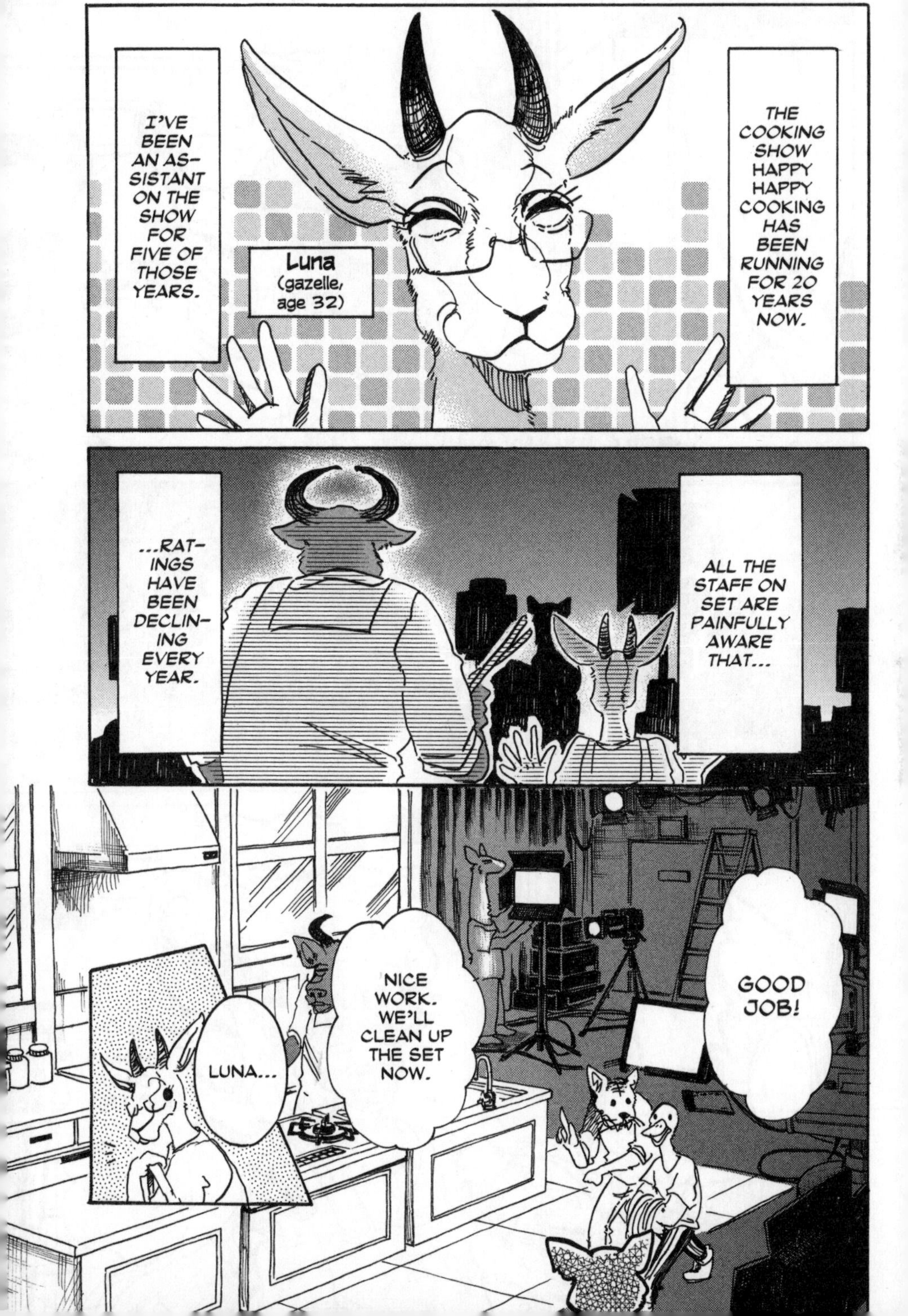
THE COOKING SHOW HAPPY HAPPY COOKING HAS BEEN RUNNING FOR 20 YEARS NOW.
I'VE BEEN AN ASSISTANT ON THE SHOW FOR FIVE OF THOSE YEARS.
Luna (gazelle, age 32)
ALL THE STAFF ON SET ARE PAINFULLY AWARE THAT...
...RATINGS HAVE BEEN DECLINING EVERY YEAR.
GOOD JOB!
NICE WORK. WE'LL CLEAN UP THE SET NOW.
LUNA...

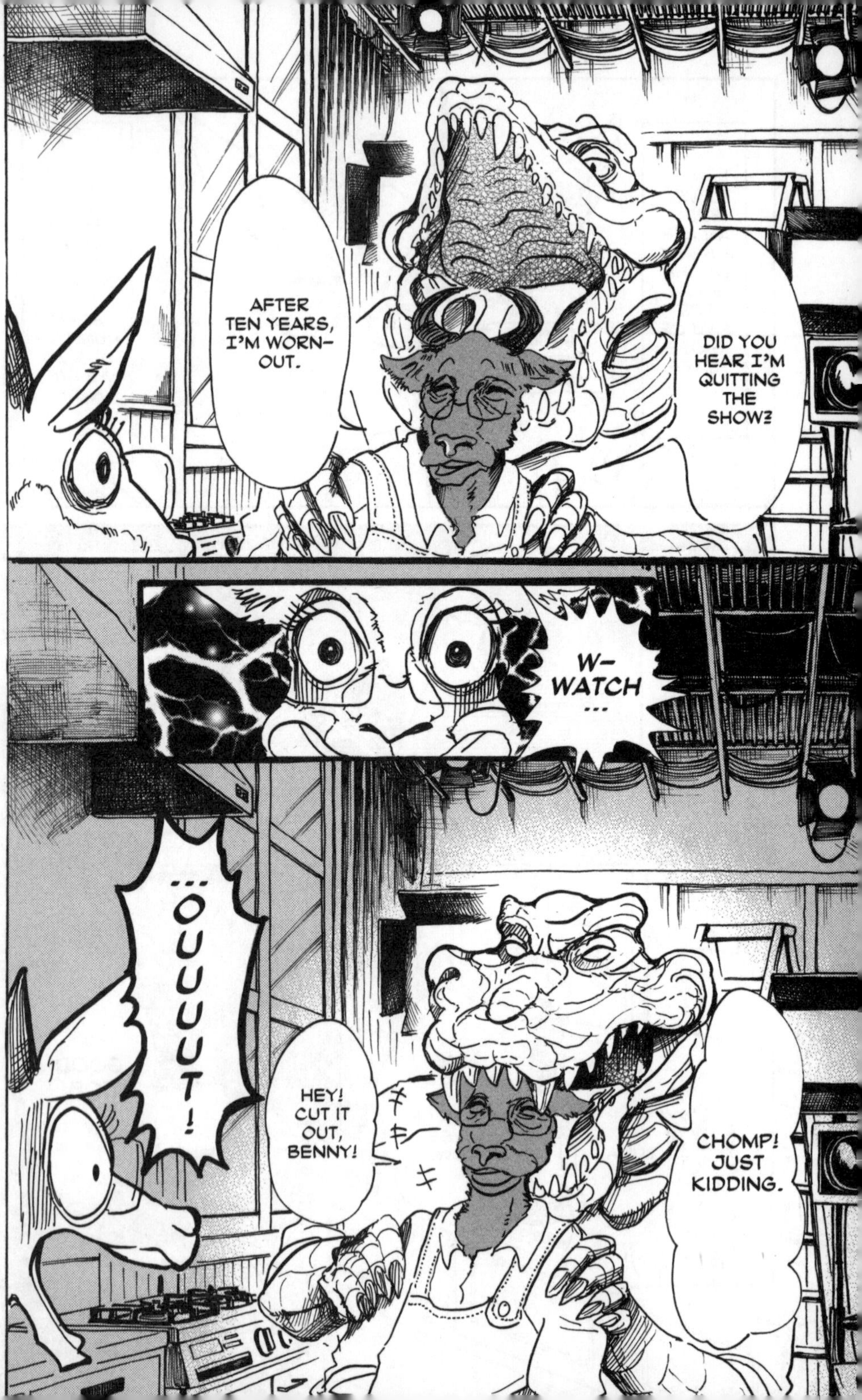
DID YOU HEAR I'M QUITTING THE SHOW?
AFTER TEN YEARS, I'M WORN-OUT.
W-WATCH...
CHOMP! JUST KIDDING.
HEY! CUT IT OUT, BENNY!
..OUUUUT!

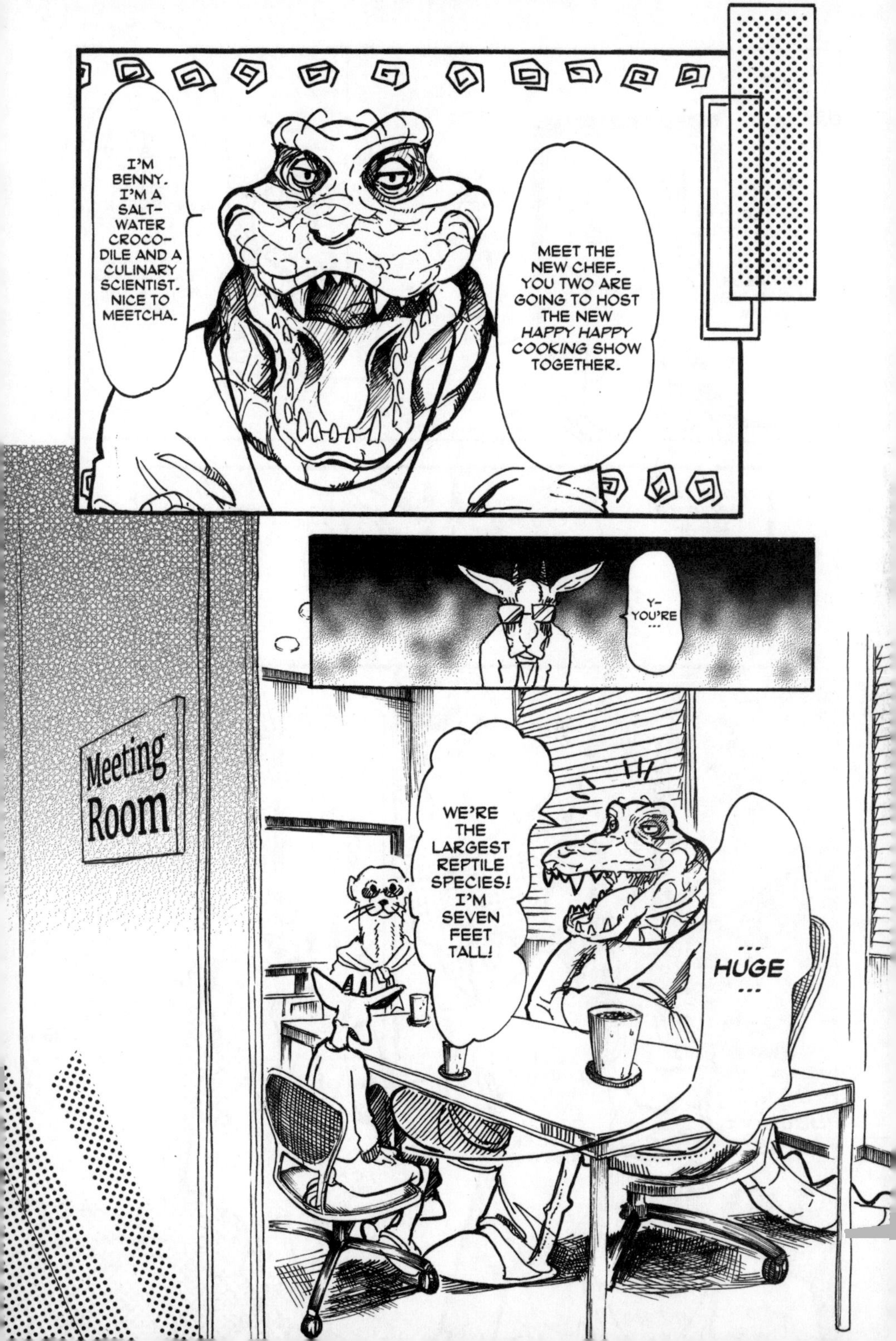
MEET THE NEW CHEF. YOU TWO ARE GOING TO HOST THE NEW *HAPPY HAPPY* COOKING SHOW TOGETHER.
I'M BENNY. I'M A SALT-WATER CROCO-DILE AND A CULINARY SCIENTIST. NICE TO MEETCHA.
Y-YOU'RE...
...HUGE...
WE'RE THE LARGEST REPTILE SPECIES! I'M SEVEN FEET TALL!
Meeting Room

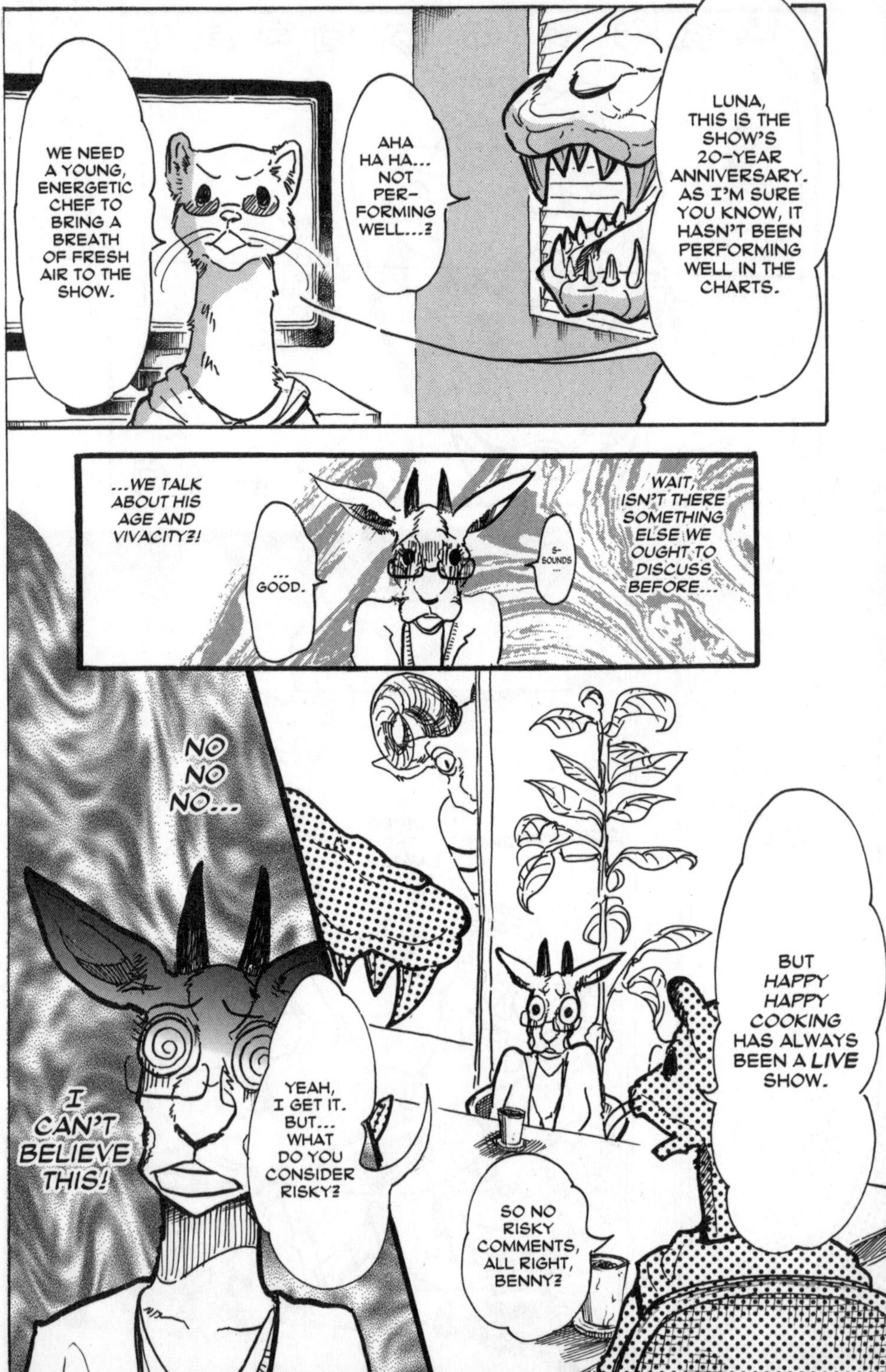
LUNA, THIS IS THE SHOW'S 20-YEAR ANNIVERSARY. AS I'M SURE YOU KNOW, IT HASN'T BEEN PERFORMING WELL IN THE CHARTS.
AHA HA HA... NOT PER-FORMING WELL...?
WE NEED A YOUNG, ENERGETIC CHEF TO BRING A BREATH OF FRESH AIR TO THE SHOW.
WAIT, ISN'T THERE SOMETHING ELSE WE OUGHT TO DISCUSS BEFORE...
S-SOUNDS...
...GOOD.
...WE TALK ABOUT HIS AGE AND VIVACITY?!
BUT HAPPY HAPPY COOKING HAS ALWAYS BEEN A LIVE SHOW.
SO NO RISKY COMMENTS, ALL RIGHT, BENNY?
YEAH, I GET IT. BUT... WHAT DO YOU CONSIDER RISKY?
NO NO NO...
I CAN'T BELIEVE THIS!

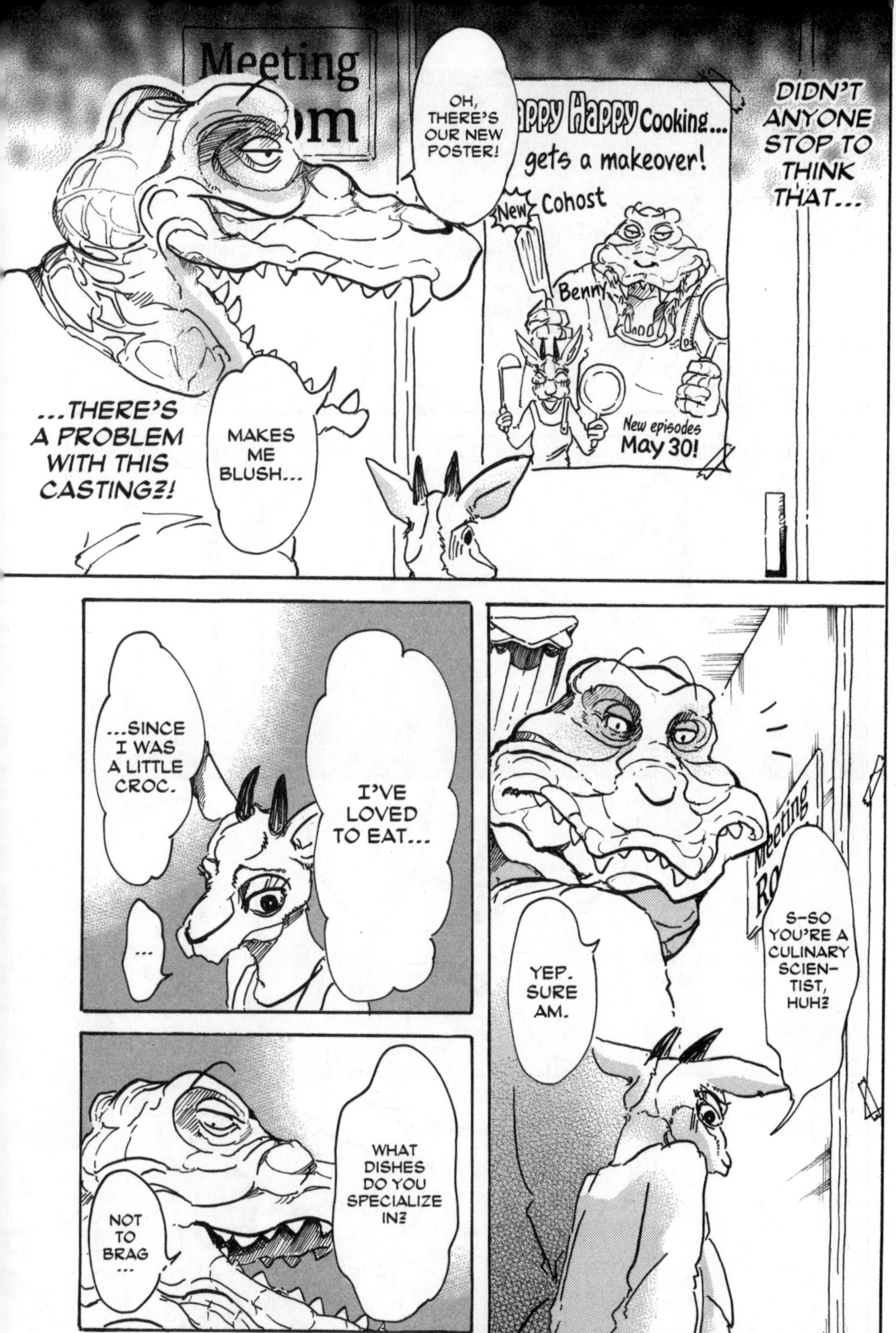

DIDN'T ANYONE STOP TO THINK THAT...
Happy Happy Cooking... gets a makeover!
New Cohost
Benny
New episodes May 30!
OH, THERE'S OUR NEW POSTER!
MAKES ME BLUSH...
...THERE'S A PROBLEM WITH THIS CASTING?!
Meeting Room
S-SO YOU'RE A CULINARY SCIEN-TIST, HUH?
YEP. SURE AM.
I'VE LOVED TO EAT...
...SINCE I WAS A LITTLE CROC.
...
WHAT DISHES DO YOU SPECIALIZE IN?
NOT TO BRAG...

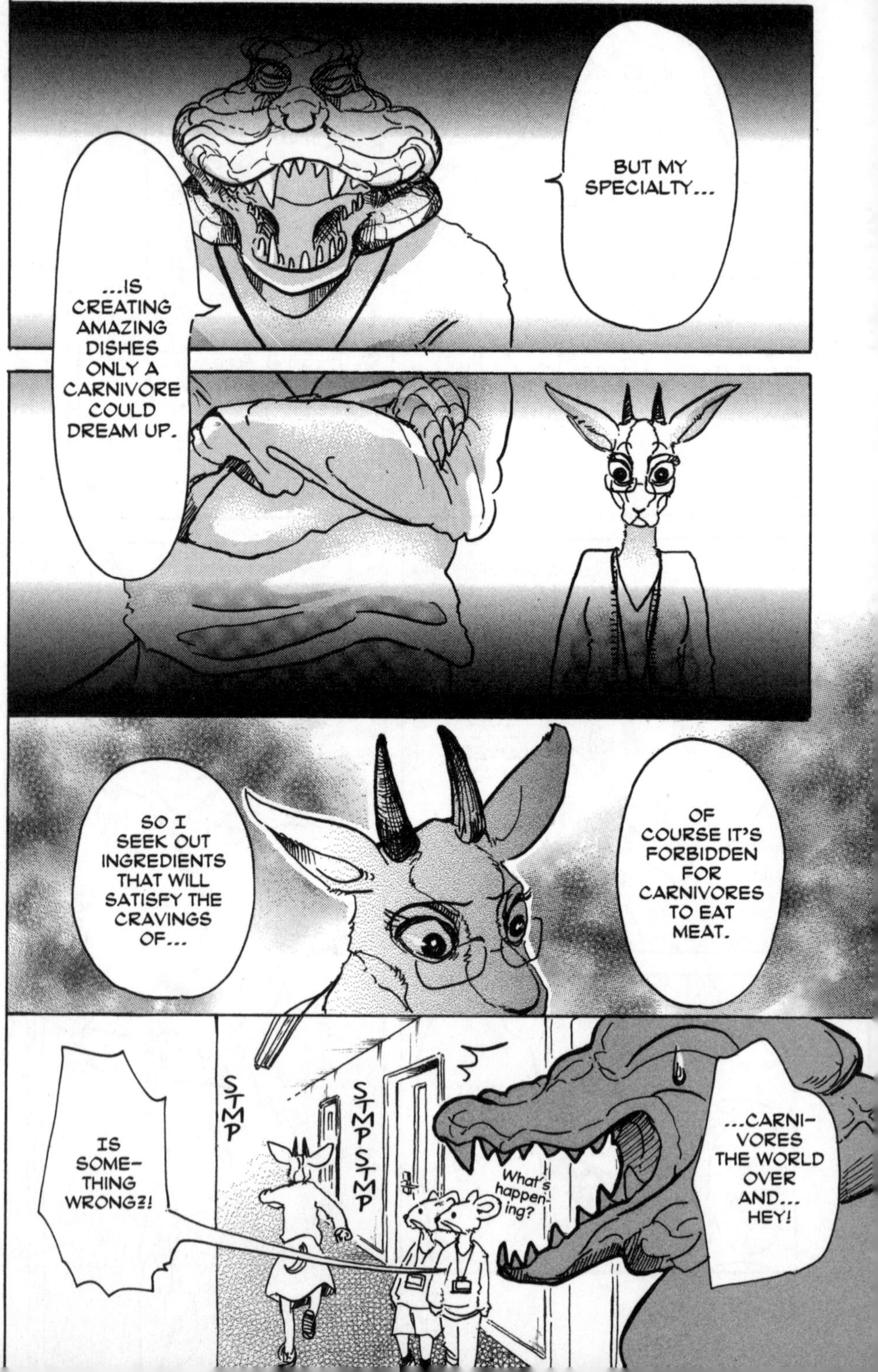
BUT MY SPECIALTY...
...IS CREATING AMAZING DISHES ONLY A CARNIVORE COULD DREAM UP.
OF COURSE IT'S FORBIDDEN FOR CARNIVORES TO EAT MEAT.
SO I SEEK OUT INGREDIENTS THAT WILL SATISFY THE CRAVINGS OF...
...CARNI-VORES THE WORLD OVER AND... HEY!
What's happen-ing?
STMP STMP STMP
STMP
IS SOME-THING WRONG?!

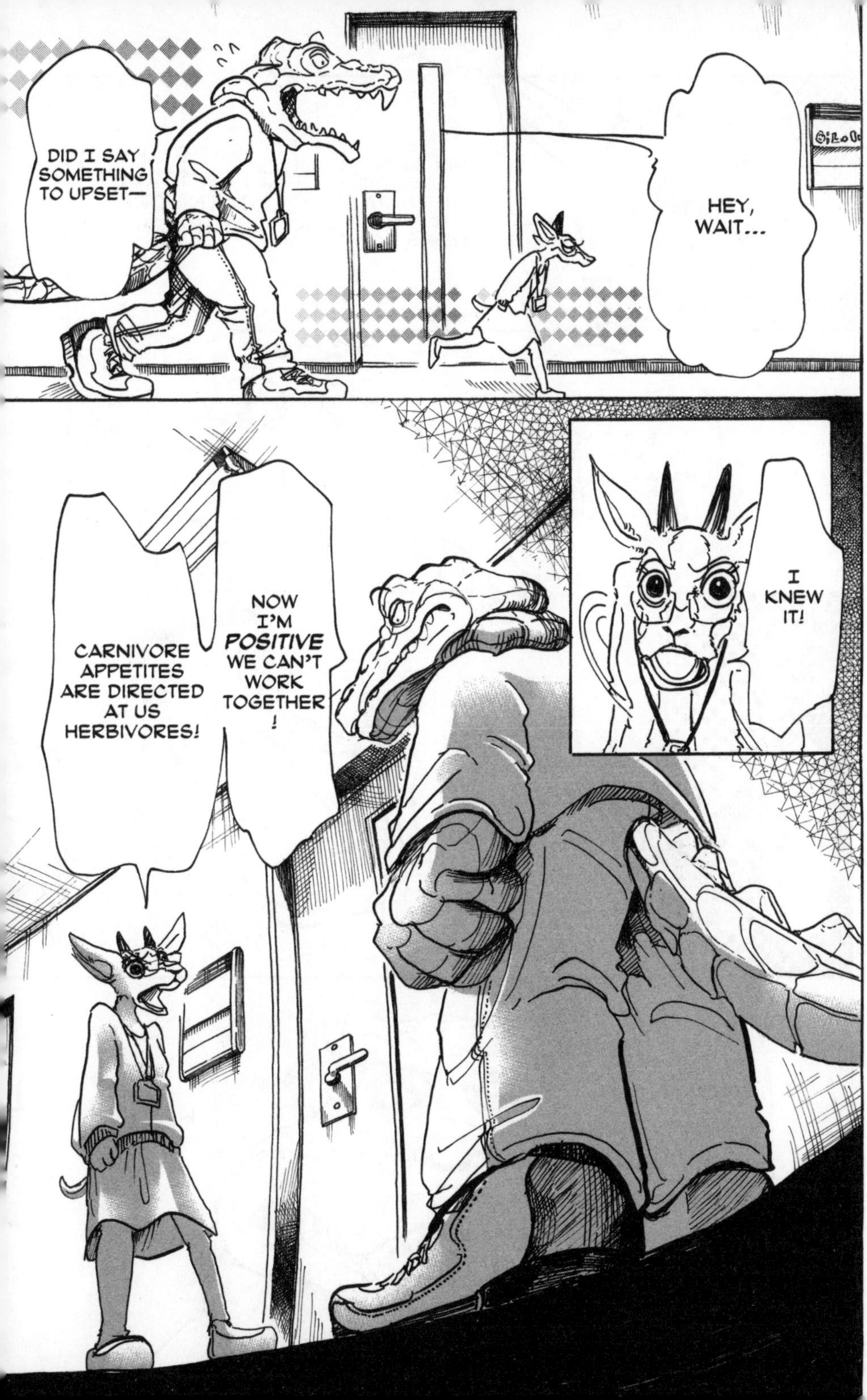
HEY, WAIT...
DID I SAY SOMETHING TO UPSET—
I KNEW IT!
NOW I'M *POSITIVE* WE CAN'T WORK TOGETHER!
CARNIVORE APPETITES ARE DIRECTED AT US HERBIVORES!

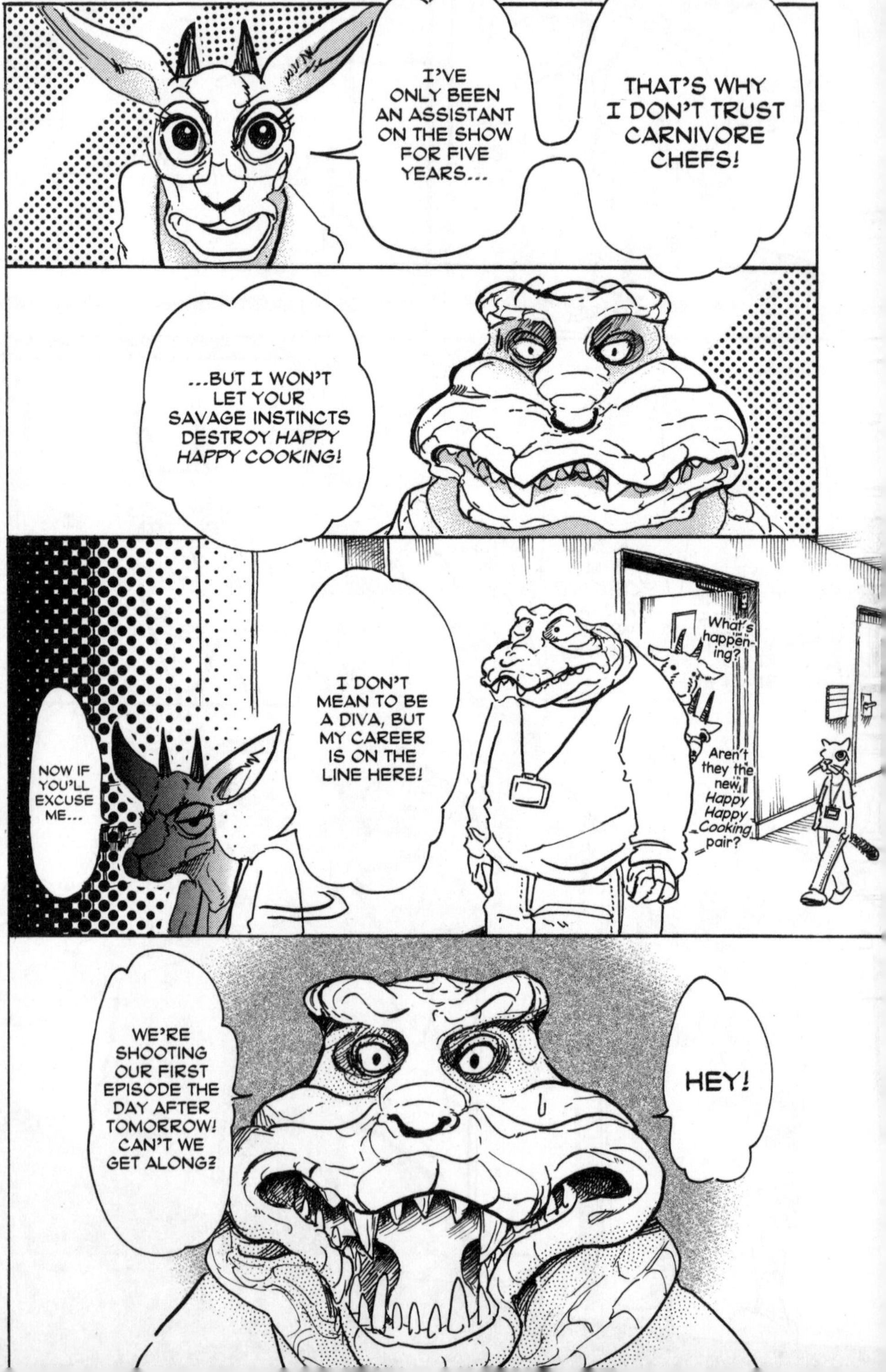
THAT'S WHY I DON'T TRUST CARNIVORE CHEFS!
I'VE ONLY BEEN AN ASSISTANT ON THE SHOW FOR FIVE YEARS...
...BUT I WON'T LET YOUR SAVAGE INSTINCTS DESTROY *HAPPY HAPPY COOKING*!
What's happening?
Aren't they the new *Happy Happy Cooking* pair?
I DON'T MEAN TO BE A DIVA, BUT MY CAREER IS ON THE LINE HERE!
NOW IF YOU'LL EXCUSE ME...
HEY!
WE'RE SHOOTING OUR FIRST EPISODE THE DAY AFTER TOMORROW! CAN'T WE GET ALONG?

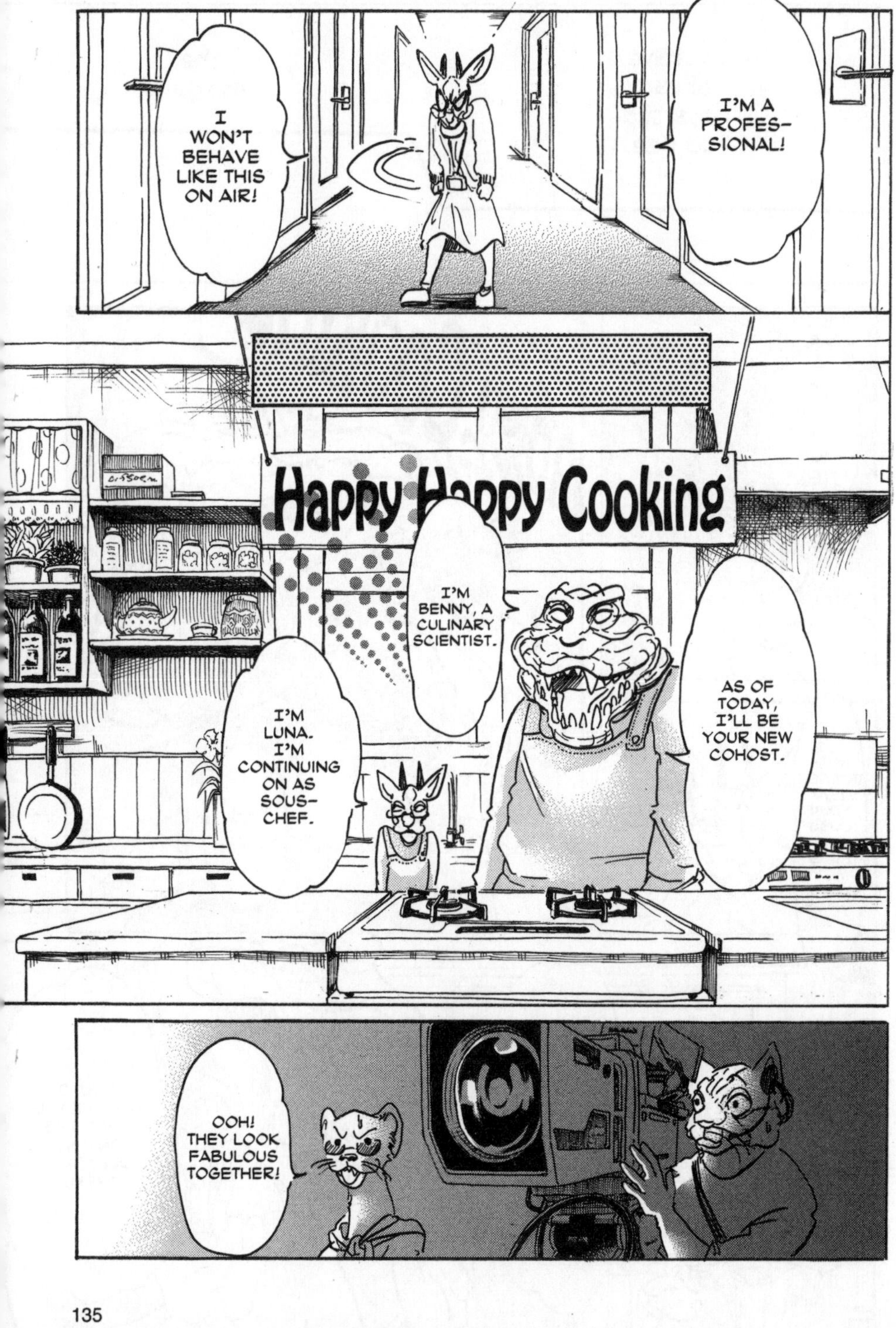

I'M A PROFESSIONAL!
I WON'T BEHAVE LIKE THIS ON AIR!
Happy Happy Cooking
I'M BENNY, A CULINARY SCIENTIST.
AS OF TODAY, I'LL BE YOUR NEW COHOST.
I'M LUNA. I'M CONTINUING ON AS SOUS-CHEF.
OOH! THEY LOOK FABULOUS TOGETHER!

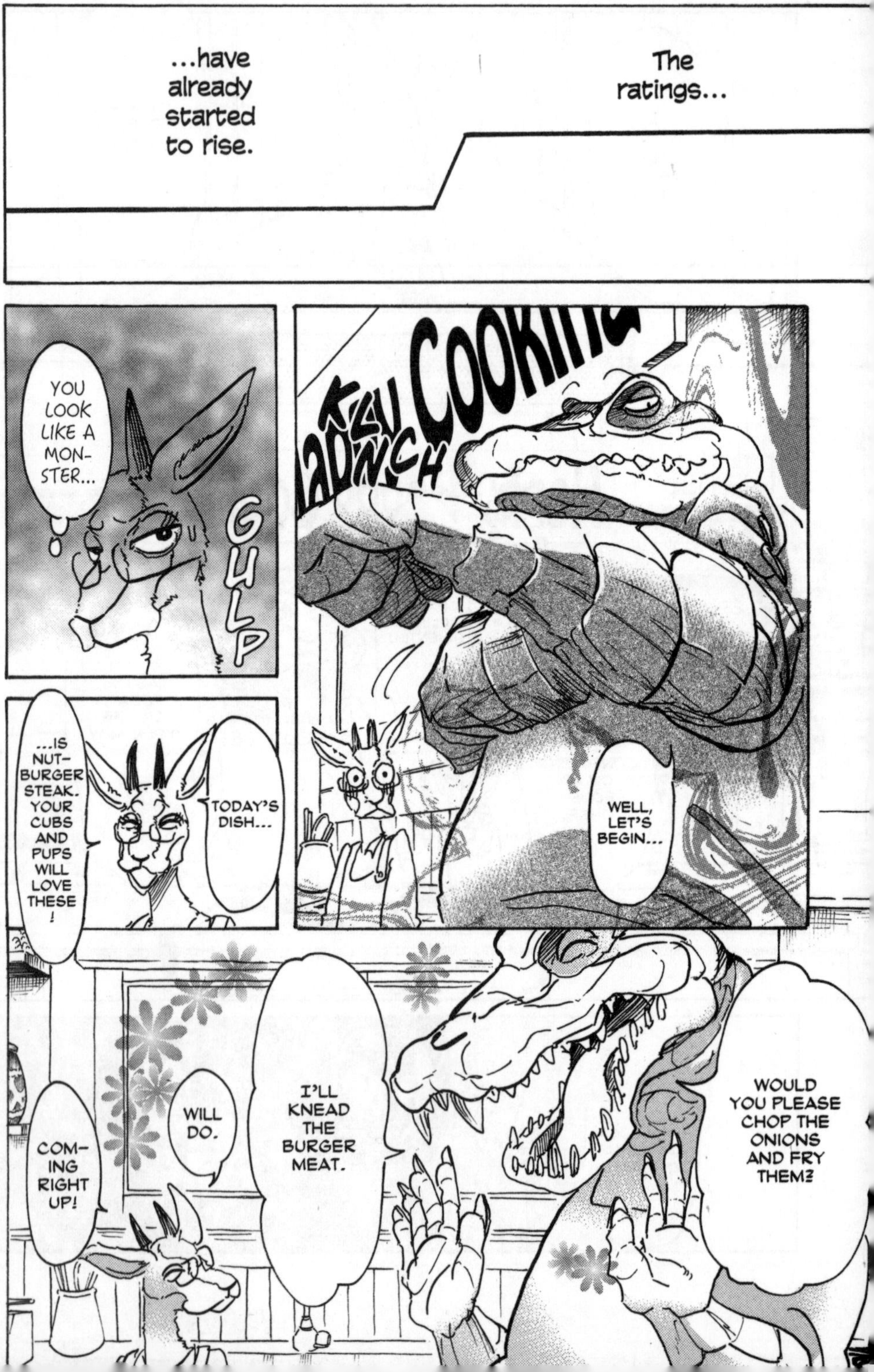
The ratings...
...have already started to rise.
WELL, LET'S BEGIN...
YOU LOOK LIKE A MON-STER...
GULP
TODAY'S DISH...
...IS NUT-BURGER STEAK. YOUR CUBS AND PUPS WILL LOVE THESE!
WOULD YOU PLEASE CHOP THE ONIONS AND FRY THEM?
I'LL KNEAD THE BURGER MEAT.
WILL DO.
COM-ING RIGHT UP!

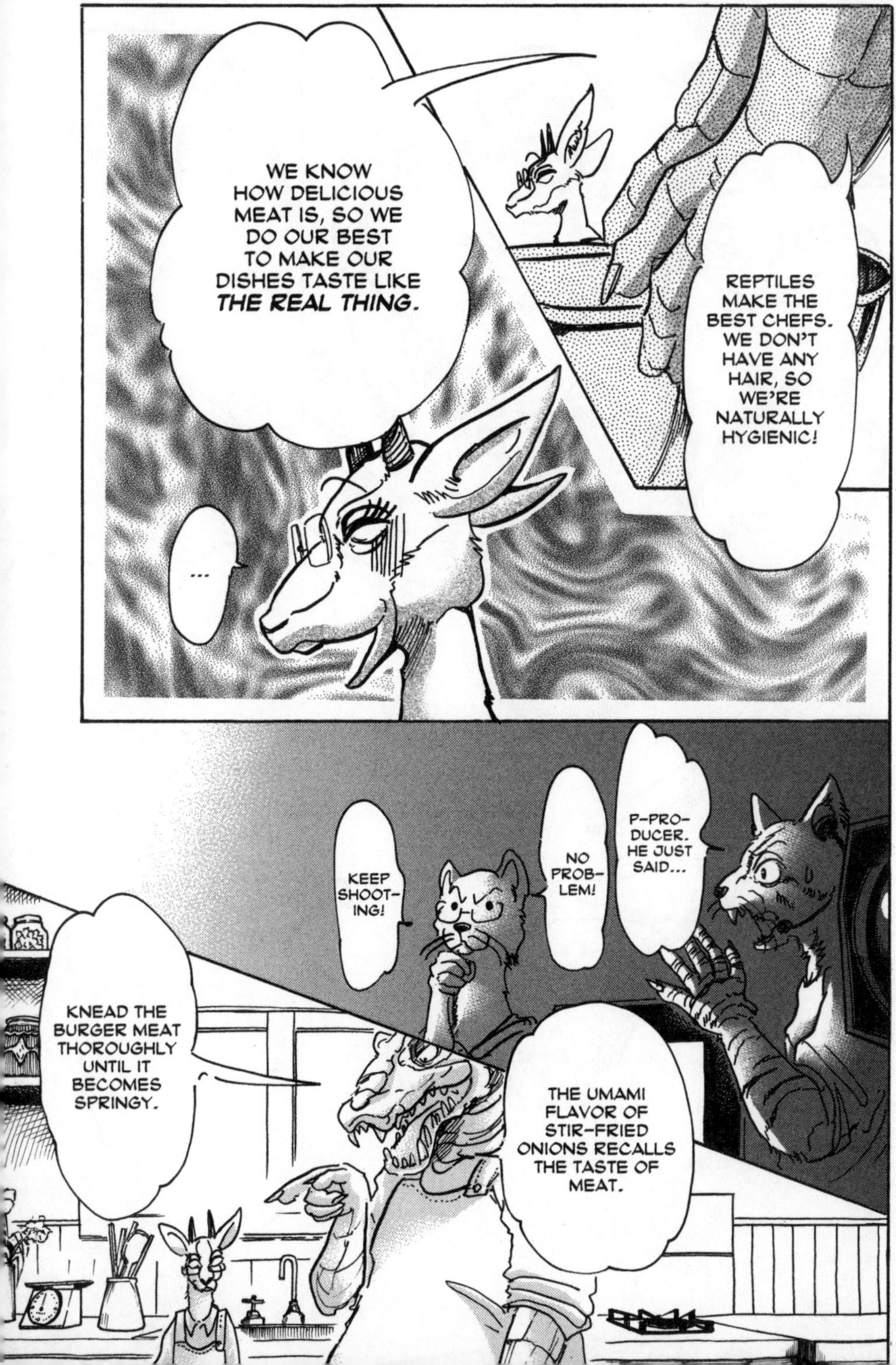
REPTILES MAKE THE BEST CHEFS. WE DON'T HAVE ANY HAIR, SO WE'RE NATURALLY HYGIENIC!
WE KNOW HOW DELICIOUS MEAT IS, SO WE DO OUR BEST TO MAKE OUR DISHES TASTE LIKE *THE REAL THING.*
...
P-PRO-DUCER. HE JUST SAID...
NO PROB-LEM!
KEEP SHOOT-ING!
THE UMAMI FLAVOR OF STIR-FRIED ONIONS RECALLS THE TASTE OF MEAT.
KNEAD THE BURGER MEAT THOROUGHLY UNTIL IT BECOMES SPRINGY.

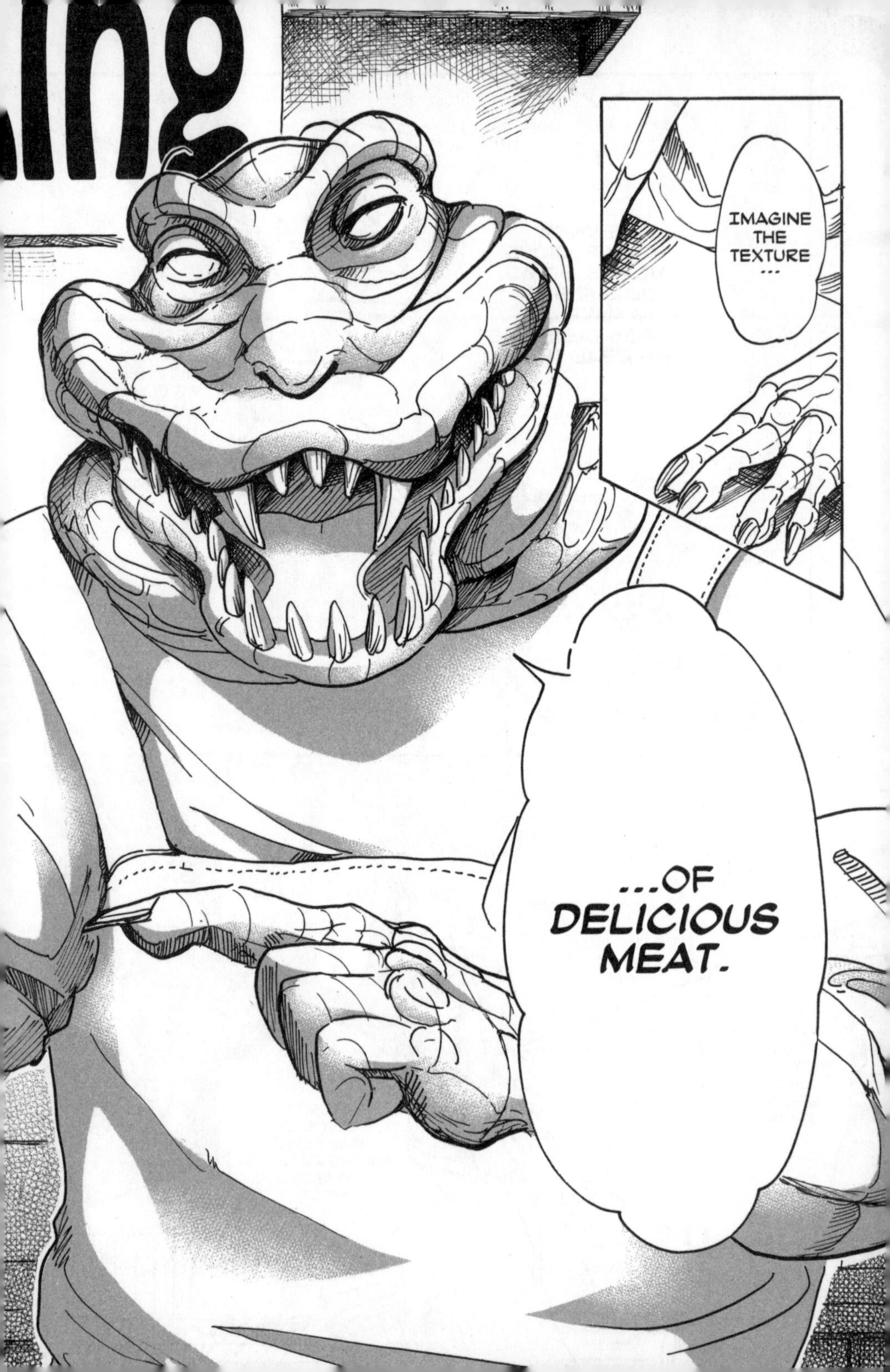
IMAGINE THE TEXTURE ...
...OF DELICIOUS MEAT.

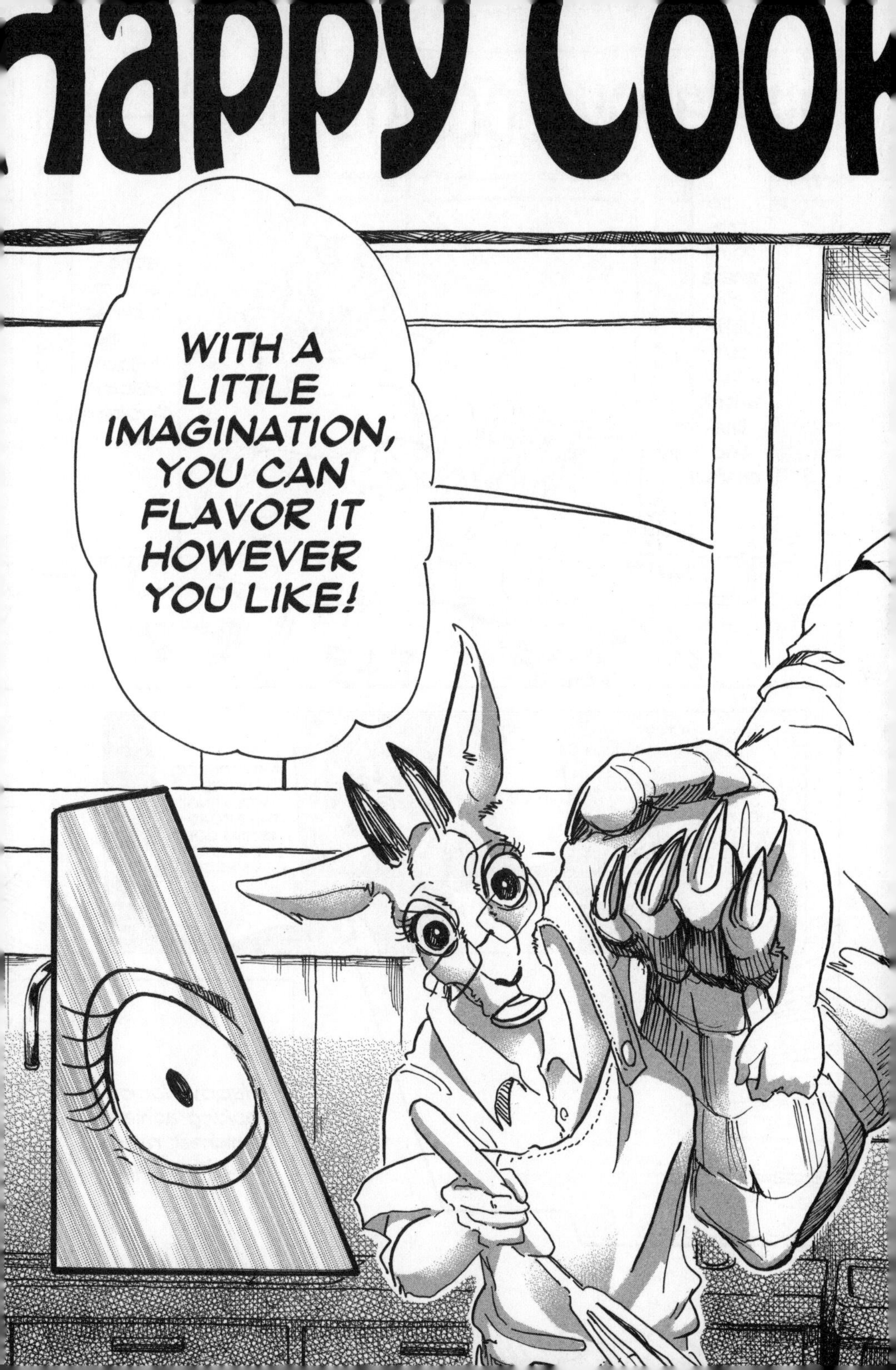
appy Coo
WITH A LITTLE IMAGINATION, YOU CAN FLAVOR IT HOWEVER YOU LIKE!

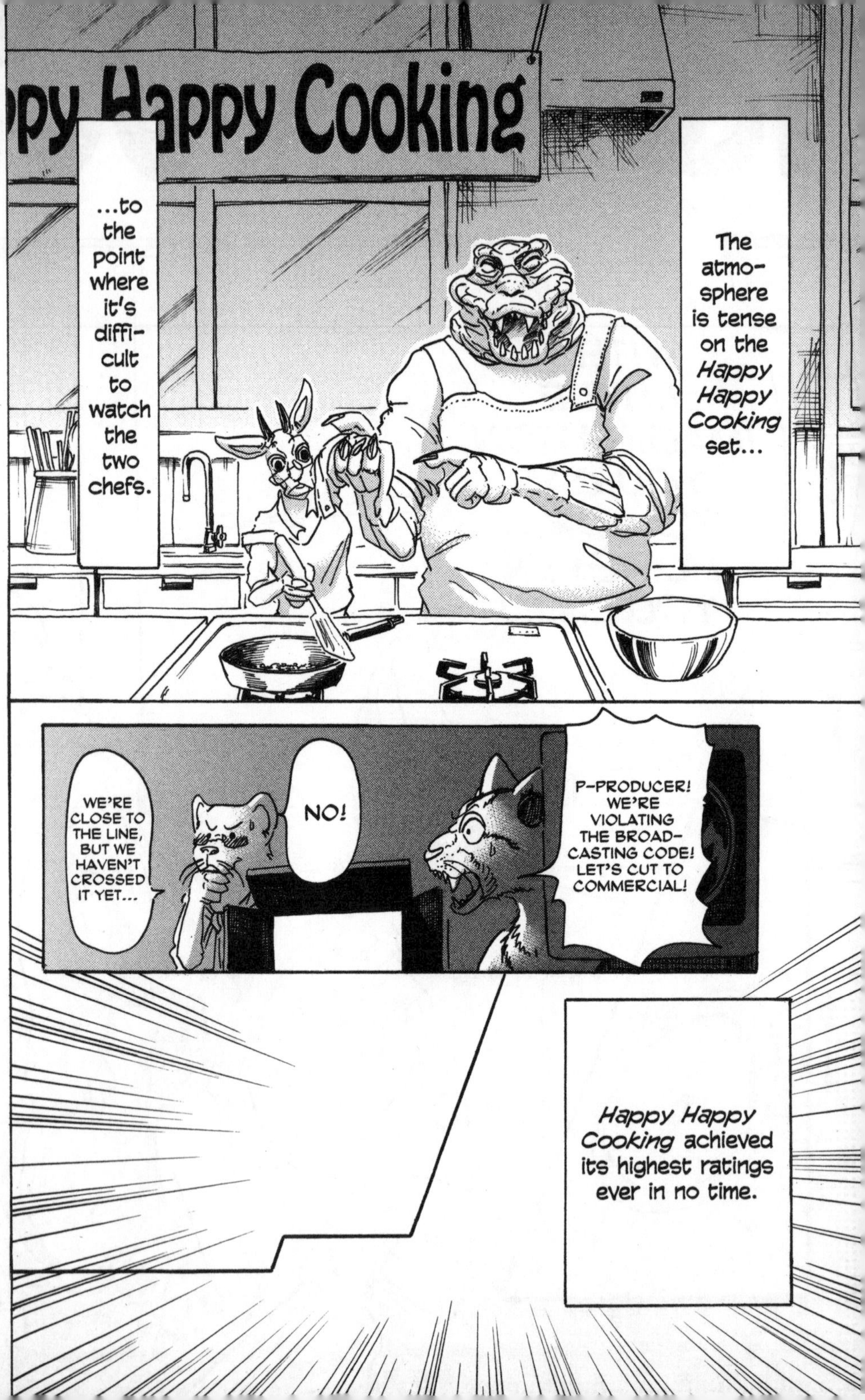
ppy Happy Cooking
The atmosphere is tense on the *Happy Happy Cooking* set...
...to the point where it's difficult to watch the two chefs.
P-PRODUCER! WE'RE VIOLATING THE BROADCASTING CODE! LET'S CUT TO COMMERCIAL!
NO!
WE'RE CLOSE TO THE LINE, BUT WE HAVEN'T CROSSED IT YET...
Happy Happy Cooking achieved its highest ratings ever in no time.

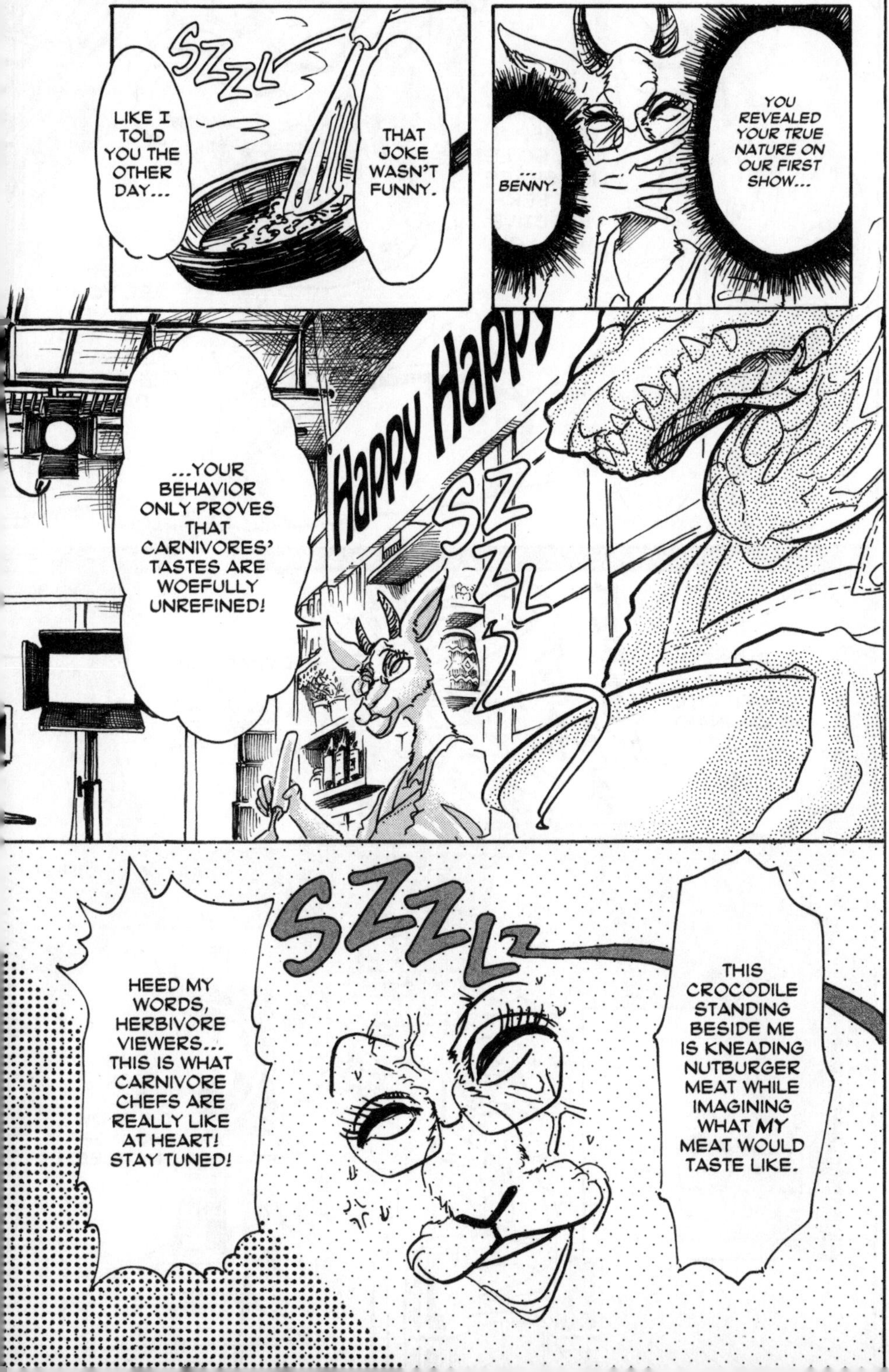
YOU REVEALED YOUR TRUE NATURE ON OUR FIRST SHOW...
...BENNY.
SZZL
THAT JOKE WASN'T FUNNY.
LIKE I TOLD YOU THE OTHER DAY...
Happy Happy
SZZL
...YOUR BEHAVIOR ONLY PROVES THAT CARNIVORES' TASTES ARE WOEFULLY UNREFINED!
THIS CROCODILE STANDING BESIDE ME IS KNEADING NUTBURGER MEAT WHILE IMAGINING WHAT MY MEAT WOULD TASTE LIKE.
SZZLZ
HEED MY WORDS, HERBIVORE VIEWERS... THIS IS WHAT CARNIVORE CHEFS ARE REALLY LIKE AT HEART! STAY TUNED!

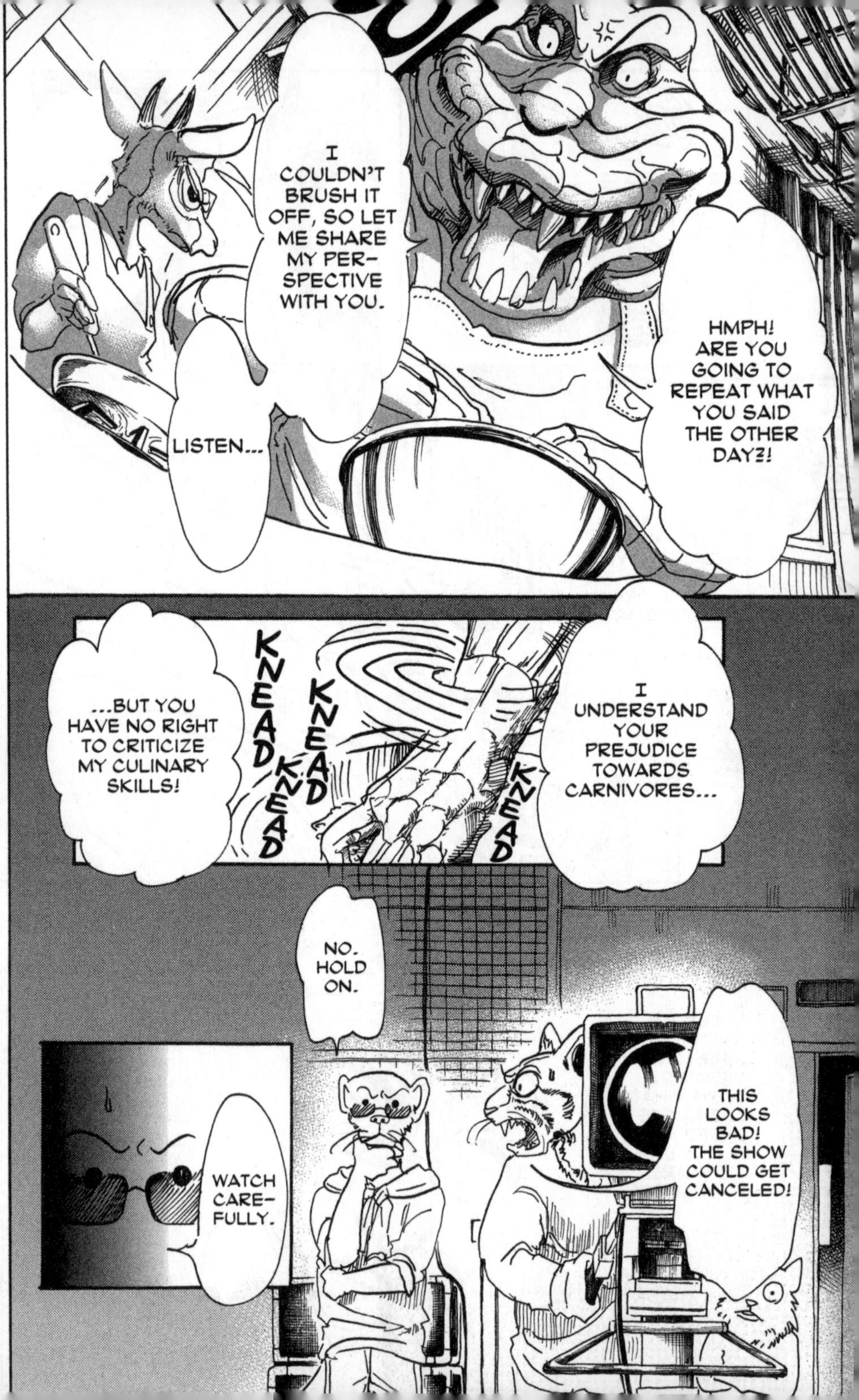
HMPH! ARE YOU GOING TO REPEAT WHAT YOU SAID THE OTHER DAY?!
I COULDN'T BRUSH IT OFF, SO LET ME SHARE MY PER-SPECTIVE WITH YOU.
LISTEN...
I UNDERSTAND YOUR PREJUDICE TOWARDS CARNIVORES...
KNEAD
KNEAD
KNEAD
KNEAD
...BUT YOU HAVE NO RIGHT TO CRITICIZE MY CULINARY SKILLS!
THIS LOOKS BAD! THE SHOW COULD GET CANCELED!
NO. HOLD ON.
WATCH CARE-FULLY.

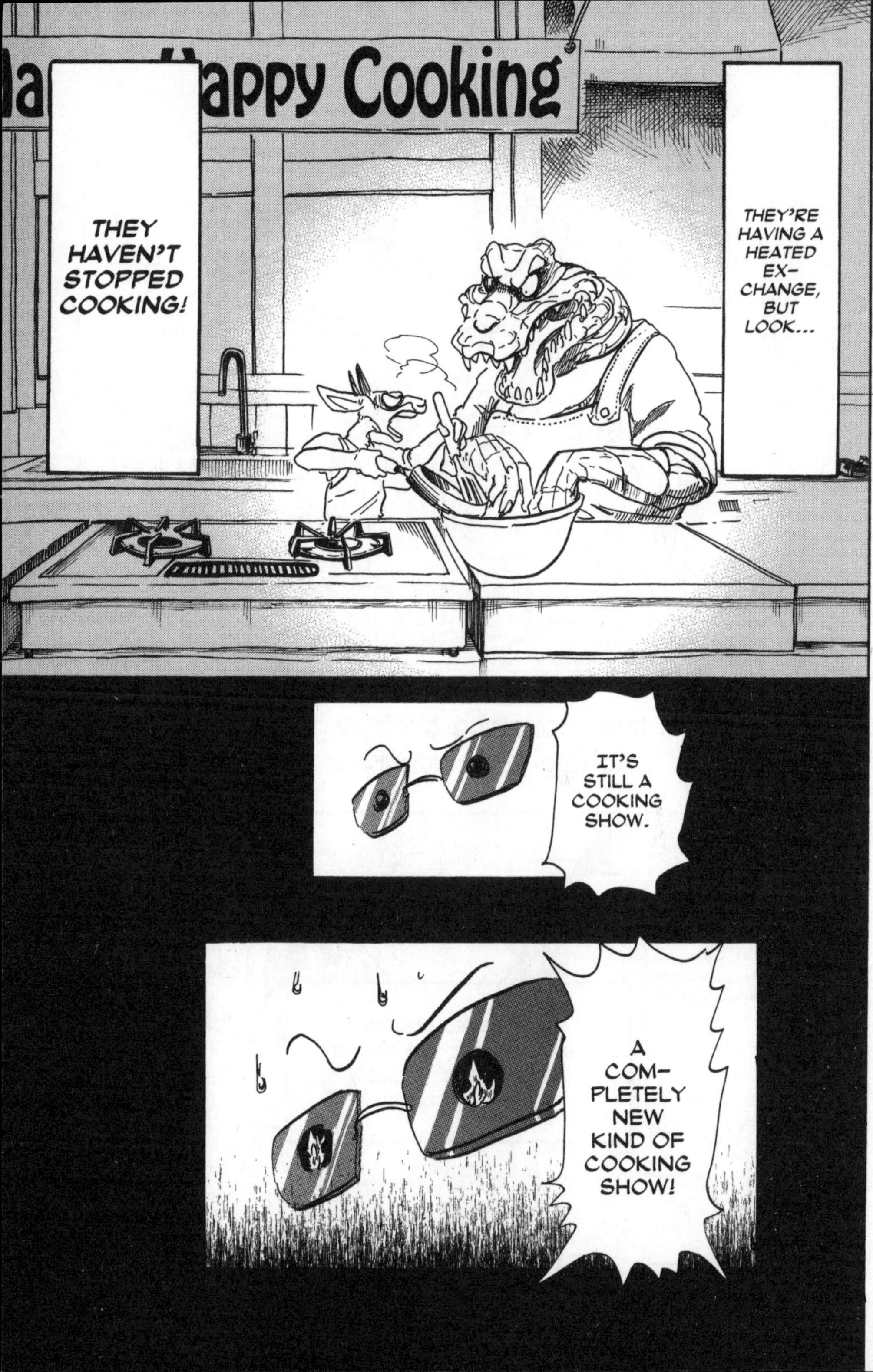
appy Cooking
THEY'RE HAVING A HEATED EX-CHANGE, BUT LOOK...
THEY HAVEN'T STOPPED COOKING!
IT'S STILL A COOKING SHOW.
A COM-PLETELY NEW KIND OF COOKING SHOW!

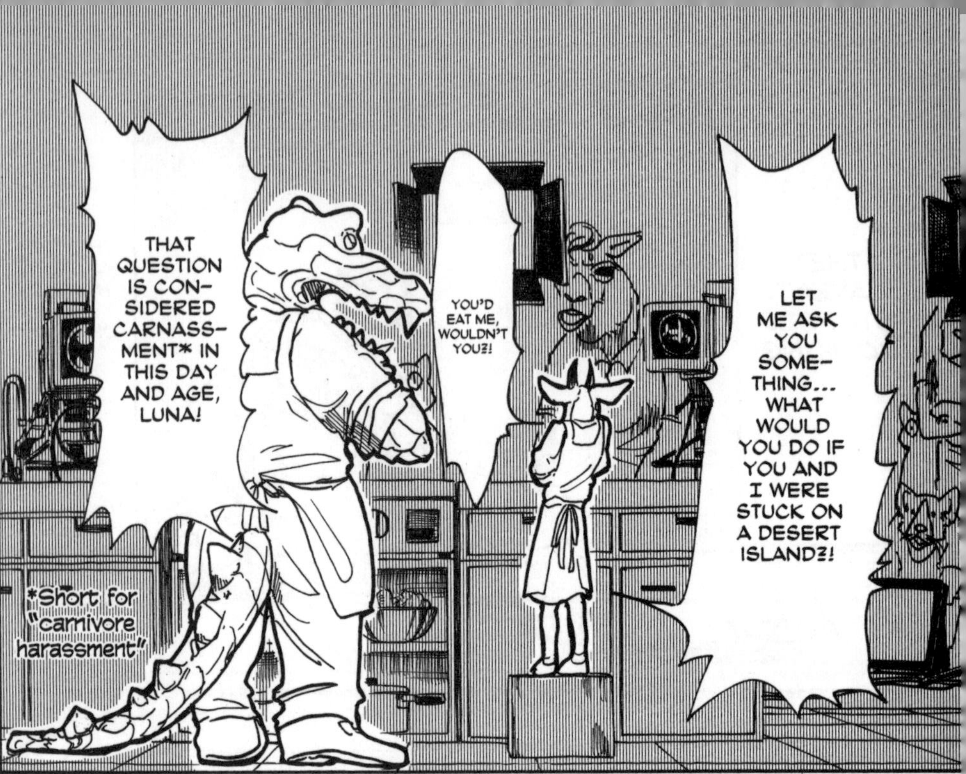
LET ME ASK YOU SOMETHING... WHAT WOULD YOU DO IF YOU AND I WERE STUCK ON A DESERT ISLAND?!
YOU'D EAT ME, WOULDN'T YOU?!
THAT QUESTION IS CONSIDERED CARNASSMENT* IN THIS DAY AND AGE, LUNA!
*Short for "carnivore harassment"

The two continue their argument while cooking the nutburger steaks.

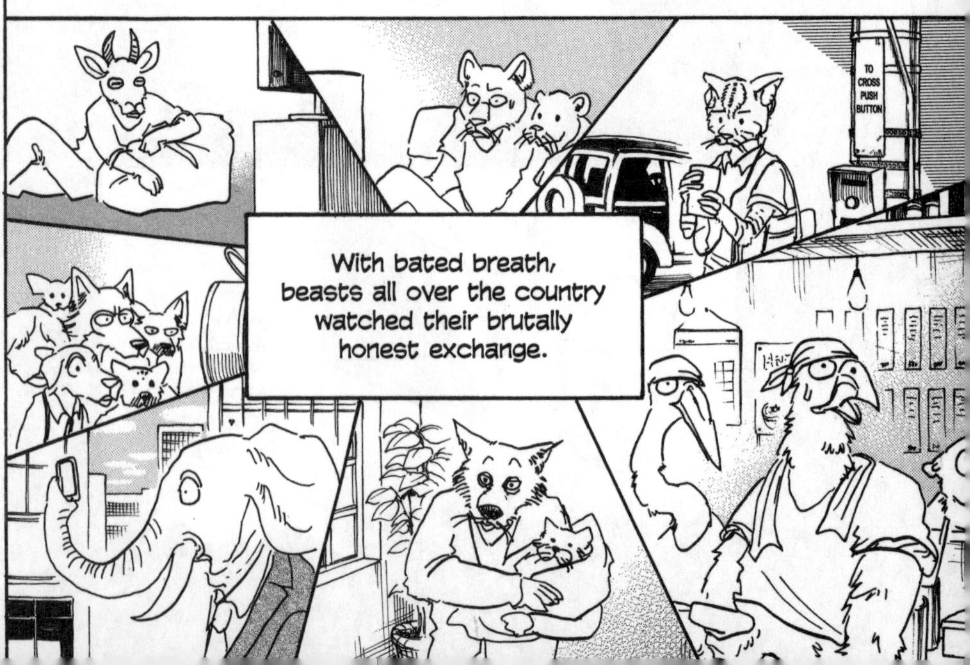
TO CROSS PUSH BUTTON
With bated breath, beasts all over the country watched their brutally honest exchange.

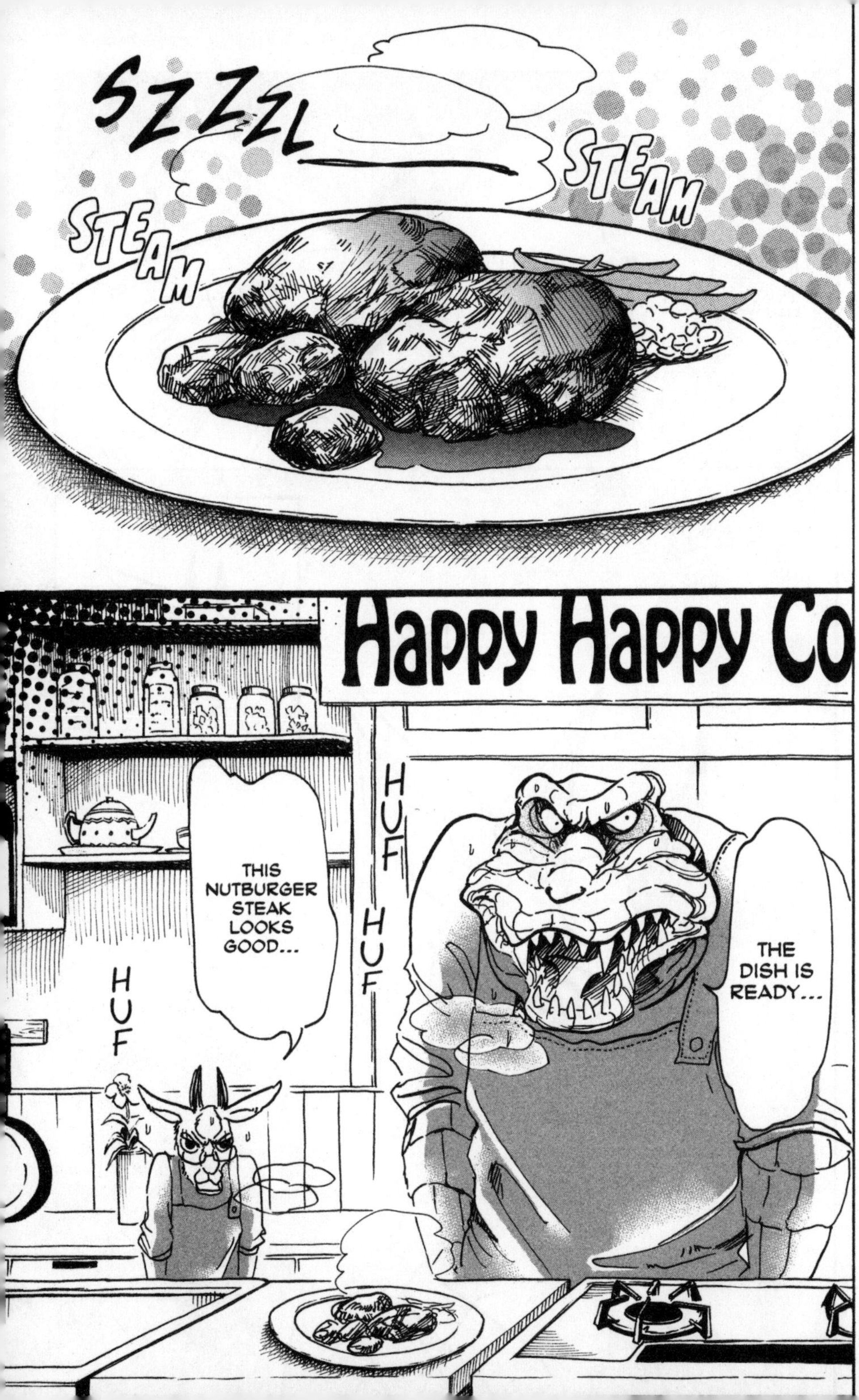
SZZZL
STEAM
STEAM
Happy Happy Co
THE DISH IS READY...
HUF
HUF
THIS NUTBURGER STEAK LOOKS GOOD...
HUF

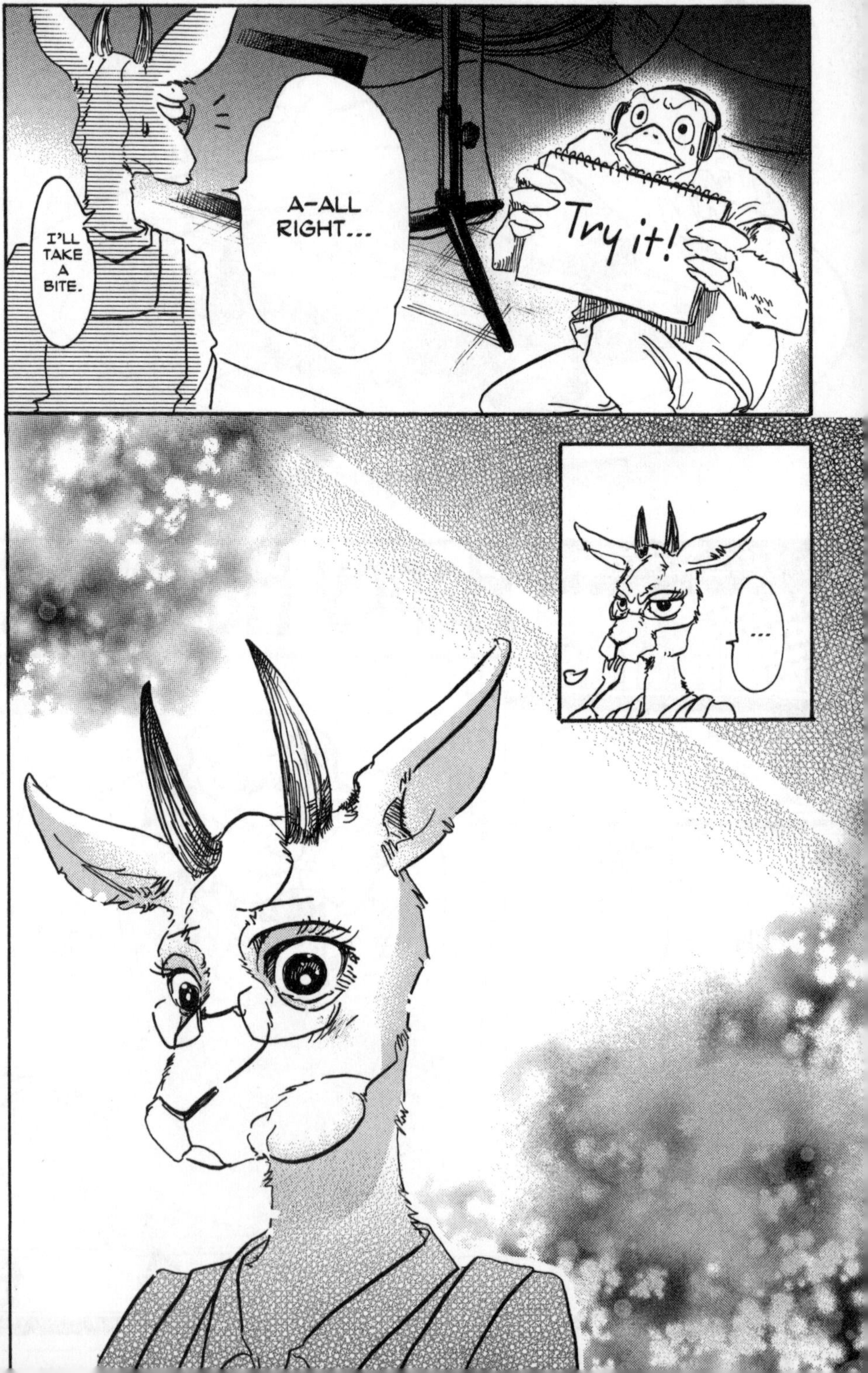
Try it!
A-ALL RIGHT...
I'LL TAKE A BITE.
...

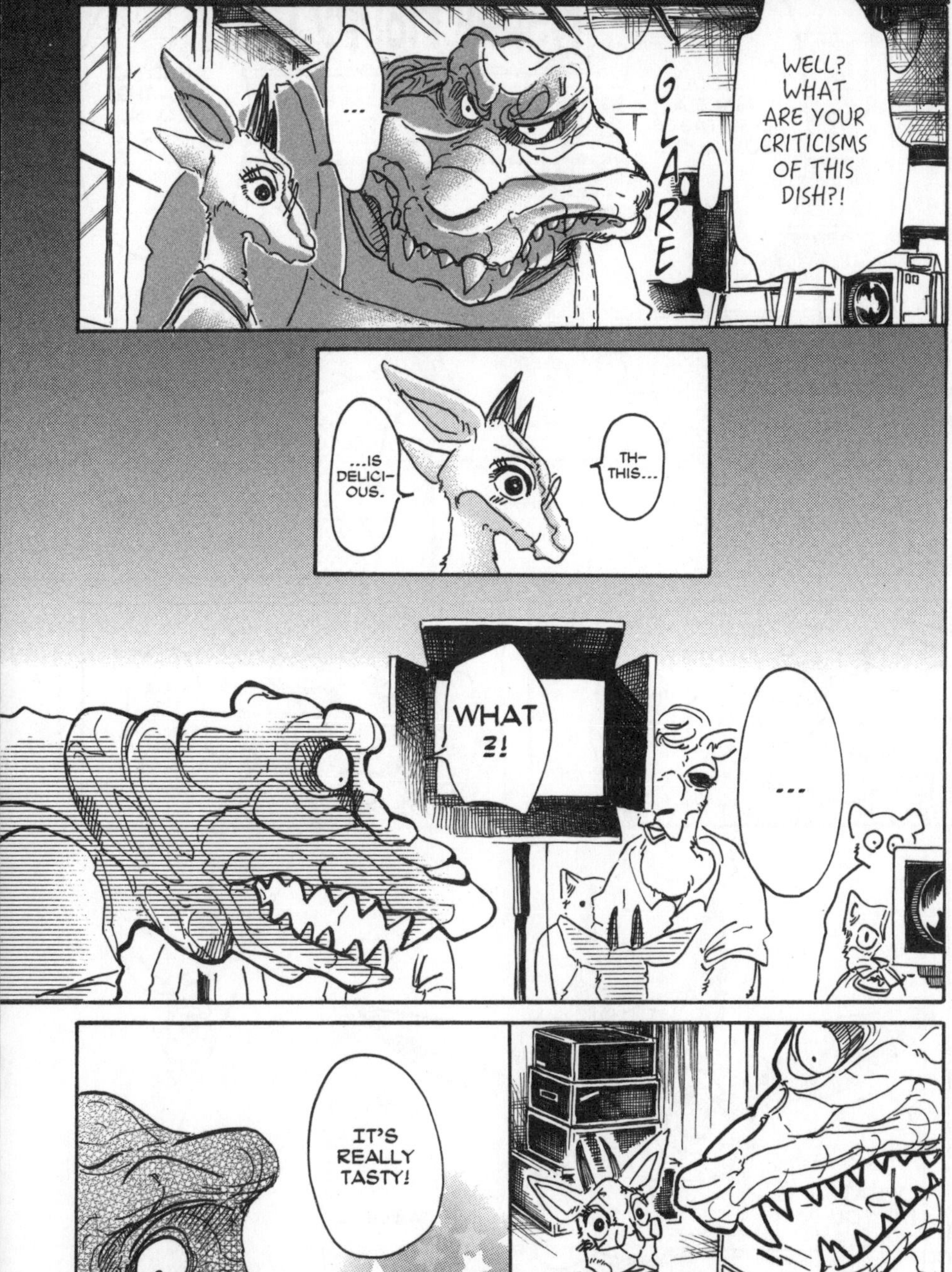
WELL? WHAT ARE YOUR CRITICISMS OF THIS DISH?!
GLARE
...
TH- THIS...
...IS DELICIOUS.
...
WHAT ?!
IT'S REALLY TASTY!

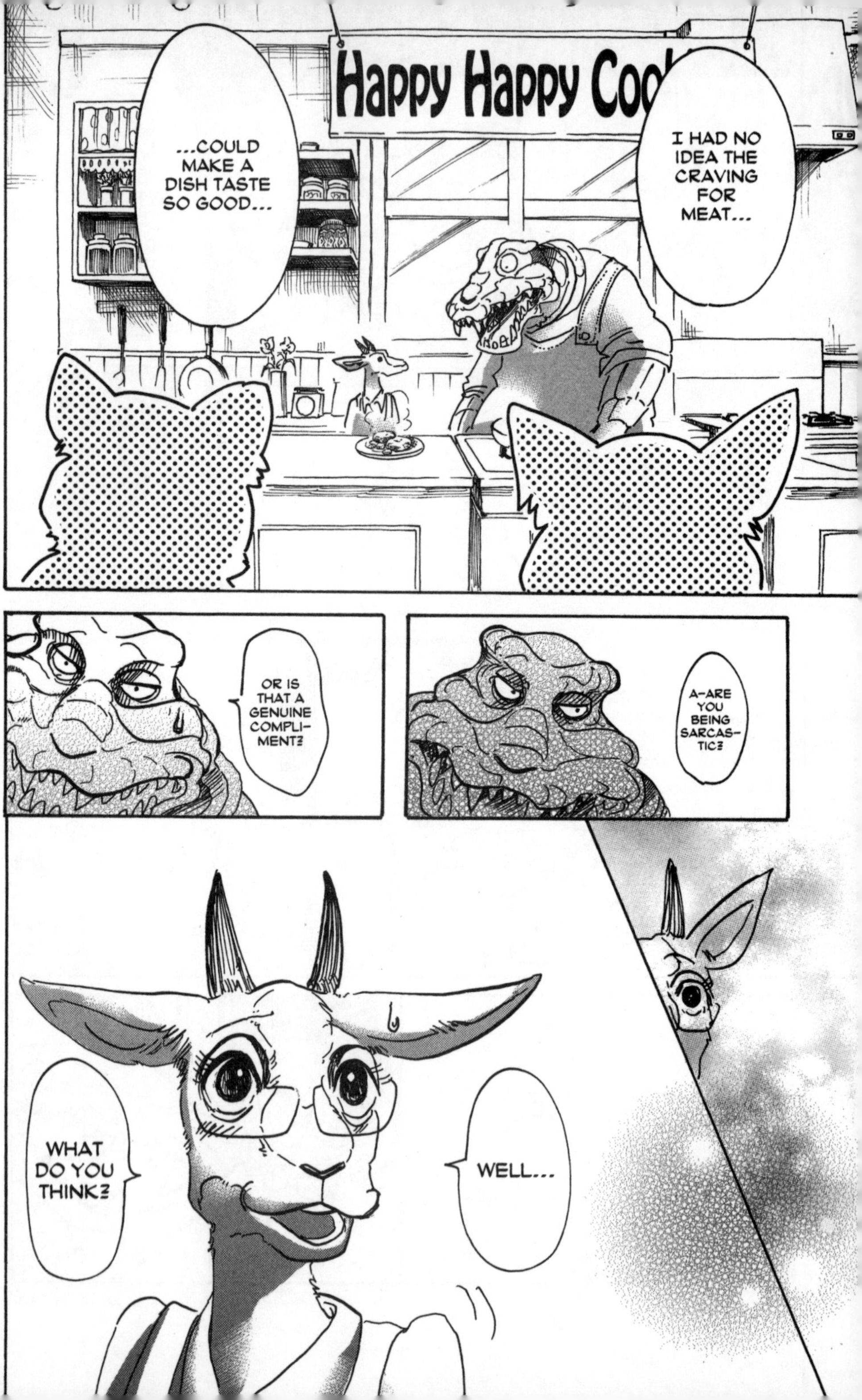
Happy Happy Coo
I HAD NO IDEA THE CRAVING FOR MEAT...
...COULD MAKE A DISH TASTE SO GOOD...
A-ARE YOU BEING SARCAS-TIC?
OR IS THAT A GENUINE COMPLI-MENT?
WELL...
WHAT DO YOU THINK?

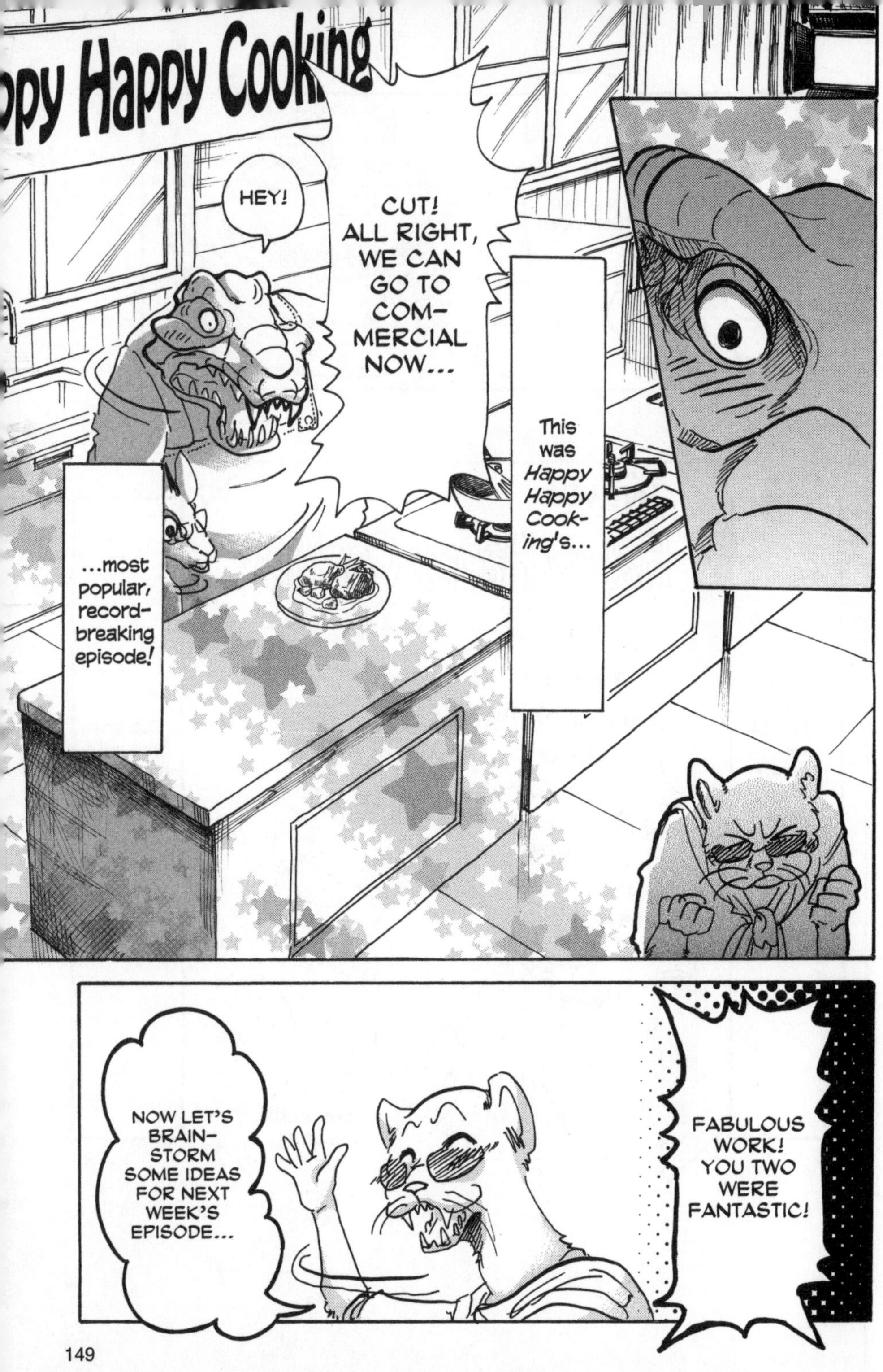
ppy Happy Cooking
CUT! ALL RIGHT, WE CAN GO TO COM-MERCIAL NOW...
HEY!
This was *Happy Happy Cook-ing*'s...
...most popular, record-breaking episode!
FABULOUS WORK! YOU TWO WERE FANTASTIC!
NOW LET'S BRAIN-STORM SOME IDEAS FOR NEXT WEEK'S EPISODE...

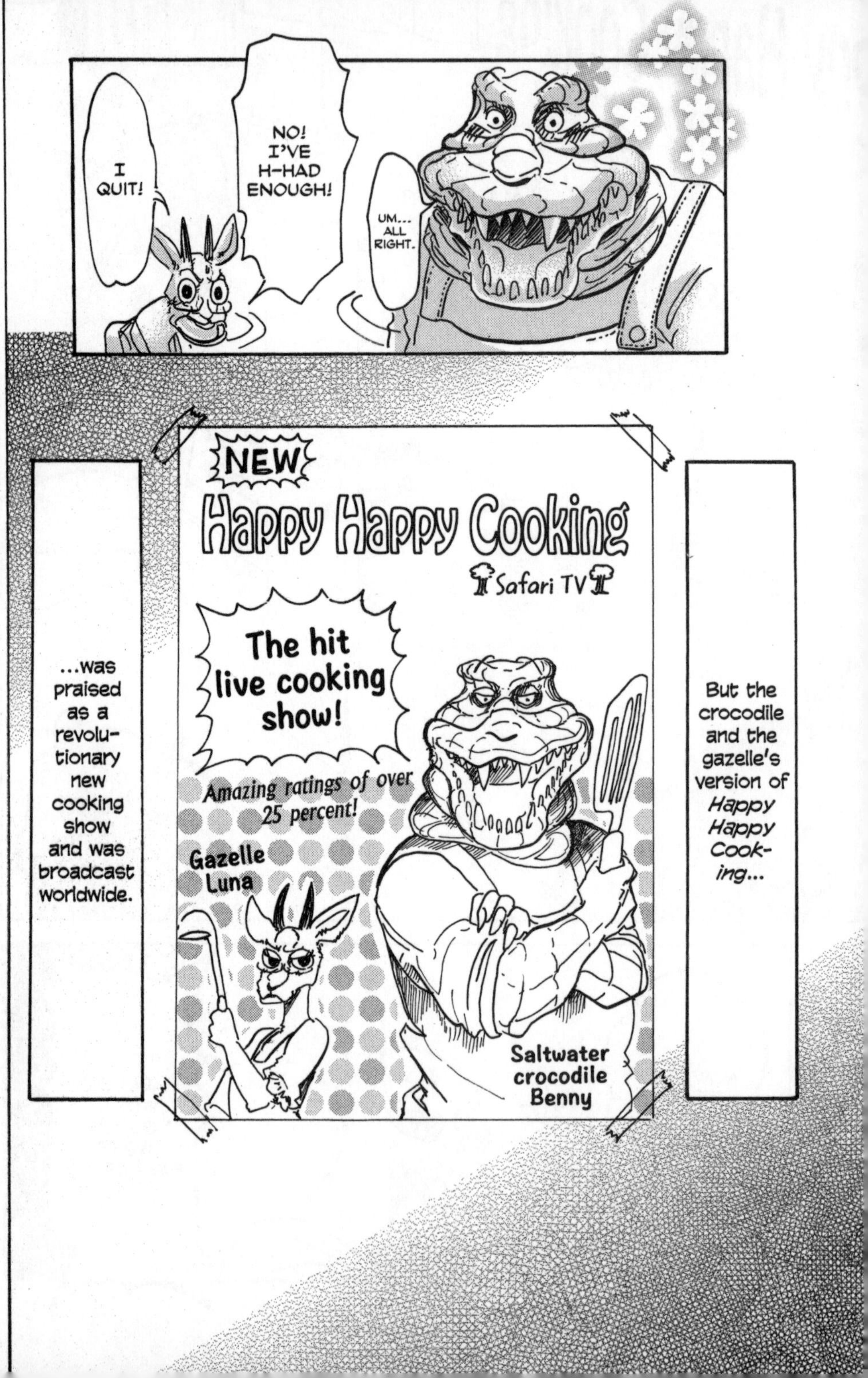
UM... ALL RIGHT.
NO! I'VE H-HAD ENOUGH!
I QUIT!
But the crocodile and the gazelle's version of *Happy Happy Cooking*...
NEW
Happy Happy Cooking
Safari TV
The hit live cooking show!
Amazing ratings of over 25 percent!
Saltwater crocodile Benny
Gazelle Luna
...was praised as a revolutionary new cooking show and was broadcast worldwide.

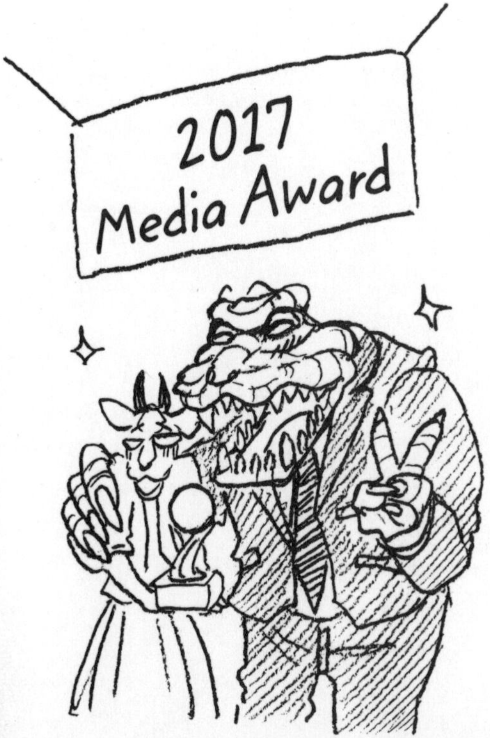
2017
Media Award

Story 6
The Fox and the Chameleon

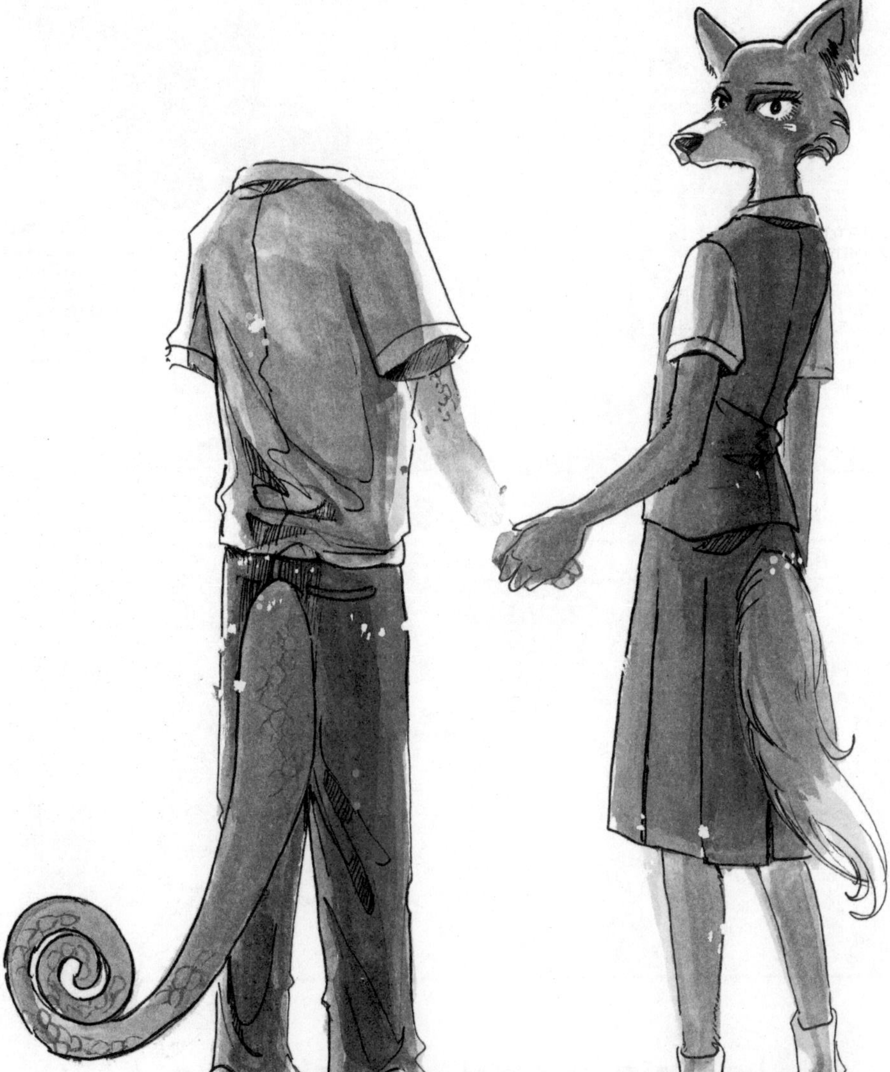

I'D LIKE A KIDNEY BEAN OMELET AND BREAD LUNCH BOX, PLEASE.
A LETTUCE SANDWICH WITH AN ASSORTMENT OF VEGETABLES ON THE SIDE FOR ME.
Herbiv
Carnivores

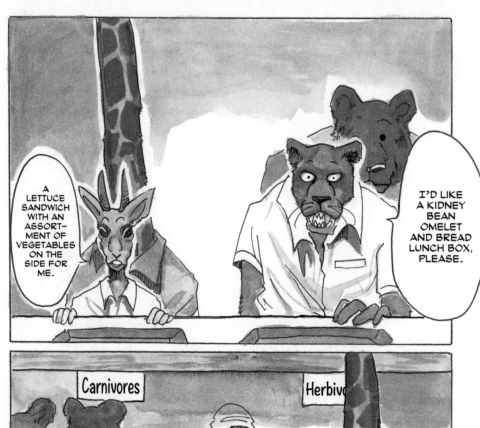

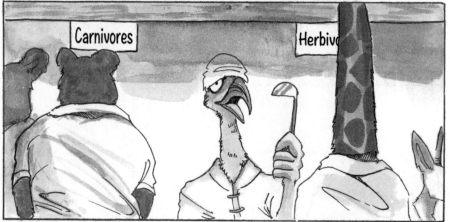

In this world, carnivores and herbivores coexist.

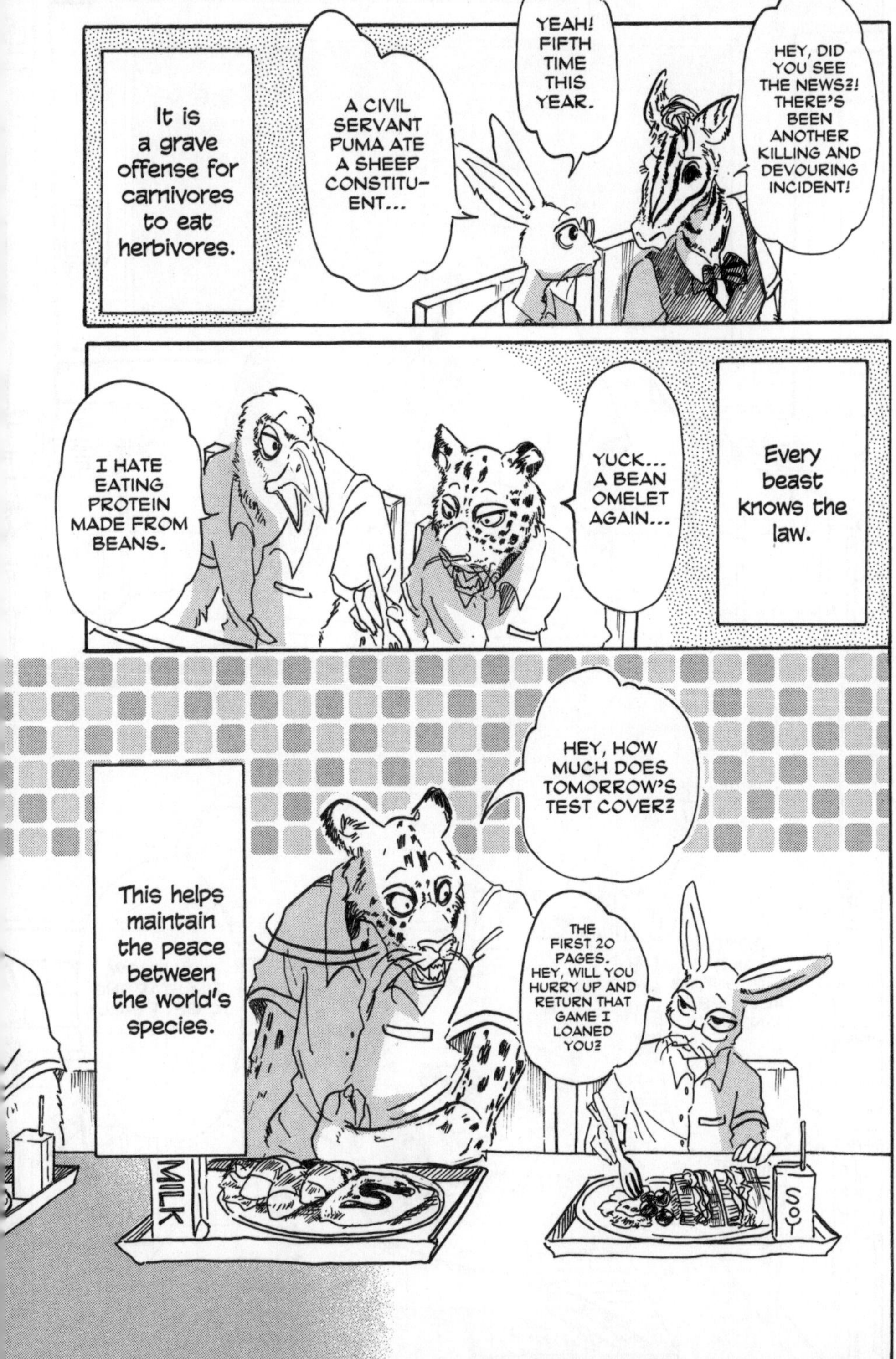
HEY, DID YOU SEE THE NEWS?! THERE'S BEEN ANOTHER KILLING AND DEVOURING INCIDENT!
YEAH! FIFTH TIME THIS YEAR.
A CIVIL SERVANT PUMA ATE A SHEEP CONSTITU-ENT...
It is a grave offense for carnivores to eat herbivores.
Every beast knows the law.
YUCK... A BEAN OMELET AGAIN...
I HATE EATING PROTEIN MADE FROM BEANS.
HEY, HOW MUCH DOES TOMORROW'S TEST COVER?
THE FIRST 20 PAGES. HEY, WILL YOU HURRY UP AND RETURN THAT GAME I LOANED YOU?
This helps maintain the peace between the world's species.
SOY
MILK

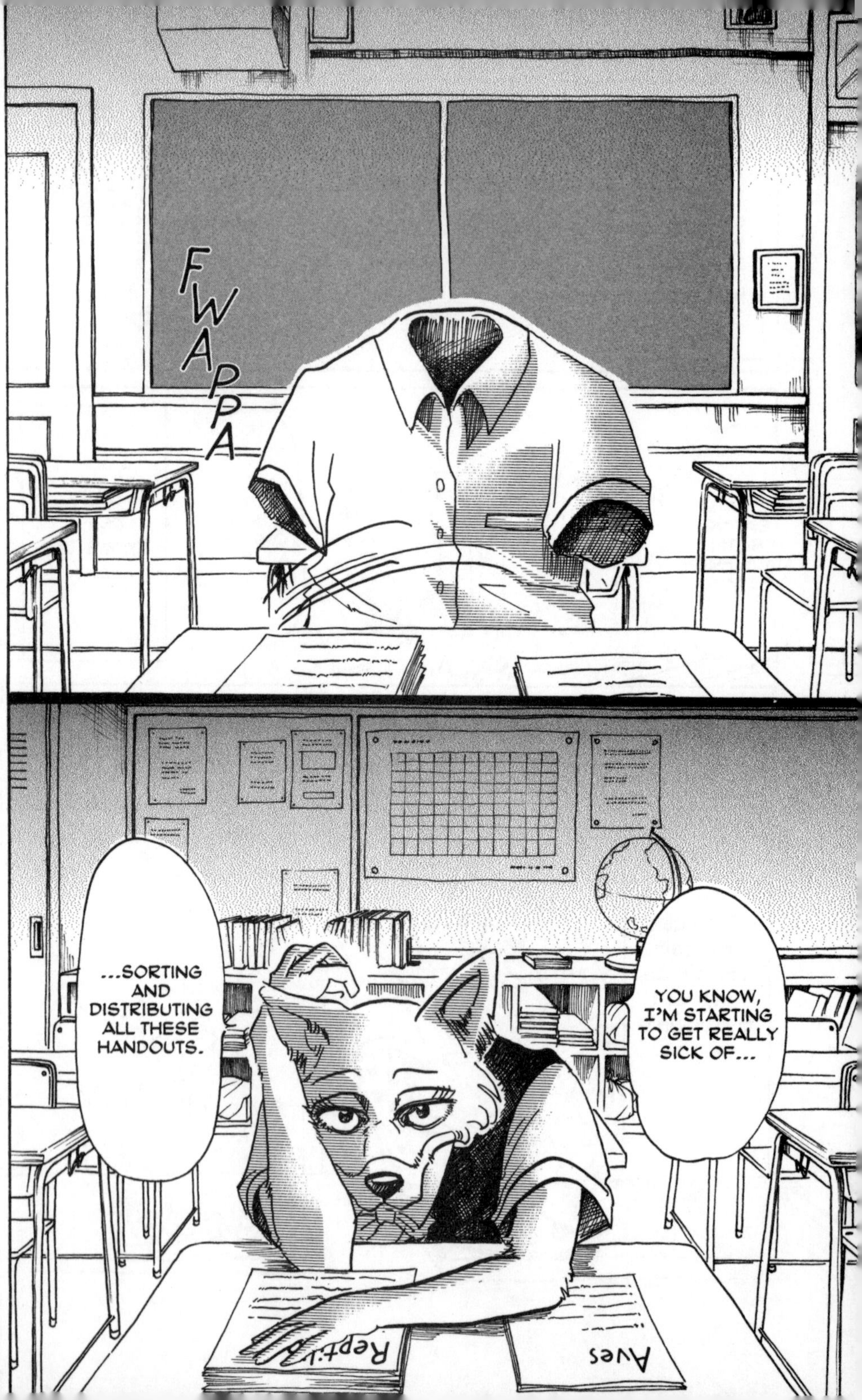
FWAPPA
YOU KNOW, I'M STARTING TO GET REALLY SICK OF...
...SORTING AND DISTRIBUTING ALL THESE HANDOUTS.
Aves

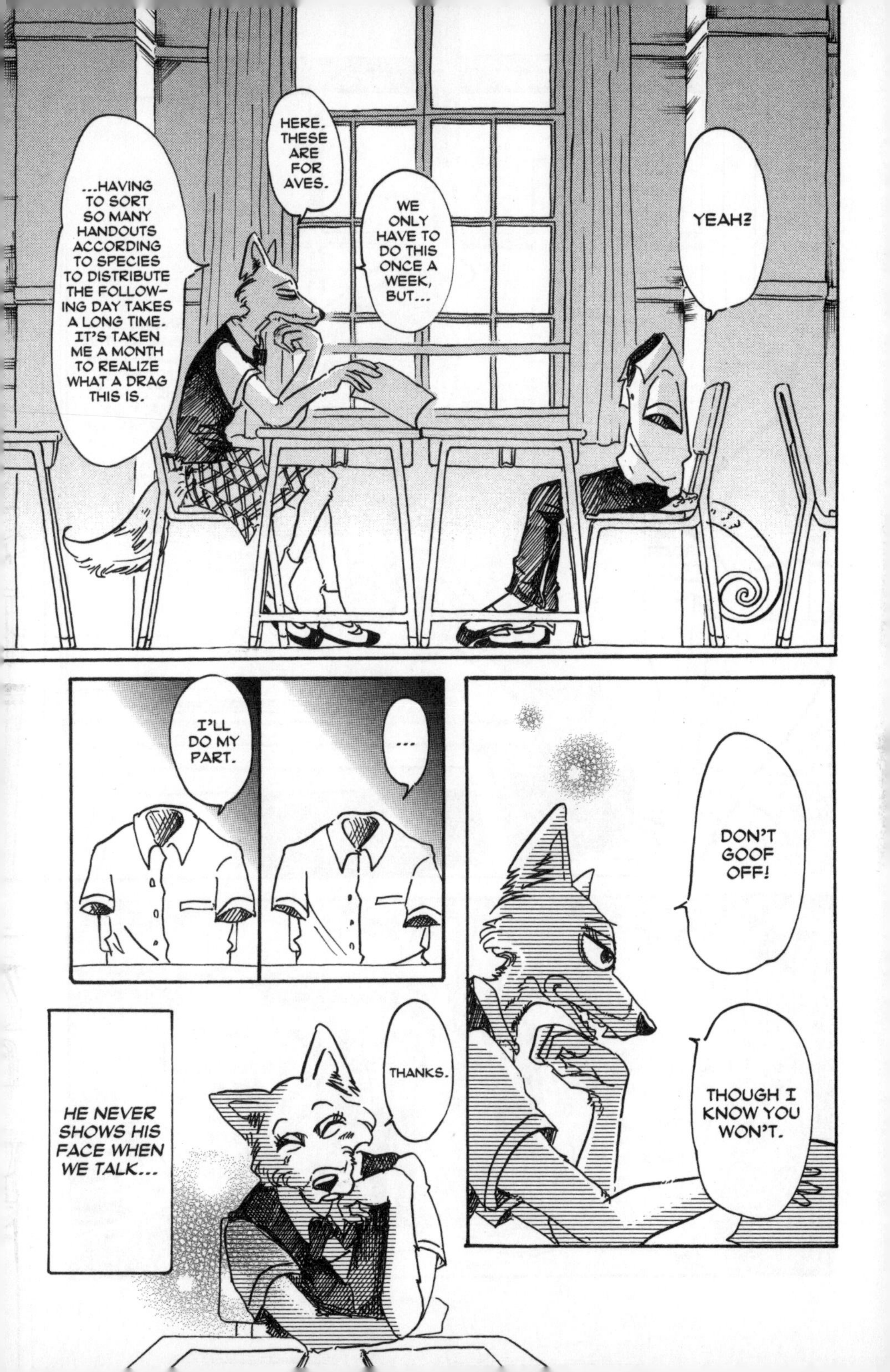
HERE. THESE ARE FOR AVES.
YEAH?
WE ONLY HAVE TO DO THIS ONCE A WEEK, BUT...
...HAVING TO SORT SO MANY HANDOUTS ACCORDING TO SPECIES TO DISTRIBUTE THE FOLLOWING DAY TAKES A LONG TIME. IT'S TAKEN ME A MONTH TO REALIZE WHAT A DRAG THIS IS.
DON'T GOOF OFF!
THOUGH I KNOW YOU WON'T.
...
I'LL DO MY PART.
THANKS.
HE NEVER SHOWS HIS FACE WHEN WE TALK...

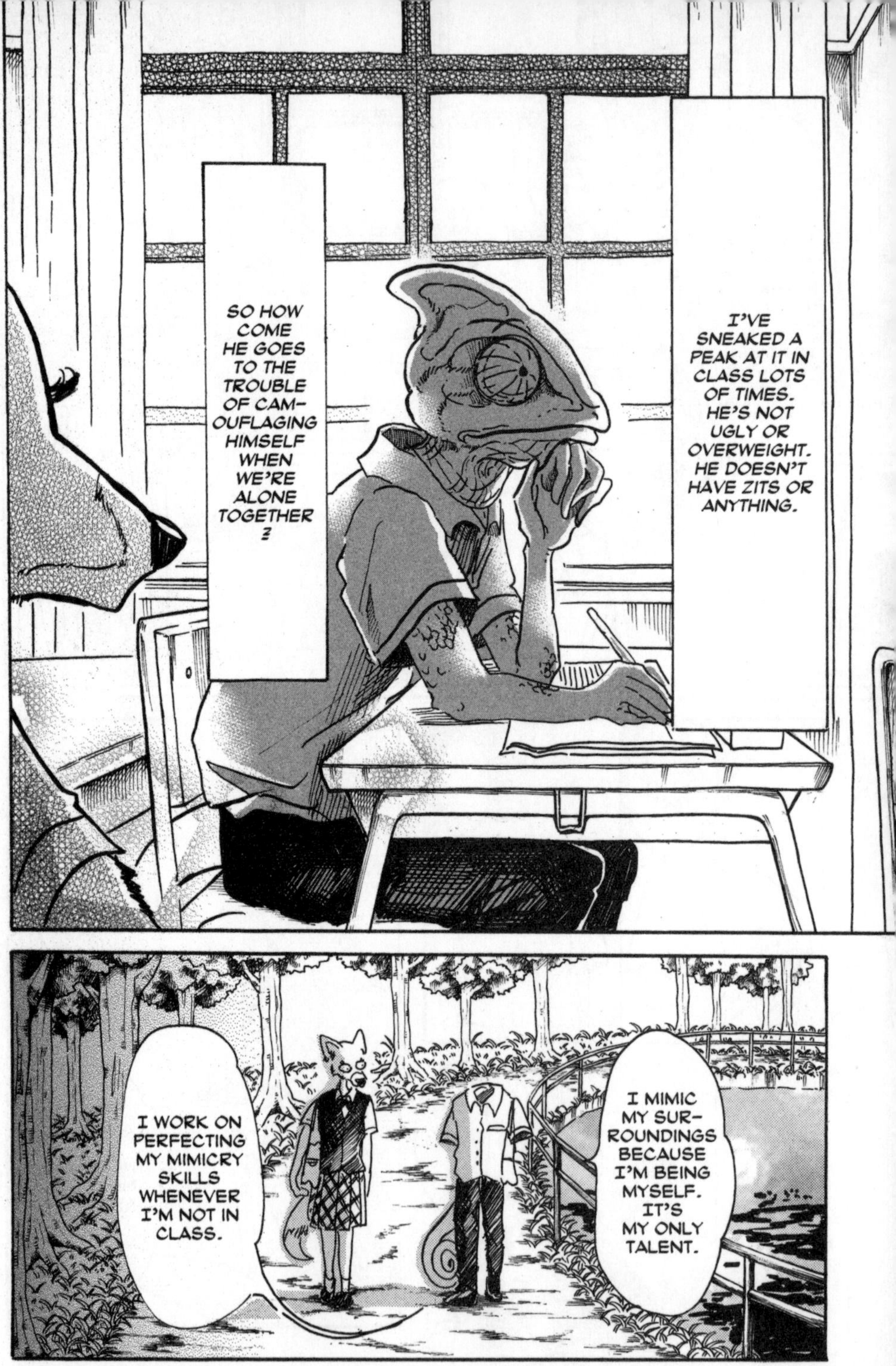
I'VE SNEAKED A PEAK AT IT IN CLASS LOTS OF TIMES. HE'S NOT UGLY OR OVERWEIGHT. HE DOESN'T HAVE ZITS OR ANYTHING.
SO HOW COME HE GOES TO THE TROUBLE OF CAM-OUFLAGING HIMSELF WHEN WE'RE ALONE TOGETHER ?
I MIMIC MY SUR-ROUNDINGS BECAUSE I'M BEING MYSELF. IT'S MY ONLY TALENT.
I WORK ON PERFECTING MY MIMICRY SKILLS WHENEVER I'M NOT IN CLASS.

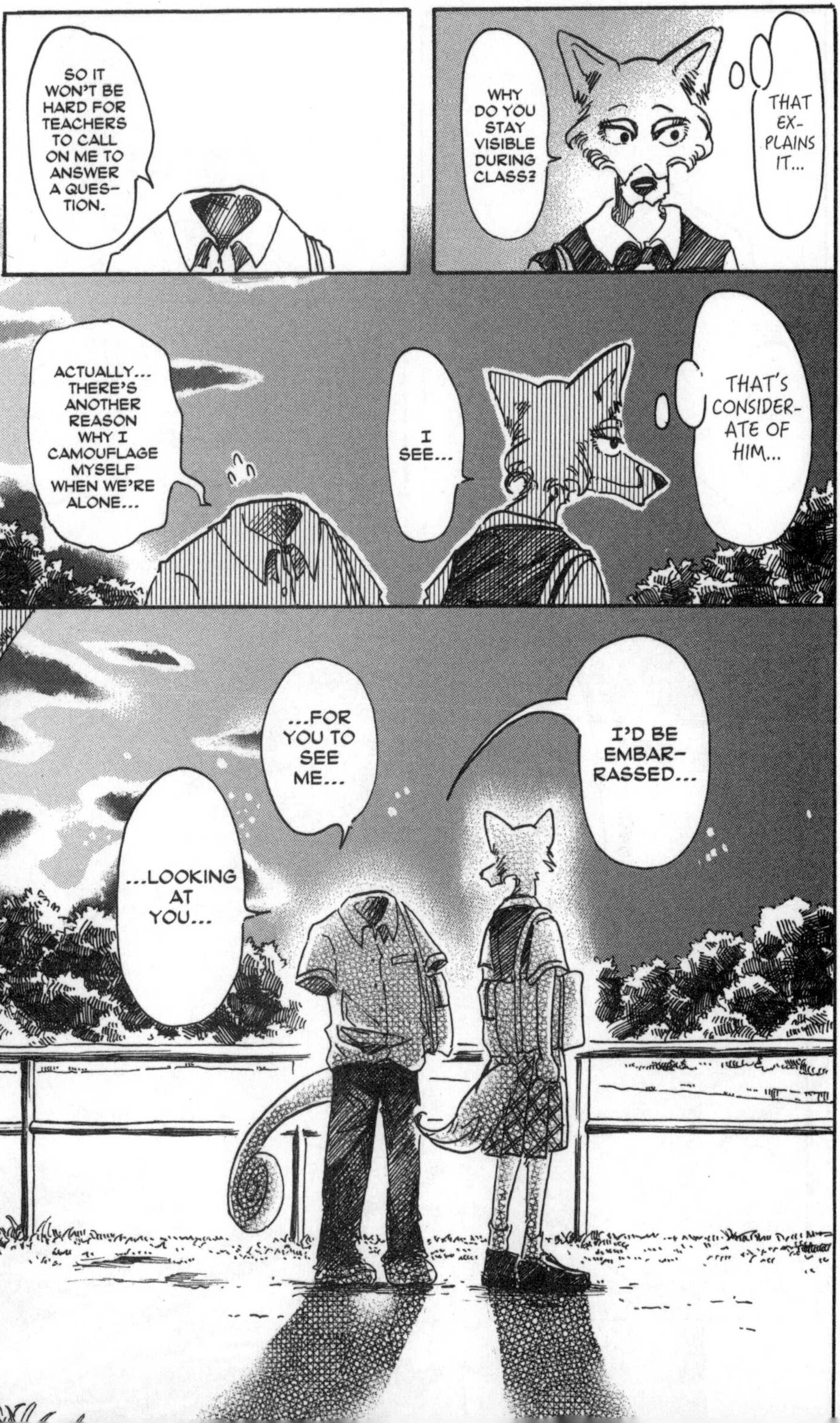
THAT EX-PLAINS IT...
WHY DO YOU STAY VISIBLE DURING CLASS?
SO IT WON'T BE HARD FOR TEACHERS TO CALL ON ME TO ANSWER A QUES-TION.
THAT'S CONSIDER-ATE OF HIM...
I SEE...
ACTUALLY... THERE'S ANOTHER REASON WHY I CAMOUFLAGE MYSELF WHEN WE'RE ALONE...
I'D BE EMBAR-RASSED...
...FOR YOU TO SEE ME...
...LOOKING AT YOU...

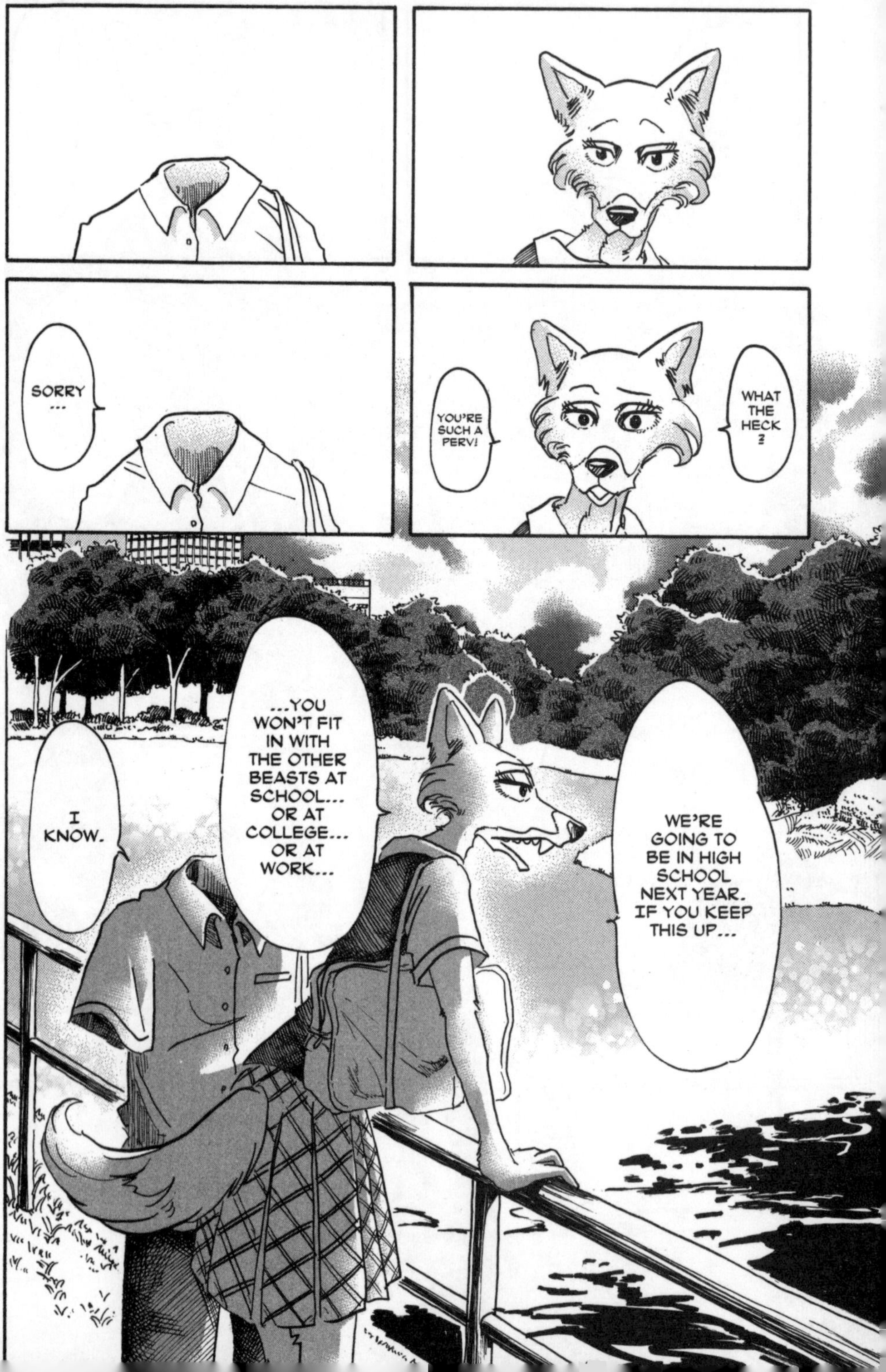
WHAT THE HECK?
YOU'RE SUCH A PERV!
SORRY...
WE'RE GOING TO BE IN HIGH SCHOOL NEXT YEAR. IF YOU KEEP THIS UP...
...YOU WON'T FIT IN WITH THE OTHER BEASTS AT SCHOOL... OR AT COLLEGE... OR AT WORK...
I KNOW.

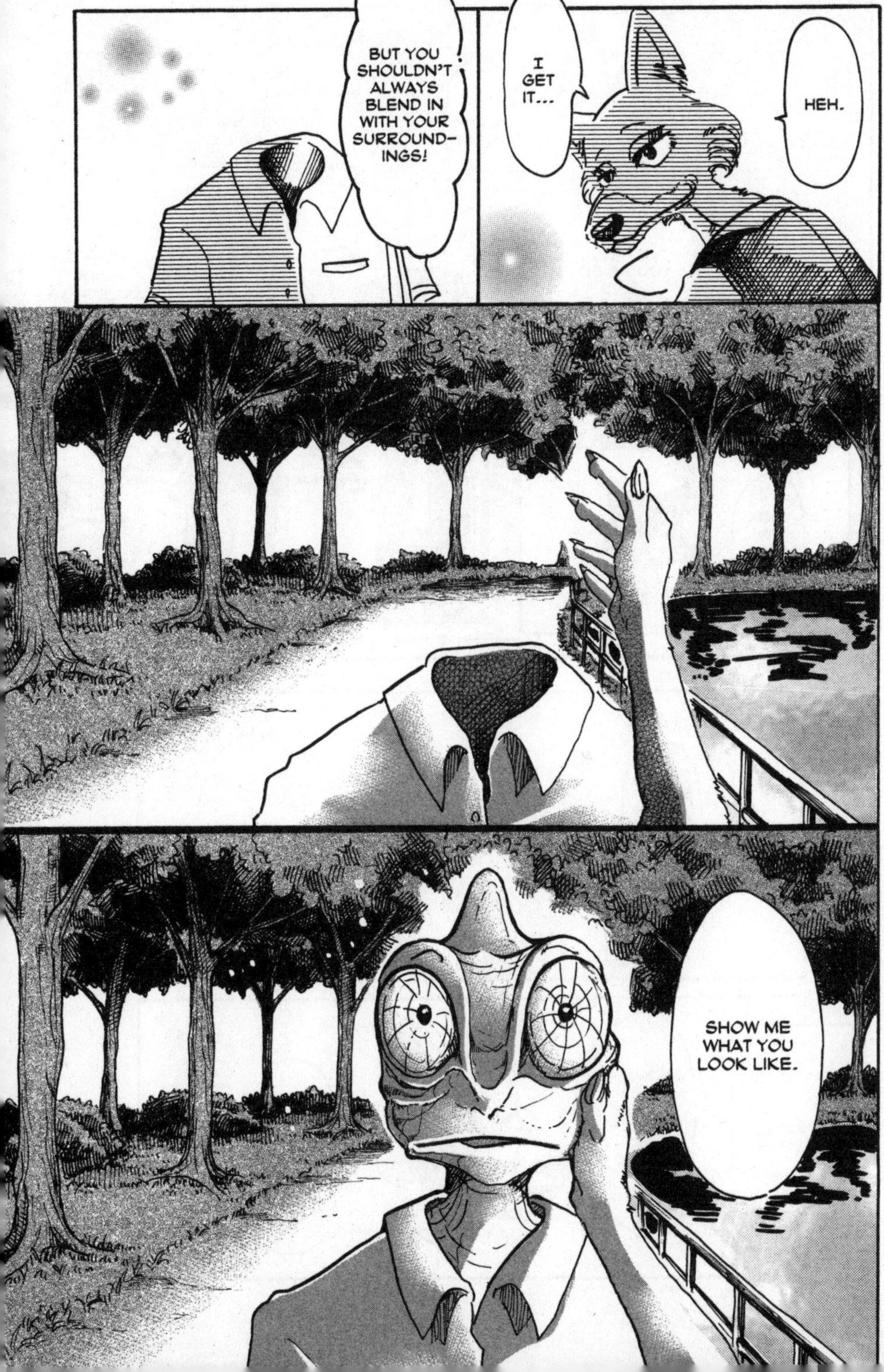
HEH.
I GET IT...
BUT YOU SHOULDN'T ALWAYS BLEND IN WITH YOUR SURROUNDINGS!
SHOW ME WHAT YOU LOOK LIKE.

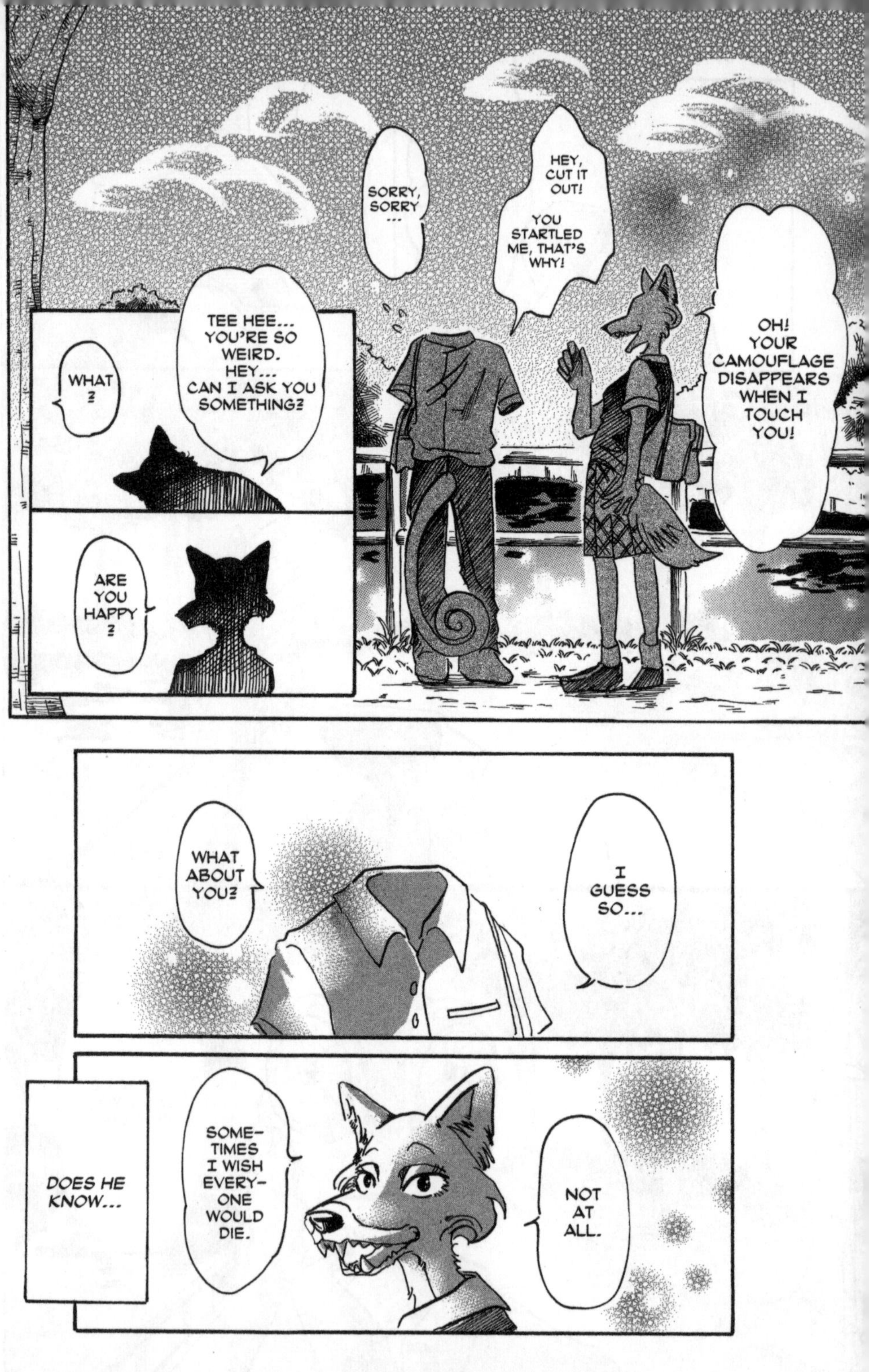
OH! YOUR CAMOUFLAGE DISAPPEARS WHEN I TOUCH YOU!
HEY, CUT IT OUT!
YOU STARTLED ME, THAT'S WHY!
SORRY, SORRY ...
TEE HEE... YOU'RE SO WEIRD. HEY... CAN I ASK YOU SOMETHING?
WHAT?
ARE YOU HAPPY?
I GUESS SO...
WHAT ABOUT YOU?
NOT AT ALL.
SOMETIMES I WISH EVERYONE WOULD DIE.
DOES HE KNOW...

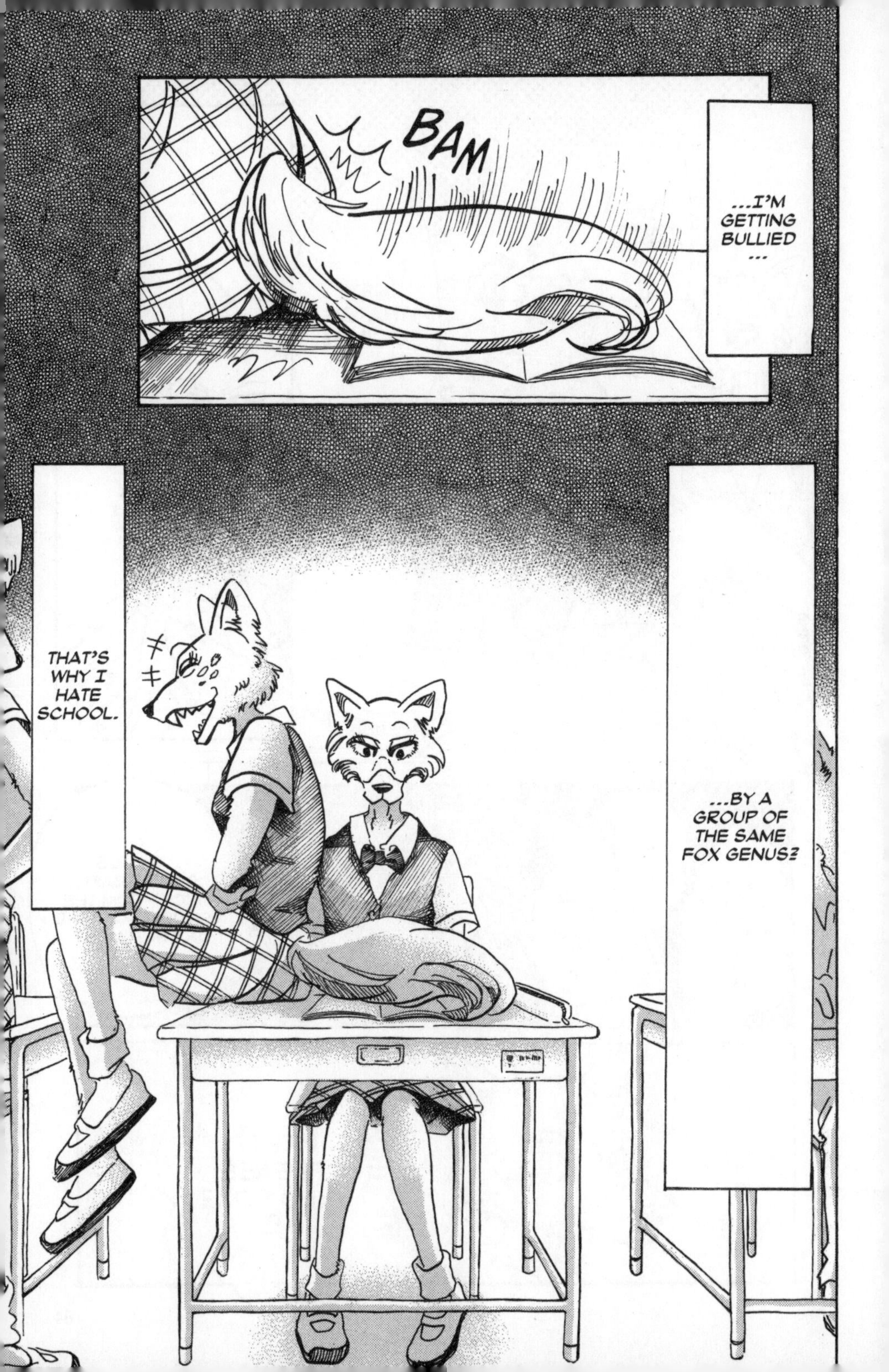
...I'M GETTING BULLIED ...
BAM
...BY A GROUP OF THE SAME FOX GENUS?
キキ
THAT'S WHY I HATE SCHOOL.

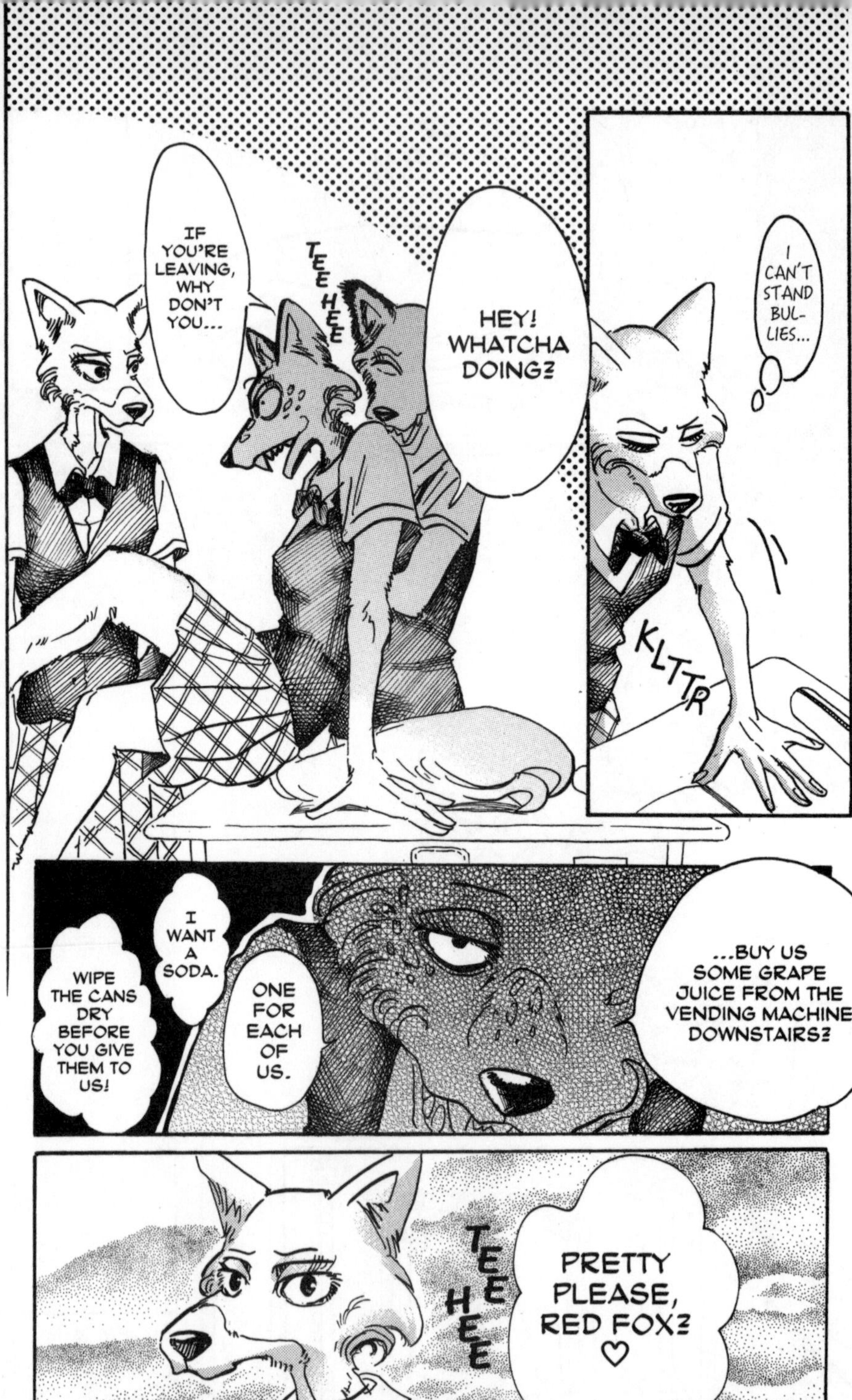
I CAN'T STAND BULLIES...
KLTTR
HEY! WHATCHA DOING?
TEE HEE
IF YOU'RE LEAVING, WHY DON'T YOU...
...BUY US SOME GRAPE JUICE FROM THE VENDING MACHINE DOWNSTAIRS?
ONE FOR EACH OF US.
I WANT A SODA.
WIPE THE CANS DRY BEFORE YOU GIVE THEM TO US!
PRETTY PLEASE, RED FOX? ♡
TEE HEE

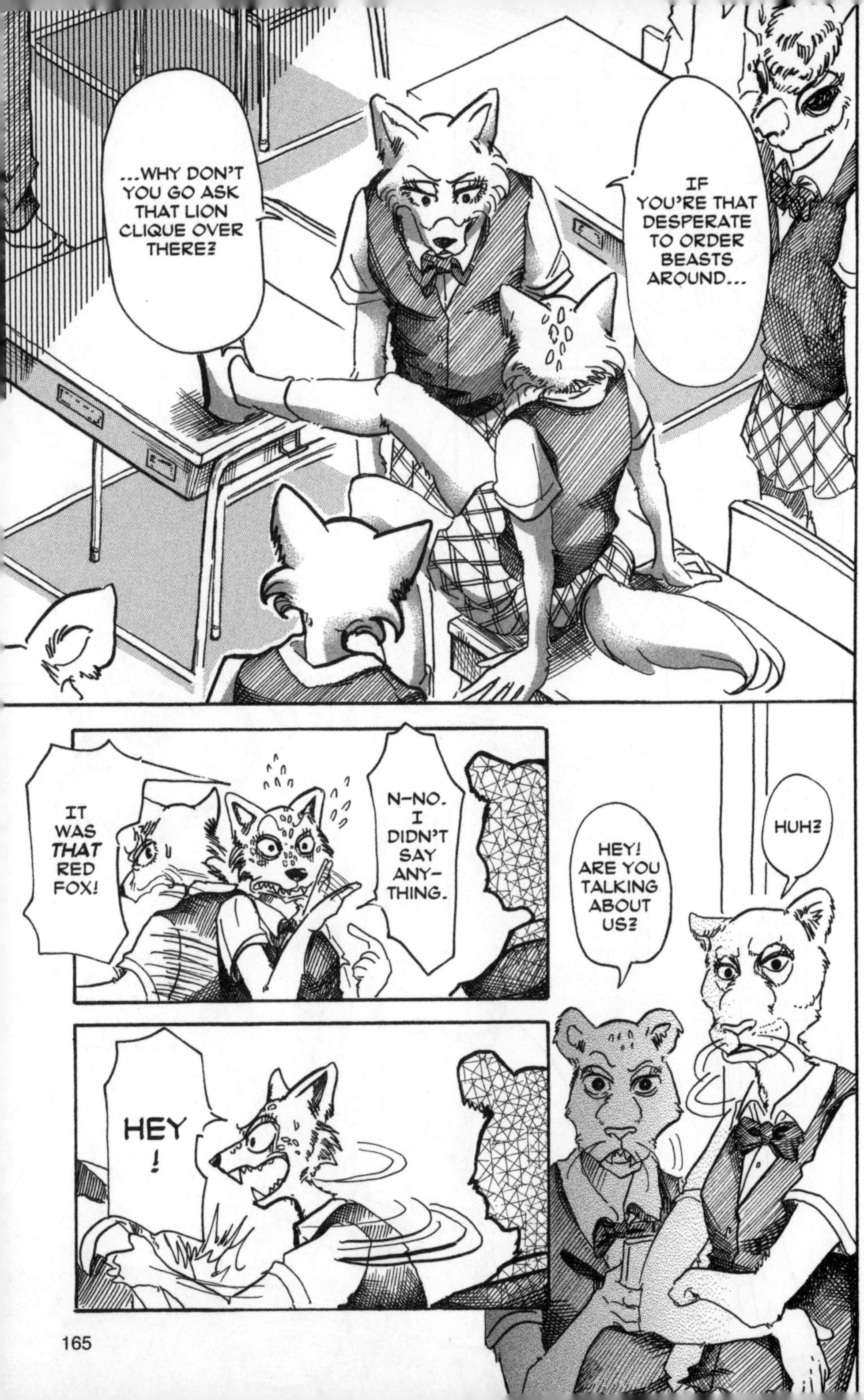
IF YOU'RE THAT DESPERATE TO ORDER BEASTS AROUND...
...WHY DON'T YOU GO ASK THAT LION CLIQUE OVER THERE?
HUH?
HEY! ARE YOU TALKING ABOUT US?
N-NO. I DIDN'T SAY ANY-THING.
IT WAS *THAT* RED FOX!
HEY!

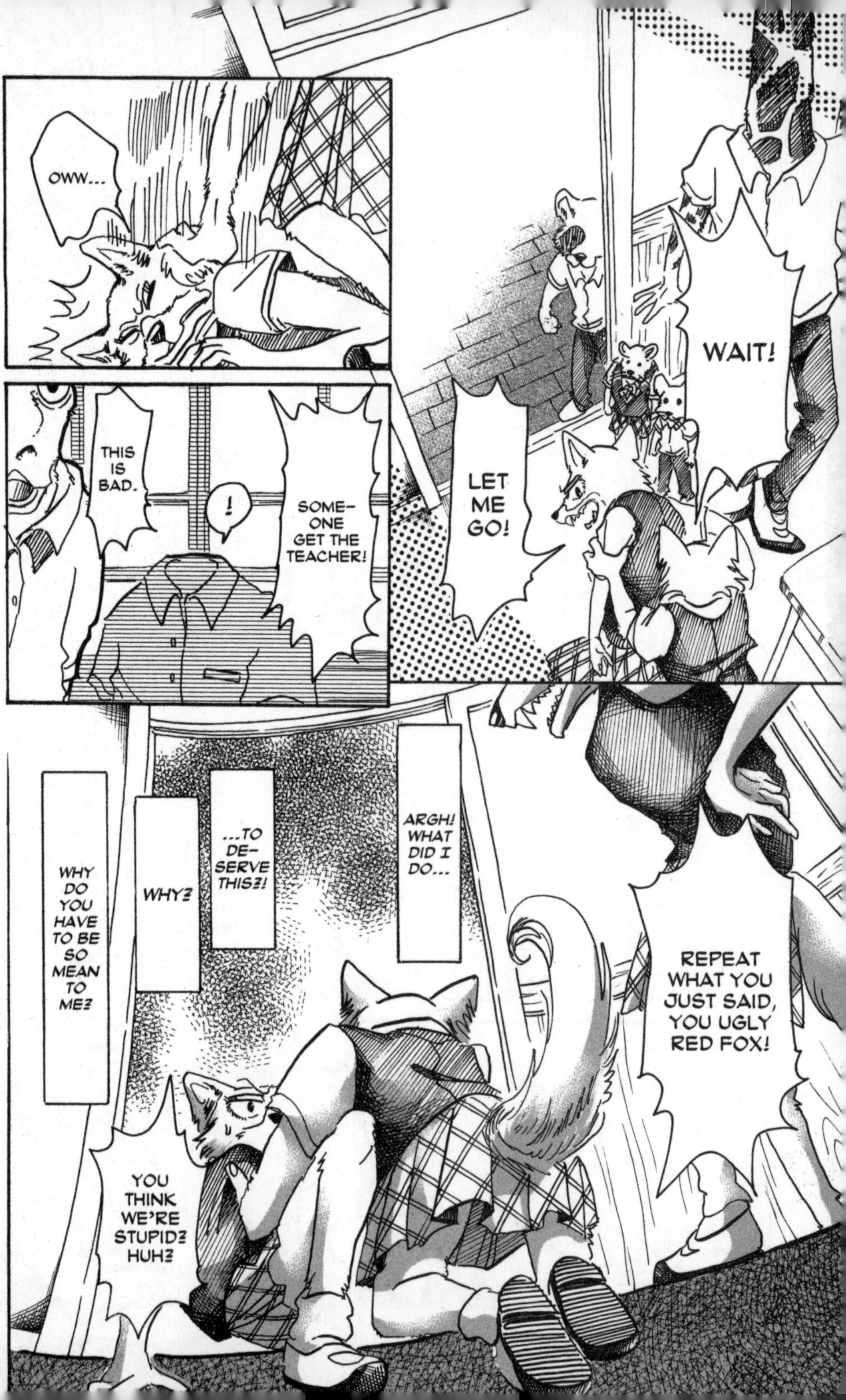
WAIT!
LET ME GO!
OWW...
SOME-ONE GET THE TEACHER!
!
THIS IS BAD.
REPEAT WHAT YOU JUST SAID, YOU UGLY RED FOX!
ARGH! WHAT DID I DO...
...TO DE-SERVE THIS?!
WHY?
WHY DO YOU HAVE TO BE SO MEAN TO ME?
YOU THINK WE'RE STUPID? HUH?

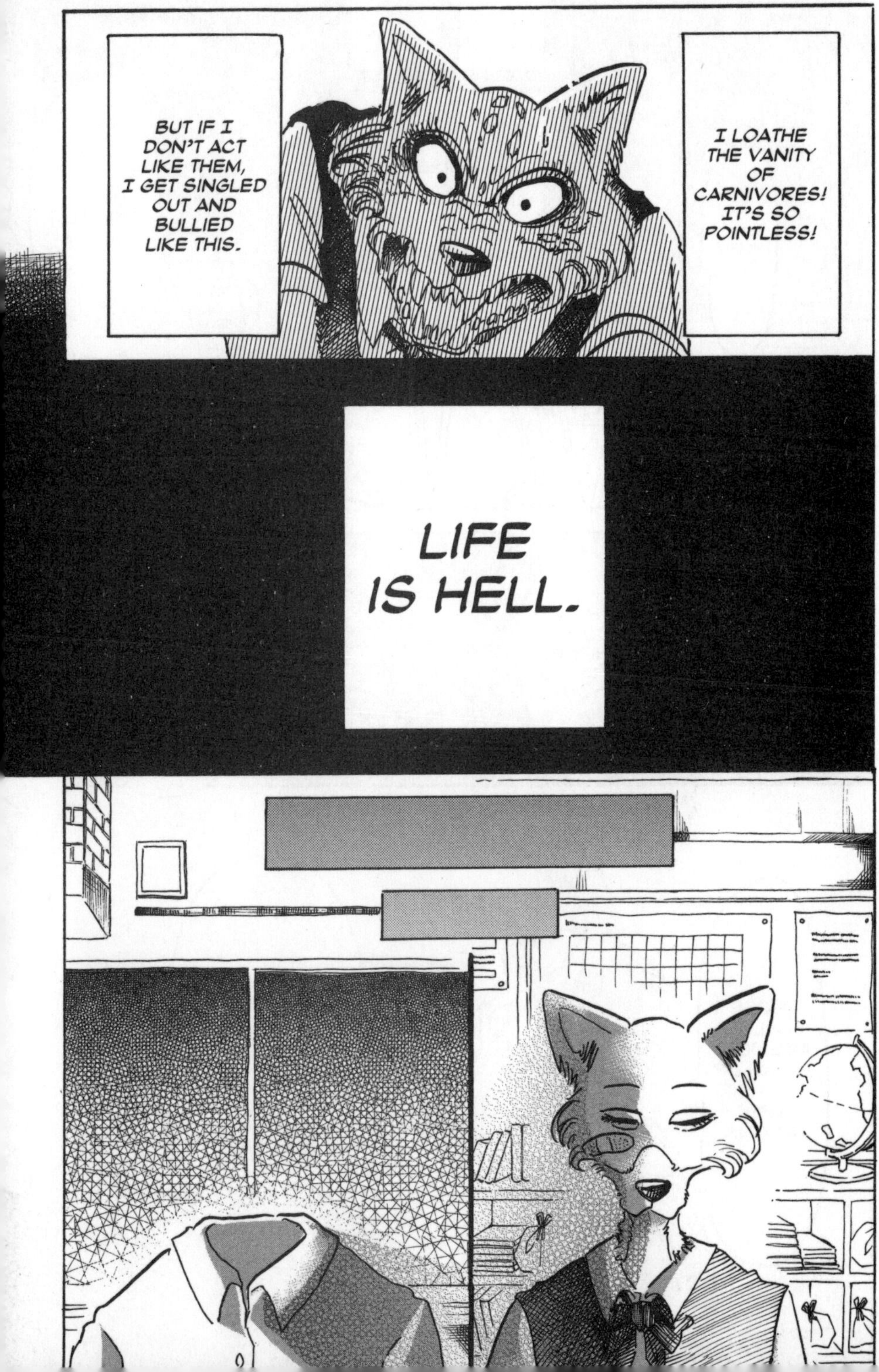
I LOATHE THE VANITY OF CARNIVORES! IT'S SO POINTLESS!
BUT IF I DON'T ACT LIKE THEM, I GET SINGLED OUT AND BULLIED LIKE THIS.
LIFE IS HELL.

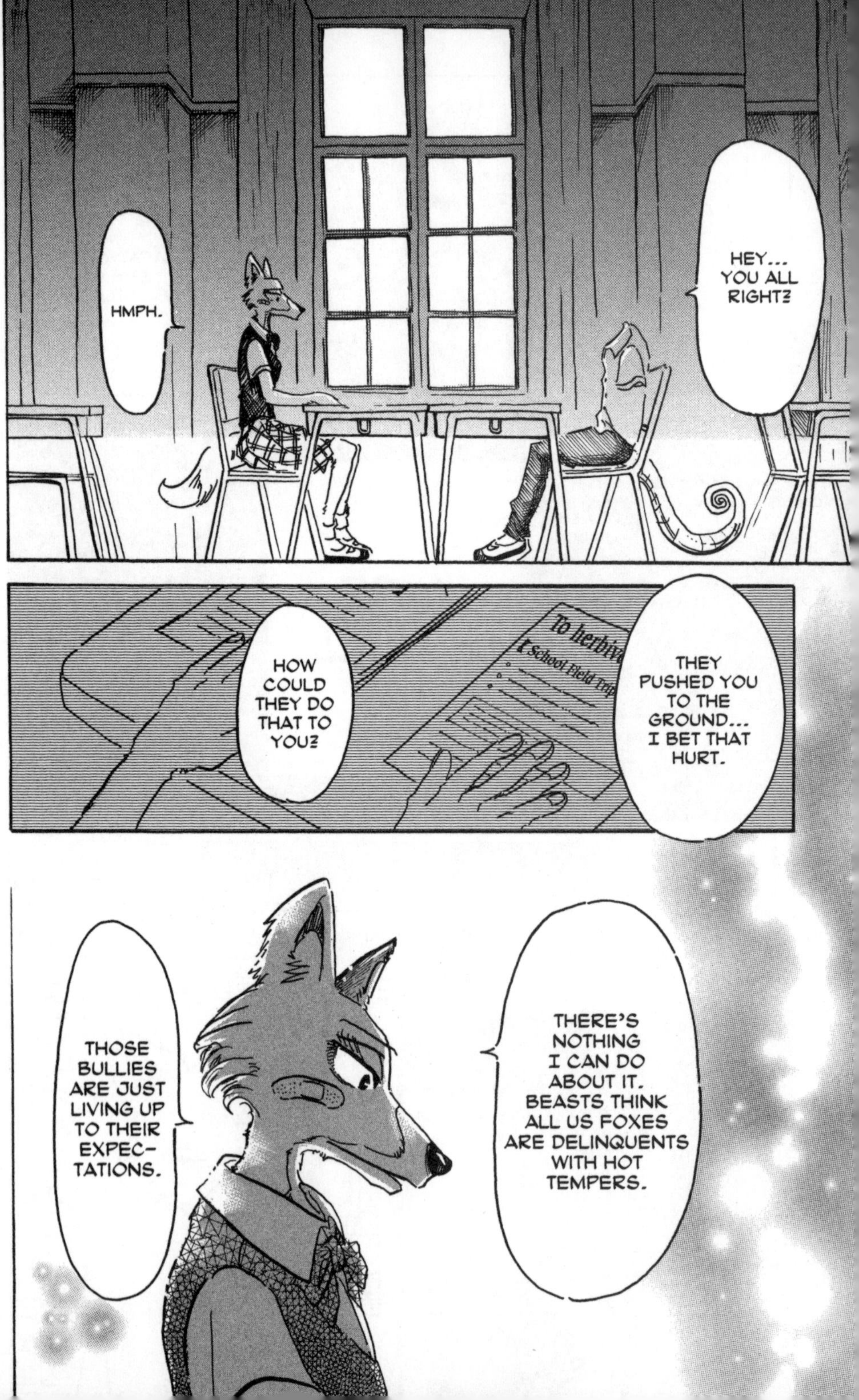
HEY... YOU ALL RIGHT?
HMPH.
THEY PUSHED YOU TO THE GROUND... I BET THAT HURT.
HOW COULD THEY DO THAT TO YOU?
THERE'S NOTHING I CAN DO ABOUT IT. BEASTS THINK ALL US FOXES ARE DELINQUENTS WITH HOT TEMPERS.
THOSE BULLIES ARE JUST LIVING UP TO THEIR EXPECTATIONS.

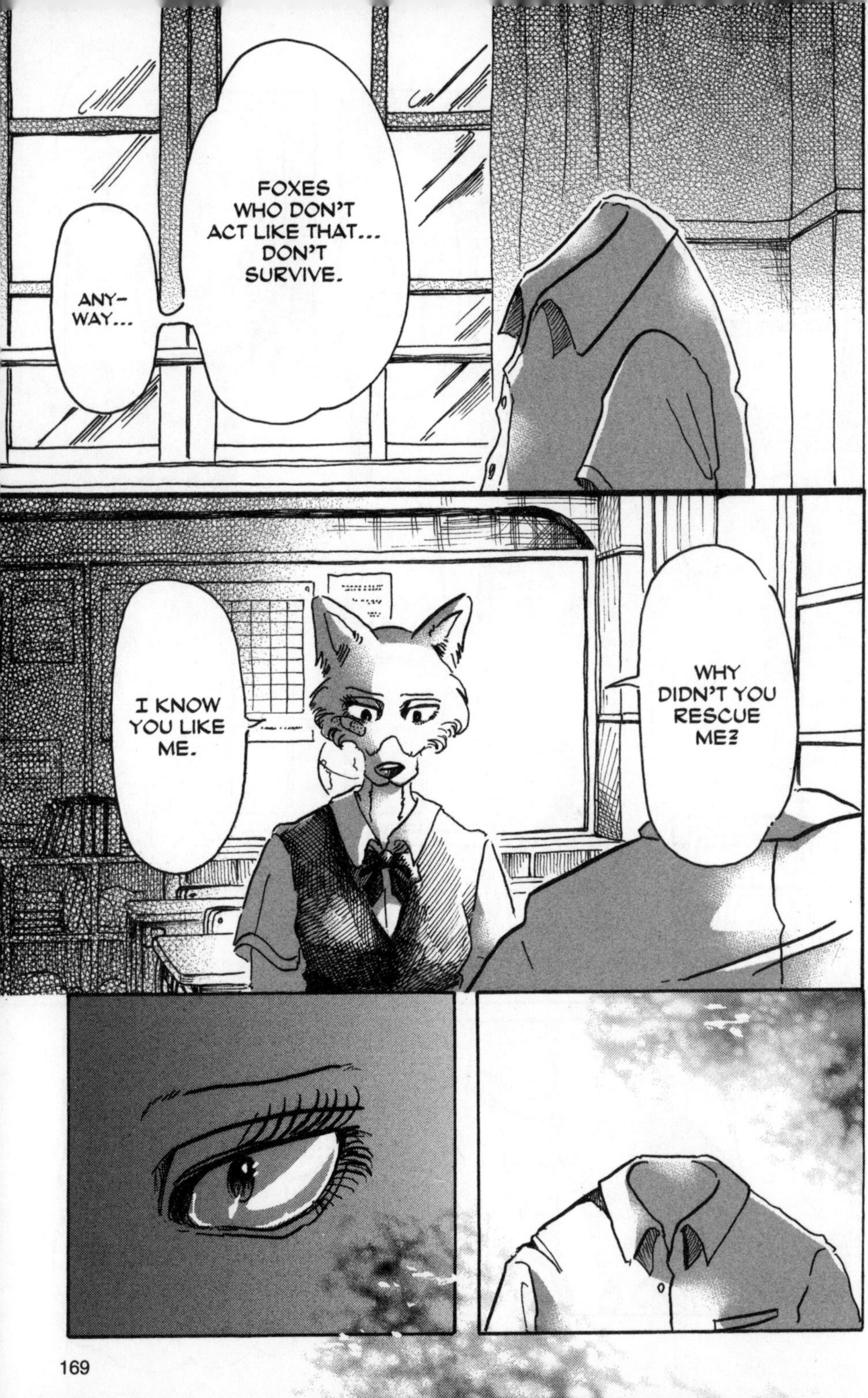
FOXES WHO DON'T ACT LIKE THAT... DON'T SURVIVE.
ANY-WAY...
WHY DIDN'T YOU RESCUE ME?
I KNOW YOU LIKE ME.

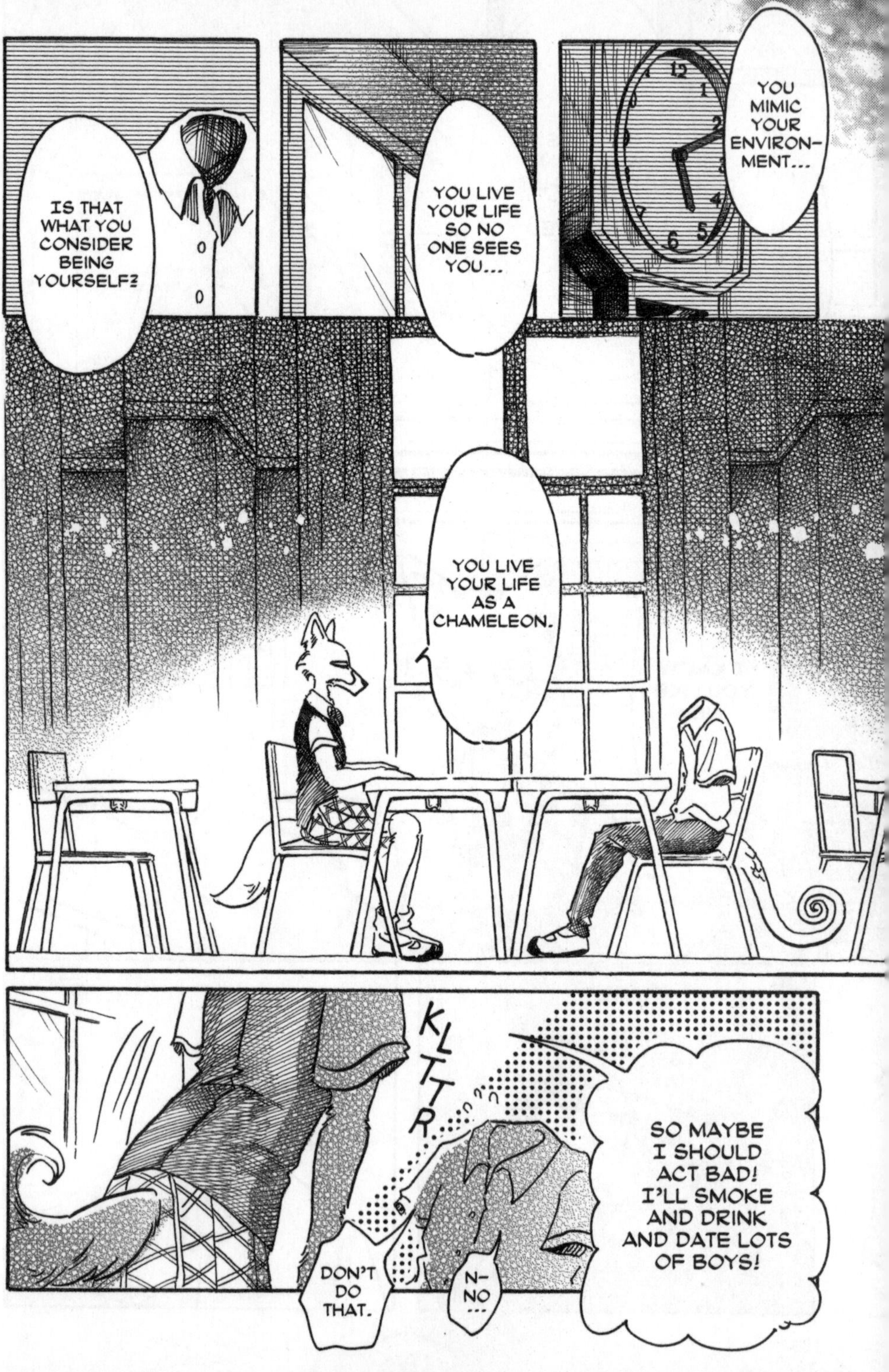
YOU MIMIC YOUR ENVIRONMENT...
YOU LIVE YOUR LIFE SO NO ONE SEES YOU...
IS THAT WHAT YOU CONSIDER BEING YOURSELF?
YOU LIVE YOUR LIFE AS A CHAMELEON.
SO MAYBE I SHOULD ACT BAD! I'LL SMOKE AND DRINK AND DATE LOTS OF BOYS!
KLTTR
N-NO...
DON'T DO THAT.

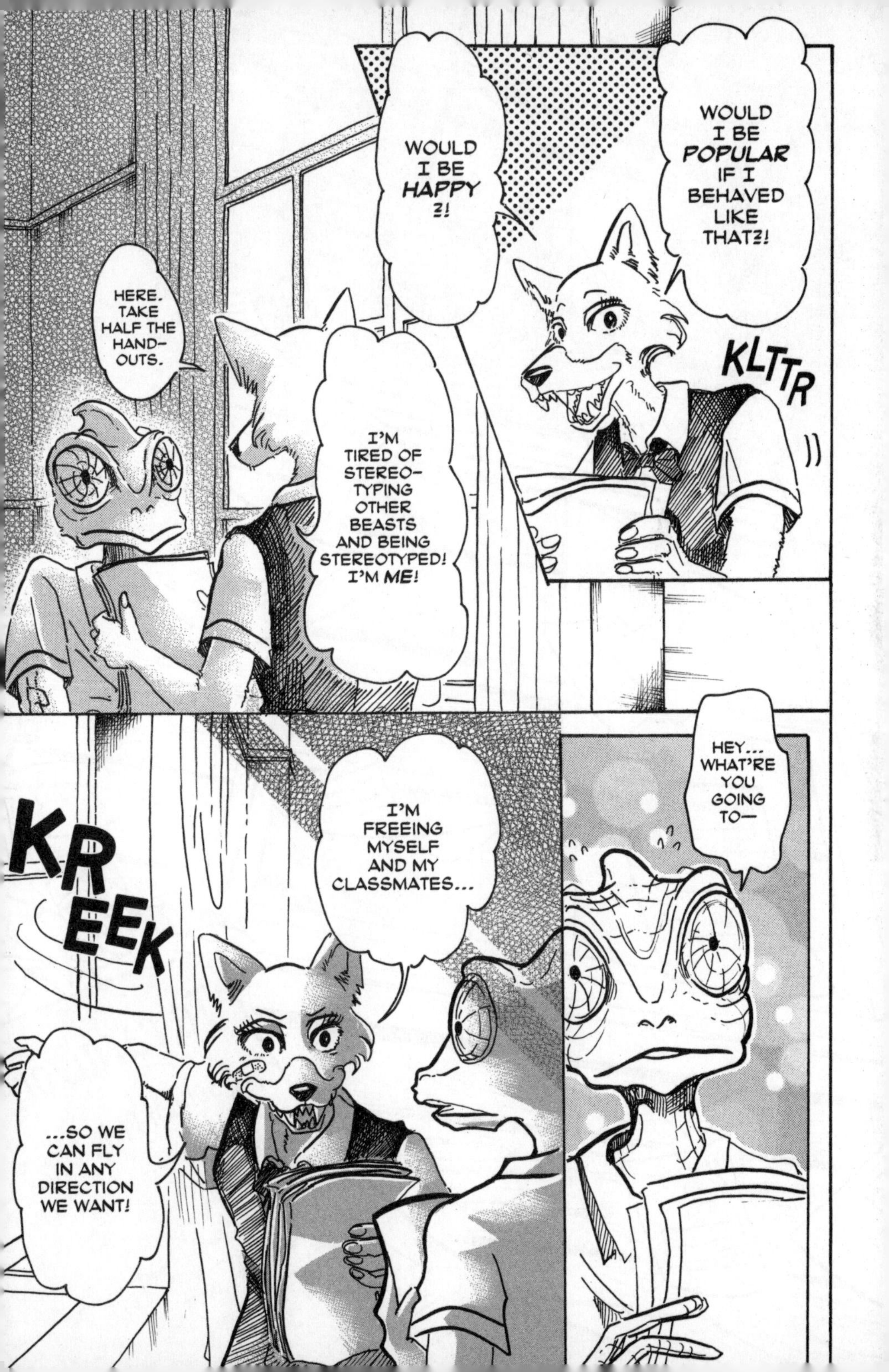
WOULD I BE *POPULAR* IF I BEHAVED LIKE THAT?!
WOULD I BE *HAPPY* ?!
KLTTR
HERE. TAKE HALF THE HAND-OUTS.
I'M TIRED OF STEREO-TYPING OTHER BEASTS AND BEING STEREOTYPED! I'M *ME*!
HEY... WHAT'RE YOU GOING TO—
I'M FREEING MYSELF AND MY CLASSMATES...
KRREEK
...SO WE CAN FLY IN ANY DIRECTION WE WANT!

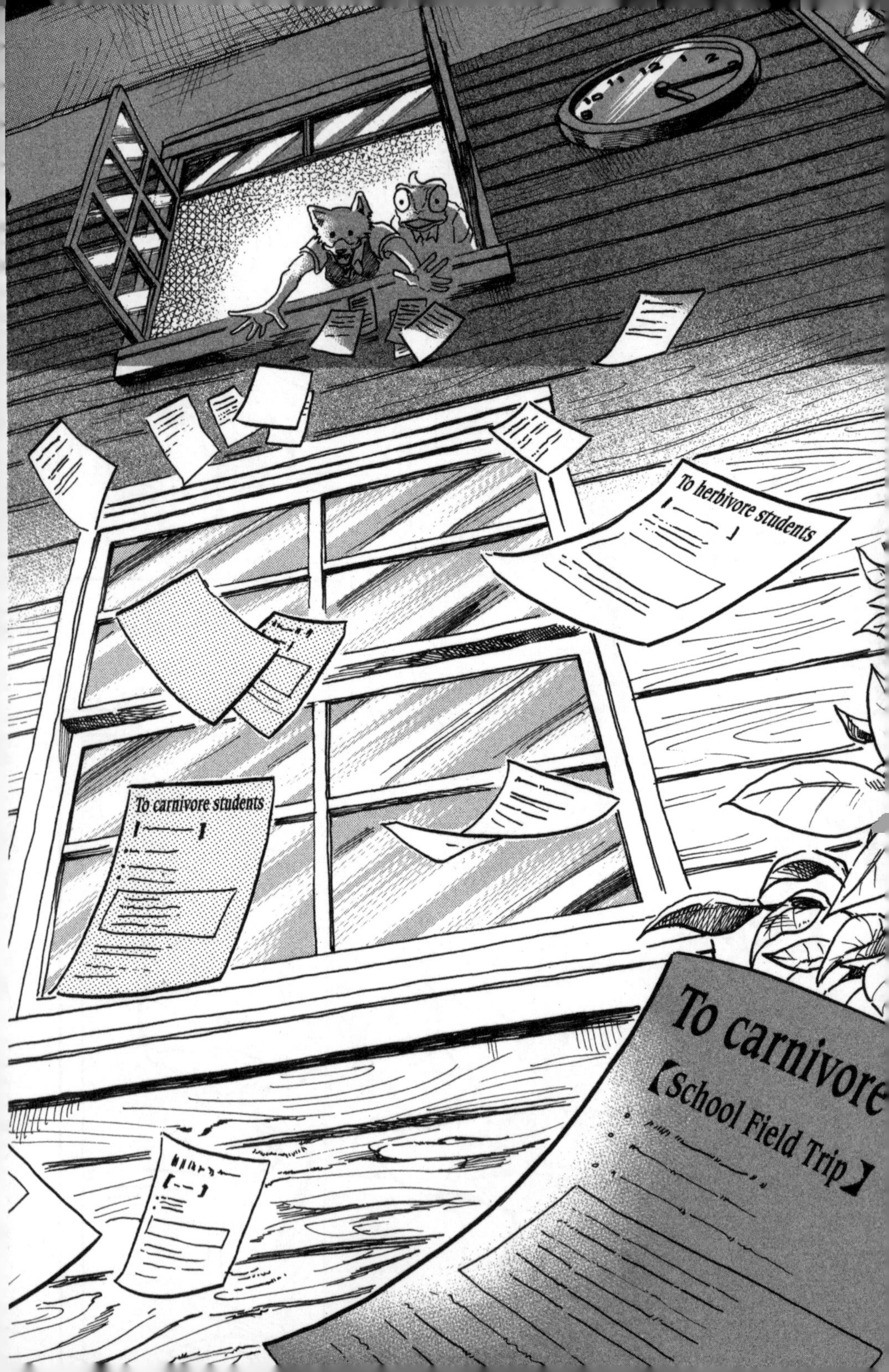
To herbivore students
To carnivore students
To carnivore
【School Field Trip】

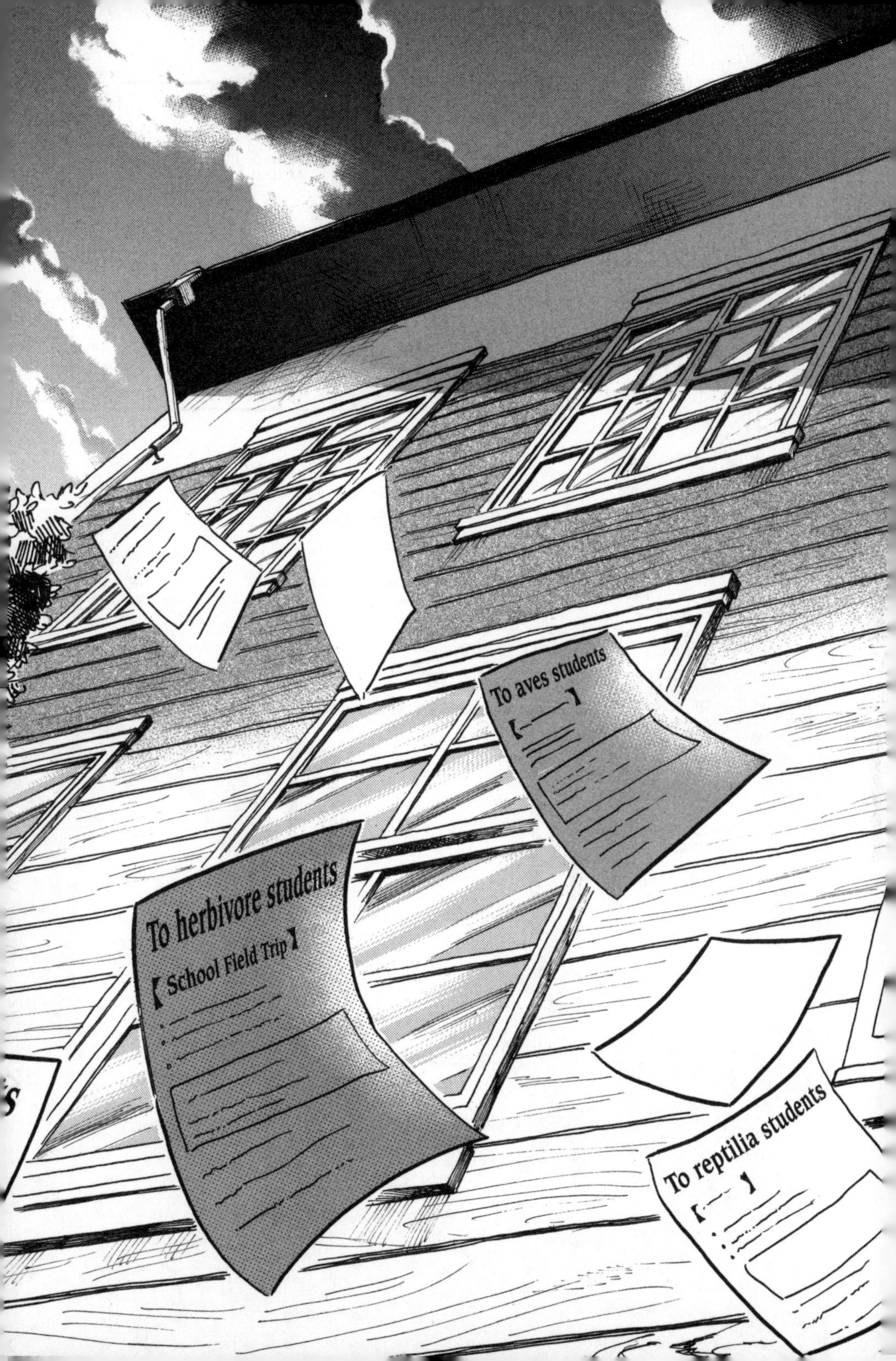
To aves students
To herbivore students
School Field Trip
To reptilia students

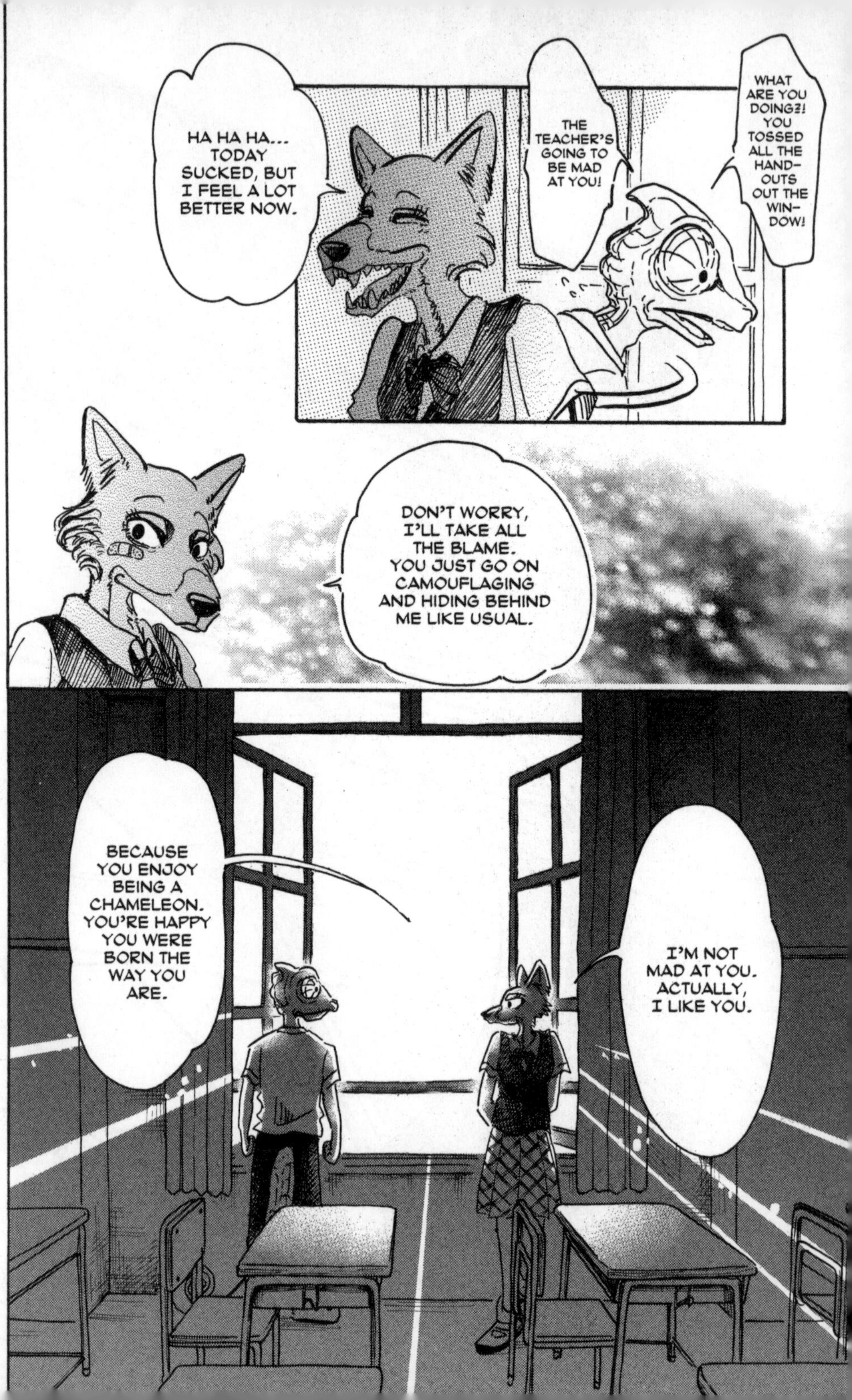
WHAT ARE YOU DOING?! YOU TOSSED ALL THE HAND-OUTS OUT THE WIN-DOW!
THE TEACHER'S GOING TO BE MAD AT YOU!
HA HA HA... TODAY SUCKED, BUT I FEEL A LOT BETTER NOW.
DON'T WORRY, I'LL TAKE ALL THE BLAME. YOU JUST GO ON CAMOUFLAGING AND HIDING BEHIND ME LIKE USUAL.
I'M NOT MAD AT YOU. ACTUALLY, I LIKE YOU.
BECAUSE YOU ENJOY BEING A CHAMELEON. YOU'RE HAPPY YOU WERE BORN THE WAY YOU ARE.

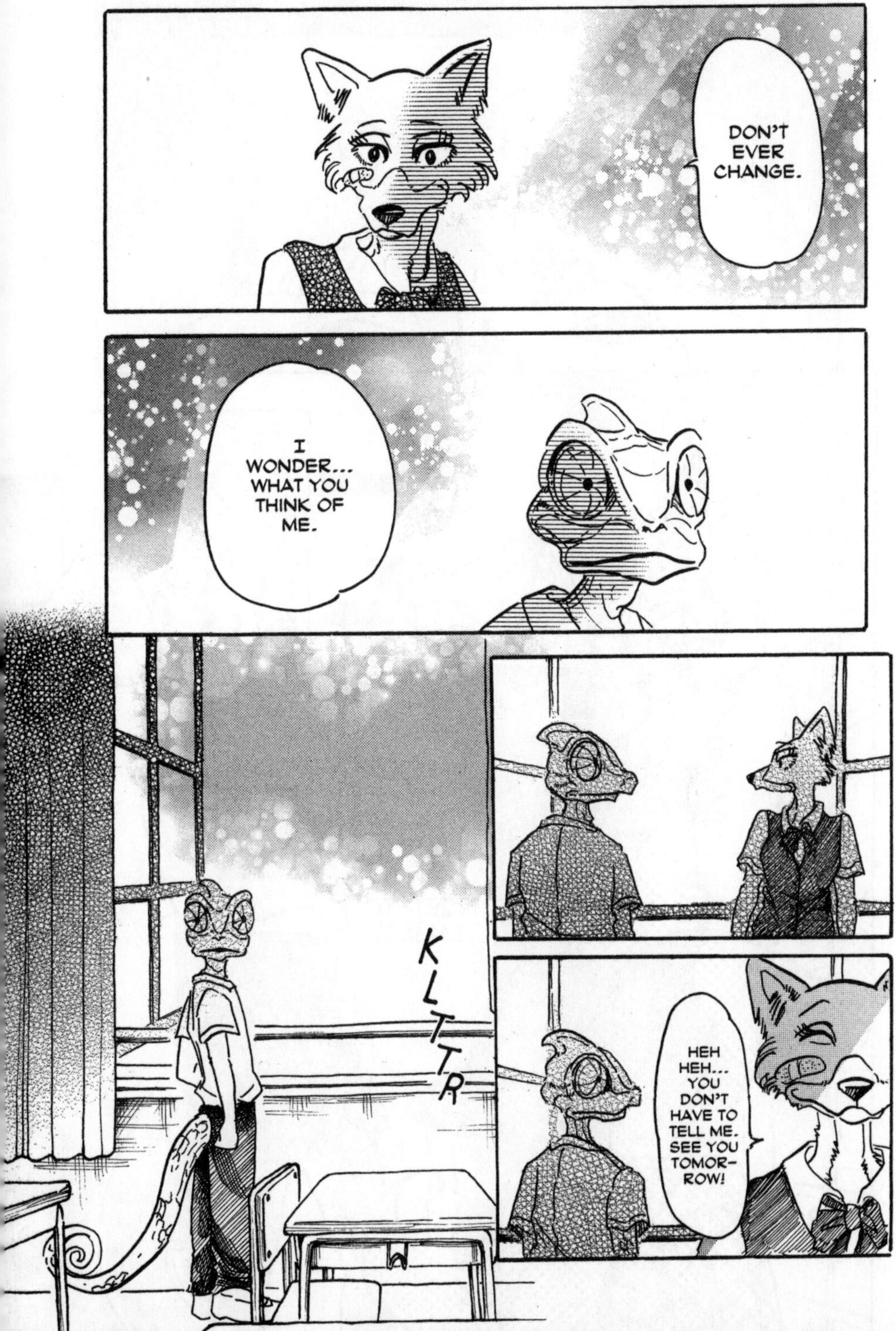
DON'T EVER CHANGE.
I WONDER... WHAT YOU THINK OF ME.
HEH HEH... YOU DON'T HAVE TO TELL ME. SEE YOU TOMOR-ROW!
KLTTR

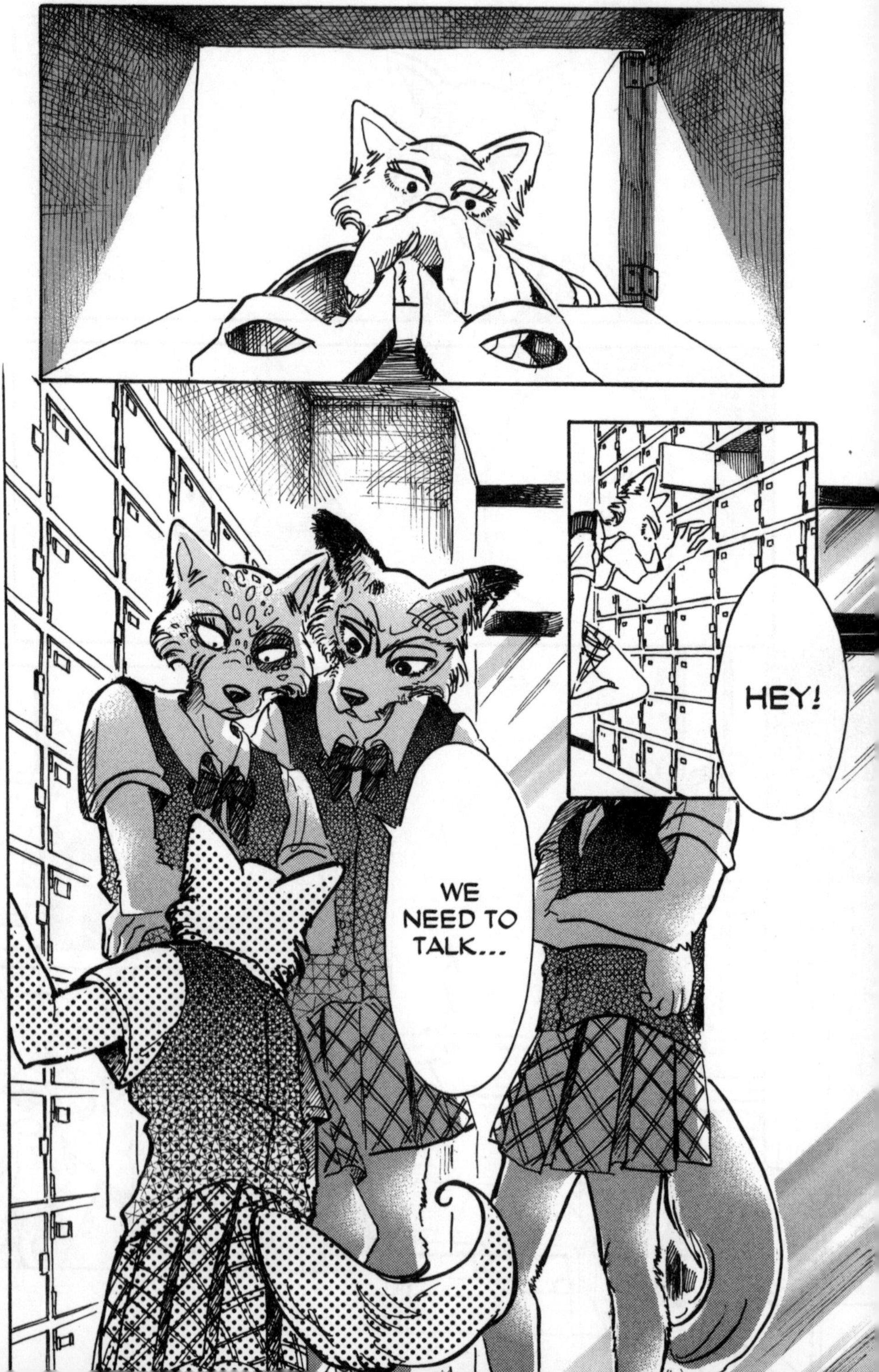
HEY!
WE NEED TO TALK...

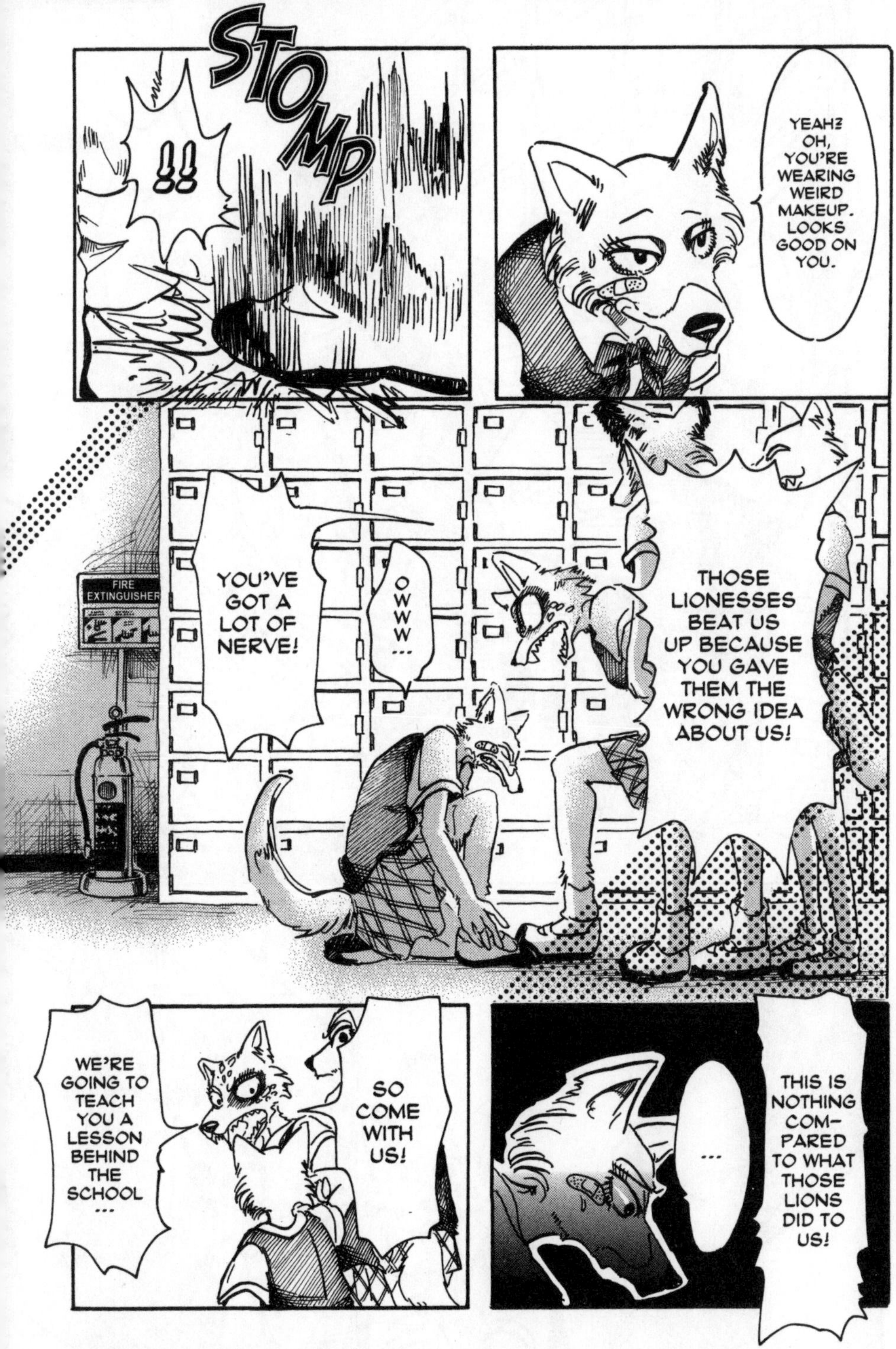
YEAH? OH, YOU'RE WEARING WEIRD MAKEUP. LOOKS GOOD ON YOU.
STOMP
!!
THOSE LIONESSES BEAT US UP BECAUSE YOU GAVE THEM THE WRONG IDEA ABOUT US!
OWWW...
YOU'VE GOT A LOT OF NERVE!
FIRE EXTINGUISHER
THIS IS NOTHING COMPARED TO WHAT THOSE LIONS DID TO US!
...
SO COME WITH US!
WE'RE GOING TO TEACH YOU A LESSON BEHIND THE SCHOOL...

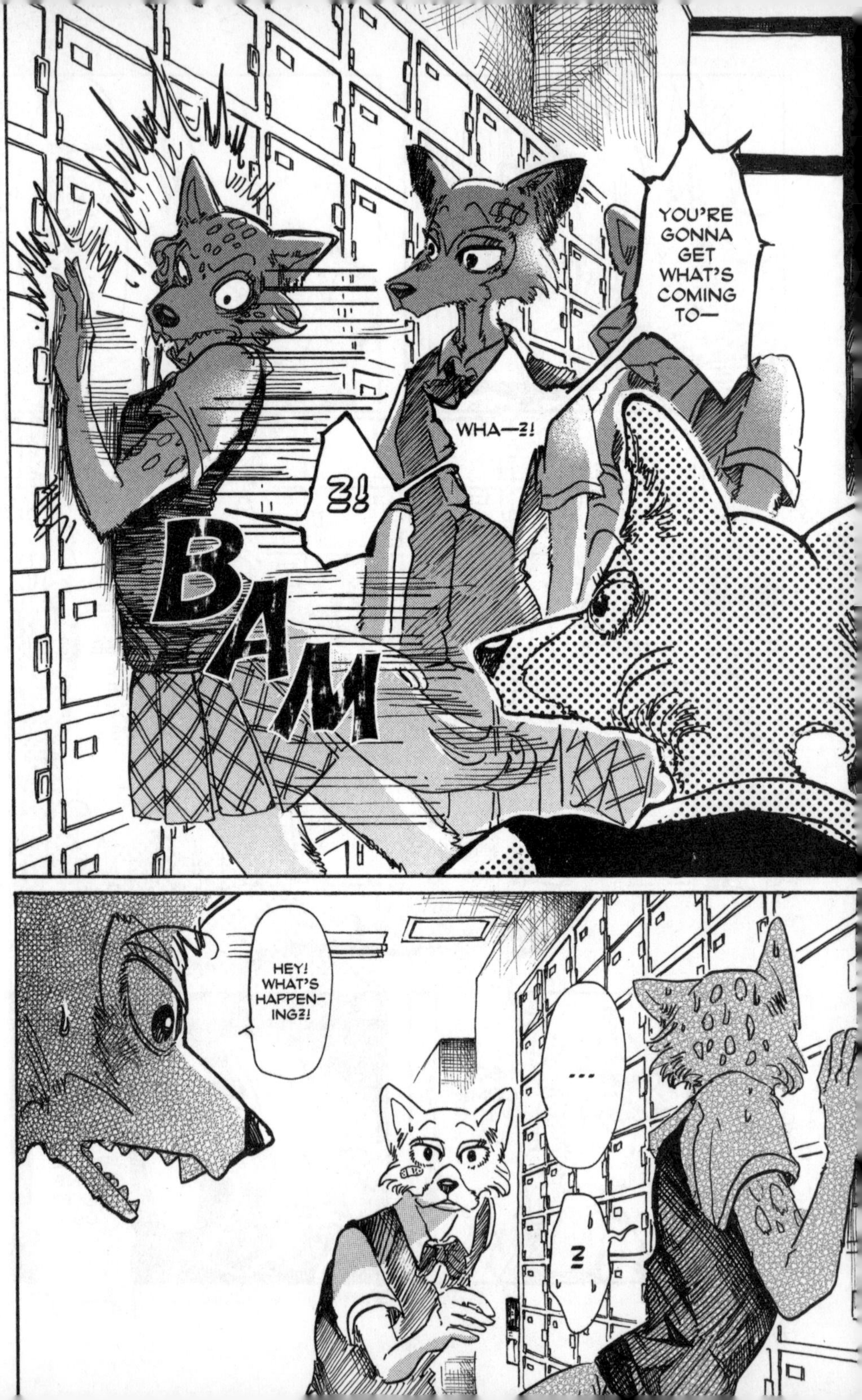
YOU'RE GONNA GET WHAT'S COMING TO—
WHA—?!
?!
BAM
...
?
HEY! WHAT'S HAPPENING?!

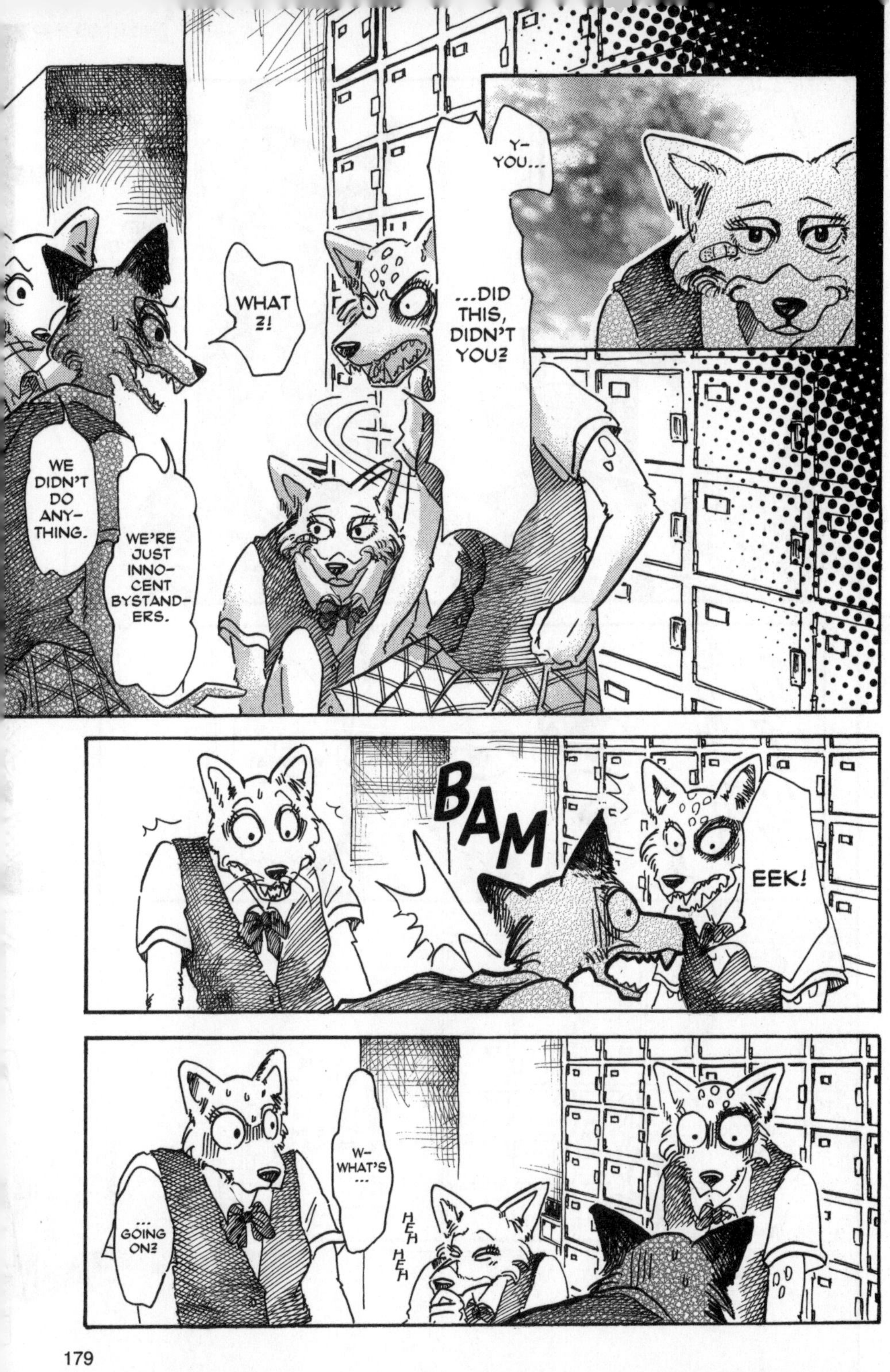
Y- YOU...
...DID THIS, DIDN'T YOU?
WHAT?!
WE DIDN'T DO ANY-THING.
WE'RE JUST INNO-CENT BYSTAND-ERS.
BAM
EEK!
W-WHAT'S...
...GOING ON?
HEH HEH

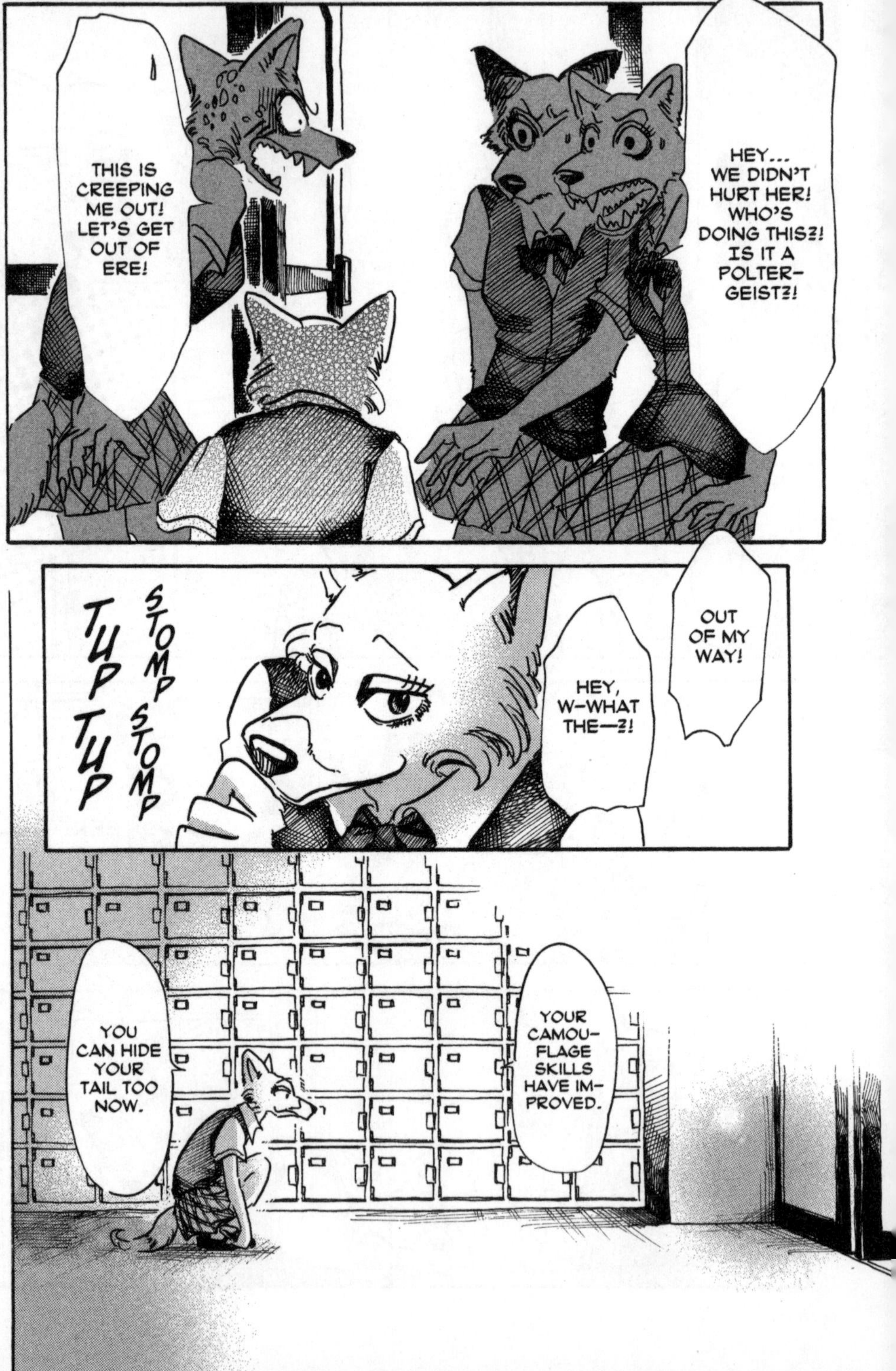
HEY... WE DIDN'T HURT HER! WHO'S DOING THIS?! IS IT A POLTER-GEIST?!
THIS IS CREEPING ME OUT! LET'S GET OUT OF ERE!
OUT OF MY WAY!
HEY, W-WHAT THE—?!
STOMP STOMP
TUP TUP
YOUR CAMOU-FLAGE SKILLS HAVE IM-PROVED.
YOU CAN HIDE YOUR TAIL TOO NOW.

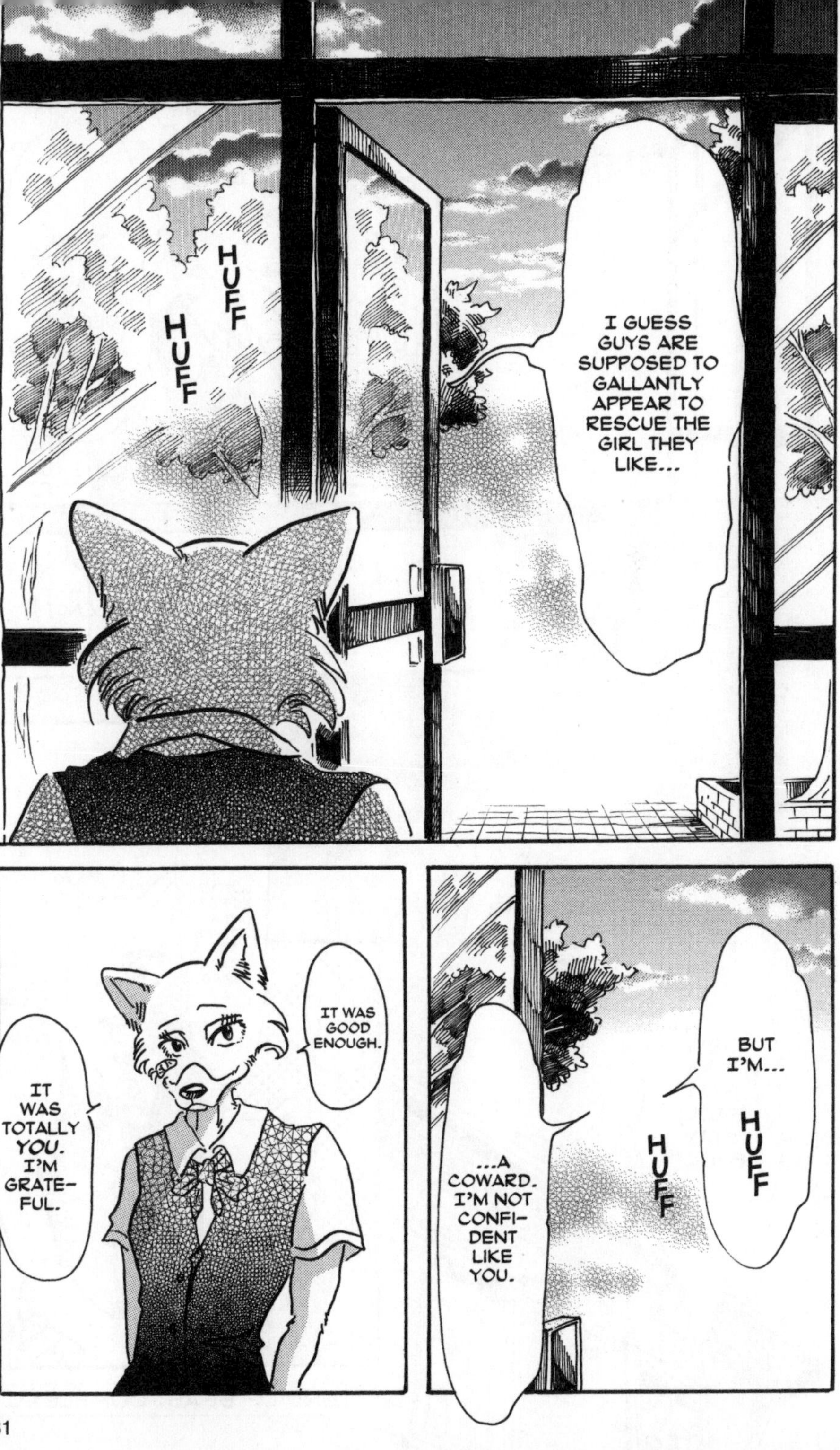
HUFF
HUFF
I GUESS GUYS ARE SUPPOSED TO GALLANTLY APPEAR TO RESCUE THE GIRL THEY LIKE...
BUT I'M...
HUFF
HUFF
...A COWARD. I'M NOT CONFIDENT LIKE YOU.
IT WAS GOOD ENOUGH.
IT WAS TOTALLY YOU. I'M GRATEFUL.

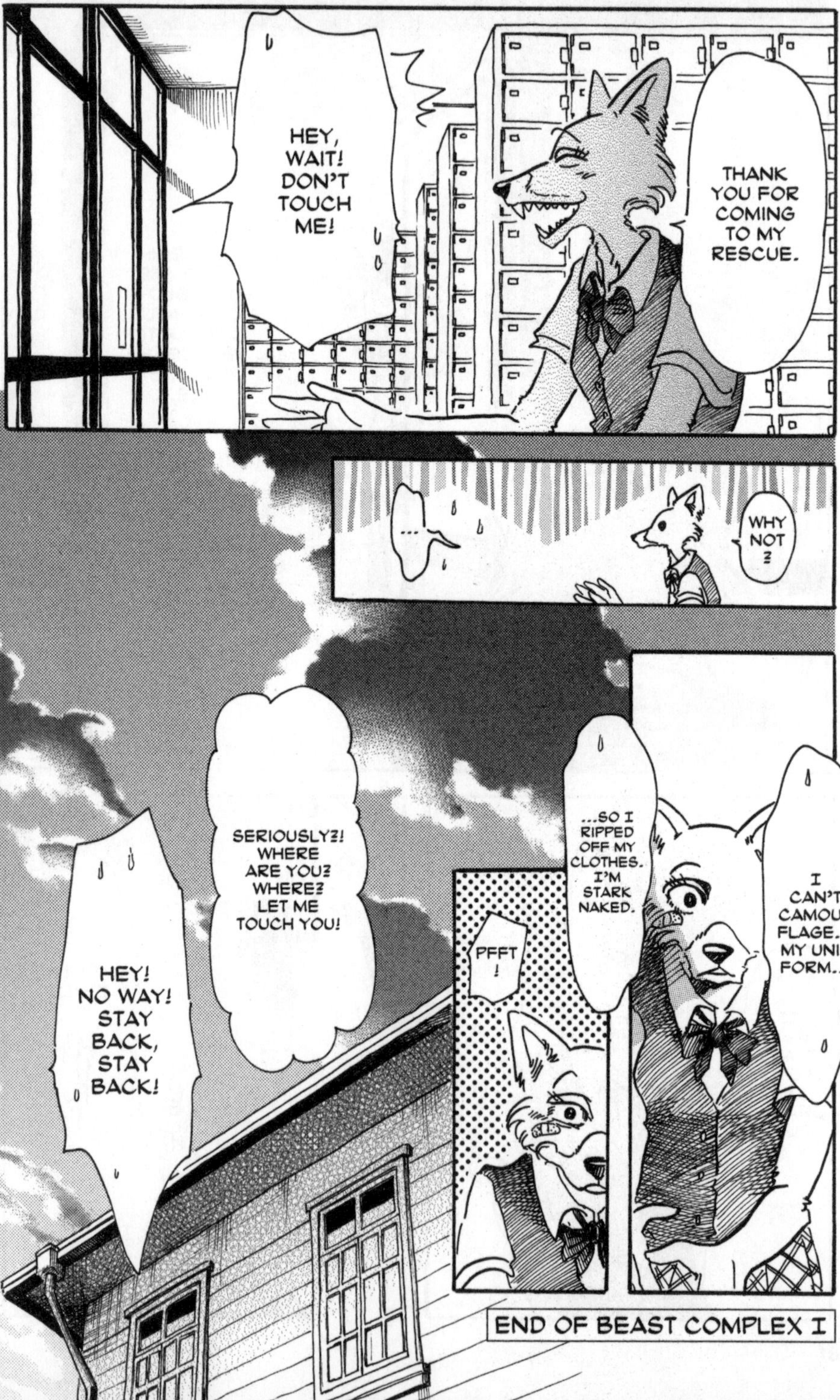
THANK YOU FOR COMING TO MY RESCUE.
HEY, WAIT! DON'T TOUCH ME!
WHY NOT?
...
I CAN'T CAMOUFLAGE... MY UNIFORM...
...SO I RIPPED OFF MY CLOTHES. I'M STARK NAKED.
PFFT!
SERIOUSLY?! WHERE ARE YOU? WHERE? LET ME TOUCH YOU!
HEY! NO WAY! STAY BACK, STAY BACK!
END OF BEAST COMPLEX I

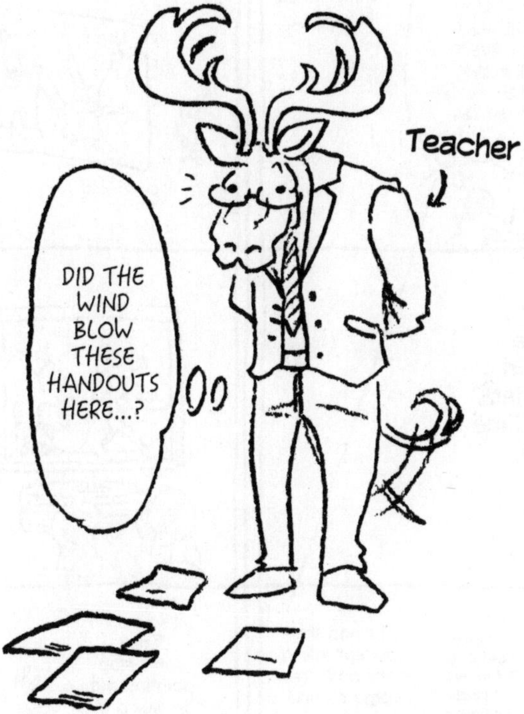
Teacher
DID THE WIND BLOW THESE HANDOUTS HERE...?

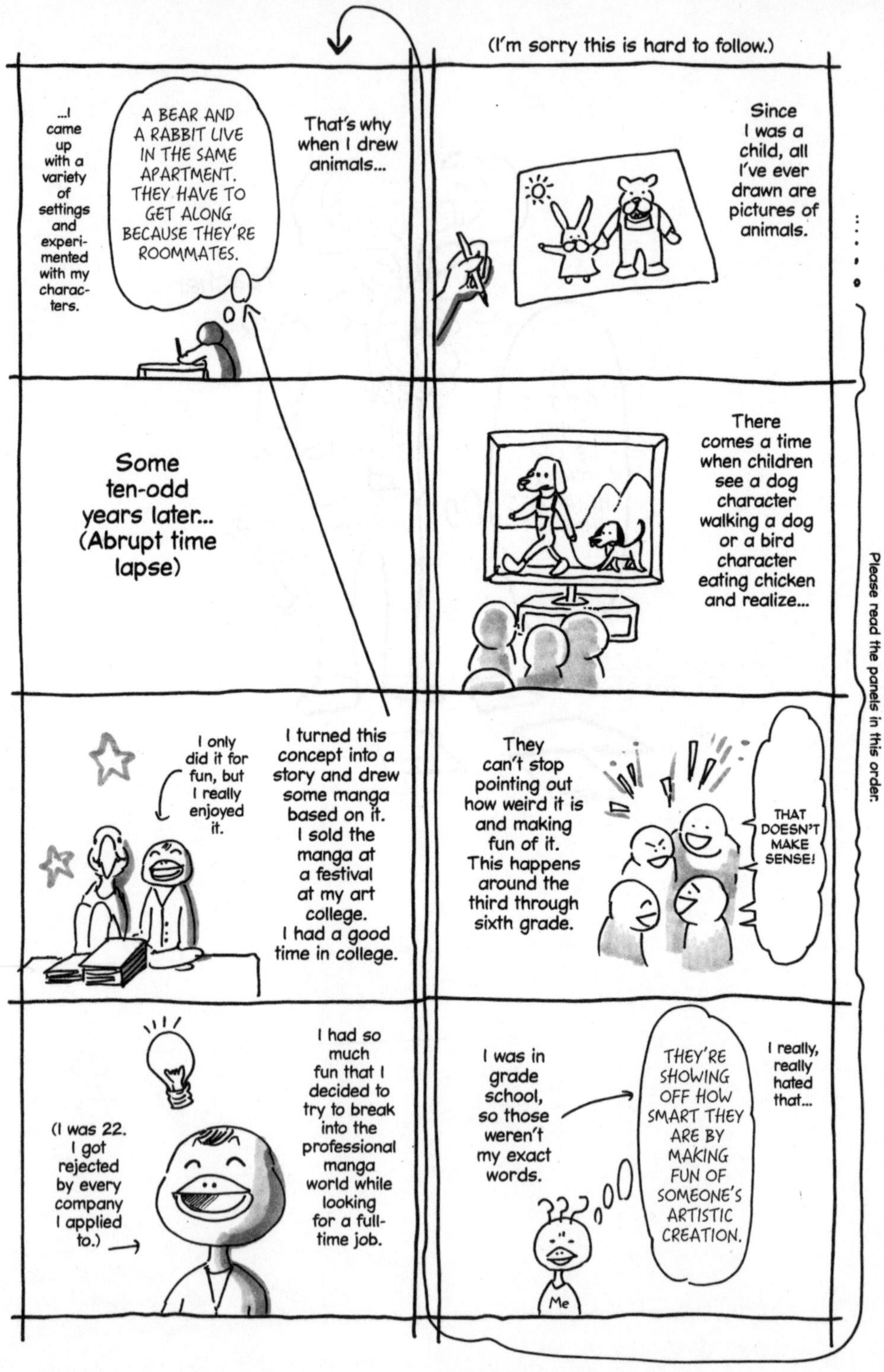

(I'm sorry this is hard to follow.)
Please read the panels in this order.
Since I was a child, all I've ever drawn are pictures of animals.
There comes a time when children see a dog character walking a dog or a bird character eating chicken and realize...
They can't stop pointing out how weird it is and making fun of it. This happens around the third through sixth grade.
THAT DOESN'T MAKE SENSE!
I really, really hated that...
THEY'RE SHOWING OFF HOW SMART THEY ARE BY MAKING FUN OF SOMEONE'S ARTISTIC CREATION.
I was in grade school, so those weren't my exact words.
Me
That's why when I drew animals...
A BEAR AND A RABBIT LIVE IN THE SAME APARTMENT. THEY HAVE TO GET ALONG BECAUSE THEY'RE ROOMMATES.
...I came up with a variety of settings and experimented with my characters.
Some ten-odd years later... (Abrupt time lapse)
I turned this concept into a story and drew some manga based on it. I sold the manga at a festival at my art college. I had a good time in college.
I only did it for fun, but I really enjoyed it.
I had so much fun that I decided to try to break into the professional manga world while looking for a full-time job.
(I was 22. I got rejected by every company I applied to.)

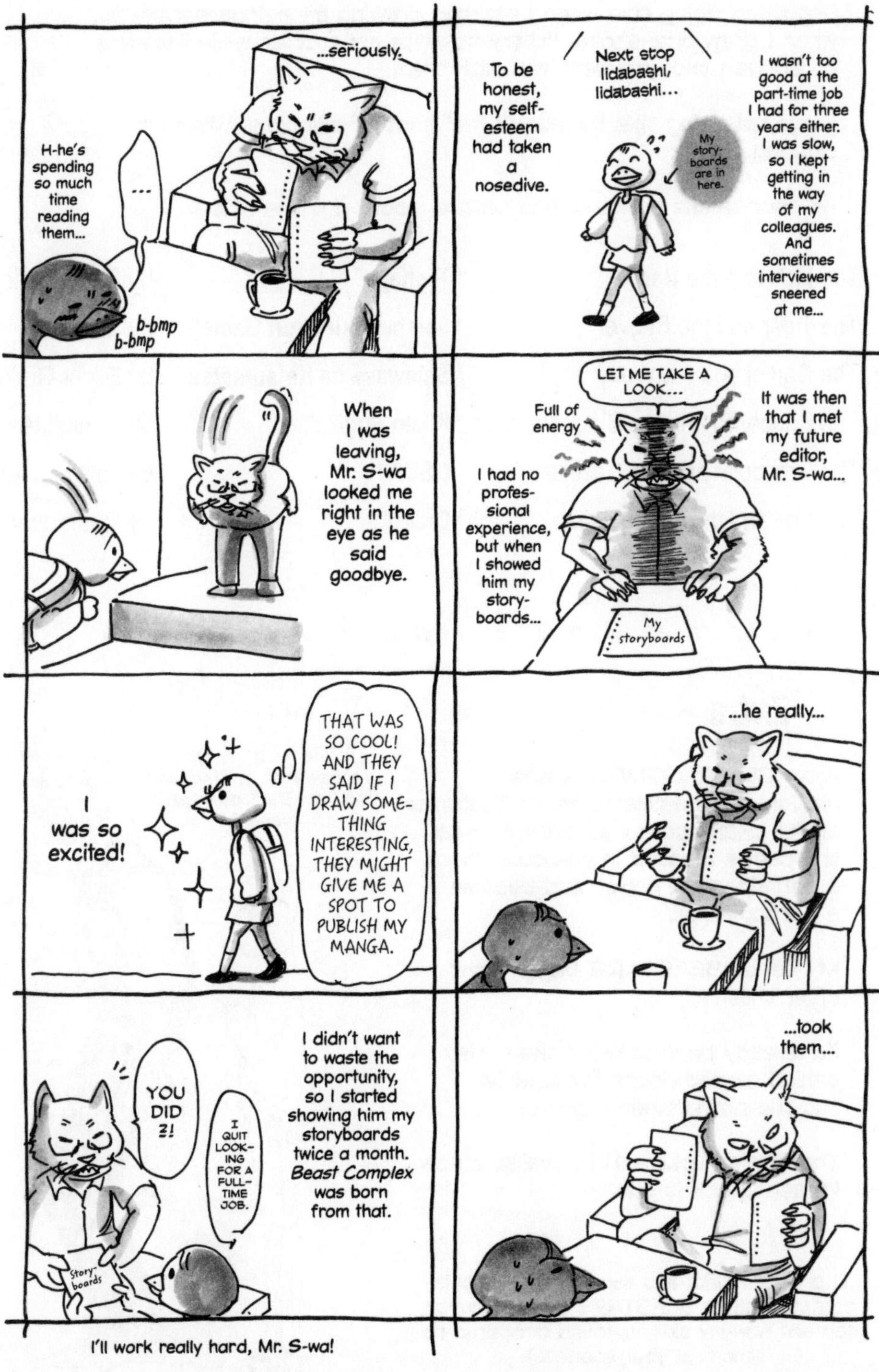
I wasn't too good at the part-time job I had for three years either. I was slow, so I kept getting in the way of my colleagues. And sometimes interviewers sneered at me...
Next stop Iidabashi, Iidabashi...
My storyboards are in here.
To be honest, my self-esteem had taken a nosedive.
...seriously.
...
H-he's spending so much time reading them...
b-bmp b-bmp
It was then that I met my future editor, Mr. S-wa...
LET ME TAKE A LOOK...
Full of energy
I had no professional experience, but when I showed him my storyboards...
My storyboards
When I was leaving, Mr. S-wa looked me right in the eye as he said goodbye.
...he really...
THAT WAS SO COOL! AND THEY SAID IF I DRAW SOMETHING INTERESTING, THEY MIGHT GIVE ME A SPOT TO PUBLISH MY MANGA.
I was so excited!
...took them...
I didn't want to waste the opportunity, so I started showing him my storyboards twice a month. *Beast Complex* was born from that.
I QUIT LOOKING FOR A FULL-TIME JOB.
YOU DID?!
Storyboards

I'll work really hard, Mr. S-wa!

～ My Manga and Music ～

I stopped doing this when I started drawing my manga series, but when I drew one-shots, I'd try to write my stories while listening to songs I thought went well with them.

I enjoyed doing this because I feel a lot of emotions when I'm drawing.

I'd choose the songs based on the mood, not the lyrics.

1. The Lion and the Bat   **"Teenage"**   by Sakanaction

2. The Tiger and the Beaver   **"Seishun Ikinokori Game"**   by Spitz

3. The Camel and the Wolf   **"Shiawase na Ketsumatsu"**   by Eiichi Otaki

4. The Kangaroo and the Black Panther   **"Kiken Sugiru"**   by Kenichi Asai

5. The Crocodile and the Gazelle   **"OSCA"**   by Tokyo Jihen

6. The Fox and the Chameleon   **"Creep"**   by Radiohead

♪ ♫ ♩ ♫ ♪ ♫ ♩ ♫ ♪ ♫ ♩ ♫ ♪ ♫ ♩ ♫ ♪ ♫ ♩ ♫ ♪ ♫ ♩ ♫ ♪ ♫ ♩

～ Extra ～

After BEAST COMPLEX was published, an animated movie featuring animal characters was created near the castle located in the country of a certain world power and became a zootopian hit.

My series BEASTARS began right after that.

I'd already been drawing the series behind closed doors for a while, but the timing wasn't good.

The English volume 11 is available now. Please check it out.

(I drew the fifth and sixth stories in this collection after BEASTARS began, so you can see how my skill improved compared to the first four stories.)

Legoshi (age 17), the hero of BEASTARS

(He made his first appearance in "The Lion and the Bat" on page 9, panel 1.)

GIVE IT YOUR ALL, OKAY?!

?

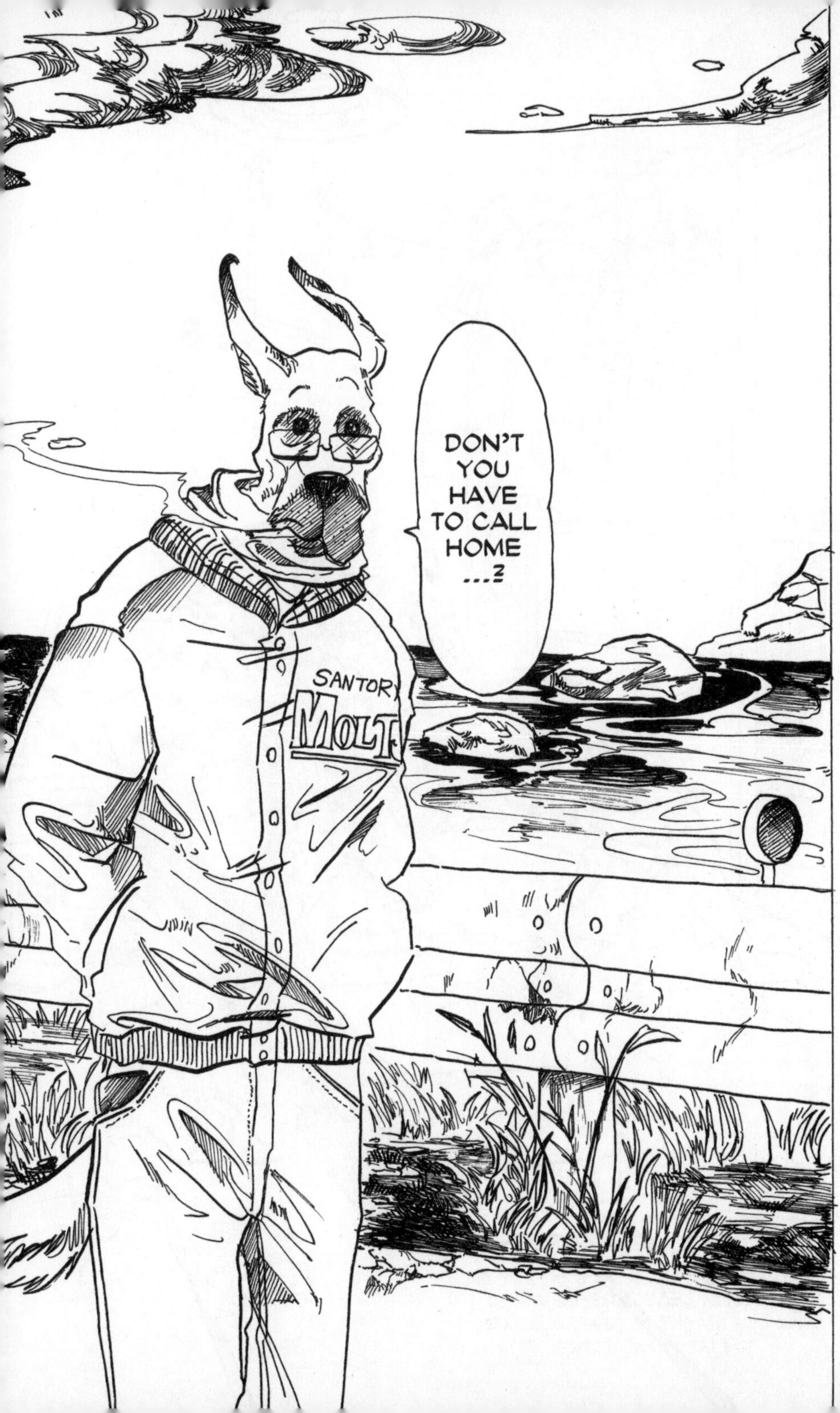
DON'T YOU HAVE TO CALL HOME ...?
SANTORY
MOLT

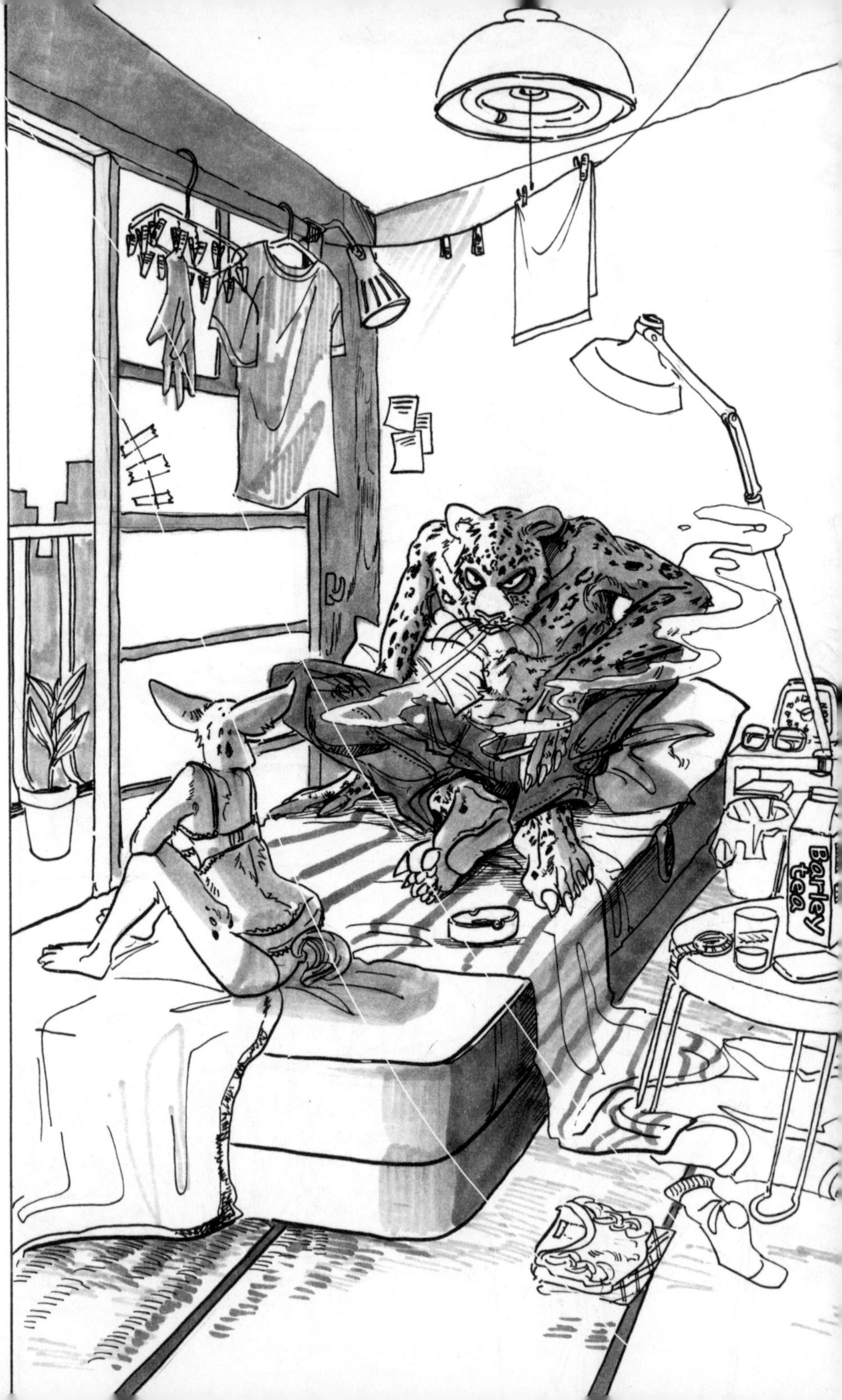
Barley tea

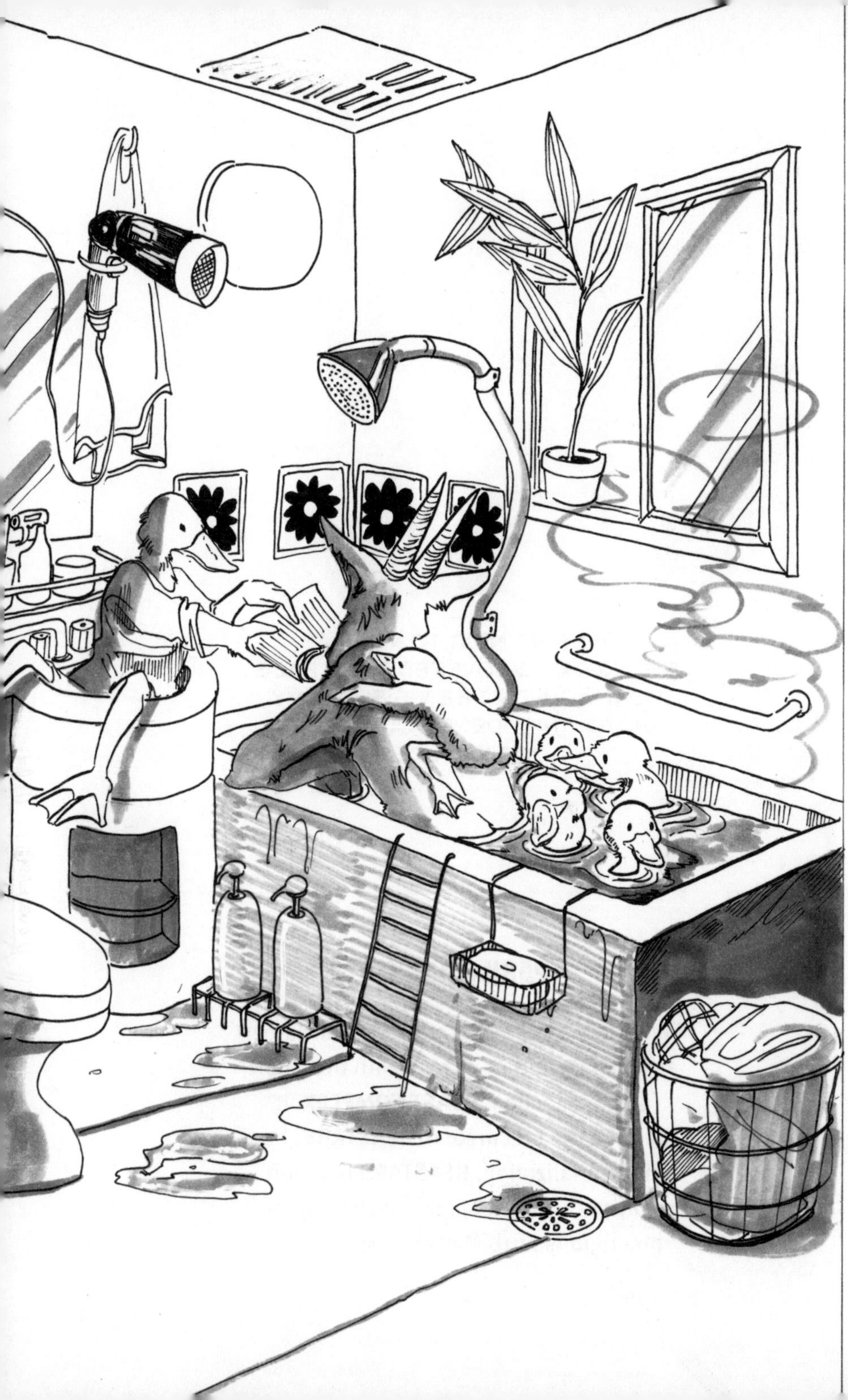

THE BIRD NEXT TO ME IS A
STRANGER—I COVERED THEIR FACE
SO IT WOULDN'T BE VISIBLE IN MY
PHOTO. THIS TURNED OUT TO BE A
GOOD PICTURE...

PARU ITAGAKI

Paru Itagaki began her professional career
as a manga author in 2016 with this short
story collection, **BEAST COMPLEX**. It
became the precursor to **BEASTARS**, her
first serialization. **BEASTARS** has won
multiple awards in Japan, including the
prestigious 2018 Manga Taisho Award.

BEAST COMPLEX
VOL. I
VIZ Signature Edition

Story & Art by
Paru Itagaki

Translation/Tomo Kimura
English Adaptation/Annette Roman
Touch-Up Art & Lettering/Susan Daigle-Leach
Cover & Interior Design/Yukiko Whitley
Editor/Annette Roman

BEAST COMPLEX Volume I
© 2018 PARU ITAGAKI
All rights reserved.
First published in 2018 by Akita Publishing Co., Ltd., Tokyo
English translation rights arranged with Akita Publishing Co., Ltd., through
Tuttle-Mori Agency, Inc., Tokyo

The stories, characters and incidents mentioned in this publication are entirely
fictional.

Printed in Italy

Published by VIZ Media, LLC
P.O. Box 77010
San Francisco, CA 94107

10 9 8 7 6 5 4 3 2
First printing, March 2021
Second printing, December 2021

 MEDIA

viz.com   vizsignature.com

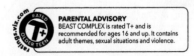

PARENTAL ADVISORY
BEAST COMPLEX is rated T+ and is
recommended for ages 16 and up. It contains
adult themes, sexual situations and violence.

This is the last page.

BEAST COMPLEX reads from right to left to preserve the orientation of the original Japanese artwork.

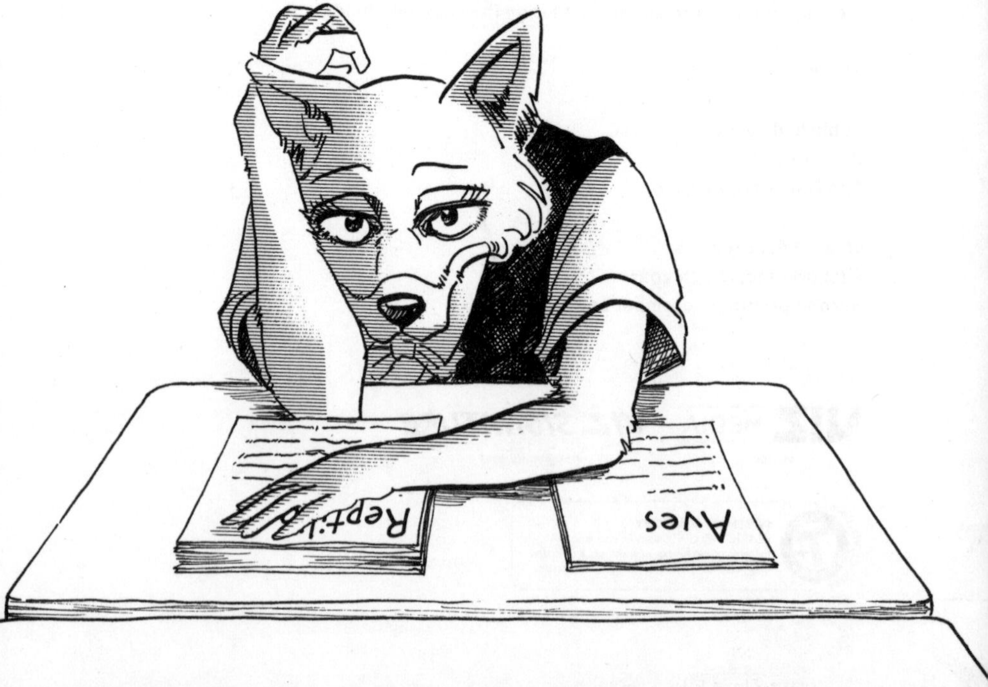

Aves